BARRON'S

Pass Key to the
GMAT®

2ND EDITION

Bobby Umar, M.B.A.
GMAT Instructor and Consultant
President, Raeallan
Leadership Speaking and Training
Toronto, Canada

Carl S. Pyrdum, III, M.A., Ph.D.
GMAT Tutor
Ivory Tower Tutoring
Atlanta, Georgia

About the Authors

Bobby Umar, MBA is a highly sought after GMAT instructor in North America. For almost 17 years, he has taught GMAT prep courses for Veritas Prep and Kaplan, global test prep companies, and his own company, Raeallan. In 2009–2010, he was awarded the "Worldwide Instructor of the Year" for Veritas out of 500+ instructors from 130 countries.

During his MBA studies at Degroote School of Business in Hamilton, Ontario, Bobby was President of the MBA Association, received awards in case competitions, academics, and leadership, and graduated at the top of his class as co-valedictorian. With a background in brand marketing, engineering, and the performing arts, he also draws on his diverse career to lead Raeallan, a transformational training and speaking company (*www.raeallan.com*). A four-time TEDx speaker, Bobby has been named one of *Inc. Magazine's* Top 100 Leadership Speakers. His talks cover topics such as leadership, personal branding, networking, and social media. With his GMAT expertise, Bobby has helped thousands of young leaders get into the best business schools.

You can connect with Bobby via Twitter, LinkedIn, or *www.GMATBobby.com*.

Carl Pyrdum, III, M.A., Ph.D. is a long-time GMAT tutor, who opened his own tutoring company, Ivory Tower Tutoring, in Atlanta, Georgia. He has worked as a teacher, tutor, and content developer for the GMAT, GRE, LSAT, SAT, and ACT for Barron's as well as for Kaplan. He has helped more than a thousand students improve their test scores and reach their undergraduate, graduate, and professional school goals.

All inquiries should be addressed to:
Barron's Educational Series, Inc.
250 Wireless Boulevard
Hauppauge, New York 11788
www.barronseduc.com

ISBN: 978-1-4380-0802-8

Library of Congress Control Number: 2016945685

PRINTED IN CANADA
9 8 7 6 5 4 3 2 1

10%
POST-CONSUMER WASTE
Paper contains a minimum of 10% post-consumer waste (PCW). Paper used in this book was derived from certified, sustainable forestlands.

Contents

The Basics

Officially, GMAT is an acronym that stands for the Graduate Management Admissions Test. The GMAT is the standardized computer-based test used in admissions decisions for most MBA programs. Since 2006, the test has been administered by Pearson VUE, with questions provided by ACT.

The GMAT dates back to 1953, when deans from nine of the most prestigious business schools formed the Graduate Management Admission Council (GMAC) and asked the makers of the SAT, The Education Testing Service (ETS), to create an objective national entrance exam for their programs. The first test, which went by the less pronounceable acronym ATGSB (Admissions Test for Graduate Study in Business), was given in February of 1954 to a few more than 4,000 hopeful business students.

In the years since 1953, some sections and question types were dropped, some added, but the underlying logic behind the test remains the same—and that's good news for prospective test takers like you! With the right guidance and a bit of hard work, the GMAT can be mastered, no matter how strange and difficult it might seem at first. Not only is there a method to the GMAT's madness, there's a system of hidden rules and expectations that the test always operates by, rules that you can learn to secure the score you need to meet your admissions goals.

THE GMAT'S STRUCTURE

When you sit down in front of your assigned computer on test day, you will face four scored sections in this order:

1. **ANALYTICAL WRITING ASSESSMENT SECTION (THE AWA).** In the AWA, you are given 30 minutes to write a response to an essay prompt, typing it into a simplified word processing interface. The prompt asks you to produce an "Analysis of an Argument," presenting a brief, fictitious argument from a made-up source and asking you to critique it.

2. **INTEGRATED REASONING SECTION (THE IR).** Here, you will be given 12 questions and 30 minutes to complete the section. IR questions ask you to use multiple sources of information—graphs, tables, charts, and

short reading passages—and to employ both your math and your verbal knowledge and skills. Four types of questions are attached to these different sources of information: Graphics Interpretation, Two-Part Analysis, Table Analysis, and Multi-Source Reasoning.

3. **QUANTITATIVE SECTION (AKA "THE MATH" OR "THE QUANT").** The Quantitative Section contains 37 questions written in two different formats, Problem Solving and Data Sufficiency (aka "the weird ones"). The questions will alternate between the two formats more or less at random. According to the test maker, both types of questions will require familiarity with arithmetic, elementary algebra, and "commonly known" concepts of geometry. You will have 75 minutes—an hour and a quarter—to answer all the questions.

4. **VERBAL SECTION.** As with the Quantitative Section, you will have 75 minutes, but here you'll face 41 questions in three different formats (Reading Comprehension, Sentence Correction, and Critical Reasoning), also in no particular order. The Verbal questions require a basic understanding of the "rules" of arguments, the ability to read and organize information presented in both long (350- to 400-word) and short (100-word) passages, and familiarity with the grammatical rules of standard written English.

Section	# of Questions	Time	Question Types
AWA	1 essay prompt	30 minutes	Analysis of an Argument
Integrated Reasoning	12	30 minutes	Graphics Interpretation, Two-Part Analysis, Table Analysis, Multi-Source Reasoning
Short Break—up to 8 minutes			
Quantitative Section	37	75 minutes	Problem Solving, Data Sufficiency
Short Break—up to 8 minutes			
Verbal Section	41	75 minutes	Critical Reasoning, Sentence Correction, Reading Comprehension

YOUR 10 (YES, 10!) TEST SCORES

When all is said and done, you will receive a lot of different scores for the GMAT—ten in total! Usually, people will just refer to one, the Overall Score (as in "I got a 720" or "I heard you need a 712 to get into Harvard" or "You get 200 points just for writing your name down!"). In actual practice, your score will come back with a little chart that looks like this:

Test Date	Verbal	Quantitative	Total	Analytical Writing	Integrated Reasoning
23 June 20XX	40/90%	50/89%	690/89%	6/91%	7/82%

Eight of your scores are calculated automatically on site, so you'll find them out on the day of your test. You have to wait a few weeks for the essays to be graded to receive the final two. The two most important scores are:

1. **OVERALL SCORE (YOUR SCALED SCORE).** This is that famous three-digit number, the first score in the Total column. It ranges from 200 to 800, in increments of 10. Two-thirds of test takers score between 400 and 600, and the median score is usually between 540 and 570. The scores are arranged on a bell curve, so scores below 300 or above 700 are relatively rare. This score is produced by a weighted average of your performance ONLY in the Quantitative and Verbal sections. (The AWA essay and the IR sections are tracked independently.) The average's weight skews toward the Math score, though the exact amount is a trade secret closely guarded by the test maker.

2. **OVERALL PERCENTILE SCORE.** The second score in the Total column, this one is actually more important than the three-digit number, although admittedly less iconic. It tells you what percentage of recent test takers your score beats. Thus, a 75th percentile scorer did better than 75% of people who've taken the test over the last three years. This score can change from year to year as the test-taking population changes, though in practice it rarely moves more than a single point in either direction.

The remaining scores are important, but a little esoteric. Performance in Math and Verbal is tracked individually, with percentiles assigned to each. The same goes for Analytical Writing and Integrated Reasoning, which each get a score and a percentile:

Score	Possible Range	Increments	Typical Range
Quantitative Subscore	0–60	1 point	7–50
Verbal Subscore	0–60	1 point	9–44
Integrated Reasoning	1–8	1 point	3–7
AWA Scaled Score	0–6	.5 point	2–5.5

	50th Percentile	90th Percentile	99th Percentile
Quantitative Percentile	29	40	45
Verbal Percentile	40	50	52
Integrated Reasoning Percentile	5	7	8
AWA Percentile	4.5	6	6

Because the scores only come in 10-point increments, it's impossible to get a 712; only a 710 or a 720—no matter what that guy at work told you he got. When you see a number in between the tens—say, on a list of scores needed for the top schools—it means multiple students' scores have been averaged to produce it.

For more information you can visit the official website: *http://www.mba.com/*

WHAT THE CAT IS AND WHAT IT MEANS TO YOU

Now that you've got the basic who, what, where, and why of the GMAT down, it's high time we moved onto the how—as in, "How am I going to improve my score on the test?" The first step is to understand how this test differs from other tests you might have taken elsewhere, not the mundane details like number of questions and how to register but the real nitty-gritty that separates the GMAT from the SAT, GRE, and ABCs: the CAT.

The C in CAT is easy enough to understand, as is the T: we all know the GMAT is a **T**est that's only offered on a **C**omputer. It's that A that bears explaining. What does it mean for a test to be "**A**daptive"?

Back when the GMAT was administered on paper, every student in the room taking it faced exactly the same questions in exactly the same order. In general, the questions were organized with the easiest ones up front and the hardest toward the end, the idea being that a student who "deserved" a 540 would be able to work only a certain percentage of the test's questions, whereas one destined for a 740 would be able to work a much higher percentage, all but a few questions, and future 800s would be able to do them all.

The paper test could be administered only a few times a year because each administration required the test makers to write an entirely new set of questions to keep those who took the February exam from telling those taking the test in April what questions they'd see. So if there were 100 questions on a test, each sitting meant a fresh 100.

Adaptive Features

An adaptive test is, instead, built from a single pool of questions much larger than the 41 Verbal and 37 Math questions a single student sees, and it's almost impossible that any two test takers would see the exact same 78 questions as any other. The pool of possible questions is organized into "tiers" of questions of similar difficulty. The first question the test taker sees is drawn from the middle tier of questions, ones that the test maker has designed to be doable by students who will end up with a score right in the fat part of the test's bell curve (and all those who exceed it) but not by those below it.

The next question drawn from the pool is determined by how the test taker performs on that first question. If the correct answer was picked, the next question will be from a slightly higher tier, and if one of the four incorrect choices was picked, a slightly lower one. Another correct answer will mean the next question is more difficult still, while an incorrect one will dial the difficulty back a notch. As the test progresses, the jumps or falls in difficulty decrease in magnitude, so missing a question in the first ten will have a greater impact on the tier your questions are drawn from than missing one of the last ten.

The idea is that the test will be able to home in very quickly on the test taker's true skill level and only offer questions appropriate to that skill level. Whenever test takers get enough questions right to raise the difficulty up into a tier that's too hard for them, they'll start missing questions, lowering it right back down to their true skill level.

If the system worked perfectly, eventually test takers should expect to reach a point where they miss every other question, wobbling back and forth around their true skill level. In practice, as you might imagine, that sort of precision is seldom the case.

NO SKIPPING AROUND

On a paper test you're free to flip back and forth from page to page, doing whichever questions strike you as easiest and quickest, leaving yourself more than an average question's allotted time to tackle the hardest ones. On the *adaptive* portions of the GMAT (Quantitative and Verbal), you have to answer all the questions in front of you before you are given the next.

EVERYONE GETS A HARD TEST

No matter what your skill level, eventually the test will throw you questions that make you work a bit more, ones that take more time or employ more difficult or complicated concepts. Once you start struggling, the questions' difficulty might dip a bit, but a question or two later you'll be right back doing the questions that give you a hard time.

Thus, if your true skill in math is in the 600 range, most of the questions you'll face will be drawn from the very top end of that range, where the questions you find most difficult live. You'll see very few "gimme" questions, and those will only appear early in the test.

YOU HAVE TO FINISH THE TEST

Because of the way GMAT's special proprietary score-calculation algorithm works, failing to complete a question counts against your score more than missing it does. Suppose two students missed exactly the same questions in the Math section and in their Verbal section up until question 39. If one student never answers question 40 and never sees question 41 whereas the other tries both but gets them both wrong, the second will get the higher score on the test. But wait, you might protest, maybe the first student was just being careful, and the second one rushing; shouldn't the careful student get more points? Not according to the GMAT's algorithm, and the algorithm is the only opinion that counts.

THE EARLY QUESTIONS ARE THE LEAST PREDICTABLE . . . BUT THAT'S ABOUT IT

There are many superstitions about the adaptive test, and many of these superstitions have been attached to the early questions. You've probably heard that the first five questions are the most important or that they "count the most"— or maybe it was the first seven or the first ten. Consequently, you've probably also heard that you should spend an extra 30 seconds on those questions—or an extra minute, or even twice as long! The important thing, these superstitions hold, is that you make sure you get the early questions right. If you're going to miss a question, miss one of the last few.

In truth, such advice is based on a misunderstanding of how the difficulty jumps between questions work. It is true that the difficulty jumps are bigger earlier in the test, so that missing an early question will have more of an immediate effect on the tier from which your next few questions are drawn, but this does not mean that they have a larger overall effect on your score. But no matter how high you climb in the difficulty tiers by giving special attention to these early questions, you would still fall right out of that tier if you were unable to continue answering questions in that tier consistently. Your fall might be slower, but it will still happen, and the remaining 32 (or 30 or 28) questions are more than sufficient for you to bottom out in the tier you're least comfortable doing.

Such advice is also based on the idea that more time is the secret to getting a question correct and that with the proper amount of time allocated to those early questions you'll be able to "make sure" that you don't miss them. But, as we all know, you might get a question wrong for any number of reasons. Maybe you misread and thought that they wanted you to calculate the final percent instead of the percent change. Maybe you thought that verbs that end in -*ing* are always wrong on the test (another superstition) and eliminated the right answer out of hand. Heck, maybe you just never studied the particular concept being tested in the question. If you encounter one of these sorts of questions in the first five, no amount of extra time would "make sure" that you got it right.

Indeed, in trying to make sure that they do those first five to ten questions correctly, many students end up without enough time to keep doing well on the later questions and find themselves rushing through the last ten, missing most of them and risking not finishing at all.

NEVERTHELESS, YOU MUST START STRONG AND BE CAREFUL

All that said, we must admit that people are absolutely correct when they say that the early questions are often the key to your performance on the GMAT. It just has little to do with the amount by which the difficulty changes from question to question. Rather, it's mostly about making sure your stress level remains low and that, consequently, you are able to shake off mistakes or confusing questions and thereby maintain momentum.

Suppose you were worried about time and rushed through the first question. Likely you wouldn't feel the best about your answer; you'd know you were cutting corners, pushing through, and that maybe you missed something—even if it was a question that you knew how to do and could do well under less stressful circumstances. When the second question pops up on the screen, you have a new challenge to attack, but you'll have to attack it burdened by the doubts and anxiety your rushing through the first question left you with. If that stress makes the second question harder than it should be, when you roll into the third, you're now doubly weighted down by the anxiety generated from the first question compounded by the uneasiness from the second. Lather, rinse, and repeat. By the middle of the test you're so out of sorts that you're missing easy questions that you know how to do, and that ever-ticking clock just keeps counting lower and lower. It's the anxiety snowball effect.

This series of little mistakes that compound each other could happen at any point in a test, of course, but if those first questions go well, you have a much greater chance of being able to halt the anxiety snowball before it rolls out of control. Being careful early gives you something to fall back on. Just don't spend time on early questions merely for the sake of spending extra time. If you're certain you isolated the right variable, double and triple checking your work isn't going to make that question count for any more than it already does, but it might steal away time you're going to need to get a harder question later on.

YOU MUST MAINTAIN AN EVEN, CONSISTENT PACE

Because the test soon learns the level of difficulty liable to give you the most trouble, the temptation to slow down and give more time to each subsequent question grows as the test goes on. Beware of the "just *one* more minute" trap because one minute can easily become two or three. You have to be willing to give the occasional question more than the one and a half or two minutes you have, on average, for each question, but put emphasis on the word *occasional*. The GMAT isn't a test suited to either tortoises or hares: slow and steady fails just as surely as quick and careless. Aim instead for brisk but careful. As St. Augustine famously wrote, "Hurry, but hurry slowly."

YOU CAN'T AFFORD TO LOOK OVER YOUR OWN SHOULDER

Because test takers know that the test is adapting to their performance, many end up trying to gauge their performance on the test with each question. If a new question feels difficult, they silently fist-pump, but if it feels easier, they start to sweat, worried that means that they missed the question they just hit "confirm answer" on. The first problem with this approach is that the more time you spend assessing your performance, the less time you're spending on the question that's actually in front of you, the one that, because there's no going back or skipping ahead, is the only question that can actually improve your performance.

The other problem is that it's actually tricky determining the difficulty of a question because there's actually no such thing as an objectively easy question or an objectively hard one. When we speak about a question's difficulty, we have to use the only ranking tool that test makers have available to them: the percentage of students who, when given the question as an experimental question on a past GMAT, answered it correctly. We say a question is "hard" when a sizable number of those past GMAT students got the question wrong; when most of them got it right, it's an "easy" question. But the reason we put scare quotes in that last sentence is that no one, not even the master test makers employed by the GMAC, has any way of knowing why any particular student got a given question right or wrong.

So what if 88% of beta-testing students got a question wrong. If you were in the 12% of students who got it right, it probably felt pretty easy to you. The same goes for easy questions. Even if 94% of people knew how to solve an equation, the 6% who didn't would probably rank the question it appeared in as hard.

Nobody aligns perfectly with the statistical average, so the reason the question in front of you feels easier than the last may have absolutely nothing to do with your performance so far.

TO DO WELL, YOU MUST KNOW YOUR COMFORT ZONE (AND WHEN YOU'VE LEFT IT)

Even though an individual question may feel easy or hard for esoteric or personal reasons, after taking a few practice exams and studying for a while, you actually should be able to get a pretty good feel for whether you're headed toward the score you've gotten in the past over a stretch of about six or seven questions (instead of from question-to-question).

As we said before, the test is designed to feel hard for everyone, regardless of their ability level. With a little reflection, you should be able to recognize how it feels to do a stretch of hard questions and how that feeling differs from doing several easy ones in a row. Thus, when the test starts to consistently "feel hard," when you've left your comfort zone—that is, once you're in the difficulty tier that is just at the edge of your ability—you know you're on track. The better you get at the test, the later this feeling will kick in, the later you'll enter what we might call your "discomfort zone."

Moreover, how well you can recognize and manage your discomfort zone will determine how high your score can go. If you consistently "freak the heck out" (to use the clinical phrase) when the test gets to an uncomfortable level of difficulty, you'll fall back into your comfort zone, just as you would if you calmly executed a triage strategy to deal with a question you didn't understand, but after a freak out you'll probably also fall further, missing a couple of hard but still manageable questions that are on the high end of your comfort zone. That means you'll have to spend a few more questions climbing back to the edge of the zone, and you won't be able to climb as high in the end, leaving you 20 points shy of your peak performance.

WHAT THE GMAT *REALLY* TESTS . . . AND WHAT IT DOESN'T

Hopefully, it's becoming clear that the GMAT isn't like most of the tests you've taken before, and consequently the study habits and test-taking strategies you've used on other tests might not be as useful to you here. That's where the book in your hands comes in. Before we go any further, let's clear up one final misconception about the test. The GMAT tests your ability to take the GMAT. It's that simple.

The GMAT is not a test of your business knowledge. There are many successful executives and managers who would absolutely fail the test, and many has-beens and never-beens who could post near perfect scores.

The GMAT is also not an intelligence test. MENSA won't let you use it to prove your IQ, and securing a 740 doesn't mean you're smarter than your friend with the 700.

The GMAT isn't a very good predictor of your ultimate success in business school, either. Even though there is some positive correlation between a high GMAT score and good grades in the first year of business school, the correlation falls away after that.

The GMAT isn't even much of a math or English test. Certain mathematical concepts appear on the test, as do certain grammatical rules and basic principles of formal logic. Ultimately, however, neither your math skills nor your deftness with the subjunctive mood will translate directly to an impressive GMAT score. So what will affect your score?

Patterns and Predictability: The Keys to GMAT Success

It's often said that the key to sales is telling the buyers what they want to hear. That jaded platitude works for the GMAT, too, when you get right down to it. The key to a higher score is learning what it is that the test makers want to hear. Test makers have certain ways of thinking that are thoroughly predictable because they've employed them time and time again on previously administered tests. Beneath every question lies a handful of patterns that have appeared in different combinations in other questions.

GMAT test takers just beginning their studies often feel as though the test makers always have another trick up their sleeve, that there's always an exception or an additional rule that they can whip out to make a weird looking statement in a Data Sufficiency question turn out to be sufficient or an answer choice in a Critical Reasoning passage look wrong when it's actually right.

The good news is that there actually is a limit to the things the test makers can spring on you. The GMAT is a small world. Indeed, odds are that any trick you fall for probably has popped up in a dozen different questions over the past year. Once you learn to spot their tricks, the little tells that are peppered throughout the GMAT, the test makers may even start to seem a little bit pathetic. "Oh, silly test makers," you'll find yourself saying instead, "the only reason to put absolute value in an equation in a Data Sufficiency question like this one is so one statement can be sufficient on its own once I plug the answers back in."

How Can We Be So Sure the Test Hasn't Changed Recently?

That's easy. Both authors of this book make a living as professional GMAT tutors, drawing clients from many different backgrounds and with score goals that run the gamut from 500 all the way to the top. The book you hold in your hands represents nearly 30 years of combined experience with the test in all its subtle nuances. What's more, with this brand new edition of the *Barron's GMAT,* the book has been completely revamped and written from the ground floor up, unlike some of those other books in your stack, which just change the number on the cover every year and call it a day. And it's loaded with helpful strategies for answering the various question types.

Let's face it: no book could cover every single facet of the test or provide the instruction to overcome every student's particular challenges—not if you want it to fit in a backpack, at least. So, think of this book as your comprehensive guide to GMAT preparation. While preparing, you'll still probably need to consult other sources for help on particular topics.

GATHER YOUR MATERIALS

As we all know, sometimes the difference between success and failure boils down to having the right tools for the job. In this respect, the GMAT is no different.

The two most important additional resources you'll need for GMAT study are sold and distributed by GMAC itself: *The Official Guides* and the GMATPrep™ Software package.

The Official Guides

Once a year, the GMAC puts out a three-volume compilation of official questions from previously administered tests called *The Official Guide for GMAT Review*, *The Official Guide for GMAT Quantitative Review*, and *The Official Guide for GMAT Verbal Review*. They're sold individually and in a three-volume set called *The Basic GMAT Study Collection*. These are the only printed books that contain actual questions from the test makers themselves. All other books (this one included) contain simulated questions written by experts from the test preparation industry. The explanations of right and wrong answers in *The Official Guides* aren't always the best, but the closer you get to your test date, the more you will want to work from official materials to ensure that you've calibrated your expectations to the exact writing style and sensibilities of the actual test.

It's important to note that even though *The Official Guides* come out every year (with a big 2017, 2018, 2019, etc., on the cover), the content within is not completely different from year to year. Indeed, the books only change out about 25% of the questions from the previous edition (and some years it's more like 10%). The remaining 75% is the same. So, don't worry too much if you're using a book that's a year or two behind. Most of the questions are the same, no matter the date on the cover. And you can usually find the previous years' volumes on drastic markdown whenever a new edition comes out. (Dutiful GMAT aficionados at places like the GMAT Club forums even compile lists of questions that are repeated in each book.)

GMATPrep™ Software

Before you take the test, you're going to want to practice taking the exam, in as close to real conditions as possible. This book has one practice test. When you sign up for the test (or for a GMAC account), you're provided with a free link to download the GMATPrep™ Software, which contains two full-length practice tests in the exact computer format that you'll see on test day, with questions taken from previously released exams.

You're definitely going to want to use these two free tests. Most students take one at the beginning of their studies and one in the week leading up to the test, using it as a "dry run" for test day.

The software also contains 90 additional free questions. And every few months, the test maker puts out new content for the software—for a price. Additional official practice tests are sold in bundles of two for about $50, and additional collections of about 150 practice questions are also released periodically. Nobody said preparing for the GMAT was going to be cheap!

Other Useful Tools

A Legal-sized Wet Erase Pad

For security reasons, the test center won't let you use paper for your scratch work. Instead, you get a noteboard, a spiral-bound booklet of six double-sided yellow legal-sized laminated sheets of graph paper. As much of a pain as it might be, you need to get used to working problems and taking notes on boards like these. Mock-ups are available from various online retailers (Amazon and the like); however, you can always have a print shop photocopy some graph paper lines onto appropriately sized pages, then laminate and spiral bind them. Either option will set you back less than $10.

A Stockpile of Wet Erase Pens

You also need the pens to go with your board, naturally. If you want to make your practice work as close to the test day experience as possible, you can even purchase the exact model that the testing centers all stock: the Staedtler Lumocolor Non-permanent #3119 Superfine black pen.

A Reliable Digital Timer

While there is great value to be had in working practice questions in untimed conditions, eventually you have to bite the bullet and add the pressure of the ticking clock to your efforts. Digital is preferable to analog, as the timer on the day of the test (found in the upper left corner of the GMAT's computer interface) will be digital.

Some Real Live People to Study With

Forget those dubious groupwork assignments from your undergrad days. Finding a study group of similarly dedicated future business school students can do wonders for your preparation. Even if you end up as the person in the group with the most advanced math knowledge, the one everyone's always asking to explain why it's important that pies aren't square, you'll still find that the very process of explaining it to someone else will further cement and deepen your own understanding of the material.

SIMULATE TEST DAY AS OFTEN AS POSSIBLE

There's a reason we asked you to get a practice noteboard. On the day of the test, it's all you'll have to write on. Remember, too, that you should use it as you answer the questions in this book. Although it's perfectly acceptable for you to take notes as you study, the first time you work a question, resist the temptation to write on the page. You won't be able to underline a telling phrase in a Reading Comprehension passage on the day of the test, so don't give yourself that luxury in practice.

Likewise, it's very easy to inadvertently provide yourself with convenient excuses for why you're having trouble with the test. Chief among these is taking practice exams and doing practice problems in loud public places or in front of the TV. You might not realize you're doing it, but by putting distractions in your environment, you're tacitly providing yourself with a fallback: you can always say, "Yeah, I was kind of distracted, that's why I missed this question." (This might be an accurate explanation, but it might also be true that you would still have missed the clue in the question stem, and you won't figure that out if you stop at distraction.) The same can be said of doing questions too late at night or when you haven't eaten.

REGISTER FOR THE TEST, ALREADY!

It's all too easy to delay taking the GMAT, to give yourself "just a few more weeks" of study, to wait until after a looming deadline, an upcoming vacation, the end of the semester exam week, Christmas break, and the list can go on forever to "really get serious about the test." There's always a theoretical better time to study that's just a few weeks away. I'll study tomorrow, next week, some day. The problem is, to quote John Fogerty, "Someday never comes."

When one someday rolls around, there's always another one, just a few weeks away.

The best way to forestall this stalling is to give yourself a deadline and put some money on the line. At $250, the GMAT isn't cheap. Schedule your GMAT for an appropriate time in the future; for most students, that's two or three months from now. Go ahead, you can sign up for the test right now. We'll wait here while you do.

Back? Good. Now you have a deadline and a $250 bet with yourself, a good reason to turn to the next chapter, where you'll begin learning about those predictable GMAT patterns and how best to turn them to your advantage. Sure, you could wait until later, but there's no time like the present . . . .

The Analytical Writing Assignment | 2

After you've navigated the testing center's security protocols and been ushered to a seat, the first test content you'll see will be the 30-minute Analytical Writing Analysis, also known as the GMAT's essay section.

The main reason that business schools had been demanding a writing section actually had little to do with writing directly. The late 1980s and early 1990s saw a huge boom in the number of applications to business schools, particularly applications from abroad, places where English was not the primary spoken or written language. Those years also saw a not-so-coincidental rise in the number of applications in which the admissions essays, writing samples, and personal statements had clearly been written by a hired gun and not the applicant in question. The best way to sort out the cheaters from the honest-to-goodness writers in the applying crowd was to get another sample of their writing on file, one produced in a controlled, secure setting, and thus the AWA was born.

Of course, it should be admitted, a good many business schools also desired a clearer picture of their applicants' writing ability. The AWA also fills this role. Admissions professionals are quite interested in your ability to write, it's just that they have many other excellent ways to gauge that: your cover letter, your TOEFL scores, the number of writing courses on your transcript and the accompanying grades in them, whether the job descriptions on your CV seem to indicate much experience writing outside of academia, samples of your previous written work, essays specific to their institution, etc.

How Schools *Actually* Use the AWA

If you're an applicant from a country where English isn't the native tongue, there's some bad news. Your AWA essay will be scrutinized a bit more heavily than an applicant hailing from the United States or the United Kingdom because business schools want to make sure you're up to the challenge presented by courses conducted entirely in English. The AWA still won't overrule more important indicators—your TOEFL score chief among them—but it will be considered.

If, on the other hand, you're a native English speaker, your AWA score is likely to get the most cursory of glances, unless your academic career or your career experience suggests some sort of deficiency in your writing skills. In that case, the AWA does allow you the opportunity to answer some of those lingering questions.

What Does an AWA Score Look Like?

As discussed in the first chapter of this book, you'll receive two scores for the AWA, and you'll have to wait about three weeks to find out what they are. Your AWA Score and its accompanying percentile score will arrive only with your Official Score Report. Your primary AWA Score will be a number from 0 to 6, either a whole number or something point five—that is, in half-point increments. The test maker almost never awards a score of .5 to 1.5, and 0 is reserved for students who simply do not write anything. Most business school applicants' scores fall between 4 and 5.5, or across only 4 different possible scores—not a lot of room to distinguish one candidate from the next.

This score, as well as the actual essay you type on the day of the test, is made available to every business school that receives your overall score.

How High an AWA Score Do I Need?

As a rule of thumb, once your AWA score is above 4, you're in the clear. If it's 4 or below, the schools will probably look more closely at your application and possibly even at the essay you wrote itself.

How Is the AWA Score Generated?

The best indication of how much schools should value your AWA score is how the score is generated. If you have images of panels of old professorial types in tweed jackets with leather elbow patches all sitting around a table in a well-appointed study discussing the relative merits of your essay, which they all have annotated heavily with red pen, congratulations, you have an excellent imagination. Alas, the truth is, unless there's some sort of problem, your essay will be read by two graders only. One of them will be a part-time employee of ACT working in a massive cubicle farm. Your essay will pop up on the computer screen for 2 minutes total. At the end of that 2 minutes, the reader—usually a current or former humanities graduate student—will enter a score for the essay, from 0 to 6 in half-point increments.

During the typical work day, these human essay graders will see about 30 essays every hour over an 8-hour shift. You don't have to have a perfect Quantitative Subscore to know that means about 240 essays each day and 1200 a week.

What the GMAT AWA Really Doesn't Test . . .

According to the GMAC's *Official Guide*, the best essays are those that exhibit:

- Exemplary critical thinking skills
- An organized argument with well-developed support
- Mastery of the language and diction of the professional English vernacular

But are those really things that you can tell about an essay that (1) is read for no more than 2 minutes and (2) is graded partially by a computer program nowhere near as sophisticated as the one that beat Kasparov? We don't think so, either.

There is, however, a silver lining. All you need to do is learn the formula, and you will be the proud owner of a robot-approved AWA score between 4.5 and 6.

The vaunted E-Rater is only going to scan your essay looking at the following:

- Structural keywords and phrases that indicate organization
- Spelling and grammar mistakes
- The general difficulty of vocabulary used
- The number and average length of phrases, sentences, and paragraphs

Attempting to match the E-Rater's assessment, the human graders will be looking for mostly the same things. So, instead of the GMAC's impressive-looking list of requirements, your essay will instead be aiming for two main things:

Length: The essay has to be long enough to give the impression that it covers the topic thoroughly and in detail.

Appropriate Vocabulary: Words that might strike your college English teacher as superfluous are absolutely essential, so you're going to need lots of transition words like *first, next, consequently, on the other hand, moreover,* and *in conclusion.*

Also, a liberal (but not excessive) dusting of "five-dollar words" can make your fluency with English rate higher with both man and machine. There is one grain of salt this advice does need to be taken with. Since one-half of the grading team actually is a person, you can bolster your chances for a score over 4 by making sure that the essay is also:

Easy to Read: Their job is not an easy or glamorous one; do the readers a favor and make sure your essay, particularly the first paragraph, glides easily from point to point.

On Topic: Though the computer algorithm can't tell lightning from a lightning bug, human readers can, and so make sure the essay actually is on the topic indicated at the top of the computer screen.

Palatable: If you think something might be offensive or alienating, then err on the side of caution. You want your essay to be easy, breezy, and comfortable for the grader.

Note the one big thing left out through all of this: content. As long as you don't write an essay about how much you love your dog when the prompt calls for an analysis of whether a particular code of ethics is likely to bring about a change in the corporate culture at Company X, *what* you say is almost insignificant compared to *how* you say it.

Indeed, it's an open secret in the test prep industry that graders of GMAT essays like to talk about essays in terms of what they call "fourness." As long as an essay *looks* like one that answers the question without having anything else to say for it—a mediocre but acceptable by-the-numbers essay—then it gets a 4. If it has any easily spotted plus, that bumps it up to a 4.5 or 5. Sixes get reserved for essays that make a great first impression and don't look at a further glance like they've committed any big errors of style or diction.

On the other hand, if there's something weird or hard to follow in the first few lines, only then do the 2's and 2.5's come out.

ANATOMY OF AN AWA PROMPT

When you finally hit that Begin Test button on test day, you'll be greeted with something that looks like this on your computer screen:

> The following appeared as part of a newspaper editorial:
>
> "Five years ago the teachers at Bellville Heights Technical School introduced interactive computer displays to their refrigeration and air conditioning classes. The proportion of students enrolled at the school who later failed their licensing exams dropped substantially. What's more, the decline followed almost immediately upon the program's introduction. Clearly, if we wish to improve education throughout our post-secondary educational system, we must allocate a greater portion of our education budget to bringing innovative technological approaches to learning into all of our classrooms."
>
> Discuss how well reasoned you find this argument. In your discussion be sure to analyze the line of reasoning and the use of evidence in the argument. For example, you may need to consider what questionable assumptions underlie the thinking and what alternative explanations or counterexamples might weaken the conclusion. You can also discuss what sort of evidence would strengthen or refute the argument, what changes in the argument would make it more logically sound, and what, if anything, would help you better evaluate its conclusion.

Notice that, much like Critical Reasoning questions, there are essentially three parts to an AWA question:

The Three Parts of an AWA Prompt

1. **THE SOURCE.** Every AWA question includes a single short line ending in a colon that gives a purported source for the argument that follows. This isn't filler, exactly, though you don't have to consider the source in making your essay if you prefer. The source does give you a handy way to refer to the argument, however. "As the editorial states," "the editorialist's position," or "the argument in the editorial" would all work if the pretend source of the question were described as "an editorial concerning the proposed tax hike."

2. **THE ARGUMENT.** Usually the argument is fewer than 100 words long and generally presents either a plan to accomplish something, a recommendation of a course of action, or an abstract evaluation of whether one thing is more important than another (both in a general way that extends to many different circumstances or in a specific, given circumstance).

3. **THE INSTRUCTIONS.** Read them now, commit them to memory soon, and once you have, never look at them again. They're not going to change, and it'll save you precious seconds on test day.

OVERALL STRATEGY FOR THE AWA

Step 1: Assess the Argument

As we will soon see, a thorough assessment of an AWA argument is a lot like untangling a Critical Reasoning question. Identify the speaker's conclusion and make a jot list of all the points of evidence the speaker employs. Unlike in the Critical Reasoning section, you're almost certainly going to want to jot this information down. You can use the noteboard or the question's response box.

While assessing the argument, take note of the usual suspects, particularly differences in the words used in the evidence and the conclusion. If a survey, study, or sample group appears (and they often do), make sure to compare every piece of information given about them and line those pieces up with the group the conclusion concerns.

Finally, don't forget that source note that comes at the top of the page. Context is always useful.

Step 2: Brainstorm

Now that you have the moving parts of the argument arrayed before you and understand the gaps in the author's reasoning, it's time to come up with all the points you think you might want to make. Though the general direction of the AWA essay is almost always the same (the speaker's argument is not convincing), be careful not to prejudge which bits of the argument will make the best hay for your essay. Very often, you'll find that something that initially seems like it might anchor one of your body paragraphs turns out to be a dud, and the point you only wrote down for completion's sake turns out to barely fit in a single paragraph once you've thought it over.

Nothing is off limits during your brainstorm. Let your mind wander free. Your essay will be the better for it.

Step 3: Outline Your Main Points

Here's a spot of good news: the outline you write for a GMAT AWA essay response will likely be shorter than one that you'd write for a paper for college credit. Forget all that old business about Roman numerals, capital letters, and so on. This can be as detailed or as scanty as you need. Keep your eyes on the prize. No one but you will ever see the outline. The essay's the only thing that can influence your score.

There is one part of the GMAT AWA outline that will differ from other essays you've written, the prewriting. Since the readers are unlikely to give careful or prolonged attention to your prose, you want to make sure that the places they will actually look are as polished and powerful as you can make them. As you finish up your outlining, you will want to convert your notes into fully completed first sentences for each of your main paragraphs. If you reach for clever turns of phrase or powerful hooks, they'll be wasted if they're buried any further in your work, so now's the time to work them out.

Step 4: Write the Essay

All told, you'll probably only spend about 15–20 of your 30 minutes typing out your essay, with the remainder devoted to the other steps, with the bulk of that time devoted to planning out the essay. Once the planning's done, it's time to get those fingers dancing across the keys—just remember, there's no spellcheck and auto-correct, so perhaps finger-dance at a slightly slower tempo than you would at home.

THE PLAN IN ACTION

Let's analyze the familiar prompt on page 21 step by step.

Step 1: Assess the Argument

Since AWA arguments follow the same rules as Critical Reasoning arguments in terms of structure, the first heavy lifting you'll have to do with an AWA prompt will be finding the argument's conclusion.

Here, the argument's conclusion is clearly flagged for us with the concluding keyword "clearly":

> "Five years ago the teachers at Bellville Heights Technical School introduced interactive computer displays to their refrigeration and air conditioning classes. The proportion of students enrolled at the school who later failed their licensing exams dropped substantially. What's more, the decline followed almost immediately upon the program's introduction. Clearly, if we wish to improve education throughout our post-secondary educational system, we must allocate a greater portion of our education budget to bringing innovative technological approaches to learning into all of our classrooms."

Whenever you're surveying the information in an argument, a good test of whether you've got it down is to reword the pieces in your own words. How would you rewrite this conclusion?

Write your rephrasing here:

_____

_____

One possible way you could go would be something like this:

> If you want to make all colleges/technical schools in the area better, spend higher % of $ in budget on classroom "technology"

Note a couple of key points:

The conclusion has a **qualification** attached; in other words, it's an **if/then** conclusion. We will need to be careful that we don't overstep the argument's conclusion in the essay and imply that our editorialist thinks that we have to follow this plan, period. It's only if we want to make the schools better that we need to spend this money. (Of course, it's not much of a qualification. Who doesn't want to make schools better?)

The scope of the argument is not just a greater **amount** of money, but a greater **percent** of the money in the budget. So, however big that budget becomes or however much it should shrink, the speaker is committed to the percentage increasing.

The reason we placed "technology" in scare quotes is that it's a relatively **vague term**. There's no way the author's evidence could possibly encompass all technological innovations, so this is an assumption waiting to happen.

Once you have the conclusion well in hand, it's time to characterize and track the evidence the author employs. With the argument less than 100 words, and so much of that taken up on that kind of lame qualification, there's not going to be much room to support the claim. That's intentional on the part of the test maker. If the argument were supported, what would you write?

Again, write your jot list of evidence points down. If you have your notes from when you took the diagnostic quiz, all the better:

A possible jot list might look something like this:

> Sample group: one school, type of class: AC/Refrig, 1 type of tech: interactive student displays, effect: lisc exams
> Effect is % of entire school; tech only in AC/Refrig. "substantial" decr
> Time frame: Incr *immediately* after tech; 5 years of history

There's a lot going on here in the evidence; or, it might be more accurate to say that there are so many places where not enough is going on in the evidence.

The argument, like so many on the AWA, draws a conclusion from a **sample group**, raising the issue of **representativeness**.

There are numerous ways the sample group can be characterized (and none of them appear in the conclusion specifically). The test case is **one school** in the district and only **one type of class** offered at that school. Likewise, as we should have expected, only **one type of technology** was involved: "interactive student displays." The **time frame of the survey** is also specified. We're only talking about 5 years of data here. Is that enough?

An even more interesting discrepancy crops up in the editorialist's description of the effect this tech had on the school. Only one type of improvement was tracked, naturally, but note that the effect is not calculated directly from the sample group. Instead of telling us that the qualifying exam scores improved for the AC and Refrigeration students—the ones in the class with the computer screens—the evidence concerns the school's students as a whole! Since we don't know how big a percent of the student body the AC students are, the possibility of both a **percent versus number** problem and an **alternate cause** emerges.

The extent of the effect is characterized as "substantial," a fairly **vague term**, all things considered. How much of an improvement will the school board or regents of this district be purchasing with their increased budget allocation?

And finally, the **time frame** is a bit suspicious. Were the students in these classrooms that received the computers all on the verge of taking their licensing exam?

As is always the case with GMAT arguments, once you have the evidence laid out (either in your head, as is usually the case in Critical Reasoning, or on paper, as here), the argument's assumptions become clear, and we have highlighted them by bolding the words above. In order for this argument to be true, we need to believe a lot that we're not told explicitly. Jot your thoughts down below and compare against the model:

_____

_____

_____

_____

The following is not meant to be an absolutely exhaustive list, but it covers the high points. For AWA prompts, our analysis of the assumptions need not be complete in any case, as we're only going to have room to write one or two as it is.

The assumptions in play:

- Bellville Heights Technical School must be similar enough to a substantial proportion of the schools in the district; otherwise, it's not going to be a good test case for making educational decisions in general.
- The students and classwork in the AC & Refrigeration courses also need to be typical, both of Bellville Heights' student body and of students in the district in general.
- These "interactive computer displays" must be sufficiently similar to the types of educational technology the editorialist believes will be purchased. And whatever their role in that AC & Refrigeration classroom, it has to be similar enough to how technology could be used in other courses throughout the district. In short, there's nothing special about these displays.
- The time frame cited requires us to take an awful lot on faith. We must assume that the displays caused the increase in passing scores on the licensing exams and that there's nothing suspicious about how soon after their introduction the scores went up.
- We must also be content to accept that 5 years of evidence is good enough to make a recommendation as large as the editorialist makes.
- The editorialist's statement that "substantial" decreases in the licensing board failure rate is a big enough benefit to count as an improvement, particularly of the sort that would change the way classes should be conducted in however many schools there are in Bellville's area.
- Since the author never discusses the actual dollar amounts, we're left to assume that however much new technology costs, it's within the budget's ability to accommodate and that moving the money around won't cause some sort of indirect harm.

The speaker in this argument sure did leave a lot of bases uncovered. And that's excellent news for us, as there are so many ways we could go with this essay. Indeed, we'd best be careful not to try chasing down each and every one of them in the next step. Though 30 minutes is a good long while to write an essay in, it's still only 30 minutes.

Step 2: Brainstorm

We've done so much in Step 1, how much could there be for us to do now? That's kind of the point, actually. If we take enough time to understand the argument, we really won't have much difficulty with the points we're going to raise in the essay.

On your whiteboard or in the text field of the GMAT CAT interface, you'd pick some assumptions and consider how best to frame them for the purposes of writing a 15- to 20-minute 500–1000 word essay.

When you wrote the essay during the diagnostic quiz, you might have focused on any number of issues. Here, we'll just go through a quick sample of a few.

> Representativeness! How big is Bellville? The AC dept? The school system? What types of schools? Are the same sort of places, students disciplines, etc.?
>
> Too soon? How could computers turn AC around? How do we know it's relevant at all? Maybe just happy to have $ thrown at them, happy students.
>
> Representativeness #2 What do "displays" do for AC? How useful in lit, history, brain surgery, law, race car mechanics?
>
> Show me the $$$ — How much do they have? How big a % of budget? Room to spare? Throwing $ at problem . . .

When you brainstorm an essay for the AWA, you're now moving beyond the things the speaker brought up to consider the sorts of facts that might change your ability to accept or cause you to reject the assumptions you've identified. Reach for specifics! You're going to need them as we enter Step 3.

Step 3: Outline Your Main Points

If you wrote your notes on your dry erase board, it's now time to move them up to the text field of the CAT interface. If you wrote your notes there on the computer, now would be the time to start deleting the lines of thought that proved less promising and to polish up the ones that you're going to go with. Of course, before you do either, you'll also need to make some decisions. What are you going to structure your essay around? Look for related points, points that will be easy to explain, and points that will flow into one another easily as you move from body paragraph to body paragraph in Step 4.

If you'd produced something like the sample brainstorming notes from Step 2, the direction is clear. If you're aiming for three body paragraphs, then the line item labeled "Too Soon" might be the one to drop, as it's a bit complicated an explanation to make in limited space and time and doesn't necessarily mesh with the other points.

If you're shooting for two body paragraphs, or an essay structured around two major points, then representativeness is clearly the way to go. Let's say that's the direction we decided to head. Our essay will be primarily about how the sample group is in many and varied ways not necessarily the best group to use to make comprehensive educational reform decisions.

Remember also that this is the part of our essay where we'll be writing out the first sentence of each of the paragraphs we're going to have in our final essay. It may seem a little bit like a cheat, but let's face it, the readers aren't likely to read past that first line anyway, and they certainly won't want to if the first lines aren't compelling.

Step 4: Write the Essay

To make sure that the reader understands the issue, the first paragraph should begin with a restatement of the argument and the situation it arises in—both should be given in your own words, though don't strain too hard to produce synonyms for every single word in the original question. There's bound to be some overlap in terminology, as there are some concepts that are hard to express any other way. After the issue has been clearly presented, it's time for the big reveal: you don't think the argument is a good one, and here's a quick sketch of why you don't.

Here are three sample first paragraphs we could write for this essay, arranged from "not quite good enough" (under 4) to "meh" (4–5), to "that'll do nicely" (6)—or, to put it in the test's argot: well under 4, 4–5, 6.

> This argument is not a good one. Its assumptions are weak and the evidence it gives is insufficient.

The good: OK, so there's not much good here. But this scant little two-sentence introductory paragraph does manage to accomplish one of our goals. It clearly lays out what the essay's main point will be: this isn't a good argument.

The bad: The biggest problem is there's no explanation of just what argument we're talking about. While there's no need for us to pretend that we're writing about school systems all through history or the higher truths of education itself, we should still take the effort to inform our reader of what we think the argument in the question says. At this rate, our hypothetical AWA writer is cruising for a 2 at best.

This argument, an anonymous editorial's recommendations for educational policy, asks us to believe that the evidence drawn from a single school is enough to make big decisions about how a school district should spend its entire budget. It supports this claim by asking us to believe without adequate support that the many differences between the pilot program's specifics and the district are inconsequential. Further, its recommendations are based only on a single type of technology. Without the addition of serious extra support, the argument should not be taken as valid.

The good: We're getting closer, but we're not there just yet. The introduction gives more specifics about the situation and the argument, and is also clear about the overall thrust of the essay. This has the whiff of "fourness" about it, though it might have an outside shot at a 5 if there's something eye-catching to follow.

The bad: The presentation of the argument and the essay's thesis statement kind of bleed together, as the hypothetical essayist seems to want to say both things at once. Hopefully, this essayist doesn't intend to call the editorial writer out for vague terminology, as this introductory paragraph is general and vague where it could easily be specific. (Pots should not call kettles black.)

This editorialist's argument recommending that an unnamed school district drastically change the allocation of money within its educational budget in order to incorporate more technology into the classrooms in its colleges and technical schools fails to convince. The main evidence offered to support the claim is quite limited, requiring us to assume that the educational improvement of students in a single school's air conditioning and refrigeration program following the introduction of interactive computer displays will be repeated throughout the district so long as those in charge of its educational budget are willing to spend extra money on technology. No regard is given to possible differences in kinds of program, sizes of school, or even the type of technology that will be purchased as the program moves from its pilot school to the entire district.

The good: Obviously, this hypothetical student's essay is going to end up longer than the other two, but notice how that length is accomplished: specific references and concrete detail. The author gives the essay's main point in the first line, fleshes out the argument in the middle of the paragraph, and then returns at its end to a preview of the sorts of issues that will be raised in the body paragraphs. It's also clear that this writer took the time to make sure that the first line of the essay was well written back in their version of Step 3.

The bad: This test taker's version of the argument is so tightly condensed into just a few phrases that it might be a little hard for the grader to grab onto. The level of diction and overall organization will probably mitigate that, however, so it's not that big a problem.

Now it's time for all three of our students to tackle the body paragraphs. Granted, it'd be hard to believe that all three of them are working from the same outline as we produced. Student 1's introduction is probably scantier, Student 3's is more developed, but not necessarily. One skill that separates the 4's from the 5.5's is the ability to take an outline and run with it.

Let's check back in with Student 1:

> To begin, how do we know whether the students in the first school are like the students all over the district? It could be that the increases in passing scores weren't even that impressive. And even if they are, that's not reason to believe that these students aren't different somehow. They're AC & Refrigeration majors, after all, and that's not exactly brain surgery. Until we know more about these guys, it's not a good idea for us to accept the editorial's argument. I mean, how do we even know that this editorialist is good at telling real educational successes from what just looks like a success after five years. You can spend ten years thinking you're doing the right thing, and only later find out that you weren't. There are too many examples of this sort of thing to list, and that's not even considering the possibility that there are a lot of schools in this district where people study all kinds of things, not just how to make sure your house is cool in the summer and your cold cuts don't spoil.
>
> That's not the biggest problem with this argument, though. We need to know a lot more about how those computer screens were used in the AC classes even. What does "interactive" even mean, and how would it help you figure out which part of the air conditioner you need to bang on when it doesn't work. And it's not like you bang on the same part when you're doing brain surgery, at least I'd hope not.

The good: Even with an inauspicious beginning, this student is managing to bring up specific reasons why the argument's underlying assumptions might not be valid. The occasional bit of color like the cold cuts in paragraph two isn't a bad idea, truth be told, though banging on the brain might be a little *too* colorful.

Also, notice that the student does manage to use transitional keywords to make sure the reader knows when the subject is being changed.

The bad: A tendency to meander and lose sight of the paragraph's purpose is this student's main flaw. The language is a bit loose, yes, but disorganization will do much more to lower a score than a casual tone. The student's body paragraphs likely mean that a 3 is not out of the question, though it is likely the essay's ceiling.

Over at Student 2's computer, body paragraphs are coming along, too:

> The program that saw the "substantial" results that so impress the editorial writer and motivate the entire proposal seems far too specific and esoteric a subject matter to use to make any drastic or far-reaching decisions about educational spending priorities. Nothing against Air Conditioning and Refrigeration Repair students, but this doesn't tend to be the program that draws the best and brightest, even at a technical school like Bellville Heights Technical. It's not clear that the results of a technical college are even relevant to collegiate education in general. Whatever the new technological improvements did for the tech school students' licensing exams, we should not be so quick to change course on the basis of their example. It is certainly within the realm of possibility that the AC Repair program at BH Technical is a comparatively small program, even at the school itself. If this were the case, it would be inadvisable for a school board to make too much of their success, however "substantial."
>
> A more compelling issue is the exact nature of the technology and the question of whether it could be usefully applied in other programs at BHT and elsewhere. The drama majors at Bellville Heights Fine Arts Academy might not know what to do with an interactive computer display, even if the business majors at a different school could use them for PowerPoint presentations that were miles above the ones they'd been able to do with noninteractive displays.

The good: The introduction of the appropriately named Fine Arts Academy is a nice touch, as is the PowerPoint example in the second paragraph. Whenever you can incorporate specific, relatable examples into your discussion, your essay will be the better for it. Student 2 is also doing a fair job of showing how the unwarranted assumptions aren't necessarily wrong, and that it will all come down to specifics that the editorial writer doesn't provide in the argument.

The bad: The problem of different points getting a bit mixed together in this student's presentation continues here. Putting the focus on the technology itself in the middle of paragraph two does mean that paragraph three is a clear extension of the overall line of thought, the original point about the HVAC students' representativeness is getting overshadowed. When writing an AWA essay, it's imperative that you finish making one point before moving on to the next.

And what sort of masterpiece has our 6-bound student produced while these last two students were sweating away?

The first and most glaring flaw with the editorial's argument is how little is told about the students in the pilot program. If the school district that contains Bellville Heights Technical is full of similar technical colleges that focus on subjects similar to air conditioning repair, we can be more confident that attempts to duplicate its success throughout the district will be met with success. On the other hand, if Bellville Heights is the only technical college in a sea of liberal arts schools, things might be different. Moreover, it is not even a certain thing that air conditioning repair itself represents a large proportion of the study body at the school in where the new computer technology was introduced. Though the drop in failure rates was substantial for students at the school in general, it is possible that the gains were found more in automobile repair or electrical engineering. The performance of the air conditioning repair students may well have gone down, for all the editorialist reveals.

This brings another problem to mind. There is very little information in the editorialist's writings about how the new "interactive computer screens" were used in the air conditioning and refrigeration repair classrooms. Without such knowledge, there is no way to determine how big a part of the increased performance was due to the computers. It could even be the case that they weren't used at all, only introduced and left to gather dust in the corner. Similarly, without knowing if there exist comparable technological advancements that could enhance the other programs in the school district, it is not possible to say whether allocating more funds to purchasing technology will bring about any increase in performance there. What helps an air conditioning repair student pass a qualifying exam might hinder a poet from creating a portfolio to send out to graduate programs.

The good: Again, it's easy to tell this essay is going to do well from the length alone, even though it is not the length alone that will determine its fate. Rather, Student 3 has clearly taken the time to think through several different points within the larger topics that serve as the focus for each of the two body paragraphs. There is little to no repetition in this student's delivery, instead detail upon detail added to flesh out the specifics of the essay's argument.

The bad: There's not much to criticize, though do notice how hard this student is having to work to keep from using personal pronouns. One wonders whose mind the problem is being brought to in the second body paragraph. At other points the diction gets a little obtuse. Great pains are being taken to keep even from abbreviating "air conditioning." This likely will not drag the essay lower than a 5.5, but if the essay seems too off putting to the human grader, it may just block the possibility of a 6.

It's time for our three students to sum their positions up in a concluding paragraph. We return to Student 1 first:

In conclusion, this argument cannot be accepted simply on the evidence that the editorial gives because we do not know enough about the other schools or about the computers the AC program used.

The good: Don't let the brevity sway your assessment too much. This is a perfectly serviceable conclusion. It wouldn't elevate an essay from a 3 to a 3.5, but it also wouldn't lower one from a 3.5 to a 3, either. In fact, Student 1 finally shows signs of clarity and focus, very cleanly reprising the two points of the body paragraphs—more clearly than the topics were presented originally, in fact.

The bad: We could easily wish for a longer conclusion, particularly one that mentions some way in which the editorialist might be able to improve the argument or answer the student's objections. Your essay on test day should avoid simply attacking the speaker's position.

Now back to Student 2, who was teetering on the edge of the acceptable score range with a rambling middle section.

Until more information about the scarcity or abundance of other, nontechnical colleges in the editorial writer's school district, and until more can be learned about the kinds of technology that fall within the potentially expanded budget, it will be hard for anyone to go along with the proposal in the editorial. Whenever someone suggests moving money around, but can only provide one limited example to back their suggestion up, we are right to be skeptical. Otherwise, we might end up with a ballet classroom full of VR helmets but no pointe shoes.

The good: Once again, Student 2 manages to rescue a substandard paragraph with a final flourish. Though beginning with the possible strengtheners as this paragraph does is a solid way to begin bringing an AWA essay to a close.

The bad: Resisting the temptation to go meandering for a sentence or two is still this student's greatest challenge. Often these shifts in subject are accompanied by shifts in tone, so that the essay oscillates unevenly between formal and casual. It would be better if this hypothetical essayist were to write an entirely casual essay than to haphazardly attempt more professional or academic sounding diction.

In the final analysis, the occasional flourishes and sparks of wit might convince the human grader to bump this essay up to 4.5 or even 5 if feeling generous. The E-Rater would probably not be as impressed and would likely suggest a 4, meaning the student's 4.5 is all but secured. It's not the most impressive AWA score, but it is good enough.

Back at Student 3's terminal, we might expect that the keystrokes have all but died down as the student dutifully follows this book's advice and is proofreading away. But what is there to show for the effort?

The holes in this argument are too many and too substantial that it remains difficult to take the editorialist seriously. Without further evidence confirming the representative quality of the air conditioning program and explaining how different technologies might improve the educational outcomes in all of the district's programs, whatever they may be, the proposal to reallocate funds to technology should be greeted with the utmost skepticism.

The good: This conclusion is perfectly serviceable, too, though not much more so than the short little conclusion that Student 1 gave. This is simply the wordy version, which is perfectly OK to do. The reader is adequately reminded of the essay's earlier points, and some suggestion for improvement is given, but there is also nothing particularly interesting or eye catching. The 6 is probably not going to happen, though Student 3 will almost certainly not score lower than a 5.5.

Step 5: Proofread

The sorts of things that our three hypothetical essayists might find on their proofreading runs won't be typos or spelling mistakes, but that does not mean that their essays could not have benefited from the time. Even Student 3's very polished essay could be further enhanced, little inconsistencies of language could be ironed out, or the vocabulary choices touched up here and there. And at the very least, the time allocated to proofreading will ensure that no one's essay cuts off abruptly.

The Final Template

Our experience with the three essayists allows us to suggest a final, fleshed out version of the potential essay template. Feel free to use it as you will. Tweak it to your own strengths and tastes, but remember that you don't have to reinvent the wheel in order to secure an excellent AWA score.

Introductory Paragraph

- Present the argument from the question in your own words.
- Clearly announce that the argument is flawed and indicate why.
- Sketch out briefly the points that form the core of the essay body.

Body Paragraphs

- In each, develop a single idea, most often a single assumption or type of assumption.
- Begin with a clear statement of the assumption to be discussed.
- Provide specific details of how certain unknown facts could weaken, others strengthen, the assumption.
- Transition to the remaining body paragraphs, if any.

Concluding Paragraph

- Begin with some indication of the sorts of evidence that might strengthen the argument.
- Proceed to reiterate your claim that the argument, as currently stated, is unconvincing.

STRATEGY TIPS, TWEAKS, AND OTHER CONSIDERATIONS

Relax!

There's no such thing as an advanced or difficult AWA question. There's nothing adaptive here and you get only one per test. And, as we've seen, all AWA prompts are more or less the same. Instead of worrying, just focus on this list of tricks, flourishes, and reminders once you've got your basic standardized test essay format down.

The "Fourth" Part of the AWA: The Interface

In general, we haven't spent too much time in this book discussing the GMAT CAT's interface, as it's not too hard to figure out that you use the mouse to move the cursor and the left-hand button to click on the answer buttons.

But with the AWA, many students do struggle a bit, spoiled by the robustness of the word processing software that they've become accustomed to using at home, at school, or on the job. The GMAT's AWA is not your old reliable word processor. You'd have to go back to the days when word processors were single-function devices that looked like fancy typewriters to find an interface this basic. It's got fewer features than Microsoft Notepad!

The most glaring lack is that function we most disdain day to day: the spell-check. No helpful red lines will appear under misspelled words, and no button will autocorrect them for you. The only buttons you'll have access to will be Cut, Copy, Paste, Undo, and Redo.

Does spelling count?!? Officially, no, spelling does not count. But do remember that one of your readers is only human, and you are trying to make a good impression; the grad students grading essays can't help but be influenced by your spelling to some degree. It might be the difference between a 5 and a 5.5.

The lack of your computerized spelling coach is very important to keep in mind when following the advice elsewhere to pepper your essay with a reasonable number of high syllable count words. You should only elevate your vocabulary to words that you are comfortable spelling. Misspelling those sorts of words will quickly give the reader the impression you're trying to manipulate them and may even assume your true facility with the language is lower than the rest of the essay might demonstrate.

However, if you don't want to use those buttons, there are a few keyboard shortcuts available. The interface designers even decided to make their bare-bones word processor agnostic to the PC versus Mac divide. Windows types will recognize these shortcuts:

Ctrl + X = Cut   Ctrl + V = Paste   Ctrl + Y = Redo
Ctrl + C = Copy   Ctrl + Z = Undo

And Mac aficionados will welcome this complementary set:

Alt + T = Cut   Alt + A = Paste   Alt + R = Redo
Alt + C = Copy   Alt + U = Undo

The AWA prompt will always take up a good bit of your screen real estate, while you'll be left to make do with the lower half. If you don't want to move your hands from the keyboard to scroll that tiny window up and down, don't forget the helpful [Page Up] and [Page Down] keys.

In Conclusion, Conclude

The 30 minutes you have for the AWA essay is a hard limit. There's no way to signal the computer that you need just one more second to finish your last sentence. When the timer in the upper right-hand corner of your screen hits 0:00, the word processing interface closes itself and punts you right into the Integrated Reasoning instruction screen. So in actual practice, you have about 29 minutes and 50 seconds in which to write your essay.

Essays that break off mid-sentence or mid-paragraph do take a grading hit from the computer and human readers alike. Prepare for this by knowing what your conclusion is going to be and, if possible, have it typed out at the bottom of your essay screen *before* you've written some of the middle paragraphs. It's easy to delete a supporting paragraph if you realize you don't have time to finish it, and so long as you've got other supporting paragraphs, they can compensate for the loss. A lost conclusion sinks the essay.

I Didn't Forget the Other Side—It's Just Wrong

Here's a simple but effective way to make your essay seem more well-reasoned and convincing with minimal extra effort on your part. You'll always be lacing your essay with pieces of information that will both strengthen and weaken particular unwarranted or under-warranted assumptions in the argument. Simply include a gracious acknowledgment that the side you find most likely is not the only possible outcome and that, indeed, many thoughtful people have disagreed.

It all boils down to one magic phrase: "There are [those/many/some] who would [say/argue/contend] . . ."

Consider the following:

> Industry alone is not sufficient to spur job growth. The Soviet political machine learned this in the last quarter of the past century, when their single-minded focus on industrial growth left villages of starving and diseased men and women who once could have entered the workforce. If only the central planners realized that if agricultural development does not keep pace with industrial, the proportion of the workforce simply unable to work will surely swell, erasing job gains in the industry.

Now, back off of that stance just a touch:

> While there are certainly economists who contend that industry alone is always sufficient to spur job growth, such an approach has often proven inadequate, as those advising the Soviet political machine learned in the last quarter of the past century, when a single-minded focus on industrial growth left villages of starving and diseased men and women who once could have entered the workforce. If only the central planners realized that if agricultural development does not keep pace with industrial, the proportion of the workforce simply unable to work will surely swell, erasing job gains in the industry.

Just one minor tweak and the author of the argument seems more engaged and even-handed, without a single jot of extra evidence!

It's possible to take the acknowledgment of other sides so far that it becomes the complete rejection of your own authority on the subject. Remember that the whole reason you're acknowledging the other side is to prove to your reader that you considered *but rejected* it.

When in Doubt, Space It Out

As many high schoolers also know, one sure way to make an essay seem longer than it is is to refrain from paragraph breaks unless they're absolutely necessary. On the GMAT, this rookie technique will likely end with your human grader's eyes glazing over. The appearance of length is important, yes, but so is making the essay as easy on the reader as possible. The human grader can be your best ally, affording you an extra bite at the apple by overruling the computer and sending you on to the final human grader, so long as you cater to them. Put an extra carriage return at the end of each paragraph. Make sure that you start your paragraphs with a full tab's worth of room, don't just hit the spacebar three times. And most importantly, if you're uncertain whether a thought belongs in its own paragraph or not, default to breaking it up.

Take a hint from the dinosaur media. Newspaper reporters have known this one for years, and even though the essay isn't as limited as their column inches, the essay is still displayed on a narrow field to the reader. Paradoxically, that means that an essay with shorter paragraph breaks seems longer than one with long chunks of text.

Don't Repeat Your Evidence

In the ever-present quest for an essay that is long enough for a 6, it can be tempting to belabor points because doing so does make the page so nice and full and paragraphs so nice and long. The problem is that human reader again. You don't want your one possibility of a sympathetic soul to turn his or her head in disgust the fourth time you pound out your example. So don't repeat your evidence.

That doesn't mean you should never repeat a structural point, however. The three phases of every successful essay boil down to the mantra *Tell them what you're going to tell them; tell them; then tell them you told them.* The structural glue of your essay might seem too repetitive, all that "first, second, third" and "for this reason, too, the argument fails to convince" isn't how the writers on *The New York Times*'s best-seller list operate—but it is how the successful GMAT AWA essayist works.

Exterminate Weasel Words

A "weasel word" is a little qualifying tweak that adds wiggle room to an otherwise straightforward statement. This is not the same as saying, "There are those who say"; rather, it's putting those squishy little asides like "sort of," "kind of," "of a sort," "so to speak," and "seems to." No responsible reader assumes that direct, forthright sentences mean that the author is some sort of pig-headed absolutist unable to see nuance, and overworked as they may be, the graders the GMAT employs are still responsible readers.

High schoolers use weasel words because they think that they make their case more compelling. Journalists do it to avoid recrimination and libel. They're both wrong, and in this you should not seek to join them.

Where to Go from Here

Now that you have an essay template to work from, examples of possible essays to draw upon, and an understanding of the actual standards that will be used to evaluate your writing, you should begin to feel a bit more confident about this small essay that begins the test. If you're still worried, or simply want extra help, there are a few extra resources readily available to you that will undoubtedly meet your needs.

Integrated Reasoning | 3

The Integrated Reasoning section has a **30-minute time limit and 12 questions**. Some of the questions may have several parts. A special online calculator is available for use only on this part of the GMAT. The Integrated Reasoning section will be scored separately from your GMAT score (from 200–800) and from your AWA score (from 0–6). This section will be scored on a scale from 1–8, in intervals of 1. **No partial points are given**, which means, for example, that if a question has three Yes/No statements, you need to get all three correct in order to get credit.

WHAT'S NEW IN GMAT INTEGRATED REASONING

The Integrated Reasoning (or "IR") section was launched in June 2012. Initially, most business schools were not familiar with it and did not assign it much importance. But with the release of the latest *The Official Guide for GMAT Review*, 2016, there are some aspects of the IR that warrant attention.

- Since a GMAT score is only valid for five years, there are now very few MBA applications with a Pre-IR GMAT score. This means business schools are more likely to use it as an assessment tool.
- The GMAC now has extensive data showing that the IR section is predictive of MBA success, independent of the quantitative and verbal scores.
- In a 2015 survey of admissions officers at more than 200 MBA programs across the United States and United Kingdom, 59% said that the IR score was an important part of their evaluation of a prospective student's overall GMAT score. In 2014, only 41% said it was important.
- Three years ago, 54% of admission officials were undecided about the IR section while only 22% felt it would become important. Given the previous point and how much the GMAC has been aggressively promoting the benefits of the scores to schools, we can expect that more admission officials would deem the IR section important.
- Now that there is enough data, we know that you do not need to answer all of the questions correctly to get a "perfect" score. Students have received a top score with only 10 of the 12 questions answered correctly.

Although less important than the quantitative and verbal sections, the IR section has become an important part of the GMAT exam. A high score on IR can give you a competitive edge, while a low score can hurt you.

The Integrated Reasoning section is designed to measure your ability to:

- review data in multiple formats using various methods,
- identify key issues and trends,
- apply high-level reasoning, and
- organize information in order to make an informed decision.

For this, you will need to be comfortable with synthesizing information from charts, tables, graphs, spreadsheets, e-mails, and letters in paragraph form. As with the rest of the GMAT, you will not need prior business knowledge to answer Integrated Reasoning questions. The Integrated Reasoning section can be best summarized as a blend of the GMAT Quantitative and Critical Reasoning sections along with some argumentative logic, thus the use of the term integrated.

Note that the Integrated Reasoning section is **not computer adaptive** like the quantitative and verbal sections, which become easier or more difficult in response to your performance. This means the questions are preselected, as in a simple paper and pencil test. Therefore, you should expect a diverse mix of question types and difficulty levels.

OVERALL STRATEGIES

The Integrated Reasoning section requires some of the same skills you will use on the overall GMAT. It also has a similar structure and format. Therefore, you can apply many of the strategies.

1. **INVEST TIME TO UNDERSTAND THE QUESTION:** For every GMAT problem, including those in the quantitative and verbal sections, you must ask yourself "What's going on?" before you dive into solving the question. Make sure you understand the question and the information given. Get a general sense of what the question is asking. Think about how you might set up your solution. Investing time up front to review the data and key insights before diving into the questions will save you from losing time by backtracking.

2. **AVOID THE TWO MOST COMMON ERRORS:** The most common errors that test takers make on the GMAT are misreading the question and making unnecessary calculation errors. Make sure you review the questions, the information, the passages, and the answer choices quickly but carefully.

When you make calculations, be sure to keep your scratch work clean, structured, and error free.

3. **KNOW HOW EVERYTHING RELATES:** Try to get a sense of how all the pieces of information—variables, numbers, and text—relate to each other. The GMAT writers don't expect you to look at all the data in great detail. Therefore, look for certain themes or trends within the data that are obvious. Most of the information given in the questions tells you the "what." Your job is to figure out the "so what." Ask yourself, "What does this tell me?" and "Why is this so important?"

4. **YOU DON'T ALWAYS NEED THE CALCULATOR:** The Integrated Reasoning section provides a calculator, but that doesn't mean you should always use it. It is an awkward tool. Most of the time, you can set up your questions to keep its use to a minimum. Most GMAT math problems can be solved conceptually and with minimal calculations. Even though you can solve all quantitative problems with a step-by-step process, there are always shortcuts. Do some mental calculations, simplify your work, and estimate whenever possible. You will be surprised by how little you need the online calculator.

5. **DON'T SKIM, SYNTHESIZE INSTEAD:** Skimming will not help you in this section. You are being tested on your ability to analyze and synthesize the data. That doesn't mean you have to look at every single detail. However, you do need to watch for important key words, note titles, headings, labels, and subject lines, along with units and key numbers.

6. **PRACTICE DATA SHUFFLING:** Since much of the navigation in Integrated Reasoning requires using tabs, scrolling, and sorting, you can practice much of this using spreadsheet software like Microsoft Excel. You can also try using a calculator on your computer for practice. Don't let the need to navigate slow you down.

7. **LEVERAGE CURRENT GMAT STRATEGIES:** Use the theory and strategies you learned in the Quantitative and Verbal sections of this book to help you. Many of the typical GMAT strategies use processes and methods that are transferable to the Integrated Reasoning section. You can apply similar skills to answering all the questions—quantitative analysis, algebra, deductive reasoning, argumentative logic and structure, identifying conclusions, and anticipating questions.

8. **LOOK FOR ALL THE HIDDEN CLUES:** The GMAT test developers like to hide clues to questions in many places. You need to know where these clues are. Start with the questions and answer choices themselves. They can give you an idea of where to look in a question and what to look for.

You can also use your work from previous questions within a section; you can use your work cumulatively to solve the next problem. Don't forget to look within the charts, tables, graphs, and paragraphs. They contain key numbers, labels, and words that provide more insight to the problem than you might originally realize. Digest every piece of the puzzle. With practice, you will begin to know what you should look for and what you can ignore.

9. **YOU DON'T NEED TO MEMORIZE:** Since you are given so much data and information, the test writers at the GMAC cannot expect you to memorize everything, nor should you try. Devote your time and energy to understanding the problem, navigating effectively, outlining a solution path, and getting to the answer. If you need to refer back, the data is always available.

10. **CONFIDENCE IS KEY:** Just like with the rest of the GMAT, confidence goes a long way to your success. When you are confident, you look at problems as a fun challenge and have the determination to solve them correctly. When you lack confidence, you second-guess yourself and you spend too much time focused on the wrong things. You use many of the skills tested on the Integrated Reasoning section every day in your professional and personal lives. Approach problems knowing that the theory, structure, and strategies you have internalized will help you succeed on the Integrated Reasoning section and on the rest of the GMAT.

Note that we will cover specific strategies for each question type in the sections ahead.

THE FOUR QUESTION TYPES

The new Integrated Reasoning section contains four types of questions:

1. **GRAPHICS INTERPRETATION:** You will analyze a graphical image and then select options in a drop-down menu in order to create accurate statements.

2. **TABLE ANALYSIS:** You will receive a sortable table of information, similar to a spreadsheet, that you must analyze to answer questions in true/false, yes/no, or other formats.

3. **TWO-PART ANALYSIS:** You will receive a paragraph of information and then answer a question in a two-part format. This requires you to look at data in two different ways in order to solve the question.

4. **MULTI-SOURCE REASONING:** You are given two to three sources of information presented in various forms—including text, charts, and graphs—on tabbed pages. You then have to answer questions in either a yes/no format or in a select one out of five format.

The following are the four Integrated Reasoning question types, along with strategies and sample questions for each.

GRAPHICS INTERPRETATION

True to its name, this section will require you to interpret graphics. The basic idea is this:

Look at this graph. Understand what it is trying to say. Extract some key information.

You will be given a graphical image—scatter plot, graph with variables, Venn diagram, bar chart, statistical curve distribution, or pie chart—and some explanatory text. There will be several statements you will need to complete using choices from a drop-down menu.

SKILLS TESTED

- Assimilating, analyzing, and interpreting data in graphical forms
- Identifying and extracting key information
- Interpreting past events and predicting future outcomes

Graphics Interpretation: Strategies

1. **START WITH WHAT YOU KNOW:** As with any GMAT question, ask yourself "What's going on?" before attempting to answer. Invest the time to get the gist of the graph. Try to look at it from a high-level or "big picture" perspective and to understand the information it is trying to convey. Think of an appropriate title for the graph in your own words (IYOW) if none is given.
2. **MAKE SURE YOU CATCH EVERYTHING:** Now focus on the details. Look at any titles, axis labels, symbols, legends, or units of measurements given. Is the graph displaying data in thousands or millions, in inches or feet, and so on? Investing time up front to understand the graph thoroughly will save you from having to analyze everything again later.
3. **IDENTIFY TRENDS AND RELATIONSHIPS:** Look for any key trends or relationships among the variables, the *x*-axis, and *y*-axis. Are there

any direct or indirect relationships? Do certain areas of the graph have spikes, a greater concentration of points, or either a positive or a negative slope? This is where we interpret the data and extract the key information.

4. **USE THE STATEMENTS TO HELP YOU**: As in the rest of the GMAT, the answer choices can provide you with some great insights. If the statements talk about slope, familiarize yourself with the slopes of any lines shown on the graph. The statements will mention certain key words that are relevant to answering the question. If you identify enough, you will be able to "connect the dots" and solve the puzzle. In other words, you can piece together all the different aspects of the graph and what it is trying to say.

5. **ANTICIPATE THROUGHOUT THE QUESTION**: Throughout your first read of the material, try to anticipate the relevant information and what the questions are going to ask. Once you see the questions, you can try to figure out the answer before you open up the drop-down menu. It's a great confidence booster if you see the answer you anticipated in the drop-down menu. If you don't see your answer there, it's a good indicator that you may have made some oversights.

TABLE ANALYSIS

In this section, you will be required to analyze tables. The basic idea is this:

Look at this detailed table. Sort the information to answer questions about it.

You will be given a table or spreadsheet that has sorting ability, much like a Microsoft Excel worksheet. Some text will be included to explain the table. The questions will have varying types of statements—yes/no, true/false, would help to explain/would not help to explain, or inferable/not inferable. You will have to select one choice for each statement. Every column in the table is sortable either numerically or alphabetically.

SKILLS TESTED

- Assimilating, analyzing, and interpreting data tables
- Sifting through and organizing a mass of information
- Identifying trends and patterns
- Extracting meaningful information to make decisions
- Understanding how data can be used to satisfy certain conditions or support either a hypothesis or principle

Table Analysis: Strategies

1. **START WITH WHAT IS GIVEN:** Look at the table and the headings. Invest the time up front to get the gist of the table. Get a sense of the data given, sorting options, rankings, columns, and highest and lowest items in the table. Think of an appropriate title for the table in your own words (IYOW) if none is given.

2. **USE THE QUESTIONS OR STATEMENTS TO HELP YOU FOCUS:** The questions will give you a good idea of what kind of information needs to be extracted from the table. Yes/no and true/false are usually easy to figure out. However, watch out for the more abstract "would help explain" questions. Ask yourself if sorting a particular column would point you toward a solution.

3. **IDENTIFY TRENDS AND RELATIONSHIPS:** Look for any key trends or relationships among the numbers given. Look at how the numbers or rankings change among columns. Do you see some obvious disparities? Are there direct, indirect, or inverse relationships? This is where you interpret the data and extract the key information. Do not spend an undue amount of time going through each piece of data. Rather, you need to get an overall sense of the table. Remember, you can always look back at the table for reference, so there is no need to memorize anything.

4. **DON'T OVERANALYZE; BE EFFICIENT:** These questions contain a lot of information. You can easily get lost on some of the larger spreadsheets and forget about the clock. If you practice sorting beforehand using a spreadsheet program, you can get a better understanding of how sorting works. When you look at numbers, you can **estimate** or use very rough numbers (for example, $23,846 is better thought of as $24k). Remember again that the questions will refer you to which columns to look at. So take the time to determine what would be the best sort to find the answer.

TWO-PART ANALYSIS

This section requires you to do two-part analysis. The basic idea is this:

Analyze a problem with two components and solve for two components.

You will be given a problem that is structured with two components. The question could be either a typical GMAT quantitative problem (two-variable, rate, or work problems), a verbal problem (two opinions on an issue, two separate aspects of research), or a combination of both. The problem will have two issues, variables, or aspects under consideration. The question will also have two components, usually as columns in a chart, with several possible answers in rows. These answer components may or may not be related. Your job is to select the one correct answer for each column.

SKILLS TESTED

- Solving complex or multilayered problems
- Recognizing relationships between two entities
- Solving simultaneous equations
- Thinking and reasoning
- Weighing trade-offs and making decisions with more than one aspect

Two-Part Analysis: Strategies

1. **START WITH WHAT YOU KNOW AND UNDERSTAND:** Write down what you know from the question, especially for multilayered or complex problems. This includes what you know and what is implied by the statements in the question. This is your starting point and helps you figure out what's going on before diving deeper.

2. **STRUCTURE WITH CHARTS OR DRAWINGS:** Typically, the more complex a GMAT problem, the more important it is to add structure to it. Lay out the data in a more organized form or use a drawing to visualize the information. Imposing structure also keeps your scratch work clean, makes your scratch work easy to follow, and helps you to extract key aspects of the problem.

3. **ALGEBRA IS YOUR BEST FRIEND:** In many of the more quantitative problems, algebra is a great tool. Algebra is the language of math. It can help you simplify the problem, understand what's going on, and unlock keys to the solution.

4. **DETERMINE THE KEY ISSUES:** In complex problems, several issues, aspects, or constraints are at play. Spend some time identifying and understanding what they are. Then you might be able to look at the answer choices and see which ones meet the question's criteria.

5. **PLUG AND PLAY:** Once you have a strong understanding of the problem, you can start trying some of the answer choices given. Many of the Two-Part Analysis problems have dependent variables. Plugging in one answer may lead to what the other answer should be. If the other answer choice is there, that is great. If not, try another answer choice and see if you can find a match.

MULTI-SOURCE REASONING

For the final question type in the Integrated Reasoning section, you will be required to use multi-source reasoning. The basic idea here is:

Look at multiple sources of information,
and pull the relevant data to solve problems.

You will be given two or three tabs that contain a large amount of information, either in text form (such as e-mails and research articles) or in table form. The idea is to give you more information than you need. Your job is to pull the relevant information from the sources and solve problems. Some of the more wordy problems resemble GMAT Reading Comprehension or lengthy Critical Reasoning questions. You may be required to use quantitative skills, verbal skills, or both. You will also have to use either deductive or inductive reasoning. Questions may be in a yes/no or a multiple-choice format.

SKILLS TESTED

- Assimilating a voluminous amount of data and extracting relevant content
- Using both deductive and inductive reasoning
- Integrating various types of information from different sources to make a decision
- Dealing with information overload
- Using both quantitative and qualitative information simultaneously
- Analyzing a case study

Multi-Source Reasoning: Strategies

1. **DETERMINE THE SCOPE OF THE QUESTION:** First determine whether the question is more quantitative or verbal, as this will determine which strategies and tactics are appropriate for the question. If the question is more verbal, first think about what the key aspect or topic is of the entire case study. Then look at each tabbed section and identify its key aspect or topic. This will help you get a better understanding of the pieces of the puzzle and the puzzle as a whole. If the question is more quantitative, make sure you know what the basic objective of the question is and what variables are at play.

2. **DETERMINE THE "SO WHAT?":** Each section, particularly for the verbal-type questions, will have conclusions, inferences, and purposes from which you can extract deductions or use inductive reasoning. Think

about each section's purpose and what the writer is trying to conclude. Again, you should do this both in context and in your own words (IYOW). Most of these questions will ask you to draw a conclusion, so understanding each section is key. The writer of each section will give you the "what," but you need to determine the "so what?"

3. **USE EACH QUESTION FOR DIRECTION:** Each question will give you a good idea of what issues or areas to focus on. The question should align with the scope and purpose you have already identified. If you are confused with all the information, you can first determine the main gist of the information and then look at the question. Depending on the question, you should be able to determine which section will be the best place to start.

4. **STRUCTURE YOUR INFORMATION:** Whether the question is qualitative, quantitative, or both, you will have to digest a lot of information. Write down the key pieces of information from each section, or create a chart that helps you sort out the issues or the math. Take the time to determine which would be the best tab to find the answer.

5. **LOOK AT THE STATEMENTS, AND ASK YOURSELF WHETHER OR NOT THAT IS TRUE:** For every inference or conclusion you have to make, you will find support in the content. As a quick check, you can try two options. The first is to find the specific support from the statements. If you can find support, then you know the answer is correct. However, if you cannot find the support, the answer cannot be correct. The second option is to ask yourself whether or not the answer is true based on the statements. If you can find a plausible alternative inference, perhaps the statement is false or the answer is no.

Quantitative Section: An Introduction | 4

The good news about the quantitative or math section of the GMAT is that you've seen it before, probably in grade 11 or earlier. The chapters ahead review the fundamentals along with some of the more commonly tested topics. Go through at your own pace, making sure you have a solid understanding of each section because the learning is cumulative. The further you go, the more you build up a GMAT quantitative bag of tricks. Eventually, you will have several tools and tactics in your arsenal to defeat the GMAT—and isn't victory fun?

WHAT'S NEW IN GMAT MATH

- There are many examples of new questions where you can break down and solve the question with little or no computation.
- Some new questions have story or practical "real world" problems for which algebraic or conceptual translation is the key to solving them.
- Some new questions integrate two and sometimes three content areas. For example, the test makers might put fractions or percentages, along with algebra, into a geometry question.
- As usual, the test makers put great effort into disguising the intent of the new questions.

Understanding the fundamentals and breaking down the questions using our strategies and knowing the "game" of the GMAT will be your best weapon on test day.

PROBLEM-SOLVING STRATEGY, METHODS, AND TACTICS

We will cover several comprehensive strategies and tools for conquering the GMAT problem-solving questions. Below is a summary of what we will explore in more detail in the problem-solving chapter (Chapter 10, page 145).

Problem-Solving Fundamentals

- Careless errors be gone!
- The secret is out about minimal or no calculations.
- The math is clean.
- Know how they deceive you.

Problem-Solving Strategies

- You need strong fundamentals.
- Invest in your immediate future.
- Harvest the garden of answer choices.
- Try this concept—conceptual thinking!
- Simplicity is the Ultimate Sophistication.
- Carry 3 big sticks—picking numbers, algebra, and number properties.

Problem-Solving Methods

Use the know-want-approach method:

1. What do you know?
2. What do you want?
3. What is your approach?

Problem-Solving Tactics

1. Pick numbers . . . wisely.
2. Use your best friends (algebra and number properties) . . . forever.
3. Don't break your back solving, try backsolving.
4. Construction, construction, what's your function?
5. Break it down!
6. Estimate, guess-timate, approximate to elucidate.
7. Process of elimination (POE): return of the friend.
8. Don't get tricked. Become a trickster.
9. Stop staring!
10. Let it go.

DATA SUFFICIENCY DIRECTIONS FOR THE GMAT

Below are the official directions from the GMAC that appear before your first data sufficiency problem on the GMAT.

DIRECTIONS: This problem consists of a question and two statements, labeled (1) and (2), in which certain data are given. You have to decide whether the data given in the statements are sufficient for answering the question. Using the data given in the statements plus your knowledge of mathematics and everyday facts (such as the number of days in July or the meaning of counterclockwise), you must indicate whether:

A. Statement (1) ALONE is sufficient, but statement (2) alone is not sufficient to answer the question asked;
B. Statement (2) ALONE is sufficient, but statement (1) alone is not sufficient to answer the question asked;
C. BOTH statements (1) and (2) TOGETHER are sufficient to answer the question asked, but NEITHER statement ALONE is sufficient;
D. EACH statement ALONE is sufficient to answer the question asked;
E. Statements (1) and (2) TOGETHER are NOT sufficient to answer the question asked, and additional data specific to the problem are needed.

Numbers: All numbers used are real numbers.

Figures: A figure accompanying a data sufficiency problem will conform to the information given in the question but will not necessarily conform to the additional information in statements (1) and (2).

Lines shown as straight can be assumed to be straight, and lines that appear jagged can also be assumed to be straight.

You may assume that positions of points, angles, regions, etc., exist in the order shown and that angle measures are greater than zero.

All figures lie in a plane unless otherwise indicated.

Note: If the data sufficiency problem asks you for the value of a quantity, the data given in the statements are sufficient only when it is possible to determine exactly one numerical value for the quantity.

SAMPLE QUESTION OVERVIEW

Question Stem	What is the value of x?
Statement 1	(1) The square of x is 25.
Statement 2	(2) $x(x-5) = 0$

DATA SUFFICIENCY STRATEGY, METHODS, AND TACTICS

We will cover several comprehensive strategies and tools for conquering the GMAT data sufficiency section. Below is a summary of what we will explore in more detail in the data sufficiency chapter (Chapter 9, page 131).

1. **INVEST TIME UP FRONT, AND MAKE IT COUNT**
   - Avoid misreading the question and statements.
   - Understand the macroquestion, and know what data sufficiency type it is.
   - Determine what you know, want, and need.

2. **MANAGE THE INFORMATION IN A STRATEGIC AND TIMELY WAY**
   - Every statement implies something.
   - Know what you *know,* both direct and implied.
   - Avoid making assumptions.
   - Do not carry information from statement 1 into statement 2.

3. **MAXIMIZE THE STRUCTURE TO YOUR ADVANTAGE**
   - Do not do calculations unless you have to.
   - Start with the easier statement.
   - Statements 1 and 2 never contradict.
   - Determine sufficiency by proving insufficiency.

4. **DON'T LET THE GAME FOOL YOU**
   - The tests put the same info in each statement.
   - Do not forget that "no" can mean sufficient.
   - Watch out for the easy C.
   - When the test asks for $a + b$, you do not need individual values.

5. **USE YOUR KNOWLEDGE OF GMAT THEORY, STRATEGIES, AND METHODS TO SIMPLIFY**
   - Manipulate the equations.
   - You always have your two BFF's (algebra and number properties).
   - Do not forget about 0 (zero).
   - Pick numbers.
   - Strategy 1: Decision Tree Method.
   - Strategy 2: Know-Want-Need Method.

Arithmetic 5

The best way to deal with math is to have fun with it. One of the reasons why the quantitative section proves challenging for students is that they likely have not done this kind of math in several years. If you do a practice test and score less than the 25th percentile on the quantitative section, you are probably missing many fundamental math skills. Even if you score above the 80th percentile, you may still have some gaps in basic definitions. Regardless, know that the math concepts on the GMAT are mostly grade 11 level or earlier. You have already "been there, done that" with success. Now you can do it again and hopefully have fun in the process. This section will introduce you to the basic definitions and arithmetic fundamentals that you need for your GMAT quantitative journey.

ARITHMETIC DEFINITIONS AND OPERATIONS

INTEGER: Any whole number that is not a fraction or decimal. It can be positive or negative. For example, –1200, –43, –2, –1, 0, 1, 2, 28, and 1462 are integers, and –0.6, $\frac{1}{2}$, and π are not integers.

EVEN INTEGER: Any integer that, when divided by 2, gives you another integer. For example, –4, –2, 0, 2, 4, 6, 8, and 10 are even integers.

ODD INTEGER: Any integer that, when divided by 2, gives you a noninteger. For example, –3, –1, 1, 3, 5, and 7 are odd integers.

REAL NUMBER: Any number on the number line. This includes (but is not limited to) positives and negatives, integers, rational and irrational numbers, roots, and π (pi). For example, –4.5, $-\frac{1}{3}$, 0, 2, $\frac{7}{37}$, $\sqrt{139}$, and $3.2 \cdot 10^{87}$ are real numbers. The only numbers that are not real are called complex or imaginary numbers (e.g., $\sqrt{-1}$), and they are not tested on the GMAT.

DIVISOR OR FACTOR: For an integer N, the divisor is a positive integer that can divide into N without creating a remainder. For example, 1, 2, 3, 4, 6, and 12 are divisors of 12 while 0, 1.5, 5, and 10 are not divisors of 12.

MULTIPLE: A multiple of integer *N* results from multiplying *N* with another integer. For example, –7, 0, 7, 140, and 28,007 are multiples of 7 while –5, 1, 8, 139, and 28,005 are not.

PRIME NUMBER: An integer that is divisible by **only** itself and 1. Prime numbers have exactly 2 factors. For example, 2, 3, 5, 7, 29, and 31 are prime numbers while 4, 10, 15, and 35 are not prime numbers. Note that 0 and 1 are not prime numbers. Note also that 2 is the smallest prime number and the **only** even prime number.

DIVISION: If we look at the simple expression $\frac{7}{3} = 2$, r1, we find several terms used in division: 3 is the **divisor**, 2 is the **quotient**, 7 is the **dividend**, and 1 is the **remainder**.

STRATEGIES FOR CALCULATION SHORTCUTS

Test takers often make computational errors on the GMAT. You are expected to know all aspects of mathematical calculations and operations including addition, subtraction, multiplication, and division of integers, decimals, and fractions. You also have to do these computations quickly and efficiently but without sacrificing accuracy. The good news is that most GMAT quantitative questions require a conceptual approach with little need for calculations. Still, it is important that you master the beginner concepts.

Calculation Shortcuts

Many students have trouble with time management. Although most questions in the GMAT math section require few calculations, you can expect some. These provide you with an opportunity to save time by employing shortcuts. The seconds that you shave off each calculation will add up to minutes of extra time that you can apply to the harder questions.

For example, if you can reduce your average time per question by even 20 seconds, you will save $37 \cdot 20 = 740$ seconds $= 12\frac{1}{3}$ minutes on the quantitative section!

MULTIPLICATION TABLES: To save time, you should **memorize** the classic times table.

x	1	2	3	4	5	6	7	8	9	10
1	1	2	3	4	5	6	7	8	9	10
2	2	4	6	8	10	12	14	16	18	20
3	3	6	9	12	15	18	21	24	27	30
4	4	8	12	16	20	24	28	32	36	40
5	5	10	15	20	25	30	35	40	45	50
6	6	12	18	24	30	36	42	48	54	60
7	7	14	21	28	35	42	49	56	63	70
8	8	16	24	32	40	48	56	64	72	80
9	9	18	27	36	45	54	63	72	81	90
10	10	20	30	40	50	60	70	80	90	100

You should also **memorize** these commonly seen multiples.

Perfect Squares		Powers of 2	Cubes and Fourths
$1^2 = 1$	$11^2 = 121$	$2^3 = 8$	$3^3 = 27$
$2^2 = 4$	$12^2 = 144$	$2^4 = 16$	$3^4 = 81$
$3^2 = 9$	$13^2 = 169$	$2^5 = 32$	$4^3 = 64$
$4^2 = 16$	$14^2 = 196$	$2^6 = 64$	$4^4 = 256$
$5^2 = 25$	$15^2 = 225$	$2^7 = 128$	$5^3 = 125$
$6^2 = 36$	$20^2 = 400$	$2^8 = 256$	$5^4 = 625$
$7^2 = 49$	$25^2 = 625$	$2^9 = 512$	$6^3 = 216$
$8^2 = 64$		$2^{10} = 1024$	
$9^2 = 81$			
$10^2 = 100$			

Multiplying and Dividing Larger Numbers

Remember that the mathematical operations on the GMAT are generally clean. That is, you will not be expected to manipulate complicated numbers. Instead, the numbers can usually be broken down for simpler computations. You can also use certain tricks to help you do the math in your head.

What is 32 • 15?

Solution: You can break this down to 30 • 15 = 450 plus 2 • 15 = 30 and add them together to get 480. You can also break this down to 32 • 10 = 320 plus 32 • 5 = 160 and add them together to get 480. Note that 32 • 5 is half of 32 × 10.

What is 651 ÷ 7?

Solution: To break this down, think of the multiple of 7 closest to 651 that you can quickly figure out in your head. In this case, 7 × 90 = 630. What is left over is 21 = 7 • 3. Therefore, the answer will be 90 + 3 = 93.

Simplify when you can: Look to simplify mathematical expressions whether at the beginning, middle, or end of a calculation.

$$144x = \frac{12y}{5}$$

Simplification: Instead of multiplying 5 • 144, divide 12 out of both sides to get $12x = \frac{y}{5}$, which simplifies to $y = 60x$.

Estimate where you can: Sometimes the answer choices are such that you don't need to calculate everything, you can just estimate.

701 • 52

The correct answer is going to be just a little bit more than 700 × 50 = 35,000, so look for that value among the choices. Furthermore, we know the correct answer will have a unit digit of 2 due to properties of numbers (discussed later in this book).

USE FRACTIONS: Since you don't have a calculator, many decimal and percent calculations are much easier when you use fractions.

33.3% of 24 multiplied by 0.25 becomes $\frac{1}{3} \cdot 24 \cdot \frac{1}{4} = \frac{24}{12} = 2.$

FRACTIONS

In GMAT math, using fractions is especially important since no calculators are allowed. A fraction is made up of 2 numbers: the numerator divided by the denominator.

$$\frac{numerator}{denominator}$$

Definitions and Properties

PROPER FRACTION: When the numerator is less than the denominator. For example, $\frac{1}{2}, \frac{1}{4}, \frac{5}{13}$, and $\frac{15}{114}$.

IMPROPER FRACTION: When the numerator is greater than the denominator. For example, $\frac{2}{1}, \frac{5}{4}, \frac{13}{5}$, and $\frac{114}{15}$.

MIXED NUMBER: When a whole number and a fraction are combined. For example, $2\frac{1}{2}, 3\frac{3}{4}$, and $7\frac{1}{3}$.

A fraction cannot have 0 as a denominator because this would make the number undefined. Integers can be expressed as fractions. For example, $12 = \frac{12}{1}$ and $5 = \frac{5}{1}$.

Fraction Operations

Addition and Subtraction

Fractions need to have the same or common denominator. You can multiply all the denominators together to find a common denominator. Alternatively, you can find the least common multiple (LCM) for all denominators, which is sometimes easier depending on the complexity of your calculations.

$$\frac{1}{2} + \frac{1}{8} - \frac{1}{5} = ?$$

In this case, the common denominator is 2 • 8 • 5 = 80. However, you may notice that the least common denominator is 40, so let's use that.

$$\frac{20}{40} + \frac{5}{40} - \frac{8}{40} = \frac{(20+5-8)}{40} = \frac{17}{40}$$

Multiplication and Division

When multiplying 2 fractions, multiply the two numerators on top and then the two denominators on the bottom. When dividing 2 fractions, convert the equation to a multiplication problem by flipping the 2nd fraction.

$$\frac{3}{4} \cdot \frac{2}{7} = \frac{(3 \cdot 2)}{(4 \cdot 7)} = \frac{6}{28} = \frac{3}{14}$$

$$\frac{3}{4} \div \frac{2}{7} = \frac{3}{4} \cdot \frac{7}{2} = \frac{(3 \cdot 7)}{(4 \cdot 2)} = \frac{21}{8}$$

Fraction Conversions

On the GMAT, you will often need to convert decimals or percents into fractions. You will also need to convert fractions from one form to another.

$$225\% = 2.25 = 2\frac{1}{4} = \frac{9}{4}$$

All of these numbers are expressing similar values.

Converting Mixed Numbers

The following diagram shows the basic process.

$$3\frac{3}{5} = \frac{18}{5}, \text{ but how?}$$

$$3 \overset{\text{add}}{\underset{\text{multiply}}{\rightleftarrows}} \frac{3}{5}$$

1. Multiply the denominator by the integer of the fraction: $5 \cdot 3 = 15$.
2. Add this result to the numerator: $15 + 3 = 18$.
3. Set this result above the denominator: $\frac{18}{5}$.

Converting Decimals

Each fraction is a division problem, one number divided by another or one numerator divided by a denominator. The GMAT is not going to give you very complicated decimals that require conversion. However, learning to convert either way is helpful in calculations. So it's much easier simply to **memorize** the most commonly occurring decimal/fraction equivalents. Some of the following are approximations.

$$\frac{1}{2} = 0.5 \qquad \frac{1}{6} = 0.167 \qquad \frac{4}{9} = 0.444$$

$$\frac{1}{3} = 0.333 \qquad \frac{5}{6} = 0.833 \qquad \frac{5}{9} = 0.555$$

$$\frac{2}{3} = 0.666 \qquad \frac{1}{7} = 0.143 \qquad \frac{7}{9} = 0.777$$

$$\frac{1}{4} = 0.25 \qquad \frac{1}{8} = 0.125 \qquad \frac{8}{9} = 0.888$$

$$\frac{3}{4} = 0.75 \qquad \frac{3}{8} = 0.375 \qquad \frac{1}{10} = 0.1$$

$$\frac{1}{5} = 0.2 \qquad \frac{5}{8} = 0.625 \qquad \frac{3}{10} = 0.3$$

$$\frac{2}{5} = 0.4 \qquad \frac{7}{8} = 0.875 \qquad \frac{7}{10} = 0.7$$

$$\frac{3}{5} = 0.6 \qquad \frac{1}{9} = 0.111 \qquad \frac{9}{10} = 0.9$$

$$\frac{4}{5} = 0.8 \qquad \frac{2}{9} = 0.222 \qquad \frac{1}{11} = 0.0909$$

Note that we left out such fractions as $\frac{2}{6}$ or $\frac{4}{10}$ because they reduce to $\frac{1}{3}$ and $\frac{2}{5}$, respectively. We also didn't include all of the sevenths as you will likely need only the first $\frac{1}{7}$ fraction.

Note also that these decimal equivalents can easily be converted to percentages:

$$0.5 = 50\% \qquad 0.167 = 16.7\% \qquad 0.222 = 22.2\% \qquad 0.0909 = 9.1\%$$

Reducing Fractions

To simplify your calculations, you will often have to reduce a fraction. A fraction is reduced to its lowest term when the numerator and denominator have no common factors.

$$\frac{1000}{1200} = \frac{10}{12} = \frac{5}{6}$$

The 5 and 6 have no common factors, so you cannot reduce further.

The key to reducing fractions with large numbers is to find large common factors. In the previous example, we could have divided by 2 a few times, but that would've taken more time. Instead, we divided by 100 right away to save time.

If you aren't sure if there are any common factors, you can either break down each number into prime factors or memorize and use divisibility rules. Here is a list of the most common divisibility rules.

DIVISIBILITY RULES FOR NUMBERS

Number	Divisibility Rule	Example
2	The number is even	108 is even, 108 = 54 • 2
3	The sum of the digits is divisible by 3	108, sum of digits is 1 + 0 + 8 = 9, which is a multiple of 3, 108 = 3 • 36
4	The last 2 digits of the number are divisible by 4	108, last 2 digits are 08, which are divisible by 4, 108 = 4 • 27
5	The last digit of the number is either a 0 or a 5	1050 ends with a 5, 1050 = 5 • 210
7	Take the last digit of the number, double it, and then subtract it from the rest of the digits of the original number; if the result is divisible by 7, the original number is divisible by 7	1050, last digit is 0, double it we get 0, subtract that from the rest of the digits, we get 105 – 0 = 105, since 105 = 7 • 15, then 1050 is divisible by 7, 1050 = 7 • 150
9	The sum of the digits is divisible by 9	108, sum of digits is 1 + 0 + 8 = 9, which is a multiple of 9. 108 = 9 • 12
10	The last digit of the number is a 0	1050, last digit Is 0, 1050 = 10 • 105
11	Take the difference between sums of alternate digits; if the result is divisible by 11, the original number is divisible by 11	4,862, we get 4 + 6 = 10 and 8 + 2 = 10; 10 – 10 = 0, which is divisible by 11; so 4,862 = 11 • 442
25	The last 2 digits of the number are divisible by 25	1050, last digits are divisible by 25, 1050 = 25 • 42

Another shortcut is to find the closest multiple that is easy to calculate. For an awkward number like 7, this works nicely. For example, what if we want to determine if 1050 is divisible by 7? We know that 700 is divisible by 7. If we subtract 1050 – 700, we get 350. We know that 350 is a multiple of 7; therefore 1050 is divisible by 7.

More Powers of Numbers Rules

All powers of numbers that end in 0 will end in 0.
All powers of numbers that end in 1 will end in 1.
All powers of numbers that end in 5 will end in 5.
All powers of numbers that end in 6 will end in 6.

Powers of 2 have the following repeating pattern of four: 2, 4, 8, 6, 2, 4, 8, 6

Powers of 3 have the following repeating pattern of four: 3, 9, 7, 1, 3, 9, 7, 1

Powers of 4 have the following repeating pattern of two: 4, 6, 4, 6

Powers of 7 have the following repeating pattern of four: 7, 9, 3, 1, 7, 9, 3, 1

Powers of 8 have the following repeating pattern of four: 8, 4, 2, 6, 8, 4, 2, 6

Powers of 9 have the following repeating pattern of two: 9, 1, 9, 1

DECIMALS

Although fractions are easier to use in GMAT calculations than decimals, you still need to understand decimals. Some of the most common things to remember are below.

TERMINATING DECIMAL: Any decimal that has a finite number of nonzero digits. For example, $\frac{2}{5} = 0.4$.

NONTERMINATING DECIMAL: Any decimal that has an infinite number of nonzero digits. For example, $\frac{3}{11} = 0.2727\ldots$.

Addition or Subtraction of Decimals

When adding or subtracting two numbers with decimal places, make sure you line up the decimal points. You may need to add zeros to help you.

$$134.6 - 3.547 = ?$$

$$
\begin{array}{r}
134.600 \\
- 3.547 \\
\hline
131.053
\end{array}
$$

Multiplication of Decimals

When multiplying two numbers with decimal places, the number of decimal places in the answer must equal the sum of all the decimal places in the numbers being multiplied. Be sure to place the number with the fewest digits on the bottom.

What is 1.8 × 0.1212?

$$
\begin{array}{r}
0.1212 \\
\times\ 1.8 \\
\hline
9696 \\
+\ 12120 \\
\hline
0.21816
\end{array}
$$

Division of Decimals

When dividing numbers that have decimal points, always remove the decimal points before calculating. Determine which number has the most decimal places. Then move the decimal point to the right in both numbers as many times as is necessary to remove the decimal places.

Divide 0.0024 by 0.008.

Since 0.0024 has the most decimal places, we need to move the decimal point to the right 4 times in each number. This gives us $\frac{24}{80} = 0.3$.

FACTORS AND MULTIPLES

Prime Numbers

Understanding prime numbers is essential for GMAT questions that involve prime factorization, fractions, and properties of numbers.

PRIME NUMBER: Any positive number that has exactly 2 factors, itself and 1. For example, 2, 3, 5, 7, 11, 13, 17, 19, 23, 29, 31, 37, 41, 43, and 47 are prime numbers.

COMPOSITE NUMBERS: Numbers greater than 1 that are not prime numbers.

You should memorize all the prime numbers less than 50. They show up often on the GMAT and this will save you time.

If a number is not prime, it can be expressed as a multiple of 2 or more prime factors.

$$30 = 2 \bullet 3 \bullet 5$$

Factor (or Divisor)

FACTOR: A positive integer that can be evenly divided into another integer, N, resulting in another integer.

30 has the factors 1, 2, 3, 5, 6, 10, 15, and 30.

Factors are always positive. Remember that 1 is a factor of all integers and 0 is never a factor.

Factor Trees

The quickest way to determine the factors of a number, whether prime factors or all the factors, is to use a factor tree.

[30 broken down into 6, 5 and then the 6 broken down into 2, 3]

[280 broken down into 14 • 20, then 7 • 2 and 5 • 2^2, then $2^3 \bullet 5 \bullet 7$]

When you factor a number, first try to break it down into factor pairs that are close to the square root. Note that the 280 above could have been broken down into 140 • 2, but the prime factorization process would have taken longer.

If you are still unsure, you could check to see if 7 divides into 101, but it doesn't. There is no need to check 11 as a possible factor because $11^2 = 121$, a number greater than 101. This means that in order for 11 to be a factor of 101, it would have to be multiplied by a number smaller than itself. Since we know no other numbers less than 11 are factors except for 1, 101 must be a prime number.

GREATEST COMMON FACTOR (GCF): The largest number that divides evenly into each of the numbers given. The best way to determine the GCF is to look at the prime factors. The GCF is the product of all the prime factors the numbers have in common.

> The GCF of 42 (which is 2 • 3 • 7) and of 70 (which is
> 2 • 5 • 7) is 2 • 7 = 14

Multiples

MULTIPLE: A multiple of any number is that number multiplied by an integer.

> 6, 9, 12, 15 are all multiples of 3 because 3 • 2 = 6,
> 3 • 3 = 9, 3 • 4 = 12, and 3 • 5 = 15.

Note that if we multiply 2 and 3 to get 6, then 6 is a multiple of both 2 and 3. Conversely, 2 and 3 are factors of 6.

LEAST COMMON MULTIPLE (LCM): The smallest nonzero number that is a multiple of 2 or more given numbers. The key to finding the LCM involves prime factorization. You need to look at each individual number and make sure that the LCM includes the minimum required prime factors for each number.

> The LCM of 42 (which is 2 • 3 • 7) and of 56 (which is
> 2^3 • 7) is 2^3 • 3 • 7 = 168.

42 has 2, 3, and 7 as factors. 56 has 2, 2, 2, and 7 as factors. This means that the LCM must have at least one 7, one 3, but most importantly, it must have at least three 2s in order to be a multiple of 56.

PROPERTIES OF NUMBERS

Number properties determine how numbers work—how they increase, decrease, or change in value. For example, when you multiply two negative numbers, the result is a positive number. When you square a positive proper fraction, the number becomes smaller. Understanding number properties is essential for doing many GMAT questions. You will need them mostly on data sufficiency questions. However, with certain problem-solving questions, especially those that seem to require far too many calculations, you can use number properties to reduce your calculations and more quickly find a solution.

Even and Odd Integers

EVEN INTEGERS: Integers that are divisible by 2. For example, the integers $\{\ldots, -6, -4, -2, 0, 2, 4, 6, \ldots\}$ form the set of even integers.

ODD INTEGERS: Integers that are not divisible by 2. For example, the integers $\{\ldots, -5, -3, -1, 1, 3, 5, \ldots\}$ form the set of odd integers.

You should understand and **memorize** the following rules.

- The sum and difference of two even integers is even: $2 + 4 = 6$ and $6 - 4 = 2$.
- The sum and difference of two odd integers is even: $3 + 5 = 8$ and $5 - 3 = 2$.
- The sum and difference of an odd integer and an even integer is odd: $2 + 3 = 5$ and $5 - 2 = 3$.
- The product of two even integers is even: $2 \bullet 4 = 8$.
- The product of two odd integers is odd: $3 \bullet 5 = 15$.
- The product of an odd integer and an even integer is even: $3 \bullet 2 = 6$.

Positive and Negative

Just like with odd and even numbers, positive (+) and negative (–) numbers have specific rules. You should memorize the rules below.

Multiplication

$(-) \bullet (+)$ or $(+) \bullet (-) = (-)$

$(-) \bullet (-) = (+)$

$(+) \bullet (+) = (+)$

Division

$(-) \div (+)$ or $(+) \div (-) = (-)$

$(-) \div (-) = (+)$

$(+) \div (+) = (+)$

Units Digit

As we saw in the section on decimals, the units digit of a number is the number just to the left of the decimal point and just to the right of the tens place. Understanding how the unit digit works can greatly increase your computation speed.

What is the unit digit of 6,797 • 13,473?

The GMAT does not expect you to do the long calculation. Rather, you can use properties of numbers. The first number has the unit digit 7, and the second number has the unit digit 3. Because $7 \bullet 3 = 21$, we know that the resulting number, no matter how huge it is, will end in a unit digit of 1.

Since you have already memorized your basic times table, you can calculate the unit digit for any multiple of large numbers.

PERCENTS

Understanding percent calculations will greatly increase your computation speed and minimize mindless errors. Your ability to maneuver quickly among fractions, decimals, and percents will be a key to success on test day.

Percent, Fraction, and Decimal Conversions

Percent	Fraction	Decimal
40%	$\frac{40}{100} = \frac{2}{5}$	0.4
320%	$\frac{320}{100} = \frac{16}{5}$	3.20
0.4%	$\frac{0.4}{100} = \frac{1}{250}$	0.004

"Percent" means per 100. For example, 20% means 20 per 100. Percents are used to measure or report the change in an amount. You hear it all the time in statements like "X stock rose 22% today in massive trading" or "24% of students failed that course." To determine percent increases and decreases quickly you need to know the basic formula:

$$\text{Percent change} = \left(\frac{(\text{New value} - \text{Original value})}{(\text{Original value})} \right) \bullet 100$$

If you let NV mean "New value" and OV mean "Original value" (or "Old value"), you can write the formula like:

$$\% \text{ change} = \left(\frac{(NV - OV)}{(OV)} \right) \bullet 100$$

The percent change from 12 to 15 is $\left(\frac{(15 - 12)}{12} \right) \bullet 100 = 25\%$.

You should also be able to calculate quickly percent increases and decreases algebraically using the formula:

$$\text{Increase or decrease of a number} =$$
$$\left(1 + \frac{(\text{percent increase or decrease})}{100} \right) \bullet (\text{The number})$$

If x increases by 30%, then you get $(1 + 0.3)x$ or $1.3x$.
If x decreases by 30%, then you get $(1 - 0.3)x$ or $0.7x$.

Stock x goes up by 80% in year 1 but then decreases by 80% in year 2. By what percentage did the value of the stock change from the beginning to after year 2?

Solution: There are many ways to do this problem, but let's try using algebra.

We start at $x \rightarrow 1.8x$ after year 1 $\rightarrow (1.8) \bullet (0.2)x$ after year 2.

$1.8 = \dfrac{9}{5}$ and $0.2 = \dfrac{1}{5}$. Therefore we get $\dfrac{9}{5} \bullet \dfrac{1}{5}x = \dfrac{9x}{25}$, which is a decrease of $\dfrac{16x}{25}$ or 64%.

Another great strategy with percent questions is to pick numbers, especially 100. For this example, we would do the following.

We start with $100 \rightarrow 180$ after year 1 $\rightarrow 180 \bullet 0.2 = 36$ after year 2 or a 64% decrease.

Note that we would have gotten the same answer had the stock decreased first and then increased.

RATIOS

Ratio: A proportional relationship that compares two or more numbers. The ratio of x to y is written as $x : y$ or $\dfrac{x}{y}$, which is read as "x to y." It is a relationship of a part to a part or a part to a whole. Interpreting ratios properly is critical.

In a GMAT class, the ratio of females to males is $\dfrac{1}{3}$.
What proportion of the class is female?

Solution: Be careful when you write this out. You should get $\dfrac{\text{F:M:Total}}{1:3:4}$.

Note that we often need to keep track of the total of all the parts in order to interpret the question properly. In this case, the sum of the parts is 4. The proportion is now $\dfrac{1}{4}$ and not $\dfrac{1}{3}$ as many students might think.

If the ratio of dogs, cats, and mice in a pet store is $\dfrac{\text{D:C:M:Total}}{2:3:5:10}$,

then the percentage of dogs in the store would be $\dfrac{2}{10} = 20\%$.

If a ratio is $x : y$, the fractions of the whole that the two parts represent is:

$$\frac{x}{(x+y)} \text{ and } \frac{y}{(x+y)}$$

In other words, one must add up the numbers in the ratio proper and use the sum as the denominator to get the fraction of the whole.

ARITHMETIC: TARGETED REVIEW QUESTIONS

(A) If you can get the answer from **(1) ALONE** but not from (2) alone
(B) If you can get the answer from **(2) ALONE** but not from (1) alone
(C) If you can get the answer from **BOTH (1)** and **(2) TOGETHER** but not from (1) alone or (2) alone
(D) If **EITHER** statement **(1) ALONE OR** statement **(2) ALONE** suffices
(E) If you **CANNOT** get the answer from statements (1) and (2) **TOGETHER** but need even more data

1. If y is an integer, is $\dfrac{3^y}{10,000} > 1$?

    (1) $\dfrac{100}{3^y} < 0.01$

    (2) $\sqrt{3^y} = 243$

2. At a business superstore, Stephen spends $\dfrac{1}{3}$ of his money on software, $\dfrac{1}{7}$ on accessories, and $\dfrac{1}{10.5}$ on paper products. If he spends the remaining $90 on gift cards, how much did Stephen spend at the business superstore?

    (A) $90
    (B) $110
    (C) $140
    (D) $210
    (E) $260

3. If r and s are positive integers and $900s = r^3$, which of the following must be an integer?

 I. $\dfrac{s}{(3 \bullet 5 \bullet (2^3))}$

 II. $\dfrac{s}{((3^2) \bullet 5 \bullet 2^2)}$

 III. $\dfrac{s}{(3 \bullet 2^2 \bullet (5^2))}$

 (A) I only
 (B) II only
 (C) II and III only
 (D) I and II only
 (E) None of the above

4. If x is an odd integer and y is an even integer, which of the following must be true?
 (A) y is not a factor of x.
 (B) xy is an odd integer.
 (C) x^2 is an even integer.
 (D) $y - x$ is an even integer.
 (E) x is a prime number.

5. What is the tens digit of the 2-digit positive integer x?
 (1) x divided by 20 has a remainder of 17.
 (2) x divided by 11 has a remainder of 0.

ANSWER KEY

1. **(D)**   3. **(E)**   5. **(C)**
2. **(D)**   4. **(A)**

SOLUTIONS

1. **(D)** We can manipulate the original question stem to ask if $3^y > 10,000$.
   Statement 1 can be manipulated by multiplying both sides by 3^y, which gives us $100 < 0.01(3^y) \rightarrow$ Multiply both sides by 100 to get $10,000 < 3^y$, which is exactly what the question is asking for. *Sufficient*
   Statement 2 tell us that if we square both sides, we will get $3^y = 243^2 = (3^5)^2$, which means we can solve for y and that $y = 10$. *Sufficient*

   Each statement alone is sufficient.

2. **(D)** This is a fraction question. The key to doing this quickly is to recognize the common denominator. We get $\frac{1}{3} + \frac{1}{7} + \frac{1}{10.5}$ $= \frac{7}{21} + \frac{3}{21} + \frac{2}{21} = \frac{12}{21}$ of the total. The rest of the amount, $90, represents $\frac{9}{21}$ of the total. Therefore the total is $90 \cdot \frac{21}{9} = \$210$.

3. **(E)** This question tests your knowledge of prime factors. If we break down $900s$, we get

   $$90 \cdot 10 \cdot s = 9 \cdot 10 \cdot 5 \cdot 2 \cdot s = 3 \cdot 3 \cdot 5 \cdot 2 \cdot 5 \cdot 2 \cdot s = r^3$$

   Since s and r are positive integers and $r^3 = 2 \cdot 2 \cdot 3 \cdot 3 \cdot 5 \cdot 5 \cdot s$, then each side of the expression is a perfect cube. Therefore, s must have minimally $2 \cdot 3 \cdot 5$ as factors in order for the expression to remain a cube. It could, for example, have $2 \cdot 3 \cdot 5 \cdot 7^3$ as factors because it is still a cube. However, we should look at the least possible value. If s was $2 \cdot 3 \cdot 5$, then none of the three expressions given would be an integer.

4. **(A)** One way to solve this properties of numbers question is to pick numbers to prove four of the statements false. Alternatively, you should be able to leverage your thorough understanding of number properties, especially since you should know the theory anyway.

   (A) If y is even, it cannot be a factor of x, which is odd. True
   (B) Odd • even is always even, just like $3 \cdot 2 = 6$. False
   (C) An odd number squared is still odd, e.g., $3^2 = 9$. False

(D) Even – odd = odd, just like 6 – 3 = 3. False

(E) Most prime numbers are odd, except for 2. Regardless, if x is odd, it is not necessarily a prime number. False

5. **(C)** Start with what we **know**—x is a positive integer and has 2 digits. Then determine what we **want**—the tens digit and only one possible answer. Let's look at the statements to see if they give us what we **need**.

Statement 1 tells us that x could be 17, 37, 57, 77, or 97. 17 is here because when we divide 17 by 20, we get 0 and a remainder of 17. Regardless, we have multiple values for x. *Insufficient*

Statement 2 tells us that x could be any 2 digit multiple of 11, which means $x = 11, 22, 33, 44, 55, 66, 77, 88,$ or 99. *Insufficient*

When we combine the statements, we now know that x could only be 77. *Sufficient*

Both statements together are sufficient.

Algebra

6

Often the biggest obstacle in algebra is translating word problems. Here are some of the common keywords that you might see on the GMAT.

ALGEBRA TRANSLATION KEYWORDS

Addition	Increased by, more than, combined, together, total of, sum, added to
Subtraction	Decreased by, minus, less, difference between/of, less than, fewer than
Multiplication	Of, times, multiplied by, product of, increased/decreased by a factor of
Division	Per, out of, ratio of, quotient of, percent (divide by 100)
Equals	Is, are, was, were, will be, gives, yields, sold for

"Billy is three years older than twice Megan's age 5 years ago" translates to

$$B - 3 = 2(M - 5)$$

A rope 40 cm in length is cut into two pieces, a short piece and a long piece. The short piece is 8 cm shorter than the long piece. What is the length of the long piece?

Solution: We could let the variables be x and y or, better, s and l. However, the simplest way is to have just one variable, which we'll call L for the long piece of rope. The short piece of rope we can call $40 - L$. By using the 8 cm difference, we get:

$$L - 8 = 40 - L \rightarrow 2L = 48 \rightarrow L = 24 \text{ cm}$$

ABSOLUTE VALUE

The absolute value of a number is its value without regard to its sign. Another way to look at it is that the absolute value of a number is the measure of its distance to 0 on the number line.

The absolute value of –4, denoted as |–4|, is 4. Similarly, |+3| = 3.

Strategies for Absolute Value

- When given multiple absolute value parentheses, start inward and work outward.

$$|6 - (|-10|)| = |6 - 10| = |-4| = 4$$

- Solving an equation with absolute value requires you to consider two cases. In case 1, you open the bracket normally and set everything equal. In case 2, you open the bracket and change the expression in the absolute value brackets to its negative form. (Do not change the side of the equation that isn't in absolute value brackets.)

$$|x - 10| = 20, \text{ solve for } x$$

Case 1: $x - 10 = 20$ → $x = 30$
Case 2: $-(x - 10) = 20$ → $-x + 10 = 20 \rightarrow x = -10$

- To avoid confusion when you have absolute values on both sides, try breaking down the equation by looking at the left-hand side (LHS) and the right-hand side (RHS) separately.

$$|x| = -|-x|, \text{ solve for } x$$

Try picking numbers. If $x = 2$, LHS = 2, RHS = –2. Doesn't work!
If $x = -2$, LHS = 2, RHS = –2. Doesn't work!
Don't forget about zero! If $x = 0$, LHS = 0, RHS = 0. This works. Therefore, $x = 0$.

Later on, we will see how to solve absolute value inequality problems.

EXPONENTS AND ROOTS

Exponents are involved in a large portion of the algebra questions on the GMAT. Let's look at the most common definitions and rules for exponents.

$$x^y = 16$$

In the above expression, x is called the **base** and y is the **exponent**. Sometimes we say "x to the **power** of y." In this particular example, if both x and y are positive integers, then either $x = 2$ and $y = 4$ or $x = 4$ and $y = 2$.

BREAKING DOWN EXPONENTS

Exponent	Expanded Expression	Base	Exponent	Value
5^3	$5 \cdot 5 \cdot 5$	5	3	125
2^6	$2 \cdot 2 \cdot 2 \cdot 2 \cdot 2 \cdot 2$	2	6	64
10^9	$10 \cdot 10 \cdot 10 \cdot 10 \cdot 10 \cdot 10 \cdot 10 \cdot 10 \cdot 10$	10	9	1,000,000,000

EXPONENT RULES

$x^0 = 1$	Any number to the zero power equals 1.
$x^1 = x$	Any number to the 1 power equals that number.
$x^{-n} = \dfrac{1}{x^n}$ $4^{-2} = \dfrac{1}{4^2} = \dfrac{1}{16}$	A negative exponent changes sign when you move it between the numerator and denominator.
$2^4 \cdot 2^2 = 2^6$ $2^{(4+2)} = 2^6$	Add the exponents when multiplying two powers of the same base.
$2^6 \div 2^2 = 2^4$ $2^{(6-2)} = 2^4$	Subtract the exponents when dividing a power by another power of the same base.
$(2^2)^3 = 2^6$ $2^{(2 \times 3)} = 2^6$	Multiply the exponents when you raise a power to a power via parentheses.
$6^3 = (2 \cdot 3)^3 = 2^3 \cdot 3^3$	The exponent can be distributed among the factors of a base.
$\left(\dfrac{10}{2}\right)^3 = \dfrac{10^3}{2^3} = 5^3$	When a fraction is raised to a certain power, you can distribute the exponent to the numbers or variables in the fraction.

PROPERTIES OF EXPONENTS

$\left(\frac{1}{3}\right)^2 = \frac{1}{9}$ $\left(\frac{2}{3}\right)^3 = \frac{8}{27}$	When you apply any positive exponent to a positive proper fraction, the number becomes smaller. In this case, $x^2 < x$.
$(-3)^2 = 9$ $(-2)^6 = 64$	Any positive or negative number with an even exponent is always positive. In this case, $x^2 > 0$ and $x^6 > 0$.
$(-3)^3 = -27$ $(3)^3 = 27$	Any positive or negative number with an odd exponent could be positive or negative depending on the sign of the original number.
$x^3 = x \quad 0^3 = 0$ $x^2 = x \quad 0^2 = 0$	When $x = 0$ and x is the base, raising it to any positive power always results in 0, which is neither positive nor negative.
$2^1 = 2 \quad 2^5 = 3\underline{2} \quad 3^1 = 3$ $2^2 = \underline{4} \quad 2^6 = 6\underline{4} \quad 3^2 = 9$ $2^3 = \underline{8} \quad 2^7 = 12\underline{8} \quad 3^3 = 27$ $2^4 = 1\underline{6} \quad 2^8 = 25\underline{6} \quad 3^4 = 81$	There is a repeating pattern for all unit digits raised to a certain power. For powers of 2, the unit digit pattern is 2, 4, 8, and 6 repeating. For powers of 3, the unit digit pattern is 3, 9, 7, and 1 repeating, and so on. For more information on unit digit of powers, see page 65.

STRATEGIES FOR EXPONENTS

1. When multiplying or dividing numbers with exponents, always reduce each base to its lowest common prime number base.

$$\text{If } 25^x = 125^{x-3}, \text{ what is } x?$$

This should become $(5^2)^x = (5^3)^{x-3}$, which leads to $5^{2x} = 5^{3x-9}$. Once the bases are equal, we can set the exponents equal to each other. This gives $2x = 3x - 9$; therefore $x = 9$.

2. When adding or subtracting exponents, factor out the highest possible value and combine like terms.

$$3^7 - 3^6 + 3^5 - 3^4 = ?$$

We can factor out 3^4 from all the terms to get

$$3^4(3^3 - 3^2 + 3^1 - 3^0) = 3^4(27 - 9 + 3 - 1) = 3^4(20) = 3^4 \cdot 2^2 \cdot 5$$

3. As mentioned in the arithmetic section, you should memorize all the basic powers to speed up your calculations.

Roots are similar to exponents because they can be expressed in the same way. Therefore, the rules will also apply the same way to roots as they do to exponents.

$$\sqrt{x} = x^{\frac{1}{2}}$$

In the above equation, 1 represents the exponent of x and the 2 represents the root of x.

You should be able to move back and forth between the radical form and the exponent form.

$$x^{\frac{2}{3}} = \sqrt[3]{x^2}$$

Note that by definition, if no number is in the root symbol, a square root is implied. Secondly, the root sign implies a positive value.

Multiplication and Division of Roots

When you multiply and divide roots, you can treat them like regular numbers.

$$\sqrt{2} \bullet \sqrt{3} = \sqrt{6} \text{ and } \frac{\sqrt{10}}{\sqrt{2}} = \sqrt{5}$$

$$\sqrt{\frac{x}{y}} = \frac{\sqrt{x}}{\sqrt{y}} \text{ and } \sqrt{(x \bullet y)} = \sqrt{x} \bullet \sqrt{y}$$

Addition and Subtraction of Roots

When you add or subtract roots, you generally need to remember two things:

1. As with variables and with adding or subtracting like terms, you can only add or subtract like roots.

$$\sqrt{2} + 3\sqrt{2} + 4\sqrt{3} - \sqrt{3} = 4\sqrt{2} + 3\sqrt{3}$$

   You cannot simplify this any further.

2. Certain roots can be reduced, which can help you find like roots. The key is to find a factor that is a perfect square and then take it out of the root.

$$\sqrt{2} + \sqrt{8} + \sqrt{98} = \sqrt{2} + \sqrt{4 \bullet 2} + \sqrt{49 \bullet 2} = \sqrt{2} + 2\sqrt{2} + 7\sqrt{2} = 10\sqrt{2}$$

   You should **memorize** the most commonly occurring roots that can be reduced.

$\sqrt{8} = 2\sqrt{2}$	$\sqrt{12} = 2\sqrt{3}$	$\sqrt{20} = 2\sqrt{5}$	$\sqrt{27} = 3\sqrt{3}$
$\sqrt{50} = 5\sqrt{2}$	$\sqrt{75} = 5\sqrt{3}$	$\sqrt{98} = 7\sqrt{2}$	
$\sqrt{2} = 1.41$	$\sqrt{3} = 1.73$		

ROOTS IN A DENOMINATOR: It is considered bad form to have roots in a denominator. Therefore, you may need to remove the root by multiplying the numerator and the denominator by the root found in the denominator. Example: $\dfrac{8}{\sqrt{2}}$ is not in standard form, so we need to remove the root in the denominator.

$$\frac{8}{\sqrt{2}} \cdot \frac{\sqrt{2}}{\sqrt{2}} = \frac{8\sqrt{2}}{2} = 4\sqrt{2}$$

PROPERTIES OF ROOTS

$\sqrt{16} = 4$ $\sqrt[6]{64} = 2$	All even roots of positive numbers result in another positive number. You cannot take an even root of a negative number. For example, you cannot solve $\sqrt{-16}$.
$\sqrt[3]{-27} = -3$ $\sqrt[5]{32} = 2$	Odd roots of real numbers can be negative, positive, or zero.
$\sqrt{\dfrac{4}{9}} = \dfrac{2}{3}$ $\sqrt{25} = 5$	When you take the square root of a number between 0 and 1, the result is greater than the original number. When you take the square root of a number greater than 1, the result is less than the original number.
$\sqrt{1} = 1$ $1^x = 1$	1 to any power = 1 including the square root of 1.
$\sqrt{0} = 1$ $0^x = 0$	0 to any power = 0 including the square root of 0.

ALGEBRAIC CALCULATIONS AND OPERATIONS

Not only must you be very comfortable working with algebraic equations, expressions, and inequalities, you need to be quick with your calculations and flexible in applying the rules. These rules include simplifying, factoring, expanding, combining like terms, eliminating variables, and so on.

Order of Operations

The order in which you carry out calculations can be critically important in reaching the correct answer. For example, $3 + 5 \cdot 2$ may, at first glance, be seen as equivalent to $8 \cdot 2$. However, it is not. The correct simplification is $3 + 10$. PEMDAS is a useful acronym for remembering the correct order.

1. **P**arentheses: Work from the innermost to the outermost parentheses.
2. **E**xponents: Work from left to right.
3. **M**ultiplication and **D**ivision: Work from left to right.
4. **A**ddition and **S**ubtraction: Work from left to right

$$3 + 4^2 \cdot 2 - 10 \div (5 - 3) = 3 + 16 \cdot 2 - 10 \div 2 = 3 + 32 - 5 = 30$$

Parentheses

The biggest challenge for you when dealing with parentheses occurs when you open them up. You might forget to change the sign or multiply an outside number by all of the terms in a set of parentheses.

Rule: $a(b + c) = ab + ac$

$$-2(x + (-6)) = -2x + 12$$

Rule: $(a + b)(c + d) = ac + ad + bc + bd$

You can use **FOIL** (**F**irst, **O**utside, **I**nside, **L**ast) to make sure you multiply every term of an expression in parentheses with every other term in the other set of parentheses.

$$(2x + y) \cdot (x - 3) = 2x^2 - 6x + xy - 3y$$

ALGEBRAIC EQUATIONS

There are three main types of algebraic equations.

1. **LINEAR EQUATIONS WITH ONE VARIABLE:** The variable has an exponent of degree 1.

2. **LINEAR EQUATIONS WITH MULTIPLE VARIABLES:** Every variable has an exponent of degree 1.

3. **QUADRATIC EQUATIONS:** One or more variables has an exponent of degree 2.

Linear Equations with One Variable

The following example shows the algebraic equation in its most basic form:

$$x + 7 = 3$$

To solve these equations, you generally need to isolate the variable. You follow several general steps to do this.

1. Eliminate any parentheses.
2. Get rid of any fractions or denominators.
3. Put all numbers on one side and all terms with the variable on the other side.
4. Combine like terms.
5. Isolate the variable by dividing by its coefficient (if there is one).

Solve for the expression $x + 2(x - 3) = \dfrac{2(x+1)}{3} - 4x$

Solution:

$x + 2x - 6 = \dfrac{2x}{3} + \dfrac{2}{3} - 4x$	(Open the parentheses)
$3x + 6x - 18 = 2x + 2 - 12x$	(Multiply both sides by 3 to eliminate the denominator)
$9x - 2x + 12x = 2 + 18$	(Gather all terms with the x variable on one side and all numbers on the other side)
$19x = 20$	(Combine like terms)
$x = \dfrac{20}{19}$	(Divide by 19 and solve)

Linear Equations with Multiple Variables

Most GMAT problems have more than one variable. When you have two variables in algebra, you need to have more than one equation in order to solve. The general rule is that you need N distinct equations for N unknowns. Therefore, if you have to solve for 5 variables, then you need 5 equations. This concept is often tested in data sufficiency type questions.

There are two ways to solve multiple equations, **substitution** and **addition/subtraction**.

Substitution Method

1. Express one variable in terms of everything else in the equation.
2. Plug this expression into one of the other equations.

3. Keep repeating until you solve for one of the variables. You can then substitute the solved value into the other equations. If possible, substitute into one of the original equations.

$$(1)\ x + y = 6$$
$$(2)\ x - y = 2$$

Solution:

Express equation (1) in terms of x → (3) $x = 6 - y$

Substitute equation (3) into equation (2)   → $(6 - y) - y = 2$

Solve for the variable y → $6 - 2y = 2,\ -2y = -4,\ y = 2$

Substitute $y = 2$ into equation (1)   → $x + 2 = 6,\ x = 4$

Addition/Subtraction Method

1. Line up the equations on top of each other.
2. Look for a variable to eliminate by adding or subtracting the two equations. You may have to multiply one or more equations by a constant number so that the variables will have the same coefficient but with opposite signs.
3. Add or subtract the equations so that the variables with the same coefficients will cancel out.
4. Solve for the variable that remains.
5. Substitute the solved variable back into one of the original equations if possible and repeat until you have all the variables.

$$(1)\ x + y = 6$$
$$(2)\ x - y = 2$$

Solution: This is the same question as the one we used in the substitution method above. Since the variables all have coefficients of 1, we can easily eliminate either x or y. Let us add and so we get

$$2x + 0 = 8,\ \text{therefore } x = 4$$

Substitute back into equation (1) to get $y = 2$.

Quadratic Equations

A quadratic equation takes the form $ax^2 + bx + c = 0$, where a, b, and c are numbers of any value.

These equations are solved by **factoring**, where you break apart the equation into two or more separate parts or factors.

$x^2 + 7x + 12 = 0$ factors into $(x + 3)(x + 4) = 0$, which means that $x = -3$ and $x = -4$.

In the previous example, -3 and -4 are also known as the **roots** of the equation. When you plug them into the original equation, the left side will equal zero. Although this equation has two distinct roots, some quadratic equations have only one distinct root. For example, $x^2 + 6x + 9 = 0$ breaks down into $(x + 3)^2 = 0$. Therefore the only root is $x = -3$.

You can use three ways to solve a quadratic equation on the GMAT:

1. **You can factor the equation by inspection**, which means you find the roots just by looking at it and visualizing the solution. This is likely the preferred and quickest way.
2. **You can plug in the answer choices**, which is not preferable as it is generally time consuming.
3. **You can use the quadratic equation**, but do this only as a last resort.

How to Factor

How did we solve the equation $x^2 + 7x + 12 = 0$ in the example above so quickly by inspection? The basic idea is to look for a pair of factors of $+12$ (because the number could be negative) that will add up to $+7$. The factors of 12 are 1 and 12, 2 and 6, 3 and 4. Note that we look at the factors in pairs. In this method, 3 and 4 stand out. We can then set up the factors as $(x + 3)$ and $(x + 4)$.

Quadratic Formula

The **quadratic formula** is $x = \dfrac{-b \pm \sqrt{b^2 - 4ac}}{2a}$ for any equation in the form $ax^2 + bx + c = 0$. In most quadratic equations, x usually has two solutions. Note that if $b^2 - 4ac < 0$, there is no real solution and if $b^2 - 4ac = 0$, the equation has only one solution. Sometimes you should check the value of $b^2 - 4ac$ before solving the entire formula. This check may save you time.

Algebraic Factoring

As with any algebraic expression, you need to move back and forth between expanding expressions and factoring them. In other words, you can use FOIL to expand an expression and use factoring to bring the equation back to its pre-expanded form.

To help with your algebraic manipulation, you should **memorize** the 3 most common algebraic identities that are easily factored. You must be able to recognize these three factored forms and work quickly with them.

$$(a + b)^2 = (a + b)(a + b) = a^2 + 2ab + b^2$$
$$(a - b)^2 = (a - b)(a - b) = a^2 - 2ab + b^2$$
$$(a + b)(a - b) = a^2 - b^2 \quad \text{Also known as the } \textbf{difference of two squares}$$

INEQUALITIES

Inequalities compare two statements with different values. They are very similar to typical algebraic expressions except that the equal sign (=) is replaced by several other possible symbols. There are five main types of inequalities:

x	$>$	y	x is greater than y
x	$\geq$	y	x is greater than or equal to y
x	$<$	y	x is less than y
x	$\leq$	y	x is less than or equal to y
x	$\neq$	y	x is not equal to y

Almost all of the rules for algebraic equations also apply to inequalities. Remember this key difference:

INEQUALITIES GOLDEN RULE

If both sides of an inequality are multiplied or divided by a negative number, then you must flip the inequality sign.

What is fascinating is that the inequalities golden rule drastically increases the difficulty level of inequalities for test takers. Most of this difficulty is just confusion about the rules and how to apply them. Note that the general rule above does not apply to addition or subtraction. So let's look at the main ways you need to address inequalities.

Addition and Subtraction of Inequalities

When you add or subtract a number to both sides of the inequality, the sign is not affected.

$$2x - 3 > x - 10$$

Subtract x from both sides and add -3 to both sides

$$x > -7$$

Note that the unknown variable and the negative number have no effect on the inequality sign.

Multiplication or Division of Inequalities

This is where the golden rule of inequalities comes into play. Remember these three tips.

1. If you multiply or divide by a positive number, there's no sign change. Treat the inequality as you would an equation.
2. If you multiply or divide by a negative number, change the direction of the inequality symbol.
3. If you multiply or divide by a variable, you need to ask the question, "Is this number positive, negative, or I don't know?" Once you confirm, then proceed according to the first two tips above.

$$\text{Is } x > y?$$

(1) $\frac{x}{y} > 1$ If this were an equation, you might try to multiply the y on both sides to get $x > y$. However, this is an inequality. You don't know if y is positive or negative. Therefore, you cannot manipulate this inequality to solve it. Insufficient

Solving Multiple Inequalities

As with equations, you can solve two or more inequalities together by adding or subtracting inequalities, or by using substitution. The key difference is that the inequality signs must be pointing in the same direction.

$$x + y > 12 \text{ and } x - y < 6. \text{ Solve for } x \text{ and } y.$$

Solution: Set up the inequalities so that their signs are facing the same direction.

(1) $x + y > 12$

(2) $\underline{+ \quad -x + y > -6}$ (We did this by multiplying both sides by –1, thus changing the sign.)

$2y > 6 \rightarrow y > 3$ This means that $x > 9$ (via substitution into equation 1).

Inequalities with Absolute Value

The GMAT frequently increases the difficulty of problems by combining two separate concepts. Inequalities are often combined with absolute values, but the process to solve these is the same. You will again have to solve two separate cases.

$$|x - 5| > 3, \text{ solve for } x$$

Solution: We need to look at two cases.

Case 1: $\qquad x - 5 > 3 \rightarrow x > 8$

Case 2: $\qquad -(x - 5) > 3 \rightarrow -x + 5 > 3 \rightarrow x - 5 < -3 \rightarrow x < 2$

So we get $x < 2$ or $x > 8$. If you have time, you can check numbers just to be sure.

FUNCTIONS, SYMBOLS, AND SEQUENCES

Functions are simply an alternate way to write an algebraic expression with one variable. Test takers find functions confusing because they are more abstract. A function comes in the form

$$f(x) = 2x + 3 \rightarrow \text{This is the same as saying} \rightarrow y = 2x + 3$$

The two expressions above are identical. In each case, when we have a specific value for x we simply plug it into the equation and solve. So if $x = 1$, then

$$f(1) = 2(1) + 3 = 5 \quad \text{OR} \quad y = 2(1) + 3 = 5$$

You can solve for functions in almost the same way as you solve for algebraic expressions. To illustrate further how similar they are, let's create a T-chart for a function and an equation.

$$g(x) = x^2 - 3 \rightarrow \text{which again is the same as} \rightarrow y = x^2 - 3$$

T-charts for both

$g(x)$	x		y	x
6	−3		6	−3
1	−2		1	−2
−2	−1		−2	−1
−3	0		−3	0
−2	1		−2	1
1	2		1	2
6	3		6	3

As you can see, functions are the same as algebraic equations. Just as we would say $y = -2$ when $x = -1$ or $x = +1$, we can also say $g(-1) = -2$ or $g(1) = -2$. The **domain** of a function is the set of all possible values for the variable.

$$g(x) = \frac{\sqrt{x-3}}{x-5}$$

The variable x cannot be 5 because the denominator would be undefined. x also cannot be less than 3 because the radical would be undefined. Therefore, the domain of $g(x)$ is all values of x, as long as $x \geq 3$ and $x \neq 5$.

Function Symbol Problems

Symbol problems are challenging because of the use of unfamiliar symbols to define an expression. Despite this abstract nature, you just need to "plug and play" by inputting the values and carrying out the operations as you normally would. One effective strategy is to separate all the steps and operations with a clear and structured chart.

If the operation ¥ is defined for all a and b as the equation

$a ¥ b = \dfrac{ab}{2}$, then what is $2 ¥ (3 ¥ 4)$?

Solution: It's important to understand what the definition is. Simply put, whatever values of a and b we have, we plug them into the expression as defined. Using a chart can help here.

	a	b	$a ¥ b = \dfrac{ab}{2}$
$3 ¥ 4$	3	4	$\dfrac{3 \times 4}{2} = 6$
$2 ¥ (3 ¥ 4) = 2 ¥ 6$	2	6	$\dfrac{2 \times 6}{2} = 6$

Sequence Functions

Sequence problems are a particular kind of function question on the GMAT. In general, you are given a formula that defines the sequence, the domain, and some of the terms of the sequence. The formula is of the form: $a_n =$ (some equation with n as a variable). The terms of the sequence are: $a_1, a_2, a_3 \ldots a_n$.

$a_n = n^2 - 1$, where $n > 1$. What is the value of a_5?

Solution: The quickest way to do this is to input $n = 5$ for a_5 to get

$$a_5 = 5^2 - 1 = 24$$

There are 2 main categories of series: arithmetic and geometric.

1. Arithmetic sequence: where each term goes from one to the next by always adding (or subtracting) the same value. 2, 9, 16, 23, 30, ... → the common difference is 7, so the next number would be 37.
2. Geometric sequence: where each term goes from one to the next by always multiplying (or dividing) by the same value. $\frac{1}{3}$, 1, 3, 9, → The common ratio is 3, so the next number would be 27.

The GMAT asks 3 common types of sequence questions:

- **Sequence type 1**: Find the nth term of the sequence. (Solve by inputting values into the definition.)
- **Sequence type 2**: Find the nth term of the sequence when given two or more values for terms. (Solve using the definition to find the link.)
- **Sequence type 3**: Find the 1000th term of the sequence. (Solve by finding a pattern with the definition to figure out the far away term.)

Sequence Strategy

1. Make sure you understand the definition of the sequence.
2. Line up the terms in order vertically.

   - If you are given the value of a few terms, make sure to leave gaps for the terms that you do not know but may need to solve.
   - If you are not given any terms, try to input the first 3–5 terms of the sequence.
   - If you can't find any terms to put in, use algebraic terms.

3. Use the definition to fill in the gaps and solve.
4. If that doesn't work, try to find a pattern to help you solve the problem.
5. Make sure you do not violate any given domain.

ALGEBRA: TARGETED REVIEW QUESTIONS

1. If $3^x - 3^{x-2} = 2^3 \bullet 3^{17}$, what is x?
    (A) 15
    (B) 17
    (C) 19
    (D) 20
    (E) 23

2. If the operation £ is defined by $q \pounds p = \dfrac{(q-p)}{(q+p)}$ for all positive integers q and p, then $3 \pounds (-4 \pounds 5)$ is
    (A) -9
    (B) -4.5
    (C) -2
    (D) 1.5
    (E) 6

(A) If you can get the answer from **(1) ALONE** but not from (2) alone
(B) If you can get the answer from **(2) ALONE** but not from (1) alone
(C) If you can get the answer from **BOTH (1)** and **(2) TOGETHER** but not from (1) alone or (2) alone
(D) If **EITHER** statement **(1) ALONE OR** statement **(2) ALONE** suffices
(E) If you **CANNOT** get the answer from statements (1) and (2) **TOGETHER** but need even more data

---

3. A convenience store bought an item for C dollars, then sold it for D dollars. The cost of the item was what percent of the gross profit that the convenience store realized?
    (1) $\dfrac{D}{C} - 1 = \dfrac{2}{3}$
    (2) $D - C = 8$

4. If the sequence S has 1000 terms, what is the 777th term of S?
    (1) The 4th term of S is -26.
    (2) The 977th term is 16,515, and each preceding term of S before the last is 17 less than the current term.

5. If a and b are integers and $a = |b + 11| + |12 - b|$, does a equal 23?

   (1) $b < 12$

   (2) $b > -11$

ANSWER KEY

1. **(C)**   3. **(A)**   5. **(C)**

2. **(C)**   4. **(B)**

SOLUTIONS

1. **(C)** When you first look at this question, you may second-guess yourself because you're wondering why there is a 2 on the right side of the equation. The rules and tactics for exponent manipulation are the same, which are to reduce everything to a prime factor base (already done) and to factor out like terms when you see addition or subtraction. So in this question, let's take out 3^x from each term on the left-hand side

$$3^x\left(1 - 3^{-2}\right) = 3^x\left(1 - \frac{1}{3^2}\right) = 3^x\left(1 - \frac{1}{9}\right) = 3^x\left(\frac{8}{9}\right) = 3^x\left(\frac{2^3}{3^2}\right)$$

Now we know where the 2^3 comes from. This gives us

$$3^x 2^3 3^{-2} = 2^3 \bullet 3^{17} \rightarrow 3^{x-2} 2^3 = 2^3 3^{17} \rightarrow \text{Thus } x - 2 = 17,\ x = 19$$

2. **(C)** This is a symbol problem. The key is to make sure to structure it clearly, plug in the numbers correctly, and follow the order of operations.

$$q\ \pounds\ p = \frac{(q - p)}{(q + p)} \rightarrow \text{Thus } -4\ \pounds\ 5 = \frac{(-4 - 5)}{(-4 + 5)} = -\frac{9}{1} = -9$$

$$3\ \pounds\ -9 = \frac{(3 - (-9))}{(3 + (-9))} = \frac{(3 + 9)}{(3 - 9)} = \frac{12}{-6} = -2$$

3. **(A)** What we want in this question is the proportion of cost to gross profit on the item or $\frac{(D - C)}{D}$ or $1 - \frac{C}{D}$. So what we need is either 2 distinct equations or the ratio $\frac{C}{D}$.

Statement 1 tells us, with a bit of manipulation, that $\frac{D}{C} = \frac{5}{3}$. This is sufficient, because we can plug into $1 - \frac{C}{D}$ and get $1 - \frac{3}{5} = \frac{2}{5}$. *Sufficient*

Statement 2 gives us a distinct equation. However, there's no other information, such as another distinct equation, to help us solve or to manipulate in order to get the ratio $\dfrac{C}{D}$. *Insufficient*

Statement 1 alone is sufficient.

4. **(B)** In order to determine the 777th term of sequence S, we either need the definition of the sequence or some way to find a pattern.

Statement 1 gives us only one term. Therefore, there is no way to determine the pattern for the definition. *Insufficient*

Statement 2 gives us a term and a definition. This means we could take the number 16,515 and subtract 17 as many times as needed in order to get to the 777th term. The GMAT test makers don't expect you to calculate this number. You just have to know that you can. *Sufficient*

Statement 2 alone is sufficient.

5. **(C)** The best way to do this question is to pick numbers and prove insufficiency by finding one example that works and one that does not.

Statement 1   → If $b = -20$, then
$$a = |-20 + 11| + |12 - (-20)| = |-9| + |32| = 9 + 32 = 41$$

      → If $b = 11$, then
$$a = |11 + 11| + |12 - 11| = |22| + |1| = 22 + 1 = 23$$
Insufficient

Statement 2   → If $b = 20$, then
$$a = |20 + 11| + |12 - 20| = |31| + |-8| = 31 + 8 = 39$$

      → If $b = 11$, then
$$a = |11 + 11| + |12 - 11| = |22| + |1| = 22 + 1 = 23$$
Insufficient

When we combine statements 1 and 2 together, we know that $-11 < b < 12$. Pick numbers.

If $b = 11$, then $a = |11 + 11| + |12 - 11| = |22| + |1| = 22 + 1 = 23$

If $b = -10$, then $a = |-10 + 11| + |12 - (-10)| = |1| + |22| = 1 + 22 = 23$

Try a 3rd number if you are not convinced.

      → If $b = -1$, $a = |-1 + 11| + |12 - (-1)| = 10 + 13 = 23$

Both statements together are sufficient.

Geometry

7

G eometry is fun! Now you may wonder where our enthusiasm comes from. Simply put, geometry is all about making drawings and a bunch of rules. In other words, you get to doodle! Some students, having forgotten most of the rules, decide to skip geometry altogether, thinking they can make up their score with the other questions. This is a bad idea. As mentioned before, there is a finite amount of underlying theory on the GMAT. There is an end in sight. In addition, the tested quantitative theory is from high school or earlier. Geometry is often taught even earlier, likely in junior high or middle school (oh those fun, awkward years). So you may find it more difficult than other quantitative topics because you were exposed to it so long ago. Geometry makes up about 10% to 15% of the quantitative questions. This represents at least 4 to 6 GMAT questions that you should be getting right!

Basic Geometry Strategy

1. **KNOW ALL THE RULES:** Geometry is rule based. To solve geometry problems, you need to know the rules and be able to recognize which ones apply. You already know most of the rules, such as the area of a circle or the angles of a triangle. The key to success is to know the more obscure rules as well as the common ones.

2. **ALWAYS MAKE A DRAWING:** Visualizing will help you greatly in geometry. Even if the GMAT provides a diagram, you should draw it again on your scratch pad. Draw it neatly and large enough to work with effectively. In many cases, you will need to draw more than what you are given.

3. **LEVERAGE SPECIAL TRIANGLES:** Most quantitative problems have a key insight that helps you understand and solve the problem efficiently. In geometry, you will often find that the key insight involves special triangles such as isosceles triangles, equilateral triangles, Pythagorean right triangles, 30-60-90 triangles, and 45-45-90 triangles.

LINES AND ANGLES

A **line** is defined as a geometric object that is straight and can be either finite or infinite.

A fixed portion of a line is often called a **line segment**, as is AB in the diagram below.

When 2 lines intersect, we create 2 pairs of angles. The angles opposite each other are equal. The sum of the angles on one side of the line is 180°.

$$x + y = 180° \qquad x = z$$

Parallel and Perpendicular Lines

Parallel lines are those in the same plane that never intersect. As shown in the diagram, $L1$ and $L2$ are parallel.

Perpendicular lines are those that intersect, creating 90° angles. In the diagram, $L3$ is perpendicular to $L1$ and $L2$.

When two parallel lines are intercepted by a third line, as shown below, we create two sets of four identical angles. Again in this case, $x + y = 180°$.

TRIANGLES

The GMAT test makers love to use triangles. In fact, you will find triangles in the majority of geometry questions. Special triangles are often the key to solving more difficult problems.

In the triangle below, the sum of the interior angles is always 180°, no matter what the shape. Therefore, when you know 2 angles, you can determine the 3rd angle.

$$x + y + z = 180°$$

The perimeter of a triangle is the sum of the length of its sides. $P = A + B + C$

The area of a triangle is its base multiplied by its perpendicular height divided by 2.

$$A = \frac{B \times H}{2}$$

Note that any side can be the base. However, you must make sure that you use the perpendicular altitude from that base for the height.

The shortest side of a triangle is opposite the smallest angle. The longest side is opposite the largest angle.

The sum of any 2 sides of a triangle must always be greater than the 3rd side.

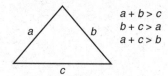

$$a + b > c$$
$$b + c > a$$
$$a + c > b$$

The exterior angle of a triangle is equal to the sum of the 2 interior angles of a triangle that are not next to that exterior angle.

$$x + y + z = 180°$$
$$a + z = 180°$$
$$\therefore \quad a = x + y$$

Right Triangles

The most important triangle in the GMAT quantitative section is the right triangle. In a right triangle, one angle measures 90°. This angle is opposite the longest side of a triangle, which is known as the hypotenuse. We can calculate the length of the third side of a right triangle when given the length of the other two sides using Pythagoras's famous formula:

PYTHAGOREAN THEOREM

$$a^2 + b^2 = c^2$$

where c is the hypotenuse while a and b are the other two sides of a right triangle

The most well known Pythagorean triangle identity is the 3-4-5 triangle. Not only should you know this right triangle, but you should also know common multiples of it such as 6-8-10, 9-12-15, 15-20-25. There are also a few other common Pythagorean triangle identities shown below.

The Pythagorean theorem is a fundamental building block for everything about right triangles, but rarely would you need to use it in calculations. Knowing some of the different right triangle identities, especially the triplets presented above, will save you time on your calculations.

Special Triangles

There are 4 special triangles that are critical to success in GMAT geometry:

1. **EQUILATERAL TRIANGLES**
2. **ISOSCELES TRIANGLES**
3. **45-45-90 TRIANGLES**
4. **30-60-90 TRIANGLES**

Equilateral Triangles

All sides of an equilateral triangle are the same length. All angles in an equilateral triangle are the same—60°. An equilateral triangle is also by definition an isosceles triangle. If you cut an equilateral triangle in half, you create 2 identical 30-60-90 right triangles. What is not commonly known about this special triangle is that you need only one side length to calculate the area by using the following formula.

$$A = \frac{s^2\sqrt{3}}{4}$$

These properties of equilateral triangles are key in both problem solving and data sufficiency type questions.

Isosceles Triangles

Isosceles triangles have 2 angles and 2 sides that are the same. So if 2 sides of a triangle have the same length, then the 2 opposite angles are also equal to each other and vice versa. Sometimes you will find isosceles triangles cleverly hidden in circle problems where the radius is involved. This is because 2 radii are of equal length and thus can be used to create isosceles triangles.

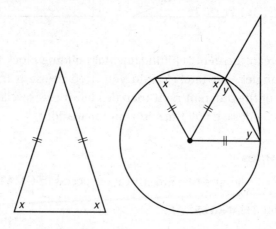

30-60-90 and 45-45-90 Triangles

These triangles are special because they have specific proportions for each side. You need to know only the length of one side in order to find the length of the other 2 sides. This is especially important to know for data sufficiency type problems.

In a 30-60-90 triangle, the ratio of the lengths is fixed at $1:\sqrt{3}:2$. This means if the side opposite the 30° angle measures 1, the side opposite the 60° angle measures $\sqrt{3}$, and the hypotenuse measures 2. Note that you can also create this triangle when you split an equilateral triangle in half. When dealing with this type of triangle, the best way to calculate the other sides is to use a chart as on the next page.

In a 45-45-90 triangle, the ratio of the side lengths is fixed at $1:1:\sqrt{2}$. This means that if either leg measures 1, the hypotenuse measures $\sqrt{2}$. This triangle is also an isosceles right triangle. Note that 45-45-90 triangles are created when you split a square in half by the diagonal. You should also be familiar with common multiples of this ratio such as $\sqrt{2}$, $\sqrt{2}$, and 2.

30-60-90 Triangle

45-45-90 Triangle

EXAMPLE 1

30	60	90
1	√3	2
↓× $\frac{4}{\sqrt3}$	↓× $\frac{4}{\sqrt3}$	
4	$\frac{8}{\sqrt3}$	

$x = \frac{8}{\sqrt3}$

EXAMPLE 2

45	45	90
1	1	√2
↓× 2√2	↓× 2√2	
2√2		4

$x = ?$ $x = 2\sqrt2$

In Example 1, we are given a 30-60-90 triangle, a length of 4 for the longer side, and we need to find the hypotenuse x. By using the chart above, we can first input the standard ratios for 30-60-90. Then we need to figure out what multiple of $\sqrt3$ will give us 4. In this example, we need to multiply by $\frac{4}{\sqrt3}$. We multiply this number to the standard ratio of the hypotenuse to get:

$$2 \cdot \frac{4}{\sqrt3} = \frac{8}{\sqrt3}$$

We take a similar approach to Example 2. See if you can follow along with the same process to solve for a square with diagonal 4.

Similar Triangles

Over the years, the GMAT has become more sophisticated and complex. The test makers use a variety of ways to complicate questions whether through tricky wording or by using advanced concepts more frequently. Similar triangles are one such area where savvy test takers need to have a better understanding.

When two triangles are similar, they share the same angles and thus share similar proportional properties. In other words, any two triangles with the same angles have their sides and heights in proportion.

Triangles *ABC* and *DEC* are similar because they both have one right angle and they share the same angle at *C*. Note that we need only two pairs of equal angles to know that the third pair is also equal. If we take any ratio of two sides of one triangle, it must be the same for the other triangle.

$$\frac{AB}{AC} = \frac{ED}{DC}, \frac{BC}{AB} = \frac{EC}{ED}, \text{ and } \frac{BC}{AC} = \frac{EC}{DC}$$

There are three standard ways to determine that triangles are similar.

- **AAA (ANGLE, ANGLE, ANGLE):** If the angles are the same, then the triangles are similar. This is the most common type found in the GMAT.
- **SAS (SIDE, ANGLE, SIDE):** If the triangles share two sides with corresponding ratios and the angle in between those two sides is the same in both triangles, these triangles are similar. This type is less frequent on the GMAT.
- **SSS (SIDE, SIDE, SIDE):** If there are constant ratios of corresponding sides for two triangles, then the triangles are similar. This type is rarely seen on the GMAT, usually because most geometry questions won't give you that much information (all the lengths of six different sides!).

The most common similar triangle identity you might see is the following.

$$\triangle ABC \approx \triangle ADB \approx \triangle BDC$$

QUADRILATERALS

Quadrilaterals are 4-sided polygons. The four most commonly occurring quadrilaterals on the GMAT are the square, rectangle, parallelogram, and trapezoid.

QUADRILATERAL TYPES AND PROPERTIES

	Square	Rectangle
Properties	All opposite sides are parallel; All sides are the same length; All angles are 90°; Diagonals are the same length, intersect at 90°, and bisect each other; interior angles add up to 360°	All opposite sides are parallel; Opposite sides are the same length; All angles are 90°; Diagonals are the same length and bisect each other; interior angles add up to 360°
Area	$A = s^2$	$A = l \bullet w$
Perimeter	$P = 4s$	$P = 2l + 2w$
Key shapes	Diagonals create two 45-45-90 isosceles right triangles	Diagonals create 2 right triangles

	Parallelogram	Trapezoid
Properties	All opposite side are parallel; Opposite sides are the same length; Opposite angles are equal; Diagonals bisect each other; interior angles add up to 360°	2 sides are parallel; Interior angles add up to 360°
Area	$A = b \bullet h$	$A = \frac{1}{2}(b + c)h$ or (Avg. base) $\bullet$ h
Perimeter	$P = 2a + 2b$	$P = a + b + c + d$
Key shapes	Right triangle needed to find the height	Right triangle needed to find the height

OTHER POLYGONS

Polygons are two-dimensional, closed plane figures that are bound by straight lines. You may see other polygons on the GMAT besides triangles and quadrilaterals such as pentagons, hexagons, or more complicated figures. You need to know a few things about polygons.

1. The sum of the interior angles of any polygon is $(n - 2) \cdot 180°$, where n is the number of sides.
2. A regular polygon is one where all sides are the same measure and all angles are the same measure.
3. All polygons can be broken down into smaller triangles, which can be a quick way to determine the sum of all interior angles.

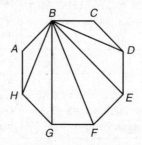

Here we have a regular octagon, with all sides and angles equal.

Sum of angles is $(8 - 2) \cdot 180° = 1080°$

You can also see that we can draw 6 triangles within the octagon. Since triangles have interior angles that add up to 180°, then octagons have $6 \cdot 180 = 1080°$.

When you see an irregular polygon on the GMAT, the key is to break the shape down into polygons that you recognize and can solve. For example, a shape like the front of a house can be broken down into rectangles and triangles.

CIRCLES

A circle is an infinite set of points that are all equidistant from a point called the center. Circles are often involved in some of the harder geometry problems on the GMAT, mostly because test makers combine circles with other geometric shapes such as triangles and quadrilaterals. Circles also have a large number of properties that can be used for a variety of GMAT questions. Let's first understand the basic definitions.

Definitions

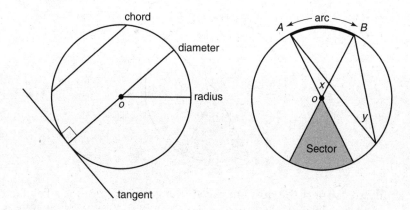

RADIUS: The distance from the center of the circle to the outside edge. The radius is usually the most important piece of information that you need for circle problems.

DIAMETER: The largest distance from one side of a circle to the other, going through the center. The diameter is twice the length of the radius.

CHORD: A line that connects any 2 points on the circle. Note that the diameter is also a chord.

CIRCUMFERENCE: The distance around the circle, which has a standard formula $C = 2\pi r$, where r is the radius.

ARC: Any portion of the circumference. The points A and B on the diagram create 2 arcs, which are the minor arc (shorter length) and the major arc (longer length).

CENTRAL ANGLE: An angle with its vertex at the center of the circle. These angles are used to calculate arc lengths and sector areas. This is angle x in the diagram.

INSCRIBED ANGLE: An angle with its vertex on the circumference of the circle. This is angle y in the diagram.

SECTOR: A portion of the area of a circle, defined by 2 radii and an arc.

TANGENT: A line that touches a circle at just one point. This tangent line is perpendicular to the radius at the point of tangency.

Circle Formulas and Properties

Your ability to connect the dots among all the geometry rules is a key factor to success. Therefore, you should know the main formulas in some of the commonly tested properties and relationships of circles. Know the following three most commonly used formulas for GMAT circles:

1. $A = \pi r^2$

2. $C = 2\pi r$

3. Arc length $= 2\pi r \left(\dfrac{x}{360°} \right)$

A = area, C = circumference, r = radius, and x = central angle measure.

Note that arc length is the proportion of the circumference where x represents the angular proportion. The total number of degrees of arc in the circle is 360°. You must know the relationship among arcs, inscribed angles, and central angles.

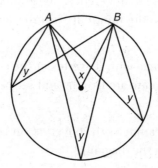

- **SIMILAR INSCRIBED ANGLES:** All inscribed angles that extend to the same arc or same 2 points on a circle are equal to each other. This can be seen with angles *y* in the previous diagram.

- **CENTRAL ANGLE VS. INSCRIBED ANGLE:** Any central angle that extends to the same arc or the same two points on a circle as does an inscribed angle is twice the size of the inscribed angle. Therefore as shown in the diagram, $x = 2y$.

- **TRIANGLES INSCRIBED IN A SEMICIRCLE:** Any triangle that is inscribed in a semicircle where the longest length is the diameter of the circle is always a right triangle.

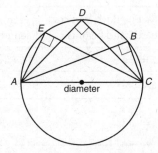

- **RADII CREATE ISOSCELES TRIANGLES:** Note that in some difficult circle problems, you can sometimes use 2 radii to create isosceles triangles and thus create 2 angles that are equal to each other.

VOLUMES AND 3-D FIGURES

The most common three-dimensional (3-D) figures in the GMAT geometry are cubes, rectangular solids, and cylinders. You may also see spheres, cones, or figures that are a combination of these. You will need to understand volumes, surface areas, and line segments within 3-D figures. A simple way to think of most volumes is that you are multiplying an area by a new dimension.

Volume = (Area of 2-D surface) × (Height)

The chart below outlines the most commonly needed formulas and properties of 3-D figures on the GMAT.

	Cube	Rectangular Solid
Visualize as	Dice	Box
Definitions	Faces, edges, vertices, bases, and heights	Faces, edges, vertices, bases, lengths, widths, and heights
Volume	$V = s^3$	$V = lwh$
Surface area	$SA = 6s^2$	$SA = 2lw + 2lh + 2hw$
Longest length within	$L = \sqrt{(3s^2)}$	$L = \sqrt{(l^2 + w^2 + h^2)}$

	Cylinder	Sphere
Visualize as	Soda Can	Ball
Definitions	Base, heights, radius	Radius, surface
Volume	$V = \pi r^2 h$	$V = \left(\dfrac{4}{3}\right)\pi r^3$
Surface area	$SA = 2(\pi r^2) + 2\pi rh$	$SA = 4\pi r^2$
Longest length within	$L = \sqrt{(4r^2 + h^2)}$	$L = 2r$

Note that a sphere would be considered a more unusual shape, as would be cones. However, we've added it to the chart because there have been a few sphere questions where the volume formula was not given. In general, the GMAT test makers will give you the formulas required for unusual shapes. If the question gives you a more complex figure, look for ways to break it down into more common 3-D shapes.

With your knowledge of basic geometry and areas, you should be able to calculate the volume of most 3-D figures such as the triangular solid below.

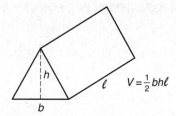

$$V = \frac{1}{2}bh\ell$$

COORDINATE GEOMETRY

Coordinate geometry is simply the mapping of points, lines, and shapes on a coordinate plane. It has become more important in recent years. Coordinate geometry questions are often combined with algebraic equations. Below we review the basic equations and properties of coordinate geometry.

The figure above is called the **coordinate plane**. The horizontal line is called the **x-axis**, and the vertical line is the **y-axis**. The point O is the **origin**. The axes divide the planes into four **quadrants**, I, II, III, and IV as shown above.

Every point in the plane has an *x*-**coordinate** and a *y*-**coordinate**, which is expressed (x, y).

Linear Equations

The line drawn in the diagram can be expressed using an algebraic equation. In coordinate geometry, the equation of a line is usually expressed using the slope-intercept formula.

> ### SLOPE-INTERCEPT FORMULA
>
> $$y = mx + b$$
>
> where *m* is the slope, *b* is the *y*-intercept, and $\frac{-b}{m}$ is the *x*-intercept

Slope

The slope of a line is an expression of its steepness. In the slope-intercept formula, it is *m*. We can think of the slope from left to right as a hill, where uphill is positive and downhill is negative. A straight horizontal line, which would be no hill at all, has a slope of 0. A straight vertical line has an undefined slope. The slope of a line can be found by calculating the following:

$$\frac{\text{Change in } y\text{-coordinate}}{\text{Change in } x\text{-coordinate}} = \frac{\Delta y}{\Delta x} = \frac{(y_2 - y_1)}{(x_2 - x_1)} = \frac{rise}{run}$$

Note that the slope is the same for all lines that are parallel to each other. Lines with the equations $y = 2x$, $y = 2x + 7$, and $y = 2x + 11$ all have a slope of 2. Lines that are perpendicular to each other will have slopes that are the negative reciprocals of each other.

The lines $y = 3x - 1$ and $y = -\frac{1}{3}x + 7$ intersect at 90° because 3 and $-\frac{1}{3}$ are negative reciprocals of each other.

x- and *y*-Intercepts

The most important skill on GMAT coordinate geometry is finding the *x*- and *y*-intercepts of an equation quickly. The *x*-intercept is where a line crosses the *x*-axis and the *y*-intercept is where the line crosses the *y*-axis. One way to find the *x*- and *y*-intercepts is to use the formula $y = mx + b$. The other way is to set *x* or *y* equal to 0.

To find the *y*-intercept, set *x* equal to 0. Then solve for *y*.

To find the *x*-intercept, set *y* equal to 0. Then solve for *x*.

$$2x + 3y = 6$$

Solution: Set x equal to 0. $3y = 6$, therefore $y = 2$.

Set y equal to 0. $2x = 6$, therefore $x = 3$.

So, the x-intercept is 3, or at point $(3, 0)$. The y-intercept is 2, or at point $(0, 2)$. If needed, we can also calculate the slope using x- and y-intercept points.

$$m = \frac{(y_2 - y_1)}{(x_2 - x_1)} = \frac{(2 - 0)}{(0 - 3)} = -\frac{2}{3}$$

Other Formulas and Properties

You will often be asked other types of coordinate geometry questions on the GMAT.

Calculate the Equation of the Line

Often in GMAT, coordinate geometry problems will ask you to determine the equation of the line. To do this, you will need any of the following:

1. Any 2 points on the line
2. Both x- and y-intercepts
3. The slope and either x- or y-intercept
4. One point on the line and the slope
5. One point on the line and the slope or equation of a line perpendicular or parallel to that line

Calculating Intersections

Whenever you are asked to calculate the intersection point of 2 lines, you need to set the equations equal to each other.

Calculate the intersection of $y = 3x - 2$ and $y = 5x - 6$.

Solution: Since both equations are set equal to y, set the equations equal to each other.

$$3x - 2 = 5x - 6$$

We get $4 = 2x$. Therefore $x = 2$. Now substitute $x = 2$ into either of the original equations.

$$y = 3(2) - 2 = 6 - 2 = 4$$

So $y = 4$.

If you use the other equation, you get the same answer.

$$y = 5(2) - 6 = 10 - 6 = 4$$

The intersection is at (2, 4).

Distance Formula

When you have 2 points on a coordinate plane, you can usually find the distance between them using the Pythagorean theorem. (You can't use this formula for 2 points on the same axis.) The distance is found by drawing a right triangle between the 2 points.

Distance between any 2 points (x_1, y_1) and (x_2, y_2) =

$$\sqrt{(\Delta x)^2 + (\Delta y)^2} = \sqrt{(x_1 - x_2)^2 + (y_1 - y_2)^2}$$

Midpoint Formula

When you have 2 points in the coordinate plane, you can find their midpoint, which can save you time on some of the more complex geometry questions. The basic idea is to calculate the average of the x- and y-coordinates.

$$\text{Midpoint} = \frac{(x_1 + x_2)}{2}, \frac{(y_1 + y_2)}{2}$$

Nonlinear Equations—Curved Lines and Circles

Sometimes on the GMAT you will see quadratic equations and circles in the coordinate plane. In these cases, your knowledge of intercepts and algebraic manipulation will be most useful.

$$y = x^2 - 3x + 2 \qquad \text{or} \qquad x^2 + y^2 = 100$$

When $x = 0$, the y-intercept is 2.

When $y = 0$, we get $(x - 2)(x - 1) = 0$; thus the x-intercepts are 1 and 2.

Note that this equation creates a circle of radius 10.

Using algebra, we can also calculate the x- and y-intercepts to be at ± 10.

Note also that the equation for a circle with a center at (a, b) is $(x - a)^2 + (y - b)^2 = r^2$.

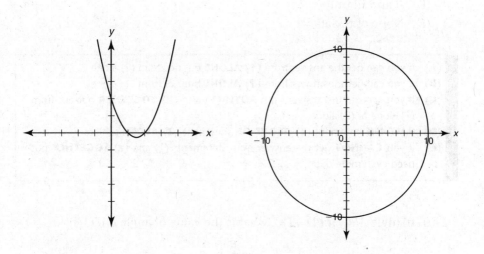

The axis of symmetry of a parabola is given by $x = \dfrac{-b}{a}$ if the equation is $y = ax^2 + bx + c$.

As you can see, graphing quadratic equations creates curved lines. If you still have trouble, try using a T-chart to get a better visual understanding. You can also use your knowledge of algebraic manipulation to simplify the equation.

GEOMETRY: TARGETED REVIEW QUESTIONS

1. If $\ell1$ is perpendicular to $\ell2$ and $\ell2$ is perpendicular to $\ell3$ in a three-dimensional space, what do we know about the relationship between $\ell1$ and $\ell3$?

   I. $\ell1 \parallel \ell3$
   II. $\ell1 \perp \ell3$
   III. $\ell1$ is equal to $\ell3$

   (A) I only
   (B) II only
   (C) I and III only
   (D) II and III only
   (E) None of the above

   (A) If you can get the answer from **(1) ALONE** but not from (2) alone
   (B) If you can get the answer from **(2) ALONE** but not from (1) alone
   (C) If you can get the answer from **BOTH (1)** and **(2) TOGETHER** but not from (1) alone or (2) alone
   (D) If **EITHER** statement **(1) ALONE OR** statement **(2) ALONE** suffices
   (E) If you **CANNOT** get the answer from statements (1) and (2) **TOGETHER** but need even more data

---

2. In triangle ABC, if $BD = DC$, what is the value of angle BAD?

   (1) Triangle ABC is equilateral.
   (2) AD bisects angle BDC.

3. If x and z are the centers of 2 circles x and y, respectively, what percent of the area of circle x is the area of circle z?

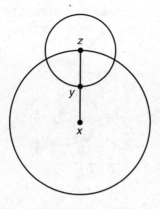

(1) $yz = \left(\dfrac{1}{2}\right)xz$

(2) The circumference of circle x is 49.

4. Rhombus *ABCD* of side 6 has perpendicular line *ED* intersecting side *AB*. What is the area of trapezoid *BCDE*?

(1) $\dfrac{AE}{EB} = \dfrac{1}{1}$

(2) Angle *EDA* is 30°.

5. In the diagram below, the 4 circles intersect each other at a point tangent to their centers, forming a shaded region. Line *BD* has a length of $8\sqrt{2}$. What is the area of the shaded region?

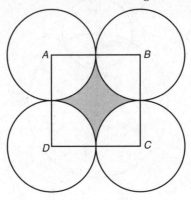

(A) $16 - 4\pi$
(B) $64 - 16\pi$
(C) $128 - 32\pi$
(D) $128 - 16\pi$
(E) 128

ANSWER KEY

1. **(E)**   3. **(A)**   5. **(B)**
2. **(A)**   4. **(D)**

SOLUTIONS

1. **(E)** The best way to solve this question is to visualize it with a drawing.

The trick here is to understand that perpendicular lines are not necessarily in the same surface plane. In other words, you should consider 3 dimensions instead of 2 dimensions. As you can see from the drawing, $\ell3$ is not necessarily parallel to or perpendicular to $\ell1$. It is also not necessarily the same length.

2. **(A)** In data sufficiency questions, we cannot assume that figures are drawn to scale. Even though it may look like an equilateral triangle, we cannot be certain unless information tells us so. We do know angles DBC and DCB.

Statement 1 confirms for us that the triangle ABC is an equilateral triangle. We are given angle DCA and thus can calculate angle DCB because the entire angle ACB must equal 60°. From this we get

$$\angle DCB = \angle DBC = 40° \rightarrow \angle DBA = 20° \rightarrow \angle BDC = 180° - 40° - 40° = 100°$$

Since triangle ABC is equilateral, $\angle DCB = \angle DBC$ and $BD = DC$. The point D is at the midpoint of line BC if it were to extend to D. This means that the line AD will bisect $\angle BDC$ (making statement 2 redundant).

$$\angle BDA = \angle ADC = \frac{(360° - \angle BDC)}{2} = \frac{(360° - 100°)}{2} = 130° \rightarrow$$

$$\angle BAD = 180° - 130° - 20° = 30° \quad Sufficient$$

Statement 2 tells us that line AD bisects BDC. However, we don't know what $\angle DCB$ and $\angle DBC$ are so we cannot solve for any other angles. *Insufficient*

Statement 1 alone is sufficient.

3. **(A)** What we know is there are two circles, x and z. What we want is $\frac{A_z}{A_x}$. What we need is A_z and A_x, $\frac{A_z}{A_x}$, r_z and r_x, or $\frac{r_z}{r_x}$ because the radius will also give us the area.

Statement 1 tells us that the radius of z is half the radius of x, giving us $\frac{r_z}{r_x} = \frac{1}{2}$. *Sufficient*

Statement 2 gives us information about circle x but no information about circle z. *Insufficient*

Statement 1 alone is sufficient.

4. **(D)** Since this figure is a rhombus, we know that all four sides are of length 6. What we need to solve for the trapezoid is the length of the two bases EB and CD as well as the height ED. We already have $CD = 6$.

Statement 1 gives us the ratio of sides AE and EB, which means $AE = 3$ and $EB = 3$. Since triangle AED is a right triangle (and a 30-60-90 one too), we can also calculate the length of ED using the Pythagorean theorem.

$6^2 - 3^2 = ED^2 \rightarrow ED = \sqrt{36-9} = \sqrt{27} = 3\sqrt{3} \rightarrow$ We could have used the 30-60-90 ratios.

To find the area of a rhombus,

$$A = \text{(average base)(height)} = \left(\frac{(3+6)}{2}\right) \bullet 3\sqrt{3} = \frac{27\sqrt{2}}{2}$$

Sufficient.

Statement 2 tells us that triangle AED is a 30-60-90 right triangle. Since we have the length of the hypotenuse, we can determine the other two sides using the ratio 1-$\sqrt{3}$-2. Sides AE and ED would be 3 and $3\sqrt{3}$, respectively. Now we can solve for the trapezoid as we did in statement 1 above. *Sufficient*

Each statement alone is sufficient.

5. **(B)** When a geometry problem seems complex, it's important to break it down into easier-to-manage steps. In order to calculate the shaded region, you need to take the area of the square and subtract the area of each sector of the 4 circles. More simply put, you just need to subtract the area of one circle from the area of the square. The problem gives the diameter of the square as $8\sqrt{2}$. Using the 45-45-90 right triangle ratio of 1-1-$\sqrt{2}$, you know that a hypotenuse of $8\sqrt{2}$ means you have a side of 8. Thus the radius of the circle is 4. This gives:

area of square – area of the circle = $s^2 - \pi r^2 = 8^2 - \pi 4^2 = 64 - 16\pi$

Statistics

8

Statistics is a topic that was very relevant to you even before you became a business school student. We see statistics cited every day in our professional and personal lives. Now here is your chance to appreciate them even more! If you are unfamiliar with statistics theory, know that you have to learn it for your MBA anyway, so you might as well start learning now. Mastering statistics will increase your confidence and will help you on some of the harder problems. The GMAT has lately been including more statistics problems. However, the depth of theory is not too complex. For example, you don't need to know how to calculate standard deviation, just how to maneuver it or understand its magnitude. You should expect to see at least a couple of statistics questions if not more.

AVERAGE (ARITHMETIC MEAN)

The **average** or the **mean** is the most common statistical concept on the GMAT. The basic formula is straightforward.

$$\textbf{Average} = \text{arithmetic mean} = \text{mean} = \bar{x} = \frac{\text{the sum of the terms in the set}}{\text{the number of terms in the set}}$$

Note that you may see the words **average**, **arithmetic mean**, and **mean** used interchangeably on the GMAT. They all mean the same thing. The test makers are not likely to give you the sum of the terms and the number of terms. That would be way too easy. If you do get that, then you're probably doing pretty badly on the test. What you will likely see is any of the following:

- An average and a way to find the sum of the terms
- An average and a given number of terms
- An abstract mix of the sum of the terms and the number of terms

Strategies for the Arithmetic Mean

1. **LOOK AT THE ANSWER CHOICES FIRST.** The answer choices tend to give clues for many GMAT quantitative problems, but this is especially true for questions involving the mean.
2. **THINK CONCEPTUALLY.** Although this advice applies to most quantitative problems, it is particularly important for questions involving the mean. Look for a way to solve without calculations, especially if you see the keyword "approximately" or "estimate" in the question stem.
3. **USE YOUR "BEST FRIENDS": ALGEBRA AND NUMBER PROPERTIES.** Understanding arithmetic mean problems may require you to set up algebraic equations or leverage number properties to unlock a shortcut or key insight.

SETS OF NUMBERS

A **set** is a collection of things. In math, a set usually refers to a set of numbers.

An **element** is one of the things or numbers in a set. A set can have a finite or an infinite number of elements.

If we take part of a set made up of elements, we have a **subset**.

If set $S = \{-3, 2, 7, 10, 100\}$, and if set $T = \{2, 7, 10\}$, then T is a subset of S.

Remember these few things about sets of numbers:

1. Rearrange the order of elements from smallest to largest. Not every set is given to you in the proper order. The first step when you see any set of numbers is to fix this.
2. When you multiply or divide a set by a constant, you must multiply or divide every element in the set.
3. Several commonly seen sets of numbers appear on the GMAT. Be familiar with them. Remember n is any interger.

   - **CONSECUTIVE INTEGERS:** $\{-3, -2, -1, 0, 1, 2, 3\}$. This can be written as $n, n + 1, n + 2, \ldots$
   - **CONSECUTIVE EVEN INTEGERS:** $\{-10, -8, -6, -4, -2\}$. These can be written as $2n, 2n + 2, 2n + 4, \ldots$
   - **CONSECUTIVE ODD INTEGERS:** $\{1, 3, 5, 7, 9, \ldots\}$. These can be written as $2n + 1, 2n + 3, 2n + 5, \ldots$
   - **PRIME NUMBERS:** $\{2, 3, 5, 7, 11, 13, 17, \ldots\}$
   - **CONSECUTIVE MULTIPLES** of any number: e.g., $\{7, 14, 21, 28, 35\}$

4. To find the number of elements in a larger set of consecutive numbers, you can do the following calculation: (largest number) – (smallest number) + 1

   How many numbers are between 50 and 175, inclusive?

Solution: $175 - 50 + 1 = 126$ numbers

Note that if we wanted the numbers between 50 and 175 but not including 50 and 175, we would take (largest number) – (smallest number) – 1 $\rightarrow$ $175 - 50 - 1 = 124$ numbers.

5. To find the number of multiples in a set, use

$$\frac{(\text{largest number}) - (\text{smallest number})}{\text{multiple}} + 1$$

Be careful that the largest and smallest numbers are actual multiples themselves so that they fit the criteria.

   How many even integers are between 520 and 300, inclusive?

Solution: $\dfrac{(520 - 300)}{2} + 1 = 111$ even integers.

If the question above had asked about even integers between 521 and 299, we still would need to use 520 and 300 in the equation. What if the questions wanted the number of multiples of 3 between 520 and 300 exclusive? You would get

$$\frac{(520 - 300)}{3} + 1 = \frac{220}{3} + 1 = 73\frac{1}{3} + 1$$

In this case, take $73 + 1 = 74$ multiples of 3.

MEDIAN

The **median** is the middle value of a set of numbers when the numbers are arranged in order. If the set has an even number of terms, it is the average of the two middle terms in the set.

> The median of the set {2, 3, 5, 7, 11} is 5 because it is the middle term. The median of the set {2, 3, 5, 7, 11, 13} is 6 because the average of the two middle terms, 5 and 7, is 6.

Note also:

- When data points are evenly spaced—consecutive integers, multiples of 5, etc.—the median is equal to the mean (more on that below).
- Even if data points are not evenly spaced, but arranged symmetrically around the mean, the median is equal to the mean (e.g., 10, 20, 60, 70).
- The median can range anywhere from the lowest number in the data set to the highest number (e.g., 10, 10, 10, 60, 70) or (10, 10, 70, 70, 70).

Median and Mean

For consecutive sets, otherwise known as evenly distributed sets, the median and the mean are equal. This statistics concept is tested often on the GMAT. One great tactic to determine the mean and median of a consecutive set quickly is by taking the average of the first and last number.

> What is the mean and median of set Z: {6, 12, 18, 24, 30, 36, 42, 48}?

Using the first and last elements $\rightarrow \dfrac{(48+6)}{2} = 27$

RANGE

The **range** is the difference between the largest value of a set and the smallest value of a set.

> The range of the set {–7, –2, 6, 9, 10} is 17, which we get from 10 – (–7) = 17.

Remember a few things about the range of a set.

1. The range is always a positive number.
2. If you add numbers to a set that are between the highest and lowest numbers, the range is not affected.

3. A range of zero means that all numbers in the set are the same, e.g., {3, 3, 3, 3}.

MODE

The **mode** is the most frequently occurring number in a set. A set can have multiple modes. If all the numbers in a set are distinct from each other, then there is no mode.

> A: {2, 4, 4, 8, 8, 10, 10, 12} has three modes: 4, 8, and 10.
> B: {2, 4, 4, 8, 10, 12} has only one mode: 4.
> C: {2, 4, 8, 10, 12} has no mode.

On their own, each statistics concept is relatively straightforward. So then how can the test makers create difficult questions? Often the GMAT will present statistics problems that combine concepts from mean, median, mode, and range.

STANDARD DEVIATION

Standard deviation is a measure of the **spread** of numbers in a set. Another way to say this is that it is the **dispersion** or **deviation** of numbers. More specifically, the standard deviation looks at how closely terms in a set are spread out around the set's mean. You will not have to calculate standard deviation on the GMAT. However, you should know how it is calculated, what exactly it stands for, and what aspects are tested on the GMAT.

1. Analyze and compare magnitudes of different sets and their standard deviations
2. Determine what happens to a standard deviation when changes are made to the elements of the set

The formula for standard deviation is

$$S.D. = \sigma = \sqrt{\text{variance}} = \sqrt{\frac{\sum (X_i - \bar{X})^2}{N}}$$

Note that you will *not* have to use this formula on the GMAT. However, it's a good idea to know how to calculate standard deviation in order to understand it better for the GMAT.

Calculating Standard Deviation

The steps to calculating the standard deviation are in the following example.

$$\text{Set } S: \{2, 4, 9, 10, 15\}$$

1. Calculate the mean of the set: $\frac{40}{5} = 8$.

2. Find the difference between each term and the mean. Then square that difference.

Term	Difference from Mean	Square of Difference
2	$(2 - 8) = -6$	$(2 - 8)^2 = 36$
4	$(4 - 8) = -4$	$(4 - 8)^2 = 16$
9	$(9 - 8) = 1$	$(9 - 8)^2 = 1$
10	$(10 - 8) = 2$	$(10 - 8)^2 = 4$
15	$(15 - 8) = 7$	$(15 - 8)^2 = 49$

3. Calculate the sum of the differences between each value and the mean squared:

$$36 + 16 + 1 + 4 + 49 = 106$$

4. Divide the previous sum by the number of terms:

$$\frac{106}{5} = 21.2 \rightarrow \text{This is also known as the \textbf{variance},}$$
$$\text{or the \textbf{mean of the squares}.}$$

5. Take the square root of the previous value:

$$\sqrt{21.2} = 4.604$$

Here are some other things to keep in mind about the standard deviation.

- Standard deviation is never negative. If it is zero, this means that all numbers in the set are equal, such as in the set $\{2, 2, 2, 2, 2\}$.
- Adding or subtracting a constant to or from each number in a set does not change the standard deviation.
- If you multiply each term in a set by a number greater than 1, the standard deviation will increase. Conversely, if you divide each term in a set by a number greater than 1, the standard deviation will decrease.
- The variance is the square of the standard deviation.
- Numbers that are tightly clustered around an average have a smaller standard deviation than numbers that are spread out.

- When analyzing the standard deviation among sets, the first thing to look at is the relative spread of the numbers. This usually is enough. If you are still not sure, look at the range of the set as a tiebreaker. If you still aren't sure, then you may have to calculate the average and look at how spread the numbers are around the mean.

Finally, note that the following happens when all of the terms of a data set are:

1. Multiplied by a factor, such as 2, 5, 10, $\frac{1}{4}$, etc.

   All terms multiplied by 2:

   - Mean doubles
   - Median doubles
   - Range doubles
   - Mode doubles
   - Standard deviation doubles

2. Increased or decreased by a number, such as adding 10, subtracting 3, etc.

   Add +10 to all terms:

   - Mean +10
   - Median +10
   - Mode +10
   - Range—same
   - Standard deviation—same

STATISTICS: TARGETED REVIEW QUESTIONS

1. The table shows the maximum and minimum recorded temperatures for City X.

	April	May	June	July	Aug.	Sept.
Minimum	29	30	31	33	31	30
Maximum	42	54	65	70	63	53

Which of the following measures is greater for the maximum recorded temperatures than for the minimum recorded temperatures during the months shown for City X?

  I: The average (arithmetic mean)
 II: The range
III: The standard deviation

(A) I only
(B) III only
(C) I and II
(D) II and III
(E) I, II, and III

(A) If you can get the answer from **(1) ALONE** but not from (2) alone
(B) If you can get the answer from **(2) ALONE** but not from (1) alone
(C) If you can get the answer from **BOTH (1)** and **(2) TOGETHER** but not from (1) alone or (2) alone
(D) If **EITHER** statement **(1) ALONE OR** statement **(2) ALONE** suffices
(E) If you **CANNOT** get the answer from statements (1) and (2) **TOGETHER** but need even more data

---

2. Is the standard deviation of set X greater than the standard deviation of set Y?

(1) Set X has no mode, and set Y has consecutive terms.
(2) The range of set X is greater than the range of set Y.

3. The median monthly rental income of a commercial real estate property with 17 different stores is $5,000. If the average rental income increases by 20% in the next month, what will the median rental income in the real estate property be next month?

(A) $5,000
(B) $5,500
(C) $6,000
(D) $6,500
(E) It cannot be determined from the information given.

4. For set T: {100, 102, 101, 103, 102, 100, 101, 103, Y}, which of the following values would increase the standard deviation the most?

(A) 100
(B) 101
(C) 102
(D) 103
(E) 104

5. The median of the four terms a, b, $a + b$, and $b - a$ is 3. If $a > b > 0$, what is the arithmetic mean (average) of the four terms?

(A) 4

(B) $\dfrac{(2b+a)}{2}$

(C) $\dfrac{3b}{2} + a$

(D) $3 + \dfrac{(b-a)}{4}$

(E) $4 + \dfrac{(b+a)}{2}$

ANSWER KEY

1. **(E)**   3. **(E)**   5. **(D)**
2. **(E)**   4. **(E)**

SOLUTIONS

1. **(E)** Let's look at each statement carefully one at a time.

    I: The average temperature for the maximum recordings is clearly greater than that for the minimum recorded temperatures. There is no need to calculate when it is so obvious from the chart. True

    II: The range of the maximum temperatures is $70 - 42 = 28$. The range of the minimum temperatures is $33 - 29 = 4$. True

    III: Remember that standard deviation is simply the spread or dispersion of numbers and you do not need to know how to calculate it. If you look at the spread of numbers for the maximum temperatures, they are far more spread out than those of the minimum temperatures. True

2. **(E)** What we really want to know in this question is if the numbers in set X have a larger spread or dispersion than the numbers in set Y. The statements talk about modes, consecutive terms, and range, which may or may not affect the standard deviation. Our best bet is to come up with examples of sets in order to disprove sufficiency for each of the statements.

    Statement 1 essentially implies that neither set X nor set Y has a mode. We can come up with 2 examples.

$$X: \{2, 4, 5\} \text{ and } Y: \{2, 3, 4\} \text{ or } Y: \{3, 6, 9\}$$

    These 2 different sets of Y have standard deviations less than or greater than that of set X. *Insufficient*

    Statement 2 suggests that a greater range will always lead to a greater standard deviation, but this is not true. Again, let's come up with a specific example.

$$X: \{2, 4, 6, 8\} \text{ and } Y: \{2, 3, 4, 5, 6, 7\} \text{ or } Y: \{2, 7\}$$

    Again we come up with 2 different sets of Y where both have a smaller range than X. The first set has a smaller standard deviation, and the second set has a larger standard deviation. *Insufficient*

    When we combine statements 1 and 2, we can take the example we just used above to disprove sufficiency. *Insufficient*

Both statements together are still not sufficient.

3. **(E)** Often our assumptions can trip us up. For example, just because the average rental increase was 20% doesn't mean that each property had a 20% increase on its rent. We are given 17 properties, so the median would be ranked 9th among the rental incomes, leaving us with 7 rental incomes on either side of the set. We could increase all the rental incomes by 20% and the median would become $6,000. However, we could also increase fewer or even one rental income by a much larger amount to give us the same average increase. So we really don't know what the exact rental distribution is. There is no way to determine the answer to this problem.

4. **(E)** Standard deviation is a measure of the spread of numbers and, more specifically, the distribution of numbers around the mean. When we put the set in the question in correct order, we have {100, 100, 101, 101, 102, 102, 103, 103, Y}. Of the answer choices, the only number outside our current group is 104. Just to be sure, we can check the mean of this set, which is 101.5. The number that is most likely to affect the standard deviation will be the one that's farthest from the mean. The number 104 will make this set as widely distributed as possible.

5. **(D)** The first thing we need to figure out is how these numbers rank in value. We know that a and b are both positive and that $a > b$. This means that $a + b$ is the largest number and that $b - a$ is a negative number and thus the smallest. This gives us the ordered set {$b - a, b, a, a + b$}. Since the median is 3, we know that it is the average between a and b so

$$\frac{(a+b)}{2} = 3 \rightarrow a + b = 6$$

The arithmetic mean is the (sum of terms)/(number of terms), which gives us

$$\frac{((b-a)+(b)+(a)+(a+b))}{4} \rightarrow \frac{((b-a)+(a+b)+(a+b))}{4}$$

$$\rightarrow \text{ substitute } a + b = 6$$

$$\frac{(b-a+6+6)}{4} = \frac{(12+b-a)}{4} = 3 + \frac{(b-a)}{4}$$

Data Sufficiency 9

▄▃▄▃▄▃▄▃▄▃▄▃▄▃▄▃▄▃▄▃▄▃▄▃▄▃▄▃▄▃▄▃

Data sufficiency problems ask a simple question: are the data provided sufficient to solve the problem? Determining the answer may not be so simple. Data sufficiency problems test your mathematical knowledge in a unique way. Because the setup is somewhat abstract, many students are intimidated by this section. The good news is that once you understand the structure, data sufficiency problems are easy to break down. In addition, you don't always have to perform calculations in order to solve them. You only have to know whether you **can** solve a problem via calculations. Therefore, data sufficiency questions generally take less time to answer than problem-solving questions.

WHY DATA SUFFICIENCY?

It's important to understand why business schools want to test you on data sufficiency. As a future manager or leader, you will be required to do several things:

1. Sort through information or data
2. Identify key issues
3. Make decisions

Data sufficiency is designed to measure your ability to think critically, identify relevant information, extract key insights, and know when you have enough information to solve a problem. These skills are important for any business school graduate and future manager.

DATA SUFFICIENCY DIRECTIONS FOR THE GMAT

Below are the official directions from the GMAC that appear before your first data sufficiency problem on the GMAT.

DIRECTIONS: This problem consists of a question and two statements, labeled (1) and (2), in which certain data are given. You have to decide whether the data given in the statements are sufficient for answering the question. Using the data given in the statements plus your knowledge of mathematics and everyday facts (such as the number of days in July or the meaning of counterclockwise), you must indicate whether:

A. Statement (1) ALONE is sufficient, but statement (2) alone is not sufficient to answer the question asked;
B. Statement (2) ALONE is sufficient, but statement (1) alone is not sufficient to answer the question asked;
C. BOTH statements (1) and (2) TOGETHER are sufficient to answer the question asked, but NEITHER statement ALONE is sufficient;
D. EACH statement ALONE is sufficient to answer the question asked;
E. Statements (1) and (2) TOGETHER are NOT sufficient to answer the question asked, and additional data specific to the problem are needed.

Numbers: All numbers used are real numbers.

Figures: A figure accompanying a data sufficiency problem will conform to the information given in the question but will not necessarily conform to the additional information in statements (1) and (2).

Lines shown as straight can be assumed to be straight, and lines that appear jagged can also be assumed to be straight.

You may assume that positions of points, angles, regions, etc., exist in the order shown and that angle measures are greater than zero.

All figures lie in a plane unless otherwise indicated.

Note: If the data sufficiency problem asks you for the value of a quantity, the data given in the statements are sufficient only when it is possible to determine exactly one numerical value for the quantity.

SAMPLE QUESTION OVERVIEW

Question Stem	What is the value of x?
Statement 1	(1) The square of x is 25.
Statement 2	(2) $x(x - 5) = 0$

Solution (in case you were curious)

We are looking for one value of x. In statement 1, the value of x could be either 5 or -5; therefore, it is not sufficient. In statement 2, the value of x could be either 0 or 5; therefore, it is also not sufficient. When we combine the two statements, the value of x could only be 5. Since we have only one value for x, we have sufficiency.

The correct answer is C.

DATA SUFFICIENCY BREAKDOWN

Based on the structure, format, and directions of data sufficiency questions, there are a few things you need to know:

- Data sufficiency accounts for at least 15 of the 37 quantitative problems. However, in recent years, test takers have seen nearly half the questions as data sufficiency, depending on how well they are doing. The better you are doing on the quantitative section, the more data sufficiency questions you will get.
- Your job is to determine when you have enough information to solve the problem. However, you rarely need to solve the problem.
- The format of the answer choices is the same, so you should memorize what each answer choice represents to save time.
- Data sufficiency tests all the same math theory that problem-solving does—arithmetic, algebra, geometry, properties of numbers, probability, statistics, and combinatorics.
- For each statement, you have to ask yourself, "Do I have enough information to determine sufficiency?" This is very similar to the real world where business leaders ask, "Do we have enough information to make a decision?" The major difference here is that in the real business world, managers rarely make decisions with 100% of the information required (usually anywhere from 20%–80%) because getting all of the information would take too long. However, the principle remains the same.
- Data sufficiency questions have a fixed format and set rules. Knowing the rules and how to exploit them is key.

There are two types of data sufficiency questions: Single Value and Yes/No. The chart on the next page describes both.

DATA SUFFICIENCY QUESTIONS—SINGLE VALUE VS. YES/NO

	Single Value	Yes/No
Description	The question asks you to solve for something.	The question asks you to answer either Yes or No.
Key words	Solve, find, calculate, what? e.g., "What is x?"	Is, does, can, will? e.g., "Is $x > y$?"
Key insight	You need only one quantity for sufficiency; multiple quantities would be insufficient.	You may have multiple quantities but just need to answer either "Yes definitively" or "No definitively."
Example	Q. What is x? (1) $x^2 = 9$ Since $x = 3$ and -3, statement 1 is not sufficient.	Q. Is $x > 0$? (1) $(x + 3)(x + 2)(x + 1) = 0$ Since $x = -3, -2, -1$, and x is always negative, we can answer "No definitively," and therefore statement 1 is sufficient.

DATA SUFFICIENCY STRATEGIES

Strategy 1: Decision Tree Method

The most common strategy is to use a decision tree to answer the following questions:

1. Is statement 1 sufficient by itself to solve the problem?
2. Is statement 2 sufficient by itself to solve the problem?
3. Are statements 1 and 2, when taken together, sufficient to solve the problem?

Depending on your answer for each question, you can follow the decision tree on the next page to determine the proper answer choice. Notice that you only have to ask the third question approximately 40% of the time. Make sure you understand why you answered "Yes" or "No" to each question.

Data Sufficiency Decision Tree

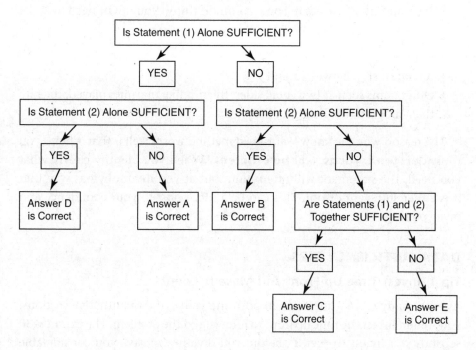

Strategy 2: Know-Want-Need Method

Another key strategy is to use the **know-want-need method**. It works well for a variety of quantitative topics—number properties, algebra, geometry, probability, weighted average, mixture, and word problems.

KNOW: What information do you know or have that is either directly given or implied? Do the statements themselves give you any extra insight about the problem?

WANT: What does the question ask for (i.e., what is the macro question)? Are there any specific units? Is this a single value or a yes/no question type? Do you need to be aware of any keywords (ratio of, percent of, number of, etc.)?

NEED: This is the link between what we know and what we want. Data sufficiency, while seemingly complex at times, can always be simplified. You are looking for a statement that gives you what you need either directly or indirectly. Every quantitative problem has a key insight, and here is where you should try to extract it. Some common things you might need include:

- x or y
- x and y
- A relationship between x and y
- Other items such as two equal sides, the number of games played, the rate that Alice ran, the height of Billy, etc.

The reason why the know-want-need method works well is that it helps you to **understand**, **focus**, and **be efficient**. When you identify clearly what you need, the statement will often jump out at you in an obvious way that it is either sufficient or not. This can be a nice boost to your confidence and save you time.

DATA SUFFICIENCY TIPS

Tip 1. Invest Time Up Front and Make It Count

As with many GMAT questions in both the verbal and quantitative sections, you should invest the time up front to understand the problem. The extra 15–30 seconds you invest to "get it" before you dive in can save you considerable time and mental energy. Make sure you:

- Avoid misreading the question and statements
- Understand the macro question and know what data sufficiency type it is
- Determine what you know, want, and need

Tip 2. Manage the Information in a Strategic and Timely Way

You can mine plenty of information from data sufficiency questions. The challenge is to know what to extract, when to extract it, and what not to extract. Keep in mind the following:

- **EVERY STATEMENT IMPLIES SOMETHING.** Determine the "what" and the "so what" for each statement. Ask yourself, "What is this telling me?" or "Why are you here?"

$$(1)\ x^5 y^2 > 0$$

This statement implies that $x > 0$ because $y^2 > 0$.
- **KNOW WHAT YOU KNOW, BOTH DIRECT AND IMPLIED.** The question often has information embedded within it.

- **AVOID MAKING ASSUMPTIONS.** Use only explicit information from the question and statement. What's given is given, and what's not given is not given.

    If y is an integer and $xy = 150$, is y a 2-digit number?

    Note that the question stem mentions y to be an integer but makes no mention of x. You can be sure the test makers will try to make you assume that x is an integer, so be careful. *Insufficient*

- **DO NOT CARRY INFORMATION FROM STATEMENT 1 INTO STATEMENT 2.** You first need to look at each statement with a clean slate.

Tip 3. Maximize the Structure to Your Advantage

Data sufficiency questions have a certain construct. The test makers have to follow the logic and process of this structure. Therefore, if you know how they set up the questions, having this insight can give you certain advantages on test day.

- **DO NOT DO CALCULATIONS UNLESS YOU HAVE TO.** Many data sufficiency questions are conceptual and do not require solving. You just have to know that you can. Often the test makers will make you think you need to do calculations when you don't have to.

    Drake's taxes were what portion of his salary?
    (1) Drake received a year-end bonus of 7% of his salary.
    (2) Drake's salary was $72,000.

    Conceptually, you need to know Drake's tax rate. Since no information about the tax rate is given in either statement, you can't solve this. *Insufficient.*

    The answer is E; both statements together are still not sufficient.

- **START WITH THE EASIER STATEMENT.** Since most test takers like to do things in order, the test makers will make statement 1 more complex than statement 2. Doing statement 2 first will not only eliminate some answer choices, but it might give you further insight into the problem and dealing with statement 1.

- **STATEMENTS 1 AND 2 NEVER CONTRADICT.** For example, in a single value type, if you find for statement 1 that $x = 2$ and for statement 2 that $x = 3$, you have made an error and need to redo your calculations. You could also use this information to gain extra insight.

> What is the value of x?
> (1) x is negative
> (2) $x^2 = 49$

If you thought here that $x = 7$, this would contradict what you learned in statement 1. This reminds you that $x = -7$ as well!

The answer is C.

If the answer to a data sufficiency question is D, then both pieces of information given, (1) and (2), must lead to the same numerical value. This is also true for Yes/No question types. They must both lead to Yes answers or both to No answers.

- **DETERMINE SUFFICIENCY BY PROVING INSUFFICIENCY.** Sometimes you can focus on proving insufficiency by picking numbers to find both a scenario that works and another that doesn't work, thus proving insufficiency.

Tip 4. Don't Let the Game Fool You

Given the previous tip, the construct of data sufficiency also gives the test makers a variety of ways to trick you. There is almost a game to how the GMAT is tested or played. Arm yourself with the knowledge of some of the traps the test makers set up for you.

- **THEY PUT THE SAME INFO IN EACH STATEMENT.** It is very easy in math to say the same thing in completely different ways (e.g., positive integer, whole number, nondecimal number greater than zero, etc.). So if you were the GMAT test maker, why not do this in data sufficiency as a way to trick test takers? If this does happen, the answer can only be either D or E. If one statement works, the other has to work. If statement 1 doesn't work, then statement 2 won't work. Putting them together adds no new information.

> Solve for x.
> (1) $x - 3y = -7$
> (2) $21 + 3x = 9y$

The equation in statement 2 is a manipulated version of the equation in statement 1. Therefore, we essentially have one equation and two unknowns. The equation cannot be solved. *Insufficient*

The answer is E.

- **DO NOT FORGET THAT "NO" CAN MEAN "SUFFICIENT."** A common thought process is to associate "No" with "Not sufficient." For Yes/No data sufficiency questions, remember that if the answer to the macro question is "no, definitively," then that is sufficient.

> Is $x > 0$?
> (1) $(x + 3)(x + 2)(x + 1) = 0$

The statement tells us that $x = -3, -2,$ or -1. We know definitively that x is not greater than 0. *Sufficient*

- **WATCH OUT FOR THE EASY C.** If the question seems to lead you to think that both statements together are sufficient, think again! You should expect the same difficulty level of questions, so getting an easy one doesn't make sense. It is likely that one (or both) of the statements have some information embedded in them or there is something in the question stem that you missed. Alternatively, there may be a hidden reason why the statements don't work even when taken together.

> If $2x + y = 5z$, what is the value of y?
> (1) $3x = -1.5 + 7.5z$
> (2) $x = 2$

Upon first glance, statement 2 doesn't work. When combined with statement 1, though, you can plug in $x = 2$ and then solve for z and y because you have 2 equations and 2 unknowns. If you look closely at the question stem and statement 1, both can be manipulated to get ① $y = 5z - 2x$ and ② $7.5z - 3x = 1.5$, respectively. If we divide $7.5z - 3x = 1.5$ by 1.5, we get $5z - 2x = 1$. We can substitute this into ① and get an actual value for y. *Sufficient*

The answer is A.

- **WHEN THE TEST ASKS FOR $a + b$, YOU MIGHT NOT NEED INDIVIDUAL VALUES.** Some data sufficiency questions seem to have too many algebraic variables, but you don't always need to solve for every variable. As long as you know what $a + b$ equals, you do not need to know what a and b are individually.

Tip 5. Use Your Knowledge of GMAT Theory, Strategies, and Methodologies to Simplify

Everything you learn in this book and externally is ammunition for beating the GMAT. All the skills and tips we share throughout the book will help you better process, understand, and approach all data sufficiency problems. You just have to leverage them when needed and be flexible whether doing data sufficiency questions conceptually or mathematically.

- **MANIPULATE THE EQUATIONS.** Just because an equation is given to you in a certain way, whether it is in the question stem or in the statement, this does not mean you can't manipulate it to serve your needs.

  Is $x - y > 0$?

  This is the same as asking if $x > y$

- **YOU ALWAYS HAVE YOUR TWO BFFS.** As we said earlier in the book, algebra and properties of numbers are your two "best friends forever" in data sufficiency as well as in all the quantitative questions. You can set up equations, simplify your work, unlock keys, break down the statements via conceptual understanding, and so much more!

- **DO NOT FORGET ABOUT 0 (ZERO).** It's so easy to forget about zero. It has unique qualities in terms of both usage and how it can change the dynamics of a question. Be wary of zero when dealing with inequalities, absolute value, and properties of numbers. Zero can also be a powerful number to use when picking numbers.

  Is $x > 0$?
  (1) $|x| = -x$

  This implies x is negative but also zero. *Insufficient*

- **PICKING NUMBERS.** We've saved the best for last and so can you (although you can try it first sometimes, too). This is the universal strategy taught by every test prep company in the world. We all can't be wrong! It helps you to understand the question better and to simplify the process. In a single value question type, you pick numbers to find more than one value. In a Yes/No type problem, you pick numbers to find both a yes and a no answer.

  If x and y are distinct prime numbers, is $x(y - 5)$ odd?
  (1) $x < 3$

Statement 1 tells us that $x = 2$. Try any prime number for y ($y = 3, 5, 7, 11$, etc.). The equation $x(y - 5)$ is always even. *Sufficient*

DATA SUFFICIENCY: TARGETED REVIEW QUESTIONS

1. If t is the tens digit and u is the units digit of a two-digit number, what is the value of this number?

    (1) $t + u = 9$
    (2) $t - u = -5$

2. An organization is showcasing an outdoor play in a park. If over the course of a two-week run, it sells $3,200 worth of tickets, all at the same price, what is the price of one ticket?

    (1) If the price of each ticket were $1 more, the total revenue would be $800 more.
    (2) If the organization decreases the ticket price by $1 and sells 25% more tickets as a result, the total revenue would remain the same as before.

3. Milk carton A and milk jug B each contain milk. The capacity of jug B is 40% greater than that of carton A. How much more milk is in carton A than in jug B?

    (1) When full, container B holds 7 L of milk.
    (2) Container A is 4/5 full, and container B is 2/7 full.

4. If x_1 and x_2 are the number of schoolchildren and y_1 and y_2 are the number of schools in Country A and Country B, respectively, the ratio of the number of schoolchildren to the number of schools is greater for which of the two countries?

    (1) $y_1 > y_2$
    (2) $x_1 < x_2$

5. If a, b, c, and d are positive prime numbers and the product of $abcd = 210$, what is the value of b?

    (1) $b + c = d$
    (2) $c + d = a^2$

ANSWER KEY

1. **(C)**	3. **(C)**	5. **(B)**
2. **(D)**	4. **(C)**	

SOLUTIONS

1. **(C)** You know that *tu* is a two-digit number. You want the value of both *u* and *t*. You need either *u* AND *t* (which of course test makers are not likely to give directly) or two equations with *u* and *t* that you can solve algebraically.

    Statement 1 means that the number could be 18, 27, 36, 45, 54, 63, 72, 81, or 90. *Insufficient*

    Statement 2 means that the number could be 16, 27, 38, or 49.

    When you combine both statements, you have two distinct equations that can be solved for *u* and *t*. Furthermore, you know that the only possible value satisfying both statements is 27. *Sufficient*

    Both statements together are sufficient.

2. **(D)** Using algebra, you know that $P \cdot n = 3200$, where P = the price of a ticket and n = the number of tickets. You want P. What you need is either P, or n, or another distinct equation with P and n.

    Statement 1 means that $(P + 1)n = 3200 + 800$. → $(P + 1)n = 4000$. This is another equation with P and n, thus giving you what you need. *Sufficient*

    You don't have to solve this, rather just know that you can. However, just by inspection you know that a $1 increase per ticket leads to an $800 increase in overall sales. Therefore, the organization sold 800 tickets.

    Statement 2 means that $(P - 1)(n \cdot 1.25) = 3200$. Again, this is another distinct equation with P and n. Therefore, you can solve it. *Sufficient*

    Each statement alone is sufficient.

3. **(C)** Let's use the know-want-need method along with algebra.

    Know: $C_B = 1.4C_A$ → Jug B's capacity is 40% more than carton A's capacity.

    Want: $A - B$ → The amount of milk in A minus the amount of milk in B

    Need: A and B or a relationship among A, B, C_B, and C_A

Statement 1 means that $C_B = 7$. The trick here is that the statement says "when full" and does not say that the container is actually full. You still don't know the amount of milk in either container. *Insufficient*

Statement 2 tells how full the containers actually are. $A = \left(\frac{4}{5}\right)C_A$ and $B = \left(\frac{2}{7}\right)C_B$. However, you don't know the actual capacity of either container. Make sure you do not mistakenly take information from statement 1 and apply it to statement 2 by itself. *Insufficient*

When you combine both statements, you know the capacities of both containers and the amount of milk in each container. Therefore, you can solve. *Sufficient*

$$C_B = 7 \text{ and } C_B = 1.4C_A, \text{ which means } 7 = \left(\frac{7}{5}\right) \bullet C_A \rightarrow C_A = 5$$

$$A = \left(\frac{4}{5}\right)C_A \rightarrow A = 4 \text{ L} \qquad B = \left(\frac{2}{7}\right)C_B \rightarrow B = 2 \text{ L} \rightarrow A - B = 4 - 2 = 2 \text{ L}$$

Both statements together are sufficient.

4. **(C)** What you want to know is if $\frac{x_1}{y_1} > \frac{x_2}{y_2}$ or if ratio 1 > ratio 2.

Statement 1 says that the denominator of ratio 1 is larger than the denominator of ratio 2. This is not helpful because you don't know the numerators. Try picking numbers to visualize this.

If $y_1 = 10$ and $y_2 = 5$ and if $x_1 = x_2 = 1$, then $\frac{x_1}{y_1} < \frac{x_2}{y_2}$ because $\frac{1}{10} < \frac{1}{5}$.

If $y_1 = 10$ and $y_2 = 5$ and if $x_1 = 100$ and $x_2 = 1$, then $\frac{x_1}{y_1} > \frac{x_2}{y_2}$ because $\frac{100}{10} > \frac{1}{5}$. *Insufficient*

Statement 2 gives you the same dilemma as above. Now you know the numerators of ratio 1 and ratio 2, but you don't know the denominators. Thus you cannot compare the ratios. *Insufficient*

When you combine both statements, you know that $y_1 > y_2$ and $x_1 < x_2$. Ratio 2 now has both the larger numerator and smaller denominator. This means that it must be greater than ratio 1. Again, you can use numbers to verify this.

If $y_1 = 10$ and $y_2 = 5$ and if $x_1 = 5$ and $x_2 = 10$, then $\dfrac{x_1}{y_1} > \dfrac{x_2}{y_2}$ because $\dfrac{10}{5} > \dfrac{5}{10}$. *Sufficient*

Both statements together are sufficient.

5. **(B)** Let's use the know-want-need method here.

Know: Direct: a, b, c, and d are positive prime numbers

                      $abcd = 210$

       Indirect: 2, 3, 5, and 7 are the prime numbers that a, b, c, and d must be because $2 \cdot 3 \cdot 5 \cdot 7 = 210$

Want: The value of b

Need: The value of b

       The values of a, c, and d.

       Three distinct equations with a, b, c, and d.

       A relationship or number property describing a, b, c, and d that allows you to determine b.

Statement 1 tells you that $b + c = d$, which means that $d = 7$ and b or c could be 2 or 5. Alternatively, $d = 5$ and b or c could be 2 or 3. You do not know the value of b specifically. *Insufficient*

Statement 2 says that $c + d = a^2$. The only way this equation could work with the given prime numbers is if you had $2 + 7 = 3^2$. So for a, c, and d the values are 3, 2, and 7, respectively. Therefore, $b = 5$. *Sufficient*

Statement 2 alone is sufficient.

Problem Solving

10

Problem solving accounts for up to 22 of 37 questions in the quantitative section of the GMAT. In recent years, some test takers have likely seen more data sufficiency questions if they were doing well. Based on this information, the number of problem-solving questions you face could reduce to about half. Problem-solving questions cover all of the theoretical topics including arithmetic, algebra, geometry, statistics, number properties, probability, and combinatorics. In this chapter, we will review the strategies, methods, and tactics for problem solving. Then we will dive deeper into the major word problems and question types.

PROBLEM SOLVING: WINNING THE WAR

The general strategy for problem solving is common among most test prep books.

1. **READ THE PROBLEM CAREFULLY.**
2. **MAKE SURE YOU ANSWER THE PROPER QUESTION.**
3. **PICK THE BEST APPROACH.** There are also dozens of tools and tactics you can use. These weapons are a significant part of your arsenal when dealing with GMAT problems. You need to be flexible, creative, and swift enough to handle any question. Below are some fundamentals, key strategies, methods, and tactics to keep in mind for problem solving on the GMAT.

Problem-Solving Fundamentals

Understanding how the GMAT test makers structure problem-solving questions will help you to process the question better and come up with a plan that works.

- **CARELESS ERRORS BE GONE!** The two most common errors test takers make are misreading and computational error. By being aware of these common errors and the fact that the test makers will try to exploit this, you can make every effort to try to avoid them. We can address both of these error types in this chapter and beyond.

- **THE SECRET IS OUT ABOUT MINIMAL OR NO CALCULATIONS.** Most GMAT problem-solving questions can be done conceptually or with several shortcut tactics that will be presented later in this chapter. This means that you should not have to do many calculations. You can often do calculations. However, if you don't have to, you would be better off just selecting your answer and moving on.

- **THE MATH IS CLEAN.** If calculations are necessary, they will not be very complex. The numbers will work out smoothly. If they don't, you either have made a calculation error or have missed a shortcut such as simplifying, estimating, or algebra.

- **KNOW HOW THEY DECEIVE YOU.** The GMAT test makers can trick you in many ways. The most common are using clever wordplay, including misleading answer choices, and making you do unnecessary calculations. After going through all of the advice in this book, you should be able to spot the deceptions.

Problem-Solving Key Strategies

- **YOU NEED STRONG FUNDAMENTALS.** If you want to get a competitive MBA score, you must have a solid understanding of fundamentals. If you struggle to reduce fractions, manipulate exponents, or translate algebra, this will slow you down big time. The information covered in the first few chapters of this book (arithmetic, algebra, geometry) provides an essential foundation for your success.

- **INVEST IN YOUR IMMEDIATE FUTURE.** Many test takers dive right into the questions by doing calculations and then quickly get lost. However, you know that many questions require minimal or no calculations. You must invest the time up front to understand the question thoroughly before attempting to solve it. You should do this for all GMAT questions, both verbal and quantitative. Don't spend too much time, though. You have 15–30 seconds to understand the question and come up with a plan of attack. This investment will save you time in the immediate future (the next 1–2 minutes).

- **HARVEST THE GARDEN OF ANSWER CHOICES.** The answer choices provide more information than you realize. They narrow the field down to five possibilities. They tell you what kind of response is required. They give you extra insight into the question. For example, if every answer choice has a π or a $\sqrt{3}$ in it, this may tell you to exploit your knowledge of circles or special triangles. If you eliminate an answer choice, you may be able to eliminate another choice or two for the same reason, allowing you to get rid of two or three answer choices at the same time.

- **TRY THIS CONCEPT—CONCEPTUAL THINKING!** As mentioned before, conceptual thinking is a big part of doing problem-solving questions quickly and with minimal calculations. Most test takers, though, have not practiced this enough. So they go back to doing small calculations on the side. We know this is hard at first. However, the more you exercise your brain, the smarter, faster, and more confident you become.
- **"SIMPLICITY IS THE ULTIMATE SOPHISTICATION."** Leonardo da Vinci said it best. Sophisticated test takers simplify problems in many ways by leveraging conceptual thinking, algebra, and number properties and by breaking down the question. Simplify your calculations, your processes, and your thinking.
- **CARRY 3 BIG STICKS—PICKING NUMBERS, ALGEBRA, AND NUMBER PROPERTIES.** Although we will discuss these tactics below, leveraging these three biggest weapons in your arsenal really counts as a strategy on its own. Every GMAT test prep book, course, and successful student will champion picking numbers, algebra, and number properties. You should too.

Problem-Solving Methods

We introduced this chapter with a basic three-step approach. We will now discuss a variety of methods and processes for some of the more common problem-solving question types later in the chapter. The main methodology you should use is the **know-want-approach method**.

When you encounter a problem-solving question on the GMAT, ask yourself the following questions:

1. **WHAT DO YOU KNOW?** You need to extract and digest everything you read.

   - What information has been given to you directly in the problem?
   - What extra information is implied?
   - What do the answer choices tell you about the question?

2. **WHAT DO YOU WANT?** You need to understand the scope clearly.

   - What is the problem specifically asking for?
   - Are there any particular keywords or hints to be aware of?
   - Are there any defined units in the question?

3. **WHAT IS YOUR APPROACH?** You need to come up with a plan of attack. For every problem-solving question, you should be able to identify the necessary components quickly.

- What theory is being tested?
- What relevant strategies, methods, and tactics do you have in your arsenal?
- What is the key insight or catch of the problem? (Most quantitative questions require a special insight for doing the problem most effectively.)
- Based on the above, what is the best approach, or mix of approaches, for you to apply?

The idea behind the **know-want-approach** method is a solid **understanding**, a strategic **focus** of your time and effort, and overall **efficiency**. In the initial stages of your GMAT studying, you may want to write down everything. Eventually, with practice, this method will become instinctive.

Problem-Solving Tactics

We've already mentioned a few tactics above in our fundamentals, strategies, and methods. However, let's look at some of the more effective and popular tactics for GMAT problem solving.

Tactic 1. Pick Numbers . . . Wisely

Picking numbers is one of the oldest tricks in the book. But it still remains one of the wisest tricks in the book. Almost every GMAT prep guide in the universe (OK, at least on planet Earth), with the ironic exception of the official guide, mentions this tactic. When you begin to work out your solution, you can pick numbers to understand the question better and to simplify your approach. As you proceed, you can pick numbers to make your calculations easier. Lastly, you can pick numbers to check your work. Just make sure you pick numbers that make sense for the question.

- In general, use simple numbers such as 2 or 3. You can also use 0 and 1 for certain problem types (such as inequalities and absolute value), although be mindful of their special properties. Don't forget about fractions, such as $\frac{1}{2}$ or $\frac{1}{3}$, or about negative values if the question allows for them.

- If the question involves a fraction with $\frac{1}{3}$, use a large multiple of 3 such as 30, 60, or 120. Similarly, if you see a $\frac{x}{5}$ or $\frac{y}{7}$ in a question, you should pick a number that is a multiple of 35.
- If the question involves percent changes in a stock, you might try using 100.
- The most likely questions where picking numbers can be a good tactic include percents, mixtures, ratios, or problems where algebraic expressions are in the answer choices.

> Company X's stock rose 30% in year 1 and declined 10% in year 2. How much did the stock increase from the beginning of year 1 to the end of year 2?

Solution: Pick 100 as your starting number → After year 1, you get 100 + 30 = 130. After year 2, you get 130 – 13 = 117. → The increase is 17%.

Tactic 2. Use Your Best Friends (Algebra and Number Properties) . . . Forever

As we have said before, algebra and properties of numbers are indeed your BFFs in math because they are always there to support you and bail you out of a messy situation. Algebra is the language of math, helping you to translate problems, unlock key insights, and simplify calculations on the majority (that's right, over half!) of quantitative questions. Properties of numbers are like the letters and words of math. These properties are how numbers work together and how they react to mathematical situations. Properties of numbers are often the key insight to questions that seem to require 10+ minutes of calculations, letting you figure things out in less than a minute.

> What is the unit digit of 2^{23}?

Solution: Clearly, multiplying the number 2 by itself 23 times is not the answer, as it would take an excessive amount of time. Properties of unit digits tell us that powers of 2 have a pattern of 2-4-8-6 as unit digits, looping every fourth power. This means that 2^4, 2^8, and thus 2^{24} have a unit digit of 6. Therefore, the looping pattern tells us that 2^{23} has a unit digit of 8.

Tactic 3. Don't Break Your Back Solving . . . Try Backsolving

If you get stuck on a problem and have already spent over a minute to no avail, backsolving or working backward from the answer choices can be a good last resort option (along with POE and guess-timating below). Start with answer choice C because almost all GMAT answer choices are in ascending order and you can likely get to the right answer within three tries. On certain GMAT questions, you should consider backsolving:

- If the problem gives you an end result and asks you to find the starting number
- When the answer choices are simple, clean, and thus easy to plug into the question
- When the math seems to get a bit too labor intensive
- When the algebra in a word problem is more complex than plugging in the answer choices or logically reasoning them out in the question

Tactic 4. Construction, Construction, What's your Function?

The more complicated a question, the more important it is for you to add structure to the problem. There are many ways you can organize the information—charts, drawings, lists, arrows, dual matrix boxes, Venn diagrams, and headings such as before/after or year 1/year 2/year 3, etc. Adding structure allows you to see and process things more clearly. It can also provide a great method for solving a problem (e.g., distance-rate-time charts, seen later in this chapter). Lastly, if your scratch work on the given GMAT yellow pad is structured, clean, and easy to follow, you can easily track your work if the answer you get is not among the 5 choices.

Tactic 5. Break It Down!

This is an excellent GMAT tactic, aside from being one of the most common expressions sung by numerous musical artists over the years (MC Hammer, Tears for Fears, or Jay-Z leap to mind). However, these words ring true for many questions, especially those that require structure as described in tactic 4. When you set up your approach to a problem, a high-level view shows you 2, 3, or sometimes even 4 steps to solve it. When you break down a problem, you separate each section into more easily solved pieces.

Tactic 6. Estimate, Guess-timate, Approximate to Elucidate

This tactic is not used enough. We know that most calculations are minimal. Therefore, some questions may test your ability to make reasonable approximations. You can approximate to simplify your calculations. You can estimate if the answer choice values are quite far apart from one another. You can guess-timate (intelligently of course!) if you are running out of time. For example, in geometry if you're stumped but you have a diagram drawn to scale, you can eyeball and guess the closest answer.

Tactic 7. Process of Elimination (POE): Return of the Friend

As we will see in the critical reasoning chapter, process of elimination (POE) is a very helpful tactic. Eliminating answer choices that are clearly incorrect increases the probability that any guesses, should you make them, will be correct. If you can get down to 2 possible answer choices, your chances are now 50% versus 20% had you not eliminated choices. While eliminating choices, you might just gain further insight to solve the problem. Again, this tactic should be considered among the last resort options. After all, we're hoping you will learn and retain all the theory and strategies to beat the GMAT.

Tactic 8. Don't Get Tricked: Become a Trickster

GMAT test makers have an unusually large bag of tricks from which to conjure smoke and mirrors and throw you off the scent of the correct answer. If you understand how and when they do this, you can become a magician yourself! You can then finesse any tricky question and pull that rabbit out of the hat. Watch for some of the common GMAT traps:

- Incorrect assumptions made when reading questions quickly
- Units of measurement that confuse you
- Wordy questions that ramble on to make you overthink
- Mixing a percent increase with an absolute percent, or misunderstanding the percent of a whole versus the percent of a part
- Good-looking answer choices that seem too easy but are meant to lead you astray
- Mistaking the distance remaining with the distance traveled
- Equation types that you are prone to set up incorrectly
- In geometry, confusing the area inside a figure with the area outside a figure
- Wasting time looking for the shortcut when sometimes you just have to do the math

Tactic 9. Stop Staring!

Many students will gaze at a question in bewilderment, trying to process where to begin. Meanwhile, an entire minute has gone by and they've done nothing.

Write down what you know, redraw the diagram, put down a relevant question, and/or map out your know-want-approach method. Just get something on paper. You might find something in the visual scratch work.

Tactic 10. Let It Go

This is one of the hardest things for even the most advanced test takers to do. Letting go of a question is hard because you want so badly to get it right. You might even know that you're pretty close. There is no reason to ever spend more than 3 minutes on a question. Sometimes it's not working out. Sometimes you are just not getting it. It's OK. This happens. You can still get several questions wrong and earn a great score. So focus on the questions you know you can get right and let go of the ones you can't get right. Make sure you really let go of a question and aren't dwelling on it 5 questions later. You need the time and energy to get the doable questions right.

CONVERSION PROBLEMS

Some questions are categorized as conversion problems. In most cases, when other questions require you to make some type of the conversion, the conversion will be given to you in the problem. However, you should be quite familiar with a few conversions, especially converting imperial to metric units.

$$1 \text{ kg} = 2.2 \text{ lb. (pounds)} \quad 1 \text{ mile} = 1.61 \text{ km} \quad 1 \text{ inch} = 2.54 \text{ cm}$$
$$1 \text{ kilometer} = 1000 \text{ meters} \quad 1 \text{ meter} = 100 \text{ cm} = 1000 \text{ mm}$$

You should also know how to calculate conversions. The key is to figure out the end result and then determine which units you need to get rid of. Keep track of numerators and denominators. Use conversion equivalents to get rid of or change units.

20 mph is how many meters per second?

Solution: $\dfrac{20 \text{ miles}}{\text{hour}} \cdot \dfrac{1 \text{ hour}}{60 \text{ min}} \cdot \dfrac{1 \text{ min}}{60 \text{ s}} \cdot \dfrac{1.6 \text{ km}}{1 \text{ mile}} \cdot \dfrac{1000 \text{ m}}{1 \text{ km}}$

Note all the different units that cancel out (miles, hour, minutes, km)

$$\left(\frac{20 \cdot 1.61 \cdot 1000}{3600}\right) \text{m/s} = \left(\frac{20 \cdot 1.61 \cdot 10}{36}\right) \text{m/s} = \left(\frac{50 \cdot 1.61}{9}\right) \text{m/s} = 8.944 \text{ m/s}$$

MIXTURE PROBLEMS

Most mixture problems involve two or more solutions mixed together or a solution with two or more parts going through changes. Often you'll need to create algebraic expressions to solve these problems. However, there are many shortcuts and tactics you can use.

1. **ALGEBRA.** If you can set up an algebraic equation to start, then do it. If the answer choices are in algebraic form, then this is a pure algebra question. You'll likely have to manipulate the equations.
2. **DRAWING.** It's easy to do mixture problems if you can visualize them with a drawing.
3. **TRACK EVERYTHING.** In many mixture problems, you need to keep track of units, amounts, percentages, total volumes, or a mix of all of them.
4. **CHARTS.** For mixtures that go through changes (e.g., adding 2 L of water to an existing solution), a chart is a good way to lay out the information clearly.
5. **WEIGHTED AVERAGE LINE GRAPH.** If two solutions are mixed together, the resulting solution may have a weighted average mixture. Thus, you can use the line graph to your advantage.
6. **MEASUREMENT PROBLEMS ARE OFTEN CONCEPTUAL.** Whenever you see a classic measurement problem, which is a form of mixture problem where "Jar A is half-full and half of it is poured into Jar B," your best bet is to solve conceptually by visualizing and using logic and reason to figure it out.

RATE PROBLEMS

Rate problems include mostly work/rate and distance/rate questions. The basic formula is

$$\textbf{Work = Rate} \bullet \textbf{Time or } \boldsymbol{W = RT}$$

where W is the amount of work done, R is the speed or rate at which the work is done, and T is the time it takes to do the amount of work.

> Robert peels potatoes at a rate of 3.5 per minute.
> How many potatoes will he peel in 1 hour?

Solution: $W = (3.5 \text{ potatoes/min}) \bullet (60 \text{ min})$ Note that we converted 1 hour to 60 min = 210 potatoes

Note that for work problems, the rate for each pipe, drain, machine, etc., remains the same.

Whenever you deal with rate problems, here is what you need to know:

1. **KEEP TRACK OF UNITS.** Often in work/rate problems, several units are at play, which can often get lost in your calculations.

2. **ALWAYS CONVERT TO UNIT RATES OF COMPLETE JOBS.** If you're told that a machine can produce 300 papers in 2 hours, you should convert that to 150 papers per hour. For rate questions, the unit rate means you are converting to per hour (or per days, minutes, or seconds) or converting to per job. If you are given the time for a partial job, calculate the rate for the complete job.

3. **YOU CAN ADD RATES TOGETHER.** If you know the unit rates of 2 different people or 2 different machines, you can add them to come up with a combined rate of the 2 people or the 2 machines. This is another reason why it's important to convert to unit rates.

4. **WHEN STUCK, USE $W = RT$.** If the rate problem is unfamiliar to you, try starting with the basic equation and look for the pieces.

5. **CHART IT OUT!** For more complex rate problems and most distance/rate/time (DRT) problems, a chart is a great method for sorting the information and solving. We'll visit this further in the DRT section.

Work/Rate Problems

There are 3 main types of work/rate problems—single jobs, batch jobs, and triple aspect types. We will explore them all and work for a sample problem for each type.

Work/Rate Type 1: Single Jobs

> Hose A fills a pool in 3 hours, and hose B fills the pool in 4 hours. How long will it take hose A and hose B, working together, to fill the pool?

Solution: For this type of problem, there are 2 methods. We will show them side by side.

Method 1: Combine Unit Rates

Calculate the unit rates for each hose.

Hose A: unit rate = $\frac{1}{3}$ pool/hr

Hose B: unit rate = $\frac{1}{4}$ pool/hr

Add the rates to get the combined rate:
$\frac{1}{3} + \frac{1}{4} = \frac{7}{12}$ pool/hr

Flip the equation to get the total time

$\frac{12}{7}$ hours/pool.

Method 2: Use the Work/Rate Formula

The standard work/rate formula is

$$\frac{1}{A} + \frac{1}{B} = \frac{1}{\text{Both}}$$

where A = the time A takes to do something

B = the time it takes B to do something

Both = the time both A and B take to do something

Plugging in we get

$$\frac{1}{3} + \frac{1}{4} = \frac{7}{12} = \frac{1}{x}$$

Therefore $x = \frac{7}{12}$ hours/pool.

The big question is which method is better? Unfortunately the answer is, as always, it depends. The formula method is quicker if the test makers give you specific times for all the people or machines in the question. For more complex rate questions, tracking and combining unit rates might be better.

Work/Rate Type 2: Batch Jobs

> Machine A prints 350 newspapers in 7 hours, and machine B prints 2400 newspapers in 6 hours. How long will it take both machines working together to print 1800 newspapers?

Solution: For this type of question, you need to calculate unit rates. Depending on the question, you would either calculate a rate per hour or rate per thing, such as, per newspaper. Given the way that the question is laid out, you should calculate the hourly rate.

Machine A: unit rate = 50 newspapers/hr
Machine B: unit rate = 400 newspapers/hr

Therefore, the combined rate is 450 newspapers/hr. You should be able to see that the math works cleanly and the total number of hours is 4 hours. However, if you cannot see this, then use the formula

$$W = RT \rightarrow 1800 \text{ newspapers} = (450 \text{ newspapers/hr}) \bullet T$$

$$\rightarrow T = \frac{1800}{450} = 4 \text{ hours}$$

Work/Rate Type 3: Triple Aspect

A common format for this type is "*X* people can do *Y* things in *Z* hours. How long will it take *A* people to do *B* things?"

Here you have three aspects at play in the question, which makes it a bit harder. Let's look at a specific example.

> 10 people can paint 6 houses in 5 days. How long would it take 2 people to paint 3 houses?

Strategy for Type 3 Work/Rate Problems

1. **FOCUS ON 2 ASPECTS AT A TIME.** The work/rate problem asked above has 3 aspects. Look at 2 aspects, and decide which one you want to adjust. In this example, you may want to change the 10 people down to 5 people. When you do that, keep the 3rd aspect the same and calculate how the 2nd aspect changes.

10 people	paint 6 houses	in 5 days	becomes
↓ ÷2	↓ ÷2	↓	
5 people	paint 3 houses	in 5 days	

Notice that we changed the number of houses and people but kept the time constant.

2. **BE CAREFUL OF THE INVERSE RELATIONSHIPS.** In the previous step, the number of people and the number of houses had a direct relationship. So when we reduced the people by half, the number of houses also reduced by half. The amount of time, however, has an inverse relationship with both the number of people and the number of houses. At this point in the example, we have the correct number of houses but now we want to change the people from 5 to 2.

5 people	paint 3 houses	in 5 days	becomes
↓ • $\frac{2}{5}$	↓	↓ • $\frac{5}{2}$	
2 people	paint 3 houses	in 12.5 days	

Since the number of people versus days has an inverse relationship, we multiplied the second number by the inverse. In order to get from 5 people to 2 people, we had to multiply by $\frac{2}{5}$. Therefore, for the number of days, we had to multiply by $\frac{5}{2}$, which is the inverse (or the reciprocal).

3. **UNIT RATES CAN HELP.** Sometimes if the question is a bit more complex, it can be worthwhile to bring 2 of the 3 aspects to a unit rate. (It is unlikely you can get all 3 rates equal to 1.) Using unit rates can be an easier starting point for your calculations. In the example, bringing two aspects to a unit rate would mean finding how many days it would take for 1 person to paint 1 house. Had we calculated this (feel free to have fun trying to calculate this), we would get 8.33 days.

Distance-Rate-Time (DRT) Problems

The basic formula for distance/rate problems is an offshoot of the work/rate formula:

$$\textbf{Distance = Rate} \cdot \textbf{Time} \rightarrow \textbf{\textit{D = RT}}$$

> If Jill travels 5 hours by car at a speed of 50 mph, the total distance she travels is $D = RT = (50 \text{ mph}) \cdot (5 \text{ hours}) = 250$ miles.

Most DRT problems will not be this simple. Instead, they will be broken down into 2 and sometimes 3 sections. Here are the 3 most common setups.

1. **THE MEET UP:** Alice travels from the west, and Billy travels from the east. They are a certain distance apart. When do they meet?
2. **THE OVERTAKE:** Alice travels from a certain point in a certain direction. Billy travels from the same point and same direction but a little bit later and at a faster speed. When will Billy overtake Alice?
3. **THE MIXED SPEEDS:** Alice travels at a certain speed during part of a trip but then travels at a different speed during another part of the same trip. What was Alice's average speed?

So how do the GMAT test makers make these questions more difficult?

- They make one or both persons start at different times.
- They make one or both persons have to stop or go slower for a short period of time.
- They throw in algebraic variables instead of actual numbers.
- They mix up the units, thinking that you might forget to convert them.

DRT Method: The DiRTy Chart

Regardless of the setup, the best way to deal with DRT problems is to use the "DiRTy chart method." Here's how it works.

	Route *A*	Route *B*	Total
D			
R			Average rate
T			

(STEP 1) If it helps, you may want to draw a diagram to understand the question better.

(STEP 2) Draw the DiRTy chart as per the diagram. Note that some DRT problems may split into 3 parts.

(STEP 3) Input the values given in the question.

(STEP 4) Determine what value you need to find, and let the variable equal this value. Input that variable into the chart.

(STEP 5) Fill in the rest of the chart using your chosen variable.

(STEP 6) Determine the key relationship that will help you create an equation to solve. In most cases, it will be:

- Total distance = $D_A + D_B$
- Total time = $T_A + T_B$
- D_A is equal to or is related to D_B
- T_A is equal to or is related to T_B
- Average rate = Total distance/Total time (The chart has been grayed out above so that you don't think that box might represent total rate, because it doesn't.) Calculating average rate is a special subtype of DRT problems that requires you to calculate total distance and total time in order to figure it out.

(STEP 7) Solve for the equation or relationship to get your answer.

VENN DIAGRAMS AND DUAL MATRIX BOXES

Venn diagrams and dual matrix box problems are very similar because they are a form of set theory. Simply put, these questions require you to organize information that relates to each other. They are almost like fun word puzzles! In many of these cases, when there are 2 sets of information, both of these methods work. What is important is to find the best method to use for the question in front of you. How do we tell them apart?

- Use Venn diagrams for overlapping groups and dual matrix boxes for complementary groups (parts add up to 100%). For example, if the group is made up of red and nonred boxes, this is a complementary group and should be solved with dual matrix boxes.
- For Venn diagrams, you will see keywords such as "only," "exactly," "both," or "neither."
- If there are 3 sets or groups of information, you should use Venn diagrams.

In most cases, test takers seem to prefer the dual matrix box.

1. It tends to involve less work.
2. It has more spaces and so can represent more quantities explicitly.
3. Its rows and columns are nicely aligned for automatic addition/ subtraction.

However, if you can fully grasp how Venn diagrams work, they are a much more powerful tool for the tougher problems. Of course, we recommend that you master both methods. Let's first look at Venn diagrams.

The Venn Diagram Method

The basic setup for Venn diagrams is as follows:

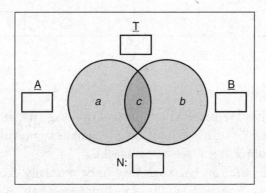

Venn formula 1: $T = a + b + c + N$
Venn formula 2: $T = A + B - c + N$

Depending on the question, you will be given values for either formula 1 or formula 2. Note that the c in formula 2 is subtracted because it was counted twice.

STEP 1 Fill in the total number of elements in the question if given. Label the 2 groups in the question.

STEP 2 Input values in the boxes or inside of circles only if they are specifically given.

STEP 3 Don't forget to consider the value of "neither" in the question. Quite often, this value is zero.

STEP 4 Determine which Venn formula is appropriate. If you are given a value for "*a* only," then you would use formula 1. If you are given a value for "all of *A*," then you would use formula 2. Make sure it is clear from the precise wording what the values are.

STEP 5 Manipulate the equation to solve.

The Dual Matrix Box Method

For the dual matrix box, we use a similar input approach as we did for the Venn diagrams. Essentially, we create a 2 × 2 box to input our values. This is why it's often referred to as a double matrix. We also have a third column and a third row for our totals. When we combine that with another row and column for descriptive headings, we get the following dual matrix box.

DUAL MATRIX BOX

	Description *A*	Description *B*	Total
Aspect *X*			
Not aspect *X*			
Total			100%

Matrix Box Tactics

- You can have 2 separate descriptions, *A* or *B* (e.g., the animals are either dogs or cats). You can also have aspect *X* and its complementary opposite (e.g., the animals are black or not black).
- The column and row headings have to be mutually exclusive. In other words, they cannot occur at the same time. Therefore, using our previous example, we cannot have a dog and a cat at the same time nor can we have a black and a nonblack animal at the same time.
- If the question gives you awkward percentages or fractions, try the Picking Numbers tactic. Start with a total number that makes sense, such as a number that is divisible by all the denominators, if you were given fractions in the question.

- Remember that the right-most columns must equal the sum of the columns to the left of them. Similarly, the bottom rows must equal the sum of the number above them.

MINIMUM/MAXIMUM PROBLEMS

A common requirement on GMAT problems is to find the maximum or minimum value. This can also be written as "least," "smallest," "most," and "largest" to name just a few synonyms.

> Harry is running for President of his club against two others, Stephen and Gillian. If 31 people are in the club, including Harry, what is the minimum number of votes with which he could actually win?

Solution: To find the minimum number of votes Harry needs, we need to find the minimum number of votes that Stephen and Gillian could get such that Harry would need only one extra vote. Ironically, if we think about the maximum spread of votes, we should just divide $\frac{31}{3}$ and get a spread of $10\frac{1}{3}$. This means that the maximum spread of votes would be 10, 10, and 11. Therefore, Harry needs a minimum of 11 votes.

Minimum/Maximum Strategies

- Figure out first whether you need to maximize or minimize and what variables are at play in the question.
- If you're asked to maximize something, you will usually need to minimize the remaining variables in the problem. If the problem asks you to minimize something, you will usually need to maximize the remaining variables.
- Even though most of the time you can use logic to understand these abstract questions better, you still should do the math and look at the scenarios that exploit the minimum or maximum values.

INTEREST RATE PROBLEMS

GMAT math questions involving interest rates fall into two categories: simple interest and compound interest. These are calculated on a starting loan or investment called the principal. Let's first understand the definitions.

INTEREST: The amount paid for the use of lent or invested money, usually given as a percentage.

PRINCIPAL: The amount of the loan or investment.

SIMPLE INTEREST: Interest that is calculated on only the original principal.

COMPOUNDED INTEREST: Interest that is calculated on the original principal *plus* all accumulated interest.

SEMIANNUAL: Twice a year.

BIANNUAL: Every other year.

SEMIMONTHLY: Twice a month.

BIMONTHLY: Every other month.

Simple Interest Rate Problems

Simple interest is the most basic type of interest rate question tested on the GMAT. The formula is

Interest earned = (Principal invested) • (interest rate) • (Time) = Pit

> If you invest $2,000 at an annual interest rate of 8%, your
> interest earned at the end of year is 2000 • 0.08 • 1 = 160

Another way of looking at this calculation is using the more formal equation

$$A = P(1 + In)$$

where A = amount, P = principal, I = interest rate, n = number of periods

Total amount of investment =
Principal • (1 + (Interest) • (number of time periods))

Interest Rate Tactics

1. Make sure you express the rate of interest in decimals rather than percentage.
2. Make sure you are clear about whether you are solving for the interest or for the new amount due to the interest. These two different things can be easily confused.
3. When you deal with periods of the loan or investment that are not full years and if you adjust the time period, do not adjust the rate of interest or vice versa. For example, if the calculation is to be made on

a semiannual basis, then adjust either the time period or the rate of interest, not both.

4. Know how to interpret between simple interest and compound interest. The key is to see in how many periods the interest is paid. If interest is paid in one period, that is simple interest. If interest is paid on interest in multiple periods, that is compound interest.

5. Some questions can be solved conceptually by applying concepts such as weighted average or by backsolving.

Compound Interest Rate Problems

Often interest rates are compounded monthly, quarterly, or semiannually. This means that the interest at each period of compounding is added to the original principal. Compounded interest will yield a bigger return than does simple interest at the same rate. The standard formula is:

$$A = P(1 + \frac{r}{n})^{nt}$$

where

A = Amount currently in the investment (principal plus interest)
P = Original principal amount
r = Interest rate (yearly) in decimal format (i.e., 8% = 0.08)
n = Number of times per year the interest is compounded
t = Number of years

There are some common question types when it comes to compound interest rate problems.

Type A Example

If Alice invests $2,000 at an interest rate of 10%, how much money will she have at the end of a year?

Answer: $2000 • 1.10 = $2200

Type B Example

If Alice invests $2,000 at an interest rate of 10%, compounded semiannually, how much money will she have at the end of a year?

Since the annual interest rate is compounded twice during the year, you need to calculate interest at $\frac{10}{2}$ = 5% every 6 months. This is how compounding gets you more money on your investment than does simple interest.

(STEP 1) At 6 months, the principal becomes $2000 • 1.05 = $2100.

(STEP 2) At 12 months, the new principal balance of $2100 earns another 5% interest, or $2100 • 1.05 = $2205.

Type C Example

> If Alice invests $2,000 at an interest rate of 12%, compounded quarterly (or bimonthly or monthly), how much money will she have at the end of a year?

You can take the step-by-step approach to solve for the 4 quarters, but it will take you time. The calculating would be even more time consuming for bimonthly or monthly compounding questions. This is where using the formula helps. Remember that 12% = 0.12.

$$\text{Quarterly compound: } A = P\left(1+\frac{r}{n}\right)^{nt}$$

$$\rightarrow A = 2000 \cdot \left(1+\frac{0.12}{4}\right)^{4 \cdot 1} = 2000 \cdot (1.03)^4$$

The GMAT test makers won't require you to make lengthy calculations, so look for the answer choices to be in the format above.

PROFIT AND REVENUE

Profit, revenue, and cost questions are relatively common on the GMAT, usually in the form of arithmetic or algebra word problems. You need to know two main equations:

Profit = Revenue − Costs   or $\pi = R - C$

Revenue = Price • (Number of units sold)   or $R = P \cdot Q \rightarrow$ Note that $P = R/Q$

P stands for price, while π stands for profit, just so you can avoid any confusion. Other terms you might hear about include the following.

BREAK-EVEN POINT: The point when the profit is zero. If $\pi = 0$, then $R = C$.

GROSS PROFIT: This is Selling price – Cost, usually on a per unit basis.

PER UNIT: This is the most important GMAT trick to understand on these questions. Sometimes the test makers will give you values in cost per unit while revenue is expressed in total number of unit sales. Make sure you convert to per unit revenue or convert the unit cost to a total cost value.

DATA INTERPRETATION

Data interpretation questions are occurring less frequently on the GMAT. This is because some of the core skills are now being tested on the graphical interpretation section of integrated reasoning. However, you still may see some. If you do, here are some strategies to keep in mind.

- **FIRST, ANALYZE THE DATA CAREFULLY:** Note labels, units, and trends. Avoid misreading.
- **BE QUESTION DRIVEN:** Use the question given in the stem to ask yourself, "What data do I need to solve?"
- **ESTIMATE WHEN POSSIBLE:** Just as in the integrated reasoning section, the GMAT test makers don't expect you to make lengthy or precise calculations. Estimating will simplify your process and reduce the time you spend.

PROBLEM SOLVING: TARGETED REVIEW QUESTIONS

Rate Problems

1. Daniel can paint the fence in 10 hours. When Mr. Miyagi helps, they can both paint the fence in $3\frac{1}{3}$ hours. How long would it take Mr. Miyagi to paint half the fence by himself?

   (A) $2\frac{1}{3}$

   (B) $2\frac{1}{2}$

   (C) 3

   (D) 5

   (E) $6\frac{1}{6}$

2. Machine 1 produces 1000 bolts in 5 hours, while machine 2 can complete 75% of the same job in 3 hours. How much time is required for both machines to produce 1750 bolts if machine 2 stops producing after 3 hours?

   (A) 5

   (B) 5.75

   (C) 6

   (D) 7.5

   (E) 8

Venn Diagrams

3. 500 dormitory residents eat daily in a campus cafeteria with a prepurchased meal plan. On an average day, 320 residents have soup with their meal and 160 residents have salad with their meal. If at least 100 residents have neither soup nor salad, then the number of residents who have both soup and salad must be between:

   (A) 40 and 100

   (B) 80 and 120

   (C) 80 and 160

   (D) 100 and 160

   (E) 160 and 320

4. Molly's high school focuses on the performing arts. In her year, 40 students can sing, 60 students can dance, and 24 students can act. No student is a triple threat (someone who can sing, dance, and act). However, 16 students can sing and dance, 12 students can dance and act, and 8 students can sing and act. How many students have only one performing talent?

   (A) 44
   (B) 52
   (C) 60
   (D) 66
   (E) 72

Mixture/Measurement

5. In a lab experiment, the number of bacteria cells produces double the amount of new bacteria cells each day for each of the 4 days since initiation. If the total number of bacteria cells after 4 days is 54 million, how many bacteria cells did the experiment begin with?

   (A) 1.5 million
   (B) 2 million
   (C) 4 million
   (D) 5.5 million
   (E) 7 million

Matrix Boxes

6. At *A Magazine's* Oscar party, $\frac{7}{12}$ of the guests are its employees, and $\frac{1}{2}$ of the guests at the Oscar party are men. If $\frac{1}{5}$ of the guests are men who are not employees of *A Magazine*, what percent of the guests are male employees of *A Magazine*?

   (A) 12%
   (B) 20%
   (C) 24%
   (D) 30%
   (E) 36%

Minimum/Maximum

7. On a hot day in July, an ice cream man sold an average of 14 ice cream products per hour over 5 consecutive hours. If during each hour, this ice cream man sold at least 7 ice cream products, what is the greatest possible range of the number of ice cream products sold in any hour?

   (A) 14
   (B) 28
   (C) 35
   (D) 42
   (E) 49

Interest Rates

8. Kumar's parents bought him a $5,000 GIC investment that paid interest at an annual rate of 6 percent compounded semiannually. What was the total amount of interest paid on the investment in one year?

   (A) $150
   (B) $300
   (C) $304.50
   (D) $618
   (E) $10,300

9. Just Lamps Inc. sells only lamps and bulbs. Lamp sales revenue was 8% higher in 2011 than in 2010 while bulb sales revenue was 12% lower. If Just Lamps Inc. saw its overall revenue decline by 2% during the same period, what was the ratio of lamp revenues to bulb revenues in 2010?

   (A) 2 : 3
   (B) 3 : 4
   (C) 1 : 1
   (D) 3 : 2
   (E) 5 : 3

ANSWER KEY

1. **(B)**   4. **(B)**   7. **(C)**
2. **(A)**   5. **(B)**   8. **(C)**
3. **(C)**   6. **(D)**   9. **(C)**

SOLUTIONS

1. **(B)** Use the $\dfrac{\text{work}}{\text{rate}}$ standard formula:

$\dfrac{1}{10} + \dfrac{1}{M} = \dfrac{1}{\frac{10}{3}}$, where M is the number of hours Mr. Miyagi takes to paint the fence

$$\frac{1}{M} = \frac{3}{10} - \frac{1}{10} = \frac{2}{10} \rightarrow M = \frac{10}{2} = 5 \text{ hours}$$

However, you need Mr. Miyagi's time to paint half the fence, which is 2.5 hours.

2. **(A)** First determine unit rates

$$\text{Machine 1 unit rate} = \frac{1000}{5} = 200 \text{ bolts/hr}$$

$$\text{Machine 2 unit rate} = (75\%) \bullet \frac{(1000)}{3} = \frac{750}{3} = 250 \text{ bolts/hr}$$

The two machines' combined rate is $200 + 250 = 450$ bolts/hr.

Now break down this problem into the first 3 hours and the rest of production.

In 3 hours, the machines produce $450 \bullet 3 = 1350$ bolts $\rightarrow$ leaving $1750 - 1350 = 400$ bolts.

Machine 1 can produce the rest of the 400 bolts in

$$400 \text{ bolts}/200 \text{ bolts/hr} = 2 \text{ hours}$$

The total time is $2 + 3 = 5$ hours.

3. **(C)** Let's start by drawing a Venn diagram.

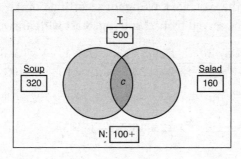

In this case, use the formula $T = A + B - c + N$, which gives

$$500 = 320 + 160 - c + (100+) \rightarrow \text{By isolating the } c,$$
$$\text{you get } c = 480 - 500 + (100+)$$

$c = 80+ \rightarrow$ The range is limited by the number of people who can have salad, which is 160.

4. **(B)** Because you have overlapping sets, this is a Venn diagram problem. However, this is a triple diagram since there are 3 different performing disciplines. Don't get too stressed out. The process is the same and the GMAT test makers typically make these triple Venn diagrams easier than the standard ones. First, fill in what you know

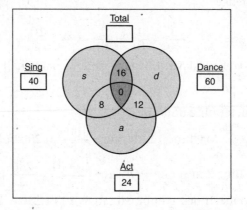

Now calculate the number of students with a single performing talent by subtracting the double threats from the whole of each performance type.

$$\text{Singing: } 40 - 16 - 8 = 16$$
$$\text{Dancing: } 60 - 16 - 12 = 32$$
$$\text{Acting: } 24 - 12 - 8 = 4$$

This gives $16 + 32 + 4 = 52$ students with a single performing talent.

5. **(B)** Given that you are looking for a starting point number, this question could best be served by backsolving. Start with answer choice C.

Day 1	Day 2	Day 3	Day 4	Total	
4	+ 8 = 12	+ 24 = 36	+ 72 = 108	108	→ Too high! Try a lower number
2	+ 4 = 6	+ 12 = 18	+ 36 = 54	54	→ On target!

Algebraically, you could have let the starting amount be x, which would give you

$$x + 2x + 6x + 18x = 54 \rightarrow 27x = 54 \rightarrow x = 2 \text{ million}$$

The algebra here is relatively straightforward. In a harder question, though, it's good to have two different tactics up your sleeve.

6. **(D)** This is a dual matrix box problem because there are 2 • 2 elements at play and there is no overlap. Guests are either male/female or employee/nonemployee. Also, because of the fraction $\frac{7}{12}$, let's pick the number 120 total. Your box should look like this (**bold** is for original values: *italics* are calculated values):

	Male	Female	Total
Employee	*36*	*34*	**70**
Nonemployee	**24**	*26*	*50*
Total	**60**	*60*	**120**

From the dual matrix box, you can see that the number of male employees is 36 out of 120 or $\frac{36}{120}$, which reduces to $\frac{3}{10}$ or 30%.

7. **(C)** In order to find the greatest number of ice cream products sold in any hour, you need to minimize the number sold in all the other hours. This means that you should let the ice cream man sell 7 ice cream products in each of 4 different hours, or 7 • 4 = 28 ice cream products sold. You also need to look at the average for the 5 hours.

$$\text{Average} = \frac{(\text{Sum of terms})}{(\text{Number of terms})} \rightarrow 14 = \frac{(28 + x)}{5}$$

$$70 = 28 + x \rightarrow x = 42 \rightarrow \text{You want the range,}$$
$$\text{though, which is } 42 - 7 = 35.$$

8. **(C)** You can use the formula $A = P\left(1 + \frac{r}{n}\right)^{nt}$, where

A = the amount of money after t or 1 year
P = the principal amount invested of \$5,000
r = the annual interest rate of 6% or 0.06
n = the number of times compounded, which is 2

$$5000\left(1 + \frac{0.06}{2}\right)^{(2)(1)} = 5000(1.03)^2 = 5000(1.0609) = \$5304.50$$

Therefore the interest paid is $5,304.50 – $5,000 = $304.50.

An alternative solution: Simple interest would be $300.

The correct answer must be just a bit over $300, so C is the answer.

9. **(C)** Since you are given two different years, it's a good idea to sort out this information. Second, since you're dealing with percents and no actual numbers, picking numbers for one of the revenues would be a good tactic here. Use algebra for the rest. Use $100 for the starting bulb revenue in 2011 and x for the starting lamp revenue in 2011. When you draw a chart, you get

	2010	% chg	2011
Bulb revenue	100	–12	88
Lamp revenue	x	+0.08x	1.08x
Total revenue	100 + x	–0.02(100 + x)	0.98(100 + x)

The 2011 column gives the equation $88 + 1.08x = 0.98(100 + x)$

$$88 + 1.08x = 98 + 0.98x \rightarrow 0.1x = 10, x = 100$$

What this means is that in 2010, lamp revenues = bulb revenues, so the ratio is 1: 1.

You could also have used the weighted average line graph. Instead, you could have noticed that the overall decline of 2% (–2%) is exactly between +8% and –12%. It still is a good exercise to try this out and utilize algebra and picking numbers as a solid strategy.

Probability

11

―▬◣◣◣◣◣◣◣◣◣◣◣◣◣◣◣◣◣◣◣◣◣―

Probability is the likelihood that a certain event or multiple events will occur. The questions that show up on the GMAT range from easy to very difficult. This topic is broken down into three main probability formulas along with several key topics that are used to increase the difficulty. Some basic elements to remember are the following:

- Probability values range from 0% to 100%, inclusive. You cannot have a probability of 150% to win a game (no matter what LeBron James or other professional athletes might tell you).
- Probability can be measured in decimals, fractions, or percents. Be sure to check the answer choice format before starting to solve.
- Many probability questions use decks of cards, coin tosses, or dice rolls. So if you're not a card shark and have no idea how many aces or spades are in a deck of cards, you should probably buy a set or watch some Texas hold'em poker on TV.

BASIC PROBABILITY OF A SINGLE EVENT

The simplest probability question would ask, "What is the probability of rolling a six on one roll of a die?"

The answer, of course, is $\frac{1}{6}$. This realization stems from the basic formula for probability of a single event.

$$P(A) = \text{(The number of outcomes where } A \text{ occurs)/} $$
$$\text{(The total number of possible outcomes)}$$

This is the starting point for all probability questions. The difficulty of the questions is increased by adding further obstacles such as multiple events or restrictions.

PROBABILITY OF ONE EVENT OR ANOTHER

Although we gave you the basic formula for probability, there is also the general case formula for probability of one event or another.

$$P(A \text{ or } B) = P(A) + P(B) - P(A \text{ and } B)$$

MUTUALLY EXCLUSIVE AND COMPLEMENTARY EVENTS

The best way to explain and compare mutually exclusive and complementary events is with a chart.

MUTUALLY EXCLUSIVE AND COMPLEMENTARY EVENTS

Aspect	Mutually Exclusive Events	Complementary Events
Definition	Events that can never occur together; the occurrence of one event eliminates the possibility of the other event occurring	Events are complementary if one or the other must occur but they can never occur together
Examples	• Scoring both 780 and 800 score on the same GMAT test • Coming in 1st and 3rd place in an Olympics marathon • Getting both heads and tails on the same coin toss • The Miami Heat and the LA Lakers winning the NBA Championship in the same year	• Getting into the MBA school of your dreams or not • Winning the Olympics marathon or not • Getting heads or tails on the same coin toss • Winning at least one game of the NBA Championships or not winning any games
Why is this important?	If events are mutually exclusive, then you simply add the probabilities of each event.	The probability of complementary events always adds up to 1. You can use the mirror rule to solve some difficult problems. The probability of complementary events occurring simultaneously is 0.
How does this affect the general case formula?	$P(A \text{ and } B) = 0$	$P(A \text{ and } B) = 0$ $P(A \text{ or } B) = 1$
Other tips to consider	• Note that the probability of heads and tails in coin tosses is both complementary and mutually exclusive. • All complementary events are, by definition, also mutually exclusive	

PROBABILITY OF TWO OR MORE EVENTS

When you are trying to determine the probability of 2 or more events occurring, use this third formula. It is applicable to a large proportion of GMAT probability questions.

$$P(A + B) = P(A) \bullet P(B)$$

Let's look at this example.

---

1. What is the probability of rolling 2 sixes on two rolls of a die?

   (A) $\dfrac{1}{36}$

   (B) $\dfrac{1}{18}$

   (C) $\dfrac{1}{6}$

   (D) $\dfrac{7}{36}$

   (E) $\dfrac{1}{3}$

Solution: $P(6 \text{ and } 6) = P(6) \bullet P(6) = \dfrac{1}{6} \bullet \dfrac{1}{6} = \dfrac{1}{36}$

The answer is A.

Notice that in question 1, the second 6 we rolled had the same probability as the first. However, in question 2, the second ace drawn had a different probability than the first. This illustrates the difference between **independent** and **dependent events**.

---

2. What is the probability of drawing 2 aces from a deck of cards with no replacement?

   (A) $\dfrac{3}{676}$

   (B) $\dfrac{1}{221}$

   (C) $\dfrac{2}{52}$

   (D) $\dfrac{2}{51}$

   (E) $\dfrac{12}{221}$

Solution: $P(\text{ace, ace}) = P(\text{ace}_1) \bullet P(\text{ace}_2) = \dfrac{4}{52} \bullet \dfrac{3}{51} = \dfrac{1}{(13 \bullet 17)} = \dfrac{1}{221}$

The answer is B.

INDEPENDENT AND DEPENDENT EVENTS

The best way to explain and compare independent and dependent events (also known as conditional probability) is with a chart.

INDEPENDENT AND DEPENDENT EVENTS

Aspect	Independent Events	Dependent Events
Definition	Events where the occurrence of one event does not affect the probability of the other	Events where the occurrence of one event affects the probability of another
Examples	• Coin tosses • Dice rolls • Winning money at the casino and getting hit by a truck on the way home • Picking balls out of jars/boxes with replacement • Picking cards out of a deck with replacement	• Picking balls out of jars/boxes without replacement • Picking cards out of a deck without replacement • The probability of getting the 3rd prize in a raffle after the first two prizes are given out
Why is this important?	If events are independent, then you can easily multiply events together to calculate probability	With dependent events, you need to determine how the new probabilities are conditional to previous outcomes
How does this affect the 3rd formula?	No effect	$P(A + B) = P(A) \bullet P(B/A)$ or $P(A + B) = P(A) \bullet P_A(B)$ where $P(B/A)$ and $P_A(B)$ means "the probability of B given that A has occurred
Other tips to consider	• Watch for whether the question specifies "with" or "without" replacement when selecting objects. • Dependent events can sometimes create two or more scenarios to consider. • Whenever multiple events are said to be simultaneous, you can look at each event in turn. The word "replacement" will often determine the difference between independent and dependent probabilities, usually with balls or cards.	

MIRROR RULE PROBABILITY

Often the GMAT will ask you the probability of something "not happening" or of "at least one" thing happening. By using the complementary rules for probability, we get two equations that make the mirror rule.

$$P(A \text{ happens}) = 1 - P(A \text{ doesn't happen})$$
$$P(\text{at least one of } B \text{ happens}) = 1 - P(\text{no } B \text{ happens})$$

Let's look at the mirror rule strategy in an example.

A single coin is tossed four times. What is the probability that you will get at least one tail?

(A) $\dfrac{1}{16}$

(B) $\dfrac{1}{4}$

(C) $\dfrac{3}{8}$

(D) $\dfrac{5}{8}$

(E) $\dfrac{15}{16}$

Solution:

$P(\text{at least one tail}) = 1 - P(\text{no tails}) = 1 - P(4 \text{ heads})$

$$= 1 - \frac{1}{2} \cdot \frac{1}{2} \cdot \frac{1}{2} \cdot \frac{1}{2} = 1 - \frac{1}{16} = \frac{15}{16}$$

The answer is E.

Be sure you understand the complementary opposites of "will happen" and of "at least one happens."

In the above example, we could still have used conceptual thinking to help us narrow the choices. You are more likely to get at least one tail out of four tosses as opposed to three tails. Therefore, we can reason that the correct answer will be closer to 1 than it is to zero, leaving us with choices D and E as our possible picks.

PAIRS PROBABILITY

What if you are asked, "If you roll a die twice, what is the probability you will end up with a pair?" Let's draw.

P(die #1)

?/?

P(die #2)

?/?

A common mistake is to make the probability of the first die roll $\frac{1}{6}$. The first roll can actually be any number from 1 to 6. The question is asking the probability that the second roll will match the first. This second probability is dependent on the first roll. No matter what the first die roll is, the probability of the second roll is the same. So we would actually get:

Die #1

6/6

Die #2

1/6

Probability(getting a pair in two die rolls) = $\frac{6}{6} \cdot \frac{1}{6} = \frac{1}{6}$.

ADVANCED PROBABILITY

The GMAT creates more difficult and advanced questions by simply adding different elements of theory to the question. For example, the test makers have a probability question combined with algebra or take two probability concepts and put them both in the same question. So even though we've reviewed all the main topics of probability, the GMAT test makers will require your cumulative knowledge and adaptability in order to solve the tougher questions.

Joey and his friends played a new game that uses 20 playing cards made up of 2 suits of 10 cards each. The cards in each suit have values from 1 to 10. If Joey turns over 4 cards, what is the probability that he will find at least one pair of cards having the same value?

(A) $\frac{1}{5}$

(B) $\frac{99}{323}$

(C) $\frac{3}{5}$

(D) $\frac{224}{323}$

(E) $\frac{4}{5}$

Solution: This question is tough because it combines the mirror rule with pairs probability. Let's draw it out first.

Note that this question uses the key phrase "at least one," which tells you to use the mirror rule. So you would get:

$$P \text{ (at least one pair)} = 1 - P(\text{getting no pairs})$$

To solve P(getting no pairs), you need to make sure that for every card that gets picked, the next card cannot match the previous cards. This means you are going to have fewer cards to pick and a smaller number of cards to pick from each time.

$$\frac{20}{20} \cdot \frac{18}{19} \cdot \frac{16}{18} \cdot \frac{14}{17} = \frac{224}{323}$$

Finally, $1 - \frac{224}{323} = \frac{99}{323}$.

The answer is B.

PROBABILITY: TARGETED REVIEW QUESTIONS

1. In a raffle that sells 3200 tickets, there is only one prize. What is the probability that a man who bought 40 tickets will win the prize?

   (A) $\dfrac{1}{3200}$

   (B) $\dfrac{1}{320}$

   (C) $\dfrac{1}{80}$

   (D) $\dfrac{3}{80}$

   (E) $\dfrac{1}{8}$

(A) If you can get the answer from **(1) ALONE** but not from (2) alone

(B) If you can get the answer from **(2) ALONE** but not from (1) alone

(C) If you can get the answer from **BOTH (1)** and **(2) TOGETHER** but not from (1) alone or (2) alone

(D) If **EITHER** statement **(1) ALONE OR** statement **(2) ALONE** suffices

(E) If you **CANNOT** get the answer from statements (1) and (2) **TOGETHER** but need even more data

---

2. On a certain Little League baseball team, one player is to be selected at random as the leadoff hitter. What is the probability that a boy will be the leadoff hitter?

   (1) The total number of baseball players is 30.
   (2) There are 20 boys on the Little League baseball team.

3. Teams A, B, and C compete in a baseball league but in separate divisions. Each team is vying to win at least 100 games against division rivals in the season. The probability of each team doing so is $\frac{1}{3}$, $\frac{2}{5}$, and $\frac{3}{8}$, respectively. What is the probability that teams A and B will win 100 games against division rivals while team C will not?

   (A) $\frac{1}{40}$

   (B) $\frac{1}{20}$

   (C) $\frac{1}{12}$

   (D) $\frac{2}{15}$

   (E) $\frac{5}{8}$

4. A number is selected from the first 40 positive 2-digit integers. What is the probability that the number is a multiple of 7 or 13?

   (A) 2.25%
   (B) 12.50%
   (C) 20.25%
   (D) 22.50%
   (E) 25.25%

5. A jug contains balls with colors and numbers. Each ball has one of three colors and one of five numbers on it. If one ball is selected from the jug, what is the probability of selecting a white ball with a 3 on it.

   (1) The probability of selecting a white ball or a ball with a 3 on it is $\frac{1}{5}$.

   (2) P(a white ball) $-$ P(a ball with a 3 on it) $= \frac{1}{20}$.

ANSWER KEY

1. **(C)**   3. **(C)**   5. **(E)**
2. **(C)**   4. **(D)**

SOLUTIONS

1. **(C)** Using the basic formula for probability gives

$$\frac{40 \text{ tickets}}{(3200 \text{ tickets})} = \frac{4}{320} = \frac{1}{80}$$

2. **(C)** Statement 1 gives us the total number of players but doesn't give us the number of boys. (Don't forget that girls play baseball too!) Even if you got tricked by that, statement 2 should remind you that the team is not made up entirely of boys. *Insufficient*

   Statement 2 gives us the number of boys, but now we don't know the total number of players on the team. It's important not to take the information in statement 1 and apply it to statement 2. This is a classic GMAT trick. *Insufficient*

   When we put the statements together, we have enough information. *Sufficient*

$$P(\text{boy is a leadoff hitter}) = \frac{\text{Total number of boys}}{\text{Total number of players on the team}}$$

$$= \frac{20}{30} = \frac{2}{3}$$

   Both statements together are sufficient.

3. **(C)** Each team's probabilities are independent from each other. However, we should make sure that we use $\frac{5}{8}$ for team C's probability of not winning 100 games. Thus the probability will be

$$\frac{1}{3} \cdot \frac{2}{5} \cdot \frac{5}{8} = \frac{1}{12}$$

4. **(D)** The set of numbers are 10 to 49 inclusive. There are 6 multiples of 7 and 3 multiples of 13 in this set. Therefore the probability is $\frac{9}{40} = 22.5\%$.

5. **(E)** If we use the classic probability formula, we will get

$$P(\text{white ball or a ball with a 3})$$
$$= P(\text{white ball}) + P(\text{a ball with a 3}) - P(\text{white ball with a 3})$$

Statement 1 gives us only one part of this equation, and we are missing the other two pieces. *Insufficient*

Statement 2 gives us two parts of the equation that seem helpful. If we look closely, though, we are given a different setup (subtraction instead of addition). There is no way to manipulate the equation to solve for anything useful. *Insufficient*

Because of the awkward setup of statement 2, there is no way to solve this when you combine both statements. *Insufficient*

Both statements together are still not sufficient.

Permutations and Combinations

12

Combinatorics is one of the more difficult topics in the math portion of the GMAT. Basically, combinatorics is the number of ways we can arrange things. A simple example would be the number of ways to arrange 5 different pictures in a display or to arrange 6 guests around a dinner table. Although this content is considered advanced material, some basic problems may show up for every student.

PERMUTATIONS VS. COMBINATIONS

There are two types of combinatorics: permutations and combinations. The basic difference is that in permutations, the order of the arranged objects matters. In combinations, the order does not matter. The chart below summarizes some of the main differences.

PERMUTATION AND COMBINATION OVERVIEW

Aspect	Permutation	Combination
Does order matter?	Yes	No (anarchy!)
How do I check for order?	Switch two elements around and see if it creates a new arrangement. If it does, then you have a permutation	
Example of question types	Passwords, seating arrangements, license plates, anything where you arrange objects in a nonrepeating way	People in groups, sets of numbers
Key words	Arrangement, order, schedule, itinerary, display	Team, group, committee, set, numbers
Frequency of each type on the GMAT	Frequent	Not often
Standard formula where: N = the # of total elements K = the # of items being selected	$\dfrac{N!}{(N-K)!}$	$\dfrac{N!}{K!(N-K)!}$
Notation	$_N P_K$ or "N PICK K"	$_N C_K$ or "N CHOOSE K"

REPEATING VS. NONREPEATING COMBINATORICS

By definition, permutations and combinations require that you cannot have repetition. For example, in a race, you cannot have someone finish in both 1st and 2nd place. For the permutation and combination section, we will assume that there is no repetition. If repetition is specifically allowed, then it is sometimes just easier to draw the problem and solve by inspection. License plates offer a perfect example:

New York City wants to issue license plates with 4 letters and 3 numbers. If the numbers and letters are allowed to repeat, how many different license plates can be created?

(A) 456,976,000
(B) 258,336,000
(C) 388,800
(D) 26,000
(E) Infinite

Solution: Note that this question is by definition a nonpermutation problem. However, it is a combinatorics question because we are still counting the number of arrangements. If we draw it out and calculate the total *number of* possibilities for each group, we would get:

Now we just multiply them all together to get 26 × 26 × 26 × 26 × 10 × 10 × 10 = 456,976,000 license plates. So it looks like New York has room to grow!

The answer is A.

Note that you should always try to solve all problems first by drawings and inspection. The majority of the problems in the rest of this chapter deal with nonrepeating combinatorics, otherwise known as permutations.

PERMUTATIONS: BASIC AND WITH SELECTION

The most basic permutation is the number of ways to arrange N items when order matters and there is no repetition. This is calculated as $N!$ or "N factorial," where N is the total number of elements in the question. Factorials are calculated by taking the number N and multiplying it by every whole number below it all the way down to the number 1.

$$10! = 10 \times 9 \times 8 \times 7 \times 6 \times 5 \times 4 \times 3 \times 2 \times 1$$

$$0! = 1 \quad 1! = 1 \quad 2! = 2 \quad 3! = 6 \quad 4! = 24 \quad 5! = 120 \quad 6! = 720$$

Billy goes to the movies with 5 of his friends. There are 6 seats left in the front row. How many different seating arrangements can Billy and his friends create?

(A) 15,625

(B) 7,776

(C) 720

(D) 30

(E) 6

Solution: Since order matters, this is a permutation. The total number of elements is 6 people, so $N = 6$. The answer is

$$6! = 6 \times 5 \times 4 \times 3 \times 2 \times 1 = 720$$

The answer is C.

PERMUTATION WITH SCENARIOS

If the combinatorics question uses the keyword or phrases "or," "at least," or "at most," you may be dealing with scenarios. In this case, you will have different values for K. To resolve this type of question, you first need to determine the scenarios. For each scenario, calculate the total number of arrangements and then sum them up.

Alice is creating head tables for a wedding party of 14 people. Excluding the bride and groom, she is trying to decide whether to go with tables that seat 4 or 6 people. How many different seating arrangements can Alice have for the first table only?

(A) $\dfrac{14!}{10!}$

(B) $\dfrac{14!}{8!}$

(C) $\dfrac{12!}{8!}$

(D) $\dfrac{14!}{10!} + \dfrac{14!}{8!}$

(E) $\dfrac{12!}{8!} + \dfrac{12!}{6!}$

Solution: This is a permutation because order matters with a seating arrangement. $N = 12$ because we do not include the bride and groom. The number we are selecting can be 4 or 6 so we are dealing with scenarios. For each scenario, the K will be different.

Scenario 1: 4 person table

$N = 12, K = 4$

$$_N P_K = {}_{12}P_4 = \frac{12!}{8!}$$

Scenario 2: 6 person table

$N = 12, K = 6$

$$_N P_K = {}_{12}P_6 = \frac{12!}{6!}$$

Now we add up the scenario totals, giving us $\dfrac{12!}{8!} + \dfrac{12!}{6!}$.

The answer is E.

COMBINATIONS

Combination calculations are very much the same as permutation calculations. The only differences are that order does not matter, and that the standard formula we use is different by a factor of $1/K$!

Combinations with Selection

Bobby is studying for the GMAT, and there are 8 other students in his class. He wants to create a study group with 3 others. How many different groups can he create?

(A) 40,320

(B) 336

(C) 56

(D) 24

(E) 6

Solution: Order does not matter here because we are creating groups and the order in which the group members are selected does not matter (unless of course we are dealing with easily bruised egos).

$$N = 8, K = 3$$

$$_NC_K = {_8}C_3 = \frac{8!}{(3!5!)} = \frac{(8 \times 7 \times 6)}{(3 \times 2)} = 56$$

The answer is C.

Combination with Scenarios

John has 8 friends and wants to have a series of dinner parties. How many ways can he have a dinner party with 1 guest, 2 guests, or 3 guests?

(A) 12,544
(B) 92
(C) 56
(D) 28
(E) 8

Solution: This is a combination since we are talking about people forming groups. Thus the order will not matter. As in permutations, the keyword "or" says to us that we are dealing with scenarios. Since we are selecting from 8 guests, then $N = 8$.

Scenario 1: One Guest	Scenario 2: Two Guests	Scenario 3: Three Guests
$N = 8, K = 1$	$N = 8, K = 2$	$N = 8, K = 3$
$_NC_K = {_8}C_1 = \dfrac{8!}{(1!7!)}$	$_NC_K = {_8}C_2 = \dfrac{8!}{(2!6!)}$	$_NC_K = {_8}C_3 = \dfrac{8!}{(3!5!)}$
$= 8$	$= 28$	$= 56$

Now we add up all the scenarios giving us $8 + 28 + 56 = 92$.

The answer is C.

COMBINATORICS METHOD

Follow this basic methodology for solving combinatorics problems:

1. **DRAW IT OUT:** If you can, use a drawing to set up the problem and understand it better.
2. **SOLVE BY INSPECTION:** Simpler problems, particularly ones that allow for repetition (and are not true permutations), can be solved by simply looking at the number of possibilities for each group and multiplying them together.
3. **CHECK FOR ORDER:** If you are not sure, you can use the procedure to check, which was described in the first table in this chapter "Permutation and Combination Overview."
4. **DETERMINE N:** This is the total number of elements involved in the question.
5. **DETERMINE IF THERE IS A K:** In some examples, you will select a smaller amount from the larger amount N.
6. **CHECK FOR ANY SPECIAL CIRCUMSTANCES:** These are among the harder examples, so it's important to know which types will show up.

   - **CIRCLE:** Use $(N - 1)!$
   - **REPEATED ELEMENTS:** Use $N!/A!B! \ldots$, where A and B are the number of repeated elements in the question.
   - **COUPLES OR GROUPS:** Treat each subgroup as a single element. Then calculate the overall number of arrangements multiplied by the number of arrangements for each subgroup.
   - **SCENARIOS:** If the question uses the keyword or phrases "or," "at least," or "at most," you need to calculate each combinatorics scenario separately and then add up the totals.
   - **SPECIAL CONSTRAINTS:** The key is essentially to break them down into separate portions and calculate each piece accordingly.

7. **SET UP THE BASIC EQUATIONS:** You can set up your equations in the form $_NP_K$ (N Pick K) and/or $_NC_K$ (N Choose K).
8. **PLUG IN FORMULAS AND SOLVE:** Use the memorized formulas to calculate the total. Remember to review the answer choices to determine whether the form of the answer will be a number or a combinatorics notation.

PERMUTATIONS AND COMBINATIONS: TARGETED REVIEW QUESTIONS

1. Wayne just received 5 vases in a set from his grandmother. Although he doesn't particularly like them, he decides to display them on the mantle behind his 50-inch plasma television. That way, he hopes they won't be noticed. All the vases look the same except that there are 2 vases colored green, 2 colored red, and the last one is colored blue. In how many ways can Wayne arrange the display in a row?

   (A) 6
   (B) 18
   (C) 30
   (D) 60
   (E) 120

2. Coach Will needs to get his glee team ready for sectionals by selecting a 6-person team of 3 men and 3 women. There are 5 men and 7 women vying for the spots. How many different ways can he arrange the teams?

   (A) 35
   (B) 120
   (C) 140
   (D) 280
   (E) 350

3. Mario's Pizzeria is offering a special. Students can order a medium pizza for only $6.99 by choosing one topping from each of 4 categories: meats, veggies, cheese, and bread. Mario's has 5 different meats, 7 veggies, 4 types of cheese, and 3 varieties of bread. How many different combinations of pizzas can Mario make?

   (A) 105
   (B) 140
   (C) 275
   (D) 420
   (E) 525

4. Billy and 10 of his friends are going to the movies. There are 2 couples who insist on sitting together and another group of 4 BFFs that always sit together. How many different ways can they arrange themselves in the front row of the movie theater?

(A) 11!

(B) $11! \times 2 \times 2 \times 3$

(C) $6! \times 2! \times 2! \times 4!$

(D) $6! \times 4!$

(E) $6! \times 4 \times 2$

5. Robin Hood and 4 of his Merry Men decide to see the Renaissance Festival evening show. There are 5 seats in the front row reserved for them. Little John has told the group that he has to sit on the end so that he can stretch his long legs. In how many ways can the Merry Men arrange themselves in the front row?

(A) 48

(B) 64

(C) 84

(D) 96

(E) 108

ANSWER KEY

1. **(C)**   3. **(D)**   5. **(A)**

2. **(E)**   4. **(C)**

SOLUTIONS

1. **(C)** This is an example of permutations with repeated elements. The formula for repeated elements is $\dfrac{N!}{A!B!}$ ... where A and B are the repeated elements. In this case, the repeated elements are the red and green vases. So $N = 5$, $A = 2$, $B = 2$ and the answer is $\dfrac{5!}{(2!)(2!)} = 30$.

2. **(E)** This is a combination question since we are dealing with teams and we also have selection. We should treat the men and women as separate groups. For the men, $N = 5$ and $K = 3$. For the women, $N = 7$ and $K = 3$. So using the notation $_N C_K$ we get

Men		Women
$_5C_3$	*	$_7C_3$
$\dfrac{5!}{(3!)(2!)} = 10$	*	$\dfrac{7!}{(3!)(4!)} = 35 = 10 \times 35 = 350$ possibilities

3. **(D)** Each ingredient can be treated as a separate piece in this simple combinatory problem. Since we are choosing only one ingredient from each category, the total number of pizzas is $5 \times 7 \times 4 \times 3 = 420$ pizzas.

4. **(C)** Normally we would say that $N = 11$. In this case, though, we treat each subgroup as a single element. We now have $N = 6$ (2 couples, 1 quartet, and 3 singles). We first calculate the number of ways to arrange the grouped elements, which is

$$N! = 6! = 720$$

We also have to calculate the number of arrangements within each subgroup.
Each couple is $2! = 2$. The quartet is $4! = 24$.
The total number of arrangements is $6! \times 2! \times 2! \times 4!$

5. **(A)** In this problem, we have a constraint where Little John wants to sit only on the end. This results in 2 scenarios. Little John will be either on the left side or on the right side. Since the calculation for each scenario will be the same, we can just calculate one of the scenarios and multiply by 2.
Scenario 1: Little John is sitting on the left-hand side. To calculate the number of arrangements for the rest, $N = 4$, so it will be $4!$
The answer will be $2 \times 4! = 48$.

Introduction to the Verbal Section

13

In the Verbal section, you will have 75 minutes in which to answer 41 questions in three different formats: Sentence Correction, Critical Reasoning, and Reading Comprehension. All are multiple-choice questions and have five answer choices.

> **Sentence Correction:** These questions present you with a sentence that might or might not have a grammatical problem and four additional ways to phrase it; you have to pick the phrasing that contains no obvious errors.
>
> **Critical Reasoning:** These questions give you a very short passage to read (usually under 100 words), containing either (1) an argument for a conclusion that you're asked to evaluate or describe or (2) a loose collection of related facts from which you're asked to draw conclusions.
>
> **Reading Comprehension:** These questions give you a more substantial passage to read (either 100–200 words or 250–350 words). You're then asked a series of three or four questions about the passage's content, tone, and structure and the author's overall agenda.

There is no set order to the question formats, but the GMAT does keep track of the number of each format you have seen in a single test sitting, so that when all is said and done you will have seen about 12 Critical Reasoning questions, about 13 Reading Comprehension questions, and about 16 Sentence Correction questions.

We have to say "about," because the test maker slips a few questions into the 41 that don't count toward your score, "experimental questions" of each of the three formats that you're essentially beta-testing for future tests. Don't worry about trying to figure out whether a question is "experimental" or "real"—just know that it means you might have 14 Reading Comprehension questions and only 11 Critical Reasoning questions.

The Verbal Questions

13 Reading Comprehension

12 Critical Reasoning

16 Sentence Correction

What the GMAT *Says* the Verbal Section Tests

According to the GMAC's official documents, the Verbal section of the GMAT tests your ability to do three things:

1. read and comprehend written material,
2. reason and evaluate arguments, and
3. correct written material to conform to standard written English.

But that's just an indirect way of saying, "There are three types of questions: Reading Comprehension, Critical Reasoning, and Sentence Correction." To be sure, these three broad conceptual areas are tested, just probably not in the way you expect.

What the Verbal Section Actually Tests and What It Doesn't

The most common complaint that test takers have with the Verbal section is that it is "boring." The passages are dense, the topics chosen are not all that interesting, the arguments all sound crazy, and the questions are worded in bafflingly obscure ways that make it a challenge to keep reading them.

This is all by design.

The Verbal section comes 2½ hours into the test; by that point, most test takers are starting to feel the strain. Exhaustion is creeping in. Stress levels are high. And then along comes a Reading Comprehension passage about the mating habits of this snail in Madagascar, and how they're different from those of the snails on the continent. Zzzz . . .

The test makers put the snails there not because snails are somehow secretly the key to success in business school, but rather because they hope you'll see something unfamiliar and kind of dry and just mentally check out. When you're bored, you don't proceed with care. You don't go back and check specific parts of the text. You read listlessly and haphazardly and end up picking the answers that "kind of sound right."

Thus, the GMAT Verbal section tests your ability to pay attention even when you'd rather not. If you want to raise your GMAT Verbal subscore, you must learn what the GMAT thinks is worthy of your attention and how to get yourself to focus on that, to the exclusion of all else. You're certainly not required to master every detail or logical nuance of the presented passages in the scant time you have to read them.

OK, we do have to admit that there are going to be *some basic grammar rules you'll need to remember*. And, yes, you'll also need to be able to recognize a couple of other technical things, like the fundamental parts of an argument. You might need to pick up your reading pace a little bit. But success on the GMAT is rarely a case of speed reading, grammatical wherewithal, or deductive brilliance; it's learning to avoid all the "easy outs," pushing aside the various things meant to distract or confuse, and finding the simple concept that lies at the core of the question.

The GMAT *doesn't* test depth.

People studying for the GMAT are often surprised to learn how short the passages actually are. The longest Reading Comprehension passages just barely top 400 words, which is shorter than the essays you were asked to write in high school. Critical Reasoning prompts are even shorter. You probably read more text in a Craigslist ad. And while there might always seem to be just one more grammar rule that you needed to know to get the right answer on a Sentence Correction question you missed, only about 30 grammar rules have ever been tested on the GMAT—not on a single test, mind you, but 30 rules tested across all GMATs ever.

So put your mind at ease. GMAT Verbal questions are shallow, although they masquerade as deep. The Verbal section can be tricky, but it consists of the same simple concepts and patterns throughout.

PACING AND TIMING IN THE VERBAL SECTION

If you were to split your 75 minutes time evenly among the 41 questions, you'd be able to spend a hair under 2 minutes on each question. However, spending equal time on all the questions would be a terrible idea. Reading Comprehension will require by far the largest share of your time. For this question type you will need to budget in the time needed to read the four passages that go with the questions—two long ones (about 300 words on average) and two short ones (about 150 words). That will take most people at least 10 minutes, and that's not counting the time needed to answer the questions themselves.

Where can you get the extra time? Critical Reasoning questions require a bit of reading themselves (and much more careful reading than Reading Comprehension questions), so it's best not to steal time away from them. That leaves only Sentence Correction questions. Because of the demands elsewhere on your time, you can afford to give no more than a minute apiece to the Sentence Correction questions.

Your overall time budget will look something like this:

Verbal Section Time Allocation

Though the most numerous question type, Sentence Correction questions will account for a fifth of your time, whereas more than half of the 75 minutes will be spent tackling the Reading Comprehension questions. As a rough guideline:

Type of Question	# of Questions	Average Time Per Question
Sentence Correction	15–16	1 minute
Critical Reasoning	11–13	2 minutes
Reading Comprehension	13–14	Questions: 1–1.5 minutes
		Long Passages: 3–4 minutes
		Short Passages: 2–3 minutes

Two minutes per question can be useful, though, if used as a rough guide as you progress through the Verbal section. If you break your time into 25-minute thirds, you should be done with roughly the first 12 or so questions when 25 minutes have passed, and be on question 27 or 28 after 50 minutes. When the clock switches from counting down minutes to minutes and seconds (the 5:00 mark), you should be somewhere around question 39.

HOW TO TACKLE VERBAL QUESTIONS

Because the three big question types can appear in any order, it might seem like you're going to have to "change gears" frequently as you move through the section, but on a fundamental level the questions are a lot alike. Whether the question throws a handful of grammar rules at you, an argument against changing the zoning ordinances in Uzbekistan, or a catalog of the challenges faced by the earliest European colonists in Australia, each one consists of a discrete amount of information. Your job is to sort through that (often purposely disorganized) information to find the nugget that will allow you to pick the one point-bestowing answer choice from the available five.

THE THREE VERBAL QUESTION FORMATS

Critical Reasoning

Each Critical Reasoning question you will see on the GMAT is composed of three parts: a **Prompt**, a brief question about that prompt (which we will call the **Question Stem**), and five **Answer Choices**.

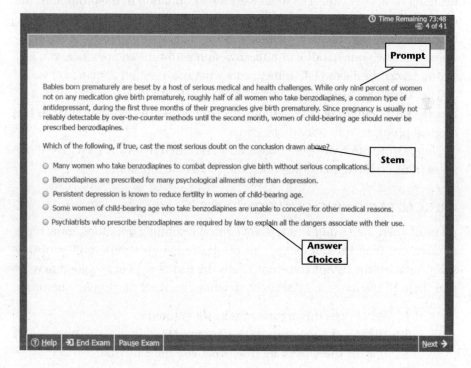

The **Prompt** contains a set of facts, opinions, and observations that create a scenario, a little self-contained world with only a handful of details sketching it out. For most of the questions, these details will be used to make an argument; for some, there will only be a series of related pieces of information. The only facts that you need to understand to find the answer can be found in the prompt. The test maker never asks you to rely on your outside expertise.

The typical Critical Reasoning prompt is about 100 words long, so you won't have to scroll to see the prompt all at once, although occasionally you will need to scroll down the page to see the fifth answer choice.

Unlike the Reading Comprehension questions, the Critical Reasoning questions will not reuse the same prompt to ask multiple questions. Each question has a unique scenario attached to it.

The information in the prompts is drawn from many different subject areas, including the arts, philosophy, the sciences, law, and business. You're not expected to know any of the material beforehand, and you should be careful if the subject happens to be one you're personally familiar with. There's no guarantee that the presented facts in these passages are actually true, and often the test maker will bend the truth in order to make the subject fit into the narrow constraints of a Critical Reasoning scenario.

The **Question Stem** that follows contains instructions from the test makers detailing what they expect us to do with the information in the prompt. In the chapters that follow, you will learn the language that test makers typically use to indicate the task they wish you to perform. Ninety-five percent of the questions reuse the same handful of phrasings, and with time and practice, you will almost always be able to tell immediately what the question demands of you.

The **Answer Choices** will always come in sets of five. Four of them will be incorrect for definite reasons, usually because of specific wording used in the original prompt. Only one will be correct.

Note: On the test, answer choices don't have letters (A), (B), etc. We'll use them in the printed questions, however, to avoid confusion.

CRITICAL REASONING QUESTION TYPES

All in all, there are 13 different types of Critical Reasoning questions, more types of questions than the number of Critical Reasoning questions you'll probably see in total on the day of your test! That's the bad news. But the good news is that these 13 questions are just slight variations on three far simpler questions:

1. What does this argument take for granted?
2. What is the structure of this argument?
3. If all of these facts are true, what else must be true?

Notice that the first two questions ask you about an **argument**. That's why we're going to classify them in the broad, cleverly named category, **Argument-Based Questions**, which we're going to immediately divide into the **Assumption Family** and the **Structure Family**, depending on whether the question asks you what the argument takes for granted (its **assumptions**) or how it's organized (its **structure**). The other Critical Reasoning questions ask you to work with a loose collection of facts, so we'll classify those as **Fact-Based Questions**.

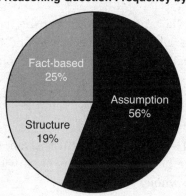

Critical Reasoning Question Frequency by Family

These question types will be discussed in detail in the Critical Reasoning chapter, but here's a quick rundown.

Argument-Based Questions

Argument-Based questions make up about three-fourths of the questions on the GMAT, so you'll see about eight in a single test sitting. Your initial approach to all of these will be the same, breaking the information in the argument down into its component parts: its **conclusion** and its **evidence**.

The Assumption Family

ASSUMPTION—In Assumption questions, an argument is given, and you must identify something that the argument relies upon but that is not stated explicitly, something that, if not true, means the argument itself must not be true.

STRENGTHEN—Here, you go one step beyond the Assumption question to find a new piece of information in the answer choices that would make one of the argument's unstated assumptions more likely to be true or that would answer a possible objection to one of those unstated assumptions.

WEAKEN—The Weaken question is the flip side of the Strengthen question. Here you would find a piece of information in the answers that, if true, would call into question or present an objection to one of the arguments' assumptions.

EVALUATE—In Evaluate questions, which are closely related to Strengthen and Weaken questions, you must select an answer choice that describes some unknown information or a question that, if known, has the potential to either weaken or strengthen the argument.

FLAW—The stem of Flaw questions calls out the speaker in the argument prompt for making a mistake and asks you to find the answer choice that best describes it. Usually, the mistake is assuming something that shouldn't be assumed.

The Structure Family

BOLDED STATEMENT—Here, an argument is given, with two sentences or phrases in **bold type**, and you are asked to identify the part that each plays in the argument as a whole.

METHOD OF ARGUMENT—An argument is given, occasionally written as a dialogue between two people, and you must explain how the argument works (i.e., what sort of evidence the author uses such as invoking a general principle or providing a counterexample) and whether that case is for or against something.

ROLE OF A STATEMENT—These questions are essentially Bolded Statement questions in which nothing is bolded. They, too, ask you to identify the role a particular part plays in the argument.

PARALLEL ARGUMENT—Very rare on the GMAT, this question contains five arguments for the price of one! You must match the argument in the prompt with the one in the answer choices that has the same structure.

Fact-Based Questions

The remaining quarter of Critical Reasoning questions do not ask about arguments. Their prompts almost always have no conclusion and no evidence. As Sgt. Joe Friday said, they want "Just the facts, ma'am." You'll probably see four or five of them in the Critical Reasoning section (SPOILER ALERT! **Inference** questions will make an appearance in the Reading Comprehension, too).

INFERENCE—These questions ask you to find the answer choice that must be true if the information in the prompt is true. (If the prompt tells you that *all dogs go to heaven* and that *Rusty is a dog*, then the correct answer could be that *Rusty will go to heaven*.)

EXPLAIN—The prompt that accompanies these questions contains an anomalous situation like "demand's up, but prices have stayed the same" or "after the law changed to require seat belts, automobile injuries went up." The correct answer provides an additional fact that can explain why the *apparent* weirdness really isn't weird at all.

Complete the Argument Questions

Wait a minute, didn't we just say there were three categories? What's with this fourth? **Complete** questions are just a different way of asking you to do one of the two question types we've already discussed. They're easy to spot because their question stem is placed above their prompt, rather than below, and because there's a big empty blank (like this: _____) somewhere in the text. You're asked to insert something into the blank that will somehow complete the argument.

COMPLETE (EVIDENCE)—If an evidence keyword precedes the blank (e.g., *for example, because, since, after all*), the **Complete** question is essentially a weirdly worded **Assumption** question. The only piece of evidence that could complete the argument is a piece that fills in the gap that is its unstated assumption.

COMPLETE (CONCLUSION)—If a conclusion keyword precedes the blank (e.g., *thus, therefore, hence, in conclusion*), the Complete question can be treated as a form of the **Inference** question. The answer choice that fills the blank will be a certainty if all the information in the prompt is taken as true.

Sentence Correction

Each Sentence Correction question you see on the GMAT will look the same: a sentence will be either partially or completely **underlined** and followed by five **answer choices** that give different possible versions of the underlined section. Voila:

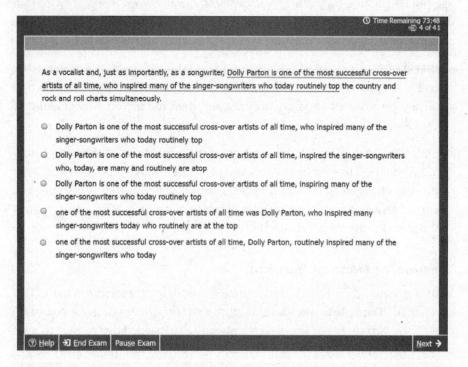

Note that the first answer choice is always a repetition of the sentence as originally written. If after analyzing the sentence and the other answer choices you conclude that there is absolutely nothing wrong with the underlined section, then you should select the first answer choice. A full fifth (20 percent) of Sentence Correction questions have no error as originally written.

Now take a moment to look at the answer choices. Don't worry about trying to find the right answer at the moment. Instead, notice how the answer choices are written. Most of the words are pretty much the same from answer choice to answer choice. Big changes tend to clump up into groups of two or three. For example, (A), (B), and (C) all start with Dolly Parton, whereas (D) and (E) move her to the middle.

In order to pick the right answer, you're obviously going to have to make a decision about where "Dolly Parton" should be. From here forward, we are going to refer to those points where the differences are clear as **Decision Points**.

There are also substantial portions of the answer choices that are identical or nearly so. The long modifying phrase *is one of the most successful cross-over artists of all time* doesn't change at all from answer to answer. Why bother to include something that big if they're not going to ask any grammatical question about it?

Usually, it's to distract you from some other grammatical question. Here, it interferes with your ability to see how Dolly is connected to that bit of the sentence that describes how influential she was. Successfully managing Sentence Correction questions requires you to identify and then ignore these **Distractors**.

SENTENCE CORRECTION QUESTION TYPES

After the 14 Critical Reasoning variations, it should come as welcome news to learn that there is, strictly speaking, just the one type of Sentence Correction question. Sure, there's some variation in how much is underlined or where the underlined section is placed in relation to the rest of the sentence, but the fundamental task is still the same each time: eliminate the answer choices that contain an obvious error until you're down to one.

Thankfully, even though the English language has numerous multivolume textbooks filled with rules and variations on those rules, the GMAT limits itself to a very small collection of errors to test in Sentence Correction questions. Six major categories of error dominate the questions; at least one of them appears in just about every question, and most questions contain two or three of them.

They are:

SUBJECT/PREDICATE AGREEMENT—The subject of the sentence (a noun) must match the predicate (the verb); singular subjects get singular predicates, and plural subjects take plural predicates.

PRONOUN REFERENCE—Pronouns must refer unambiguously to a single noun, and they must also match the noun they replace in number, gender, and case.

MODIFICATION—Modifying elements, such as adjectives, adverbs, and prepositional phrases, must be placed so that it's clear what they're supposed to modify and so that the modification makes logical sense.

PARALLELISM—Parts of a sentence that play the same role must be put into matching forms. This includes words in lists, in comparisons, and in other multipart constructions.

CLAUSES AND CONNECTORS—Clauses can be either independent or dependent. Linking them incorrectly can result in a run-on sentence or a sentence fragment.

IDIOMATIC CONSTRUCTION—Certain words are paired with other words in English not because of any logical rule but because that's just the way they're expected to be. Usually, this involves preposition choice (i.e., you sleep in a bed, not at a bed).

In the sections that follow, we will discuss each of these frequently tested errors, explaining both the formal rules and the ways that the rules tend to be tested in the context of a question. For now, let's see how to apply the Four-Step Verbal Method to all Sentence Correction questions, no matter what error they contain.

Reading Comprehension

You will know that you are dealing with a Reading Comprehension question set the moment the screen switches to a two-paned display with a scroll bar in the middle of the screen:

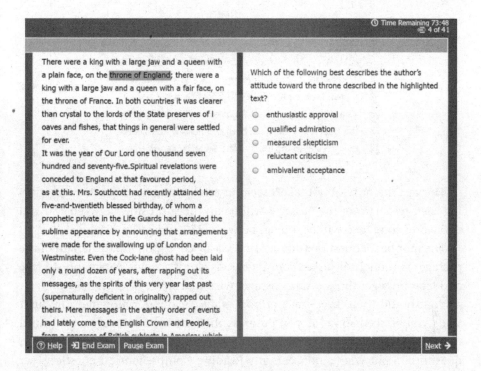

There were a king with a large jaw and a queen with a plain face, on the throne of England; there were a king with a large jaw and a queen with a fair face, on the throne of France. In both countries it was clearer than crystal to the lords of the State preserves of l oaves and fishes, that things in general were settled for ever.

It was the year of Our Lord one thousand seven hundred and seventy-five. Spiritual revelations were conceded to England at that favoured period, as at this. Mrs. Southcott had recently attained her five-and-twentieth blessed birthday, of whom a prophetic private in the Life Guards had heralded the sublime appearance by announcing that arrangements were made for the swallowing up of London and Westminster. Even the Cock-lane ghost had been laid only a round dozen of years, after rapping out its messages, as the spirits of this very year last past (supernaturally deficient in originality) rapped out theirs. Mere messages in the earthly order of events had lately come to the English Crown and People,

Which of the following best describes the author's attitude toward the throne described in the highlighted text?

○ enthusiastic approval
○ qualified admiration
○ measured skepticism
○ reluctant criticism
○ ambivalent acceptance

Help　End Exam　Pause Exam　　　　　　Next →

Like the other two formats, Reading Comprehension questions can appear at any point in the Verbal section, but they do cluster into sets every time. There's never a one-off single-question passage. Indeed, nearly every Reading Comprehension set is composed of three or four questions.

Thus, every Reading Comprehension set will be composed of a **passage** in the left-hand window on your screen and a **question** in the right. The **passage** will remain until all the questions in the set are completed. You can't skip questions; even though they're part of a set, they still appear one at a time. Each **question** is composed of a **stem** and **five answer choices**, four incorrect and one correct.

The lines of text are not numbered, as they are in a paper-and-pencil GMAT (such as those you'll encounter in the *Official Guides* and in this book). When a question makes a reference to a specific part of the passage, instead of line numbers, the interface will highlight that part of the passage in yellow for as long as the question is on your screen.

There were a king with a large jaw and a queen with
a plain face, on the throne of England; there were a
king with a large jaw and a queen with a fair face, on
the throne of France. In both countries it was clearer
than crystal to the lords of the State preserves of l

The vast majority of test takers see four total passage and question sets during their test. Two of the passages will be on the short side, between 150 and
200 words long; two will be longer, between 250 and 350 words.

The number of questions doesn't necessarily correspond to the length of the
passage. You might be asked four questions about a single-paragraph passage
and later only get three with a passage twice that size.

You should try to keep track of how many Reading Comprehension questions you've seen so far as you progress through the test because you need
to leave extra room in your time budget to read the passages. So if you're on
question 25 but you've not seen any Reading Comprehension questions yet
(a *very* unlikely situation), you'd know that almost every remaining question
was going to be Reading Comprehension. To be on pace, you'd still have the
majority of your time remaining, even though you'd be over two-thirds of
your way through the section.

The biggest mistake that novice GMAT test takers make with Reading Comprehension is reading the passages as though they were just any old piece of
text they've just happened to have come upon. "Oh, that's interesting," they
might think while reading the passage, or "Really? I didn't know that," when
what they should be thinking is "Whose side is the author on?" and "This
example is meant to prove which theory, exactly?"

Just as with the Critical Reasoning questions, the information in a Reading
Comprehension passage is drawn from many different subject areas, including
the arts, philosophy, the sciences, law, and business. You're not expected to
know any of the material beforehand, and you should be careful if the subject
happens to be one you're personally familiar with because there's no guarantee
that the things presented as facts in these passages are actually true.

Sure, the test maker generally starts with a journal article or a newspaper or
magazine report, but in order to make it into a GMAT Reading Comprehension
passage, the facts are tweaked and the descriptions of things are changed so
that the passage will fit into the specific logic they use to determine which of

the five answers is right and to ensure that there are four tempting but wrong answers.

Thus, the key to mastering Reading Comprehension questions will be learning to organize the information in the passage in your head (or on your noteboard) in such a way that you can answer the sorts of questions the GMAT asks about these passages. You're not reading for fun or just to say you've read the passage. You're reading in preparation for a very narrow range of possible tasks you might be called upon to perform.

READING COMPREHENSION QUESTION TYPES

Remember the most important ground rule for the Reading Comprehension section: every answer must be based on **specific** pieces of **information found in the passage**. You are not required to know anything about the passages nor are you expected (or allowed) to justify picking an answer because of information you know from any other source.

Now, consider how limiting that is for the test makers and how hard it makes their job. They can present information from anywhere, from any source or subject under the sun, but they can only ask you to do things with that information that someone could reasonably be expected to do solely on the basis of that information and that information alone. Thus, a lot of the things that you're accustomed to doing with a piece of text or a chunk of an article are explicitly out of bounds. So what's left for them to do?

Recall Questions

One question the test maker can still ask is simply "Hey, what did this guy say about this particular subject?" Or, to put it in the context of the question, "Which of these five different things did the passage you just read actually say?" We call this general category of questions **Recall** questions because they ask you to do just that: recall a single piece of information from the passage. There are two ways this question can be asked:

DETAIL—These questions ask you to recall or locate a piece of information that was explicitly written in the text of the passage.

INFERENCE—These questions ask you to recall or locate a piece of information that was not explicitly written in the passage but that MUST BE TRUE if you take all the information in the passage as true.

Global Questions

The test maker can also ask you, "What was the reason this passage was written?" or, phrased another way, "What did the author do with this information? Was there some sort of point to it all? Or was it just a bunch of random facts?"

MAIN POINT—These questions ask you to identify the author's agenda or the overall point of the passage.

Nearly every single passage on the GMAT will have some sort of agenda or direction to it. Something is at stake. It might be as simple as, "People used to think this, but now they think that, **and it is right to think that instead of this for these reasons**." Most often the author is explicitly siding with one of two parties or one of two interpretations. In this way, they're a lot more like Critical Reasoning questions than they might seem.

On the rare occasions that the passage does not have a point, then that means that the test maker is even more constrained than usual. The only questions in bounds would be **Detail** and **Inference** questions.

The other type of **Global** question singles out a specific piece of information presented in the passage and asks, "Why did the author mention this?" The answer to that question must always involve the author's overall goal.

FUNCTION—These questions ask you to identify the role that a particular piece of information plays in the author's overall agenda.

And that's it. There are just four questions.

RECALL QUESTIONS (ask you "What?")
Detail: "Did the author say this or that?"
Inference: "Which of these has to be true because of something the author said?"

GLOBAL QUESTIONS (ask you "Why?")
Main Point: "Why did the author write this?"
Function: "Why did the author say this here?"

Critical Reasoning Questions

Didn't we already cover Critical Reasoning questions two sections ago? Yes, but they also show up from time to time in the Reading Comprehension question sets. When one does pop up, you will treat it according to the method appropriate to whatever type of Critical Reasoning question it happens to be. If it's a **Weaken** question, then weaken; a **Strengthen** question, strengthen. That's that.

Critical Reasoning

14

A ccording to what GMAT and ACT say elsewhere, Critical Reasoning questions target three different cognitive skills:

ARGUMENT CONSTRUCTION: Questions of this type may ask you to recognize the basic structure of an argument, properly drawn conclusions, underlying assumptions, well-supported explanatory hypotheses, or parallels between structurally similar arguments.

ARGUMENT EVALUATION: Questions of this type may ask you to analyze a given argument, recognize factors that would strengthen or weaken an argument, reasoning errors committed in making an argument, or aspects of the methods by which an argument proceeds.

FORMULATING AND EVALUATING A PLAN OF ACTION: Questions of this type may ask you to recognize the relative appropriateness, effectiveness, or efficiency of different plans of action; factors that would strengthen or weaken a proposed plan of action; or assumptions underlying a proposed plan of action.

—"The GMAT—Test Structure and Overview—Verbal Section," *MBA.Com*

ARGUMENTS AND FACTS

Arguments—Understand their parts and how they work.
Facts—Understand how to draw inferences from a collection of facts.

Arguments

When the test makers use the word "argument," they mean the logician's definition: a series of connected premises meant to demonstrate the truth of a proposition.

Or, to put it another (less-jargony) way, all the arguments on the GMAT take the form of **someone making the case for something**, a contestable claim like *ABC Cola is the best cola in the world.* We call this claim the argument's **conclusion.** The conclusion will be accompanied by some information meant to prove the conclusion to be true, like, perhaps, *Studies have shown that 100 percent of people who drink ABC Cola find it to be delicious and refreshing.* We call this information the argument's **evidence**.

> **Argument**—An attempt to support a claim by giving reasons for it.
>
> **Conclusion**—The claim that an argument attempts to support.
>
> **Evidence**—The reasons given in support of an argument's conclusion.

The evidence explains the conclusion. The conclusion is explained by the evidence. When you have both, you have an argument.

Does that seem a little circular to you? It should. Logically speaking, **evidence** and **conclusion** only exist as a pair. If you don't have at least two pieces of information, it's impossible to have an **argument**. If you simply say *ABC Cola is the best cola in the world*, you have not made an argument. You've only made a claim.

And even when you have two pieces of information, if one doesn't explain why you should believe the other, then you *still* don't have an argument.

Add something explaining *why* to believe some particular *what*, and now you have an instant argument.

explains the

Evidence (Why?)   Conclusion (What?)

is explained by the

Thus, all arguments can be put into a very basic template:

[What]	BECAUSE	[Why]
[Conclusion]	BECAUSE	[Evidence]
[ABC Cola is the best cola in the world]	BECAUSE	[Studies have shown people who drink ABC Cola find it to be delicious and refreshing]

The arguments you'll encounter on the GMAT usually have only one or two pieces of evidence, and sometimes the test makers go out of their way to disguise the evidence, but whatever the trick being played, every single argument on the GMAT can be put into the form **conclusion** *because* ***evidence***.

When you finish reading a Critical Reasoning prompt containing an argument, try to rephrase the argument into that basic template before going on to the answer choices. That's your spot check to make sure you understood what you just read.

Evidence	Evidence	Conclusion
Socrates is a man.	All men are mortal.	Socrates is mortal.
Celery is gross.	You shouldn't eat gross things.	You shouldn't eat celery.
If it's Tuesday, we should eat by 12.	It's Tuesday, and it's 12:30!	We should have eaten by now.
Words in columns look cool.	These words are in columns.	How cool!

Also, don't think that the argument's conclusion has to come at the end of the argument or the evidence at the beginning. You can scramble them up however you want. As long as there's something being explained and something doing some explaining, you have an argument.

You might not have a *good* argument, though, which brings us to valid and invalid arguments!

VALID AND INVALID ARGUMENTS

Valid Arguments

Once in a while (for Argument Structure questions), the GMAT lets you stop once you've identified the parts of the argument, but more often the test also asks you to say something about whether the argument is *good* or *bad*—or to use more formal-sounding words, *valid* or *invalid*. But what makes an argument valid?

Earlier we described an argument as a "series of connected premises meant to demonstrate the truth of a proposition." The keyword there was "connected." When an argument is valid, the evidence and conclusion form a chain, a series of reasonable little steps from one idea to the next.

> ## FUN WITH SYNONYMS!
>
> **Good arguments are** valid, properly drawn, supported, logical, sound, logically correct, convincing.
>
> **Bad arguments are** invalid, improperly drawn, flawed, unsound, illogical, unconvincing.

Consider this quick argument:

> Boston is a city in Massachusetts. Susan is in Boston.
> Massachusetts is in the United States. Therefore, Susan is in the United States.

We would call this a valid argument because it's possible to arrange it into a chain where one piece of evidence is directly connected to the next:

> Susan is in Boston. Boston is a city in Massachusetts.
> Massachusetts is in the United States.

If we believe each link in the chain, there's no doubt about it. Susan must be in the United States. Our argument is valid.

Invalid Arguments

There are lots of reasons an argument might be bad. Earlier, when we professed our undying love of ABC Cola, you probably found yourself thinking "Come on, no survey's going to show 100 percent agreement. That's crazy." In effect, you were thinking, "That's a pretty terrible argument." Maybe, getting into the spirit of this section's heading, you even thought, "That argument is invalid!" Not so fast! **Invalid** is not the same as **incorrect**.

Arguments aren't invalid because their evidence is wrong. They're invalid because their evidence, as stated, does not give enough reason *on its own* for you to believe the conclusion.

Assumptions

Earlier, you learned that arguments have two parts, evidence and conclusion. To this we add a final part that is never written out explicitly: the argument's **assumptions**. In one sense, assumptions are pieces of evidence that are left *unstated*. To put it another way, an argument's assumptions consist of everything else that needs to be true in order for the argument to be true.

Assumptions—The information an argument does not state explicitly but that is required for the argument to be true.

When we say an argument is "convincing" or "well-formed" or "valid," we are actually passing judgment on the argument's assumptions. Good arguments don't require much beyond what is explicitly stated in order to be believed. Bad arguments, on the other hand—ones that fail to convince, aren't properly formed, or are invalid—require us to take too much on faith. Invalid arguments ask us to believe something that we know probably isn't the case (or that's actually impossible).

Don't take from this, however, that assumptions are always mistakes an argument makes.

If there's a question that needs an answer in order for us to be comfortable saying our evidence adds up to our conclusion, we've found an assumption. Assumptions answer questions. Assumptions bridge gaps in the evidence.

If it turns out that an assumption isn't true, then the argument will no longer be valid. Remember always:

$$\text{Evidence (+ Assumptions)} \rightarrow \text{Conclusion}$$

Facts

What is a fact? In the world outside the GMAT, that's a thorny question, but for our purposes it couldn't be simpler: a fact is any piece of information that we are asked to take as true without being given an argument to explain why.

Fact—Any piece of information that you're told to take as true on the GMAT.

Every piece of evidence in a GMAT argument is something we'll be told to treat as though it were true. Thus, all GMAT arguments are built out of facts—but not all facts on the GMAT are found in arguments.

Paradoxically, that means that a lot of things that we think of in real life as opinions, on the GMAT we're going to be taking as facts. Other than the conclusion, everything found in a prompt is, to us, simply a fact.

DISTINGUISHING FACTS FROM ARGUMENTS

Consider these two simulated GMAT prompts:

No employee who works at a major corporation wishes to anger the boss, and all major corporations are arranged hierarchically. Bad news inevitably angers the boss who receives it. Those highest in the corporate hierarchy of major corporations are often the least informed about the problems their company is currently facing.	No employee who works at a major corporation wishes to anger the boss, and all major corporations are arranged hierarchically. Because bad news inevitably angers the boss who receives it, it is reasonable to believe that those highest in the corporate hierarchy of major corporations are often the least informed about the problems their company is currently facing.

What is the difference between the two?

The prompt on the left is presented as a series of facts. The prompt on the right is, instead, arranged into an argument. The only difference between them is that the one on the right has the words "because" and "it is reasonable to believe" added, but that is all it takes to turn a collection of facts into an argument: words that indicate which of them you are meant to accept as an explanation (i.e., the evidence) for why one of them (i.e., the conclusion) is true.

As we've already said, when the GMAT gives us an argument, we're expected to think about the argument's assumptions. But what does the GMAT ask us to do with facts?

MAKING INFERENCES FROM FACTS

Primarily, the GMAT expects us to be able to make valid **inferences** from facts.

In our day-to-day lives, we make a lot of inferences.

> If someone comes back from vacation with a sunburn, we think, "I'll bet they went to the beach."

> If we hear a crash in another room followed by the pitter pat of paws beating a hasty retreat, we think, "That darn cat broke something again."

When you start from something you know and make a guess or a prediction about something you don't know, you're making an inference.

However, if somehow these examples appeared in GMAT Critical Reasoning questions, we would have just missed these questions. Each of these inferences would be considered invalid according to the GMAT's rules for inferences.

On the GMAT, the only inferences allowable are those that are 100 percent certain, things that absolutely, positively, without a doubt and without any extra information beyond what is found in the prompt MUST BE TRUE.

Arguments preceded by *probably*, *possibly*, *maybe*, and *more than likely* all fail to make the GMAT inference cut.

> **GMAT Inference**—Something that MUST BE TRUE on the basis of something else taken to be true.

Because of this narrow definition, most of the inferences you'll be asked to make on the GMAT might seem kind of pointless. For example:

> If someone comes back from a vacation sunburned, **on the GMAT** we think, "His or her skin has been damaged by the sun. It is not in the same condition it was in when it was not damaged. His or her skin has changed over the course of his or her life."

> If we hear a crash in another room followed by the pitter pat of paws beating a hasty retreat, **on the GMAT we think,** "The cat—or something that makes the same sound as the cat—has moved. I have just heard a sound that could have been caused by something breaking. The other room is not always quiet. Sometimes you can hear things that sound like a cat or like something breaking in it."

None of those inferences is interesting, but that's just it—GMAT inferences aren't interesting. They aren't clever. If we believe the first statement, we must believe all the others that follow. Very often, novice GMAT test takers miss Inference questions because they think, "But that's too obvious to be the answer!"

Too obvious is never a reason to get rid of a GMAT answer, but that is particularly true with Inference questions.

The GMAT gives us some facts that contain some categorical statements and ask us to say what follows from those statements.

Fact #1	Fact #2	Inference
Socrates is a man.	All men are mortal.	Socrates is mortal.
Celery is gross.	You shouldn't eat gross things.	You shouldn't eat celery.
If it's Tuesday, we should eat by 12.	It's Tuesday, and it's 12:30!	We should have eaten by now.
Words in columns look cool.	These words are in columns.	How cool!

OK, you caught us, we did just reuse the same table from a few pages ago. That's because inferences, arguments, and assumptions are not wholly unrelated concepts.

The conclusion to a valid argument is inferable on the basis of the evidence presented.

> If it is true that Socrates is a man and it is true that all
> men are mortal, then we can infer that Socrates is mortal.

If we are presented with an argument that we are told is valid, but there are gaps in the argument's evidence, then we may infer that the assumptions necessary to bridge those gaps are true.

> If it's true that Socrates is a man, and it's true that because
> Socrates is a man, Socrates is mortal, we can infer that all
> men must be mortal.

The GMAT will clearly indicate to you whether you need to make an inference of what must be true from a couple of facts or whether you need to look at some evidence and a conclusion and say what the conclusion assumes in order to be true.

But ultimately, making inferences and finding assumptions rely on a common skill set. You look at all the information you have and decide either what you need to get where you want to go (assumptions) or where you're going to end up given what you've started with (inferences).

THE FOUR-STEP METHOD FOR CRITICAL REASONING QUESTIONS

Time to see the **Four-Step General Verbal Method** in action on a Critical Reasoning question. We'll use the sample question from the Verbal Introduction:

> Babies born prematurely are beset by a host of serious medical and health challenges. While only nine percent of women not on any medication give birth prematurely, roughly half of all women who take benzodiazepines, a common type of antidepressant, during the first three months of their pregnancies give birth prematurely. Since pregnancy is usually not reliably detectable by over-the-counter methods until the second month, women of child-bearing age should never be prescribed benzodiazepines.
>
> Which of the following, if true, casts the most serious doubt on the conclusion drawn above?

Step 1: Identify the Question Type

The first step of the **Four-Step Verbal Method** is to **Identify the Task**. The task in a Critical Reasoning question always depends on the question **type**. The **question stem** will contain keywords that signal the question type and thus the task demanded.

After you've read the stem, first decide whether the question is **Fact-Based** or **Argument-Based**. Then narrow it down to the particular question type.

If we take a look at the stem of this question, three words allow us to decide:

> Which of the following, if true, casts the most serious doubt on the conclusion drawn above?

When a question asks us to *cast doubt* on an argument's *conclusion*, it's a **Weaken** question, part of the **Assumption** family of **Argument-Based** questions.

Step 2: Identify the Parts of the Argument (for Argument-Based Questions)

Because our question is **Argument-Based**, the best way to **Process** the information is to identify the parts of the argument.

The two basic parts of an argument are the **conclusion**, the idea that the speaker in the prompt is trying to prove, and the **evidence**, the reasons the speaker provides as proof. Start by locating the argument's conclusion.

This argument's conclusion happens to be where you might expect conclusions to come, at the very end:

> [. . .] counter methods until the second month, women of child-bearing age should never be prescribed benzodiazepines. ·

Take note of how **absolute** is the argument's conclusion—by which we don't mean that it's provocative or the sort of thing an extremist might say, rather that this argument's conclusion is not qualified in any way. There is no hedging, no *maybe* this or *possibly* that. According to this speaker, there is absolutely no reason—none, nada, zero, zilch—why these benzodiazepines should be prescribed to women in the indicated age group. Such a far-reaching conclusion would require similarly far-reaching evidence to back it up—indeed, far more evidence than you could ever fit in a 100-word GMAT prompt.

> **Absolute**—On the GMAT, something that applies to 100 percent of cases, without exception.

Once we have the conclusion, we need to take an **inventory** of the rest of the passage. After you've found the conclusion, what remains will almost always be some kind of **evidence**. Here, we should be able to tease out these pieces of evidence:

✔ It can sometimes be hard to tell a pregnancy has started.
✔ The drug whose name starts with a *b* is an antidepressant.
✔ The *b*-drug causes women to give birth prematurely.
✔ Being born prematurely is bad.

Your description of the evidence can be as general or as specific as you need; the important thing is to understand what things the speaker actually said and what was left to the speaker's audience to fill in. You can jot your evidence **inventory** down in a more abbreviated shorthand on your noteboard, or you could just keep it in your head.

Now, does all this **evidence** add up to a compelling case that benzodiazepines should *never* be prescribed to any women in this age group? Certainly not. The argument establishes only that there is *one disadvantage* associated with the drug and then makes a big leap to claim that the drug should *never* be prescribed. In other words, we've found a gap, the gap between *one disad-vantage* and *never prescribing*.

Note: When you're doing a Fact-Based question, this step is going to look a little different. Instead of breaking the argument down into parts, you'll be searching the prompt for the most definite pieces of information. See page 203.

Step 3: Prephrase the Answer

The third step of the **General Verbal Method** is to plan out your approach to the answers. Ideally, for Argument-Based questions we should have a concrete prediction in mind of what the right answer will look like.

For a **Weaken** question the right answer will contain new information about something in the argument that makes us less likely to believe the argument's **assumptions**.

We already know where this argument's assumptions lie, in that gap between finding out that this drug *has one disadvantage* and concluding that it should *never be used*. If the conclusion is correct, the speaker must assume that

> There are no possible advantages or other considerations
> that could outweigh the one disadvantage given.

So what sort of thing would make us less likely to believe that there are no other advantages? We might be moved by an answer choice that mentions an advantage the speaker neglected to bring up. Or perhaps information that defangs the disadvantage could change our mind, something showing that the disadvantage is not as bad as the speaker seems to think. As we move into the answer choices, we'll be looking for something that can change the **advantage/disadvantage balance**.

Step 4: Evaluate the Answer Choices

Let's take it from the top:

> (A) Many women who take benzodiazepines to combat
> depression give birth without serious complications.

This answer choice offers nothing new. The argument only claimed that the side effects were experienced by *roughly half of all women*, which is to say, not all of them. Thus, we already knew that there were some women who didn't experience the side effects (the roughly less than half). Something taken into account by the evidence already present can never weaken a GMAT argument. In other words, this is a **closed issue**. Eliminate.

> (B) Psychiatrists who prescribe benzodiazepines are required
> by law to explain all the dangers associated with their use.

This answer choice hopes to lead you astray by bringing up something **reasonable but irrelevant** to the situation presented in the prompt. You can probably think of several instances of required warning legislation that was passed in the real world. But there's no indication in the prompt that a patient's knowing about the dangers or not knowing would change the rate of negative outcomes significantly. (And that's why we try, whenever possible, to avoid **real-world thinking**. Limit yourself to the facts explicitly stated in the prompt.) Cross this one out.

> (C) Persistent depression is known to reduce fertility in
> women of child-bearing age.

But for the word *persistent*, this answer choice might require more thought. As it stands, we don't know anything about how benzodiazepines work or about what specific kinds of depressions they're used to treat or whether other treatments might be able to be used for the same thing. So how could we possibly say whether benzodiazepines could provide a benefit to people suffering this specific type of depression (the persistent kind)? Since we have to know more to know whether this answer choice would be relevant, we'd say it's **one step removed** from the argument we're dealing with. Out it goes.

> (D) Some of the women of child-bearing age who take
> benzodiazepines are unable to conceive for other
> medical reasons.

Aha! Finally, we have an answer choice that affects the balance of advantage and disadvantage because it both blunts the force of the disadvantage and suggests a possible advantage. The argument's conclusion, as stated, applies to all women of a certain age because of things that are dangerous only to a subset of those women—namely, the subset who can conceive. Those unable to conceive will not be directly affected by the cited disadvantage, so it might prove advantageous to allow benzodiazepines to still be prescribed, just only to those who cannot be harmed by their negative side effect. (D) is the correct answer.

> (E) Benzodiazepines have been prescribed for many years
> by doctors for most common forms of depression.

There is one answer choice left, but we've already found one that must be right. On the day of the test, you might only spare (E) a courtesy glance to make sure you didn't misread something in answers (A) through (D).

After reading (E), we could be reasonably certain that we didn't make any mistakes earlier, as it's clearly a **closed issue** like (A). We already know that *benzodiazepines* are *a common type of antidepressant*.

Click the oval by the answer choice, hit Next and Confirm. It's on to the next question.

Speaking of questions, it's time for you to try some GMAT questions on your own . . . .

Critical Reasoning Diagnostic Quiz

Try to complete the following 13 questions in 25 minutes or less. If you don't finish in that time, just take note of where you were when time was up so that you' can get an idea of how long the questions currently take you, on average, to complete.

The questions are meant to be of average difficulty, targeted at test takers whose Verbal scores would be around the 50th percentile.

Answers and explanations follow the quiz. These questions will be used throughout the sections that follow to demonstrate various techniques and concepts vital to GMAT Critical Reasoning success.

DIRECTIONS: Select the best of the answer choices given.

1. Harry: Reducing our use of fossil fuels is a matter of national security; we cannot afford to allow foreign powers to threaten our economy by reducing production.

Susan: You forget that most foreign oil is refined into gasoline and other usable products in domestic refineries. Your proposal would put thousands out of work when refineries close, and the result would be disastrous for our economy.

Which of the following best describes a weak point in Susan's response to Harry?

(A) Susan takes for granted that the refineries currently used to process foreign oil could not be refitted to allow the refining of other profitable commodities.

(B) Susan doesn't take into consideration the political disadvantages of introducing a plan to reduce the use of fossil fuels.

(C) Susan treats a possible reduction in foreign oil production as though it were inevitable.

(D) Susan's response does not consider the concern of many environmentalists that believe fossil fuels cause ecological damage.

(E) Susan wrongly assumes that Harry's proposal cannot be implemented unless new technology is developed.

2. While patients taking one 40-mg Zzzolution™ pill each night do sleep better than those who take the 20-mg pill, a new study has revealed that throughout the following morning those taking the 40-mg pill perform their daytime activities with much less efficiency and consistency than those taking the lower dose. Since the main reason people take pills to combat sleeplessness is to avoid the reduced productivity that typically follows a sleepless night, doctors now recommend their patients take no more than 20 mg of Zzzolution™ per night.

In evaluating the doctors' new recommendation, it would be most useful to determine which of the following about the study participants?

(A) Whether those taking the higher dose would have performed even worse if their dose had not been raised

(B) Whether those taking the lower dose would have experienced more sleeplessness taking the medicine less frequently

(C) Whether the lower dose would have been sufficient to reduce sleeplessness in the group taking the higher dose

(D) Whether the performance of those taking the lower dose varied more than that of those taking the higher dose

(E) Whether those taking the lower dose took their pills earlier in the evening than those taking the higher dose

3. Experts have long agreed that wearing a helmet can drastically reduce the most serious risks associated with skiing, but the recent experience of a California resort suggests otherwise. After High Hopes Family Resort made the wearing of helmets mandatory on all its slopes, the rate of skiing injuries at the resort did not go down; indeed, it actually rose a slight amount.

Which of the following, if true, most helps to explain the increase in the injury rate?

(A) The slopes at High Hopes Family Resort are much more heavily forested than those at other resorts.

(B) Helmets can only protect a skier from cranial trauma, concussions, and other head injuries.

(C) Before the new policy requiring helmets was implemented, High Hopes had a higher than average injury rate.

(D) Many of the accidents at High Hopes could be avoided if skiers were given adequate training before being allowed on the slopes.

(E) After helmets were made mandatory, many of the most skilled skiers stopped using the slopes at High Hopes.

4. Computech CEO: For over a decade, the M+ has been our flagship personal computer. But now that tablet sales are climbing, the M+ is losing market share, its sales down 25 percent in each of the past three quarters. In order to stop this decline, I propose we enhance the capabilities of the M+, doubling its processing power. Tablet computers are already underpowered, and **the difference will make the M+ obviously superior in the eyes of consumers, which is sure to increase sales**.

Consultant: The M+ is losing sales to tablets because people view tablets as cheaper alternatives to traditional desktop PCs. **Increasing the CPU's speed will raise the price of the M+,** causing even greater numbers of your customers to turn to tablets.

In the exchange above, the statements in **bold** play which of the following roles?

(A) The first presents a conclusion; the second is also a conclusion, but one that is irrelevant to the first.

(B) The first presents a conclusion; the second casts doubt on the conclusion by attacking the evidence on which that conclusion is based.

(C) The first presents a prediction; the second presents evidence that provides a reason to doubt the probability of that conclusion.

(D) The first is evidence that is provided in order to disprove the claim presented in the second.

(E) The first presents a conclusion opposite to the conclusion for which the second provides evidence.

5. Ironically, George Lucas's reputation as an artist has been hindered by the very technology that makes his films so dazzling. Many of the theaters that play his films lack top-of-the-line projection machinery. Such machinery is absolutely vital to the full display of Lucas's artistic skill.

Which one of the following can be properly inferred from the statements above?

(A) Some theaters that play Lucas's films provide support for Lucas's reputation as an artist.

(B) All theaters that play Lucas's films and that possess top-of-the-line projection machinery display Lucas's artistic skill fully.

(C) All of the showings of Lucas's films that do not display his full artistic skill lack top-of-the-line projection machinery.

(D) If a theater possesses top-of-the-line projection facilities, it will provide a full display of an artist's skill.

(E) At least some of the theaters that play Lucas's films fail to display fully Lucas's skills as an artist.

6. Which of the following answer choices, if true, best completes the argument below?

As violence in movies increases, so too do municipal crime rates in cities with large movie-going populations. To combat this, we must limit admission to violent films, only allowing those over the age of 18 because _____ and because it has been well-established that teenagers emulate the behavior they see in movies.

(A) those over the age of 18 are able to distinguish violence in movies from actual violence

(B) teenagers often lack the restraint necessary to refrain from crime when the opportunity presents itself

(C) laws restricting the display of violent films will damage the profits of the studios that produce them

(D) those under the age of 18 see more movies today than they did in the past

(E) teenagers are more likely to see movies if they contain objectionable content

7. Program Director: We designed this leadership training program specifically with your company in mind, so you can be certain that sending your employees on one of our weekend program retreats would lead to enhanced team-building and productivity in your business.

Human Resources Manager: While you may have designed it for us, your program is nevertheless poorly designed. Most of the companies that have attended your weekend retreat have seen no benefit at all, even those that are like our company in most respects.

The Human Resources Manager's response to the Program Director's pitch

(A) rebuts a central premise upon which the pitch is based by citing exceptions to it.

(B) rejects the pitch's conclusion by refuting each of its premises.

(C) accedes the pitch's conclusion, but rejects the evidence upon which the pitch is based.

(D) accepts that one of the premises on which the pitch is based may not be false.

(E) rejects the pitch on the grounds that its evidence cannot be proven.

8. The most famous protagonists in literature have always been at odds with societal norms, but it has been increasingly fashionable for postcolonial literature to glorify these iconoclastic protagonists much more than any previous genre of literature has. By presenting these characters as being worthy of emulation, postcolonial authors subtly endorse their outsider ethos and may convince their readers to adopt it. Thus, postcolonial literature can be harmful to at least some of its readers, and thereby to society itself.

Which of the following is an assumption on which the argument above depends?

(A) Some protagonists from earlier literature were better role models than any found in postcolonial literature.

(B) It is beneficial for some readers to avoid adopting an outsider ethos or to avoid emulating iconoclasts.

(C) Postcolonial protagonists who adopt an outsider ethos will harm readers more now than if they did not adopt that ethos.

(D) The aesthetic merit of some literary works cannot be judged without considering their moral implications.

(E) Postcolonial literature presents a greater number of outsider characters than did the literature of earlier eras.

9. Which of the following would best complete the argument?

Hymenoptera is the order of insects that contains all bees and most species commonly mistaken for them, such as wasps. Honeybees are the only Hymenoptera with a strongly barbed stinger, though the stingers of some wasps, such as the yellow jacket, have small barbs. Ants are also members of the order Hymenoptera, and many species of ants have stingers, and some of them, like honeybees and wasps, fly. To avoid confusing flying ants with honey bees, therefore, _____.

(A) one should not look at its stinger, unless the ant also resembles a wasp

(B) one should determine whether all the members of that stinging ant species can fly

(C) one could not look at the ant's stinger, unless it were strongly barbed

(D) one could determine whether the ant's stinger is strongly barbed

(E) one could determine whether the ant is an insect or a member of the order Hymenoptera

10. As the old saying goes, if you wish to get to Carnegie Hall, you must practice. Paula practices her cello night and day, so she has at least part of what she needs to get to Carnegie Hall.

Which of the following exhibits a pattern of reasoning most similar to that in the argument above?

(A) Surviving the audition process at Julliard requires dedication like Trent's. All the same, Trent's lack of talent will prevent his being admitted to Julliard.

(B) As the old saying goes, if you love someone, set them free; if they do not come back, they were never yours to begin with.

(C) It just might be spring, because when it is spring, I can't stop sneezing, and I've not been able to stop sneezing all day.

(D) It is a truism that the sound of thunder moves more slowly than lightning's flash, but sometimes the lightning is so close that the two phenomena appear simultaneous; thus, the truism proves false.

(E) According to the architects, nothing short of an earthquake will cause this building to fall. Last night an earthquake struck the building, so it will surely fall soon.

11. Some managers believe that the hourly wage that an employee receives ought to be proportional to the effort required by that job's typical duties, but it would be terrible if a business actually followed this advice, as it would mean that those employees with the least ability to perform their jobs adequately would be entitled to the highest hourly wages, a perverse incentive.

The claim that employees with the least ability to perform their job adequately would be entitled to the highest hourly wages is used in the argument as

(A) a general principle that provides a reason in favor of adopting a disagreeable practice illustrated elsewhere in the argument.

(B) a potentially unpopular general principle that is illustrated by a list of reasons that its adoption would be favorable.

(C) an undesirable consequence that would follow from the adoption of a general principle described elsewhere in the argument.

(D) a piece of evidence that discredits a general principle under consideration by showing that the principle could not be uniformly applied.

(E) a possible consequence said to follow from a general principle's adoption that some incorrectly describe as inevitable.

12. Some say that the funding of a large high-energy particle accelerator will benefit only the few physicists who are given direct access to it. If society had listened to such naysayers, however, today we would not have such vital technologies as radio, nuclear power, and the Internet, as at one time the research necessary to bring these about would not have been seen as beneficial to society as a whole. Clearly, therefore, we should not hesitate to build the proposed large high-energy particle accelerator.

Which of the following principles, if accepted as true, would strengthen the argument above for the construction of a large high-energy particle accelerator?

(A) When there is a conflict between nonspecialists and specialists, such as physicists, the specialists ought to be trusted over the nonspecialists.

(B) When a proposed action is opposed only by those who are anonymous, the action should not be rejected because of their opposition.

(C) Unless experts agree about the benefit of a proposal to society as a whole, that proposal ought not be carried out.

(D) If a proposed action is to be considered, it must first be determined how beneficial the action will be to society as a whole.

(E) Whenever a proposed action is opposed by those who believe the action will have only minimal impact, that opposition ought to be ignored.

13. With recent cutbacks in educational funding, the state university must reduce its expenditures or risk bankruptcy. The university's president has proposed moving several introductory-level classes online in order to save money on building maintenance and energy costs associated with a normal classroom setting. Students enrolled in these proposed "virtual classrooms" would be taught by the same instructors who currently teach these classes, and the curriculum would not be changed. Lectures would be broadcast live, not prerecorded, and students would be able to interact with the instructors in real time through a private text-based chat program.

Which of the following, if true, would weaken the case for the adoption of the president's proposal?

(A) The university will be able to enroll more students in an introductory course taught in a virtual classroom than if the course were held in a traditional classroom.

(B) Much of the value of an introductory course stems from the spontaneous exchange of ideas between students in face-to-face discussions.

(C) Many students in the university's introductory classes have jobs and other demands on their time.

(D) The students at the university are accustomed to using computers to communicate with their instructors.

(E) Prerecorded lectures have been shown to have little negative impact on the ability of students to engage with their instructors.

Your Critical Reasoning Diagnosis

ANSWER KEY

1. **(A)**	5. **(E)**	9. **(D)**	13. **(B)**
2. **(C)**	6. **(B)**	10. **(C)**	
3. **(E)**	7. **(D)**	11. **(C)**	
4. **(C)**	8. **(B)**	12. **(E)**	

There are 13 different types of Critical Reasoning questions, and it's no coincidence that there were 13 questions in the Diagnostic Quiz. Each question was drawn from a different one of the 13 types.

Obviously, you're not expected to have gotten all of the questions on the Diagnostic Quiz correct. But now that you've seen some GMAT questions up close and personal, you've got an excellent opportunity to figure out where your current strengths and weaknesses lie. Over the course of your GMAT Verbal studies, you'll need to do some work on all the different types of questions, even the ones you're already good at. As you read the following sections, which discuss the question types in more depth, use your performance on this Diagnostic Quiz as a guide to what you need to focus the most attention on initially.

In the discussion that follows, we're not going to focus solely on whether you got the question right or wrong. Picking the right answer is obviously important, but working with answers is only one of the skills you need for Critical Reasoning. It's also important for you to determine whether you understood the question as a whole, whether you were able to identify conclusions and evidence in the questions that involved arguments, and whether you were able to tell when a question was giving you an argument or when it was giving you a set of facts to make some inferences from.

The Diagnostic Quiz: Answers Explained

1. **(A)** Susan takes for granted that the refineries currently used to process foreign oil could not be refitted to allow the refining of other profitable commodities.

    Analysis: Because the stem asks us to find a *weak point* in an argument, we know this is a **Flaw** question, part of the **Assumption** family of **Argument-Based** questions. The prompt is divided up between two speakers, Harry and Susan, and Susan's statement is the argument the stem indicates is flawed. All flaws are some kind of unwarranted assumption. Here, Susan's conclusion is that *Harry's proposal (reducing the use of fossil fuels) will be bad for the economy*. She cites as evidence one possible disadvantage, that *if refineries close, lots of people will lose their jobs*.

Susan makes a kind of argument that will become very familiar as you study for the GMAT: she's making a **net calculation** about a plan. Whenever such arguments are made, the person making them must assume that *there are no other relevant advantages or disadvantages* that might change the **advantage/disadvantage** balance. Answer Choice (A) describes this unwarranted assumption exactly. Susan's assuming that the one disadvantage she cites is inevitable, and this answer shows us how it might not be.

2. **(C)** Whether the lower dose would have been sufficient to reduce sleeplessness in the group taking the higher dose

   Analysis: Zzzolution™ and the right dosage to prescribe was part of an **Evaluate** question, another member of the **Assumption** family of **Argument-Based** questions. In these questions, we're asked what piece of evidence would be "most useful to know" in order to "evaluate" the argument. We put those words in scare quotes because the wording makes it sound more complicated than it is. All the test maker wants you to do is to find an assumption in the argument and then pick an answer choice that would test whether the assumption was true or false.

   The argument's conclusion is that *this hard-to-pronounce sleeping pill should only be prescribed at a dosage of 20 mg or less*. The evidence given for this recommendation is the result of a study that found, after comparing two groups, the group taking 20 mg was more efficient and consistent when doing their normal day-to-day activities than the group that took 40 mg. Whenever an argument invokes the authority of a **study**, it brings with it lots of assumptions. The relevant one for this question is that *there's nothing special about either group that's relevant to the conclusion*.

   The correct Answer Choice (C) provides a way to test that assumption, on the issue of sleep. If the people taking the 40-mg dose wouldn't be able to sleep on the 20-mg dose, then that would be something special about one of the groups that would be relevant to the conclusion that everybody should take 20-mg doses.

3. **(E)** After helmets were made mandatory, many of the most skilled skiers stopped using the slopes at High Hopes.

   Analysis: This was your first question from the **Fact-Based** category of questions, one you'll soon learn to recognize as an **Explain** question. In these questions, instead of an argument with evidence and conclusion, you're given an information dump about a situation that, as presented, seems kind of weird. Something that ought to be happening isn't happening. With these questions, your first task is to **identify the two parts of the dilemma**. Here, the **dilemma** is an **expectation** that failed to come true. There's reason to think that (1) helmets should reduce the injury rate, but instead (2) the rate rose after helmets were made mandatory.

It's generally hard to predict what the right answer to an Explain question will look like, so once you have the dilemma's two parts in mind, you can proceed to the answer choices to perform a process of elimination. The right answer will bridge the gap between the two parts of the dilemma. Here, Answer Choice (E) does the trick: if the law requiring helmets made the ski resort less popular with the sorts of skiers who tend to know best how to avoid accidents—the experts—then it makes sense that the injury rate rose after the law. The helmets are still preventing accidents; the resort just has more accidents per capita because of the new composition of its population of skiers.

4. **(C)** The first presents a prediction; the second presents evidence that provides a reason to doubt the probability of that conclusion.

Analysis: The **bolded** statements are the tipoff. This is a **Bolded Statement** question, part of the **Structure** family of **Argument-Based** questions. This question prompt presents a two-part argument. The CEO has a plan that the Consultant disagrees with. Your job is to say what role the bolded statements play in the exchange. Often, with these questions, it's easiest to pick one bolded statement and use it to do a process of elimination with the answer choices.

The second bolded statement is probably the easier of the two. We know the Consultant disagrees with the CEO's claim, so Answer Choice (E) is out. We also know that the Consultant's conclusion is the last line, that *even more customers will be lost if the plan is enacted.* The bolded statement is evidence in support of that conclusion, not a conclusion itself, so Answer Choices (D) and (A) would also go. Left with Answer Choices (C) and (B), we can eliminate (B), because the Consultant doesn't disagree with the CEO's evidence (though the Consultant does oppose the CEO's conclusion). The Consultant just states a fact that the CEO didn't take into account.

If we'd chosen instead to use the first statement, we could eliminate Answer Choice (D), but all the rest are probably OK. Describing a conclusion as a prediction is fine when that conclusion is actually a prediction, and the CEO's certainly is. He's concluding that *sales will rise.*

5. **(E)** At least some of the theaters that play Lucas's films fail to display fully Lucas's skills as an artist.

Analysis: "Inferred" (see question on page 226) in the stem lets us know this is an **Inference** question, the most common kind of **Fact-Based** question. As with Explain questions, the information in the prompt is just a collection of facts; our job is to find an answer choice that must be true if we take those facts to be true. When you read through the prompt of an **Inference** question, look for the most definite pieces of information, the elements that are *always* or *never* the case, the things true of *everybody* or *anyone*. Here, there's one definite piece of information, the last sentence. Saying that something is *absolutely vital* is a way of saying that it is *required*. Thus, this fancy machinery is *required* for *the full display of Lucas's artistic skill*. Any theater that displays Lucas's full artistic skill must have this machinery, and any theater lacking it will be unable to display said artistic skill.

As luck would have it, the prompt also tells us something about *many theaters*. They lack this machinery. Thus, they will be unable to display Lucas's skill—and that's why Answer Choice (E) is the right answer. Apply the rule in the prompt and you get a close paraphrase of Answer Choice (E).

6. **(B)** Teenagers often lack the restraint necessary to refrain from crime when the opportunity presents itself.

Analysis: Question 6 is one of those sneaky **Complete** questions that can either belong to the **Assumption** family or to the **Fact-Based** category, depending on what the keywords near the blank tell us is missing from the argument. Here, the word *because* tells us the blank is missing some *evidence*, which makes this a **Complete (Evidence)** question and a member of the **Assumption** family. Like all its familial cohorts, **Complete (Evidence)** questions require us to find the conclusion and see how the evidence is connected to it.

In this prompt, the conclusion is a **recommendation** about what *must* be done to solve a problem (that violent crime rates are going up in tandem with the increase in violent movies). The speaker recommends banning anyone younger than 18 from seeing the films and offers a single piece of evidence in support: *teenagers emulate the behavior they see in movies*. To complete the argument, we need to provide an extra piece of evidence that covers one of the argument's assumptions.

This argument does have a lot of assumptions! Just because teens tend to emulate what they see in movies doesn't necessarily mean that they're responsible for the increase in violent crime in the city. Maybe they just act violently toward each other, or play violent video games. To cover the assumption, we need information that makes it more likely the teens actually are up to no good. Answer Choice (B) works because it addresses the *crime* issue. If teens are unable to resist criminal behavior, then it's more likely that their movie habits are the cause of the crime increase—as unlikely as that would be in the real world.

7. **(D)** The Human Resources Manager's response to the Program Director's pitch accepts that one of the premises on which the pitch is based may not be false.

   Analysis: Because this question asks us *how* someone's argument works, it belongs in the **Structure** family of **Argument-Based** questions. It's a **Method of Argument** question, to be more specific. For these questions, the right answer will describe the way that the argument's evidence is used to support its conclusion.

   The Manager's conclusion is to the point: *this program is poorly designed*. To support that claim, the Manager offers reasonable evidence, citing the terrible experiences with the program had by other companies similar to the Manager's company. The correct answer, (D), might have thrown the unwary, as it describes only a small part of the Manager's method of argument, the first few words in which the Manager accepts the Program Director's claim that the program was designed with the Manager's company in mind. Thus, (D) is the answer. Sneaky!

8. **(B)** It is beneficial for some readers to avoid adopting an outsider ethos or to avoid emulating iconoclasts.

   Analysis: The word *assumption* tells us, naturally, that this is an **Assumption** question. We'll be discussing this question in depth a bit later in this chapter. For now, the important thing is knowing whether you recognized it as an **Argument-Based** question and knew from that that you needed to find the argument's conclusion and characterize its evidence in order to find any gaps. The conclusion is stated in the last sentence: *postcolonial literature is harmful to its readers*. In support of this, the author provides no evidence that describes a harm, only some features of postcolonial literature. Thus, the argument assumes that *at least one of the things the evidence says that postcolonial literature does is harmful somehow*. Answer Choice (B) nails that assumption, though it does try to hide it under a layer of **double-negatives** (is beneficial to avoid = is bad to not avoid = is harmful).

9. **(D)** One could determine whether the ant's stinger is strongly barbed.

Analysis: Like Question 6, this is a **Complete** question, but the *therefore* before the blank classifies it instead as a **Complete (Conclusion)** question, a member of the **Fact-Based** category of questions. Because you'll be drawing a conclusion from some facts rather than identifying a conclusion, the task ahead is a lot like an Inference question. The right answer choice will follow if all the information in the prompt is taken to be true. When we read the prompt, we should be on the lookout for **definite** information, rules, and categorical statements, which are the things inferences are made of.

Here, there's a *lot* of definite information, and the challenge is just lining it all up to keep it straight. To fill the blank, we need a definite way to tell flying ants from honey bees. According to the rules above, honeybees are the *only* members of the order Hymenoptera that have *a strongly barbed stinger*. The prompt also tells us that flying ants are in the order Hymenoptera. Thus, a quick check of the ant's stinger will solve our problem. If the stinger of an insect in order Hymenoptera is not strongly barbed, then the insect in question is not a honeybee. Answer Choice (D) spells out this connection.

10. **(C)** It just might be spring, because when it is spring, I can't stop sneezing, and I've not been able to stop sneezing all day.

Analysis: When we see *a pattern of reasoning most similar* in the stem, we know we're dealing with a **Parallel Argument** question, a member of the **Structure** family that asks us to compare the argument in the prompt with five different arguments in the answer choices and find the prompt-answer pair that have the same structure. With these questions, you need to be able to describe the argument's structure in extremely abstract language, ignoring the content. The right answer choice almost never has anything to do with the original argument in subject matter, only in structure.

The argument in the prompt has a very safe conclusion: *Paula has at least part of what she needs*. It supports this conclusion with a rule that establishes a **requirement**: *in order to get to Carnegie Hall, practice is required*. It also provides information that lets us know that the requirement has been met: *Paula practices*. The correct answer, (C), has this precise structure. It has a safe conclusion (*It "might" be Spring*), which it backs up with a rule that establishes a requirement (*When it's Spring, I can't stop sneezing*) and information that the requirement has been met (*I can't stop sneezing*).

When it's Spring, I can't stop sneezing might not have seemed like much of a requirement to you when you read the argument initially. In a later section, we'll discuss the basics of Formal Logic, the rules that govern requirements and guarantees. We won't get technical about it now, but the secret is to rephrase either statement and you'll see how they're the same:

If it is Spring, I cannot stop sneezing = If you are at Carnegie Hall, you must have practiced.

11. **(C)** An undesirable consequence that would follow from the adoption of a general principle described elsewhere in the argument.

   Analysis: Here we have another **Argument-Based** question from the **Structure** family. The stem tells us to describe how a part of an argument *is used*, meaning this is a **Role of a Statement** question. To understand the role, you have to understand the argument, so identifying the conclusion and evidence is still your first step. This argument's conclusion follows a common pattern: **people who say X are wrong**—in this case, *managers who think that pay and effort should be proportional are wrong*. That conclusion is supported, in part, by the piece of the argument about which the stem is asking us. Thus, the role of that statement is that it's a piece of evidence.

   We usually have to be a smidge more specific with Role of a Statement questions, so we would also need to realize that this piece of evidence is a sort of **counterexample**, a prediction of an **undesirable consequence** that would follow if the argument were accepted. Answer Choice (C) describes that precisely.

12. **(E)** Whenever a proposed action is opposed by those who believe the action will have only minimal impact, that opposition ought to be ignored.

   Analysis: This question features another **people who say X are wrong** pattern to its reasoning, but the stem asks you to make the argument better, making it a **Strengthen** question, a member of the **Assumption** family of **Argument-Based** questions. Start by finding the conclusion. The *people who say X* are identified in the first line, those who *say that funding this particle accelerator will only benefit a few physicists;* the *are wrong* doesn't show up until the last sentence, which goes one step further than just saying these people are wrong. They're wrong, and thus the argument concludes that *this accelerator should be built immediately.*

This conclusion is supported only by the evidence that other inventions that were ultimately beneficial also had "people who say" opposed to them, which means that the argument assumes that *the particle accelerator case is similar enough to the other cases that what is true of one is true of the other.* Soon, you'll learn to call this a **representativeness** assumption, a very common GMAT argument pattern.

The stem also contains a common pattern, in this case a word that changes what we should expect from the answer choices: **principle**. When a GMAT question asks you for a principle, the right answer will be phrased as a **general rule** rather than as a description of the specific case at hand. The rule will still strengthen the argument in the same way as a specific description would, by supporting the unstated *representativeness* assumption. Answer Choice (E) does this exactly. If we follow this answer's principle, we will treat any case in which a potential action has naysayers the same, by going full steam ahead and doing the action.

13. **(B)** Much of the value of an introductory course stems from the spontaneous exchange of ideas between students in face-to-face discussions.

Analysis: Question 13 is Question 12's opposite number, a **Weaken** question, also part of the **Assumption** family of **Argument-Based** questions. Up until the final step, you'll treat Weaken questions the same as Strengthen questions, by finding the argument's conclusion, considering how the evidence is linked to the conclusion, and finding a gap that an unstated assumption is needed to cover. The only difference is that the correct answer will make the assumption *less* believable.

The stem tips off the argument's conclusion, the president's proposal to *move some intro classes online in order to save money.* When arguments present a proposal, the conclusion is almost always that *this proposal will work.* Such an argument inevitably assumes that *there are no disadvantages to the plan that would outweigh the advantages cited in the argument,* a kind of **net calculation** about the **advantage/disadvantage** balance (as we saw back in Question 1).

The advantages cited are that the online classes would be similar in a lot of ways but would still cost less overall. To weaken the assumption, we simply look for evidence in an answer choice of a possible disadvantage, and we find that in Answer Choice (B). If a lot of value will be lost, then the advantage of savings might be outweighed by the decrease in quality.

The Final Diagnostic Analysis

Recognizing the Task

Always read the stem first when attacking a GMAT Critical Reasoning question because it allows you to determine what you're supposed to be paying attention to when you read the information in the prompt.

In each of the sections that follows, the discussion will begin with a few sample stems. The keywords repeated across each type of question are relatively few in number and easily committed to memory. Note, however, that most successful GMAT test takers don't just memorize a list of keywords and apply them mechanically; instead, focus on how the keywords describe the *task* that each question demands.

For example, **Strengthen** questions and **Inference** questions use the same keywords to describe dramatically different tasks. A **Strengthen** question could ask *which of the following, if true, most supports the argument above?* An **Inference** question, on the other hand, could ask *which of the following is most supported by the argument above?* The *direction* of the support is more important than the word *support* itself. If the answers support the argument, it's a **Strengthen** question; if the argument/prompt supports the answers, then it's an **Inference** question.

Identifying the Conclusion (Qs 1–2, 4, 6–8, 10–13)

In the sections that follow, you'll learn the three most powerful techniques for identifying an argument's conclusion.

> **LOOK FOR CONCLUSION KEYWORDS**—Words like *thus*, *therefore*, and *in conclusion* usually—but not always!—indicate a conclusion. When you spot one, don't assume you've found what you're looking for; be sure to verify that what follows is actually the conclusion of the argument. For easy reference, you'll find a list of the most common GMAT argument keywords on page 247.

> **USE THE WHAT/WHY TEMPLATE**—As we discussed in the previous section on **Arguments and Facts**, all arguments can be put into the form

[CONCLUSION] because [EVIDENCE] or [WHAT] because [WHY]. If you think you've found the conclusion, but you're not sure, try rephrasing the argument so that it fits the template. If the thing you're identifying as the conclusion is never explained by the evidence, then you've probably got it the wrong way around.

RECOGNIZE THE MOST COMMON ARGUMENT PATTERNS—The more experience you get with the GMAT question writers' ticks and habits, the easier it will be to find the conclusion. While there is probably an infinite number of ways that an argument *could* be phrased, the GMAT tends to stick to only a few variations. You'll find these discussed starting on page 247.

Identifying Dilemmas and Definite Statements (Qs 3, 5, 9)

The most common difficulty test takers have with Inference and Explain questions is that they read the prompt thinking that there is no way to predict what the answer choices might bring up. On the one hand, they're right; the specific wording or new information you find in these answer choices is often designed to seem unfamiliar. On the other hand, you can't make a GMAT-approved inference with just any old piece of information. The inference must be supported by something definite, a rule or an otherwise categorical statement like *this always happens* or *this is required for that*.

Familiarize yourself with the most common Inference question setups (pages 281–290). You'll find as you work through GMAT practice problems, you're really being asked to do the same sort of inference process again and again.

The same can be said of Explain question prompts. It's true that the right answer will bring up something completely new, but you can prepare yourself for the answers by understanding what sort of information you're looking for. Practice finding the two sides of each little dilemma or paradox presented in these questions.

Understanding Information in the Prompt

"Understanding Information" is a necessarily broad category that describes several GMAT skills. When you're practicing GMAT questions, be honest with yourself during the review process, after you've worked the question, and while you're reading over the answers and explanations. How much of the argument or fact pattern did you *really* understand, and how much of it did you just have a "feeling" about? Slow down as you read question prompts, and ask yourself, "OK, so what's going on here?" If you find you don't know what an argument says, either go back and reread it or sacrifice the question by guessing and move on.

You don't pick up speed on a standardized test by short-changing your understanding of the information in the questions. Clumsy, rushed, or otherwise too-swift strategies almost always lead to earning fewer points in the long run.

Predicting Missing Assumptions (Qs 1–2, 6, 8, 12–13)

The single most important key to understanding more than half of the Critical Reasoning questions on the GMAT is the ability to see the gap between the evidence and the conclusion *before you look at the answers*.

The most common reason that test takers fail to see the assumptions beneath an argument's explicit evidence is that they don't understand the definition of an assumption. That's why we've devoted an entire section to defining assumptions in the most helpful ways.

Depending on the argument, you might think of an assumption as *anything not stated that the argument needs to be true*, or as *the information that makes the evidence relevant to the conclusion*, or as *information that rules out any possible exceptions or roadblocks*. These are three different ways of saying the same thing: assumptions are the bare minimum extra information that the argument *needs* to cover a *lack of information* about a critical idea.

Lean heavily on the most common argument structures as well when searching for an argument's assumptions. Two arguments that share the same structure likely share a similar sort of assumption. For instance, whenever an argument relies on an **analogy**, we know that at least one of the assumptions is that the two items said to be similar in one way are also *similar in all the ways needed for the conclusion to be true*. Learn to spot the GMAT's patterns and you'll have a shortcut to knowing the assumptions being tested.

Selecting the Right Answer

The reason the GMAT frustrates so many is that even when you know the task you're supposed to do, and even when you understand everything in the argument, you can still end up picking the wrong answer choice. When you look at the Answers and Explanations, you think, "Oh! How did I not see that?" A better question would be, "What did this question do to *keep* me from seeing it?"

The question writers back at GMAT HQ aren't professional psychologists or sociologists, but they do employ psychological and sociological research in order to craft answer choices that seem right when they're not or that appeal to a certain sort of test taker or a certain type of mindset. Don't let yourself be satisfied with the explanation, "I just need to read more carefully," as you could *always* be more careful. Instead, keep a record of the ways you've been fooled and during subsequent reviews, compare your performance against the record. A diary or journal is often useful for this. You'll eventually come to understand what scenarios or tricks you're vulnerable to and how to recognize them during a test session.

Also, during the discussion of each type of question in the sections that follow, we'll be sure to outline the most common ways the test maker throws you off the scent of the right answer or makes you bite too soon on a wrong answer.

I. THE ARGUMENT STRUCTURE FAMILY OF QUESTIONS

Anatomy of an Argument Structure Question

Prompt

Some managers believe that the hourly wage that an employee receives ought to be proportional to the effort required by that job's typical duties, but it would be terrible if a business actually followed this advice, as it would mean that those employees with the least ability to perform their jobs adequately would be entitled to the highest hourly wages, a perverse incentive.

Stem

The claim that employees with the least ability to perform their job adequately would be entitled to the highest hourly wages is used in the argument as

Answer Choices

(A) a general principle that provides a reason in favor of adopting a disagreeable practice illustrated elsewhere in the argument.

(B) a potentially unpopular general principle that is illustrated by a list of reasons that its adoption would be favorable.

(C) an undesirable consequence that would follow from the adoption of a general principle described elsewhere in the argument.

(D) a piece of evidence that discredits a general principle under consideration by showing that the principle could not be uniformly applied.

(E) a possible consequence said to follow from a general principle's adoption that some incorrectly describe as inevitable.

Prompt

- All contain an **argument** that has a specific **conclusion** and one or more pieces of **evidence**.
- Keywords like *therefore* or *thus* are often absent or used misleadingly.
- Often the prompt contains more than one point of view—someone is **responding** to someone else or to a **commonly held** belief.

Stem

- Most include the actual word **argument** or a close synonym like **reasoning.**
- Will make reference to the **function**, **role**, or how a piece is **used in** or **factors into** the argument.

Answer Choices

- Abstract descriptive terms and answers that differ in only small ways are the norm.
- Can often be grouped into twos and threes that share the same part.

Identifying Argument Structure Questions

There are four different ways that a GMAT question might ask about an argument's structure. Sometimes, the question will ask only about a part of the argument and the role it plays in the argument as a whole. If the part is highlighted in **boldface**, we call it a **Bolded Statement** question. If there's no boldface, but you're still only looking at a part of the argument, then you're dealing with a **Role of a Statement** question. Most Bolded Statement questions are just two Role of a Statement questions stitched together. You're asked about two roles for the price of one argument.

The other two types of structural questions ask you to describe the argument as a whole, how it comes to its evidence is used to come to its conclusion. **Method of Argument** questions ask for that description directly, whereas **Parallel Argument** questions ask you to find the argument in the answer choices that has the same structure as the one in the prompt.

Because of the specific ways each of the four questions is phrased, you'll be able to identify the task just by looking at the stem.

ROLE OF A STATEMENT

A few ways Role of a Statement stems might be phrased:

- In the argument above, the statement that all wolves born in the wild are able to recognize their pack's leader plays which of the following roles

- The claim that the comptroller has overlooked the value of the finance department is used in the auditor's response as a
- In the passage above, the reference to a possible reduction in foreign oil production serves primarily to

Occasionally, a Role of a Statement question works in the opposite direction, naming a role and asking you to find the statement that plays that role:

- Which of the following states the main conclusion of the argument above?
- In defending the position above, the inspector offers which of the following as evidence?

METHOD OF ARGUMENT

The most common stems for Method of Argument questions include:

- In the passage, the author **develops** the **argument** by
- Which of the following best describes the **rhetorical strategy** used above?
- The statement that X **plays which role** in the **argument** above?
- In making his **claim**, the judge's use of Y **serves to**

A second style of Method of Argument stem usually occurs with prompts that contain more than one point of view and uses some synonym of the word *responds*:

- The farmer **responds** to the rancher's argument by
- The rancher **addresses** the issue by

BOLDED STATEMENT

Look for the **bolded parts**. Enough said!

PARALLEL ARGUMENT

Parallel Argument stems describe both the prompt and the answer choices as containing arguments and ask you to find the two that are *similar* or *parallel*:

- The reasoning above is most similar to that found in which of the following?
- The argument above contains reasoning most similar to which of the following answer choices?
- The argument above most closely parallels which of the following arguments?

Processing Argument Structure Prompts

Obviously there's always going to be an argument in the prompt, one composed of a conclusion and the pieces of evidence given in support of the conclusion. About half the time, there will be more than one argument present. Sometimes this is done explicitly, by dividing the prompt between two different speakers:

> Trina: Fish taste like squishy salt. We shouldn't serve fish
> tonight because our guests will be disgusted.
>
> Levon: But many of our guests are fishermen. They enjoy
> the taste of fish. The question isn't whether we should
> serve fish, but how many different types of fish to serve!

Other times, the second argument is presented by a speaker who intends to present an argument to the contrary:

> Chef: While some people may believe that fish tastes like
> "squishy salt," they are wrong to try to dictate the menu at a fine
> restaurant. Anyone who would describe the taste of fish in such a
> crass way clearly lacks a refined palate and should be ignored.

In other words, you'll see a lot of speakers in Argument Structure prompts arguing against other people, sometimes given titles or other descriptions like *environmentalists* or *the distinguished councilor*, but just as often left anonymous, merely *those who would say* or *some people*.

Pay careful attention if the question stem identified someone. Often, this means that the question will be about the method of argument of the person being argued *against*, rather than the argument's main speaker.

Whenever you see a speaker say something like, "But it would be wrong to think that" or "It is absurd to believe this," you've probably just been given the conclusion. Find what the *this* or *that* is referring to, and rephrase the conclusion into the author's position. For example:

> Critics often claim that the value of a work of art is inextri-
> cably linked to the circumstances in which it was created,
> but in this they are clearly mistaken, for [. . .]

"In this they are clearly mistaken." is the conclusion. What is "this" referring to? The claim that "the value of a work of art is inextricably linked to the circumstances in which it was created." Put the two together, and the conclusion of the speaker's argument becomes

> Art is not inextricably linked to the circumstances in which
> it was created.

Attacking Argument Structure Answer Choices

Recognizing the right answer choice will depend on your ability to describe the argument's parts using abstract terminology and descriptions rather than content. Answers, both wrong and right, will look more like

> The author rebuts a potential criticism to a general rule by showing the criticism to apply only to a small minority of instances in which that rule might be applied.

than

> The author argues that buying flea collars for your dog is still a good idea even though some particularly inbred poodles are allergic to flea collars.

The same argument is being described in each; the first is just using abstract vocabulary to do so.

IDENTIFYING CONCLUSIONS AND EVIDENCE

The first step to every Argument-Based question is to locate the conclusion of the argument given in the prompt. If you can't find the conclusion, you won't be able to identify the argument's structure, nor will you be able to consider the assumptions that underlie the argument. So how do you go about finding it?

Technique #1: Look for the Keywords

Sometimes, the speaker in the prompt just comes out and says, "Hey, lookie here, this is my conclusion." OK, so they don't put it that way exactly, but they might as well. Instead, speakers direct your attention to their conclusion by tagging it with "therefore," or "thus," or, our personal favorite, "in conclusion." These are conclusion keywords, and about half the arguments on the test have them.

THE MOST COMMON GMAT CONCLUSION KEYWORDS

thus	accordingly	may conclude
therefore	as a result	in conclusion
hence	for this reason	in the end
clearly	it follows that	from this
so	this shows that	
consequently	must be that	

Of course, not every prompt is so nice. Sometimes you can find the conclusion by looking for *evidence* keywords, eliminating everything following them; what you have left is likely your conclusion. This is most often the case when the conclusion comes at the beginning of the argument.

THE MOST COMMON GMAT EVIDENCE KEYWORDS

as	in that	as we know
because	given that	the studies found that
since	due to	this can be seen from/in
for	according to	we know this by
for example	as indicated by	

Technique #2: The Types of Conclusion and Evidence

Suppose an argument lacks any identifying keywords (or that it has too many). What would you do then? One way to find the conclusion is to look for "the most conclusionary part."

While there's an infinite number of possible arguments that could be made in English, all argument conclusions can be sorted into a handful of categories that describe the *type* of claim the conclusion makes. Not just anything can be a conclusion.

THE MOST COMMON GMAT CONCLUSION TYPES

PREDICTION—A conclusion about what *will* happen, what *is going to* happen, what *ought to* occur, what *can be expected*, etc.

> The Hendersons will arrive tomorrow. Winning the bid will make a profit for the company. If Thomas enters the race, he will lose.

RECOMMENDATION—A conclusion about what someone *should* or *ought* to do, often phrased as a plan or proposal to meet a goal spelled out earlier.

> The company should invest in new machinery. People who want to be loved should learn to love others. The best way to get to Carnegie Hall is to practice.

BARE ASSERTION—A conclusion about what *is* the case, what *is true* about a situation or phenomenon, what someone *should believe* about a particular case. This is the most common type of conclusion.

> Petra is an excellent dancer. The building is structurally unsound. Hydrogen indicates contamination.

VALUE JUDGMENT—A conclusion about what is right or wrong and what is moral or immoral. These are relatively rare on the GMAT and can usually be treated as a more specific type of recommendation.

> One should never lie. Pol Pot was history's worst dictator.

CAUSAL CONNECTION—A conclusion that asserts that one thing *is responsible for*, *brought about*, or *caused* some other thing. These are usually established on the basis of a correlation between two things.

> Rain makes the flowers grow. The earthquake knocked the buildings down. Static electricity is responsible for your hair being so hard to manage.

Argument Structure questions in particular often turn on your ability to describe the argument's conclusion according to one of these categories.

But be careful when the answer choices to such questions further characterize conclusions as *recommendations, predictions,* etc., because it can be very easy to mistake one for the other. The verb used in the conclusion is the best sign as to what type of conclusion you have, but because of the way English plays fast and loose with the future tense (allowing *will, ought to,* and even *is to* as future indicators), even these can be misleading, particularly in distinguishing recommendations and predictions. As a rule of thumb, think of these examples:

> You will not shout in this room.
> You should not shout in this room.
> You cannot shout in this room.

The first is a **prediction** of what will happen. Regardless of whether shouting is allowed or not, it is not going to happen.

The second is a **recommendation**. While people might choose to ignore the rules and shout anyway, it's not *allowed* in the room.

The third is ambiguous. It *might* be a **recommendation**. You can't shout here because it isn't allowed. But it might be a simple **bare assertion**, too.

You can't shout in this room because it is in outer space and there's no air (i.e., it's impossible). Sometimes, context is still necessary to decide what type of conclusion you're dealing with.

Just as with keywords, often you can narrow down to the conclusion by identifying things that are almost always evidence.

THE MOST COMMON GMAT EVIDENCE TYPES

STUDIES, POLLS, EXPERIMENTS, AND SURVEYS—Usually evidence because the conclusion is not an argument proving what the study *said* but rather how people are interpreting it or what it means.

> Recent research found a connection between . . . , 4 out of 5 dentists surveyed . . . , We asked our listeners . . .

LONG-HELD BELIEFS—Watch for arguments that tell you that something has been thought, believed, or considered for a long time. Usually, this will be evidence for a conclusion to come.

> Scientists have long known that . . . , History tells us that . . . , It is a truism that . . .

GOALS AND PLANS—Rarely will an argument try to convince you that something *is* the goal or that a plan *is being considered*; rather, the conclusion is usually that a goal will be met or a plan will succeed.

> The city has enacted an ordinance to . . . , In order to reduce costs . . . , In response to rising unemployment . . .

RECOGNIZING SETUP INFORMATION

All three of the most common types of evidence could be grouped under a heading that we've already used in passing earlier: **setup information**.

You know by now that the GMAT forbids you to use any information from the world outside the test in order to select the right answer. Because of this restriction, you can think of each new Critical Reasoning prompt as a little world unto itself.

Consider this argument prompt:

> Because they construct such elaborate and intricate nests, male weaver birds are often considered nature's avian artists. Because weaver nests share features with those built near them that they do not share with those built by males farther away, researchers have suggested that the style of nest that a male weaver bird builds is at least partially determined by information obtained during the lifetime of the individual bird and is not completely a function of a particular sequence of genes.

The first line isn't really direct evidence for the argument's conclusion, the researchers' hypothesis found later on. Instead, it establishes that, in the world of this particular Critical Reasoning prompt, there are birds and that they do this interesting thing with their nests.

But the first line also isn't being argued. It's not at stake, so it can't be the conclusion. The argument isn't trying to convince you that weaver birds do what they do. The conclusion is an *explanation* for why they do it.

Don't think of **setup information** as "fluff" or "filler." Very often, the difference between the credited answer and an incorrect but tempting one will be a little detail from the setup. Suppose the prompt above had a stem attached that asked you what the argument assumes. A wrong answer might well try to distract you by bringing up details from the setup.

> (A) Artistic species are seldom found in nature.

As stated, the argument doesn't require us to believe that the behavior of these birds is rare, even though it seems reasonable to believe it is. Reasonable but irrelevant answers, as always, are opportunities for the lazy reader to take an easy out.

The right answer might use vocabulary from the setup in order to disguise its correctness:

> (B) Elaborate or intricate features found in the work of geographically proximate species are unlikely to be similar purely by chance.

Answer Choice (B) is probably not how you would have prephrased the assumption, but a part of learning how to use your prephrased prediction is learning how to adapt it to the vocabulary used in the passage.

Technique #3: Further Characterizing the Evidence and Conclusion

Both **Role of a Statement** and **Bolded Statement** questions single out part of an argument and ask what role it plays. Since there is little to no fluff or filler in a GMAT Critical Reasoning prompt, everything that appears in the prompt of an Argument-Based question is either part of the **evidence** or part of the **conclusion**.

As you sort through answer choices, look for the words that indicate what type of evidence is used:

> finding, explanation, objection, judgment, standards, methods, data, etc.

or what type of conclusion:

> position, explanation, prediction, recommendation, hypothesis, interpretation, objection, contrary conclusion, implication, etc.

IS THE CONCLUSION POSITIVE OR NEGATIVE?

Sometimes the difference between the right answer and the wrong ones comes down to a simple word like *not*. Some authors arrive at positive conclusions; others reach negative conclusions.

HOW DEFINITE IS THE EVIDENCE OR CONCLUSION?

The basic parts of an argument can be **extreme** or **qualified**.

Extreme evidence takes the form of rules that are always true, characteristics that are never shared, things that are impossible or the only way to proceed:

> The shark, as scientists have long known, is **unable** to survive if it remains still.

> . . . because there **can be only one** definition for a word in the Burundi language.

> **No** Ps are Qs, but **all** Qs are Js.

Qualified evidence leaves wiggle room:

> There was a forty percent **likelihood** that the participants would not survive.

> **Many** fields of study require specialized lingo or jargon.

> It **occasionally** can be seen from the north side of the mountain.

Extreme conclusions make all-encompassing claims that admit no exception:

> Therefore, **everything** in the universe is composed of either energy or matter.
>
> Thus, **all** the items on this table are edible.
>
> Hence, **there is only one** way to skin a cat.

Qualified conclusions hedge with weasel words like *some, probably, to an extent, in many cases.*

> So, the mail **will likely** be here by Tuesday.
>
> The researchers concluded that heart disease **is often** linked to diet.
>
> Consequently, **at least some of** the food in the refrigerator is rotten.

To determine whether the evidence and conclusion are qualified or definite, be on the lookout for keywords like:

> all, every, most, many, some, several, few, only, never, probably, not necessarily, rarely, etc.

IS THE SCOPE LIMITED?

Sometimes, the argument throws out a limitation on the applicability of its evidence or its conclusion, admitting that there are some cases to which it doesn't apply or some exceptions to the rule:

> This research, **if accurate**, suggests that people form opinions on such subjects immediately.
>
> **To the extent that** a species' range is limited, it will always adopt this behavior.
>
> **Inasmuch as** the goal of such programs is financial stability . . .
>
> **If** you want to secure a seat by Tuesday, you must act now.

IS THE EVIDENCE USED TO PROVE OR DISPROVE SOMETHING?

Most of the time, evidence presented on the GMAT is positive.

> this shows, this confirms, an example would be, etc.

On the other hand, sometimes a fact is used as a counterexample or evidence to disprove a claim, often accompanied by keywords such as:

> but, yet, however, admittedly, by way of contrast,
> although, even still, whereas, despite this, in spite of, after
> all, and our favorite, on the other hand

HOW MANY PIECES OF EVIDENCE ARE USED?

Does the author cite only one rule or are multiple rules linked together? Does the author add a second premise that supports the conclusion indirectly, eliminates some possible misinterpretation, or answers an objection?

In these cases, you'll often see keywords like:

> furthermore, as well, besides, after all, moreover, in addition, what's more

HOW MANY CONCLUSIONS ARE THERE?

The most common way to complicate an argument in a Structure question is to present two arguments that oppose one another within the same prompt. This can be done implicitly:

> **There are those who say** that contentment is
> impossible if desire persists; **however, . . .**
>
> **Some argue** that we always hurt the ones we love, **but . . .**
>
> **A number of students** often maintain that they cannot
> arrive on time, **but . . .**

Or explicitly:

> **The esteemed councilperson claims** that we should
> elect him to the judgeship, **but . . .**
>
> I **oppose** the suggestion of **these environmentalists**
> **who believe** that we should limit its use.

Another way to throw more than one conclusion into an argument is to tack an **additional implication** or suggestion onto the **end** of an argument.

> Because Chemical X harms small children, it should be
> banned. **Further**, those who developed it should be fined.

Moreover, these extra conclusions are almost always present only to set up a wrong answer choice, not to be a part of the right one.

The final way an argument might have more than one conclusion is when the argument has a **complex** or **nested** structure. By this, we mean that it arrives at an **intermediate conclusion**, taking that conclusion as evidence for a **final conclusion** given later. An example:

> Because no other military in the world possesses even a single "supercarrier," there exists no real threat to any naval operation. Consequently, the suggestion that we increase the Navy's budget to allow the purchase of three additional "supercarriers" is absurd.

The first sentence presents a miniargument with both a conclusion and evidence:

> **Evidence:** No one else has a supercarrier.
> **Conclusion:** No one can threaten our naval operations.

This conclusion is itself used as evidence for the argument's final conclusion:

> **Evidence:** No one can threaten our naval operations.
> **Conclusion:** We shouldn't buy three new supercarriers.

If you're having trouble sorting evidence from conclusion because it seems like two different parts are being explained by evidence, you're likely facing a complex argument with a nested structure.

COMMON WRONG ANSWER TRICKS AND TRAPS FOR ARGUMENT STRUCTURE QUESTIONS

There are always four wrong choices and one right choice; those four wrong choices display patterns of their own specific to each type of question. For Structure Family questions, whose answer choices tend to be abstract descriptions that are very similar from answer choice to answer choice, these tend to be the most common ways that wrong answers are constructed:

MISPLACED DETAIL—An element that is a feature of one part of the argument is used to describe the wrong part, usually a distraction written in language that is very similar to the actual language in the passage.

REASONABLE BUT WRONG—When an argument is confusing, unwary test takers gravitate toward descriptions that are sensible and easy to understand but don't correspond to the text of the argument. Beware of this "default answer choice." In structure questions, the reasonable but wrong answer choice is usually a description of the sort of argument that tends to be made when this subject is brought up but that isn't actually made in the prompt.

For example, an argument's subject might be global warming, and a tempting trap might say that the argument *seeks to establish the extent to which humans contribute to temperature change*, when the actual argument was just a debate over the applicability of one specific case to one specific principle.

EXACT OPPOSITE—This is perhaps the most frustrating trap to fall for. The conclusion was that a rule *should not* be applied, but you end up picking the answer choice that says that the rule *should* be applied. Often, these answer choices will use the language that "sounds better" than the real answer choice, which uses obfuscating synonyms that are nevertheless correct descriptions of what has occurred in the argument.

BUT FOR ONE WORD—A lot of answer choices that are **exact opposites** would qualify for this category as well (the tricky *no* or *not* you missed), but there are also answers that line up all the pieces correctly only to misdescribe a single element of the argument. For example, you might be looking for "The author uses a counterexample to disprove a suggested interpretation" and pick instead "The author employs a counter*conclusion* to disprove one interpretation of a given set of facts." But for the word *counterconclusion*, this answer would have been right.

HALF-RIGHT/HALF-WRONG—You see this trap in **bolded statement** questions most often. The first part of the answer choice correctly describes the first bolded statement and describes it in the way that feels most natural, the likely phrasing of a concept—but the description of the second statement goes off the rails. The test maker is counting on your having an "Aha!" moment when you read the first half, such a strong "Aha!" that you don't bother to read the full answer.

So read the full answer!

II. THE ARGUMENT ASSUMPTION FAMILY OF QUESTIONS

Anatomy of an Argument Assumption Question

Prompt

The most famous protagonists in literature have always been at odds with societal norms, but it has been increasingly fashionable for postcolonial literature to glorify these iconoclastic protagonists much more than any previous genre of literature has. By presenting these characters as being worthy of emulation, postcolonial authors subtly endorse their outsider ethos and may convince their readers to adopt it. Thus, postcolonial literature can be harmful to at least some of its readers, and thereby to society itself.

Stem

Which of the following is an assumption on which the argument above depends?

Answer Choices

(A) Some protagonists from earlier literature were better role models than any found in postcolonial literature.

(B) It is beneficial for some readers to avoid adopting an outsider ethos or to avoid emulating iconoclasts.

(C) Postcolonial protagonists who adopt an outsider ethos will harm readers more now than if they did not adopt that ethos.

(D) The aesthetic merit of some literary works cannot be judged without considering their moral implications.

(E) Postcolonial literature presents a greater number of outsider characters than did the literature of earlier eras.

Prompt

- All contain an **argument** that has a specific **conclusion** and one or more pieces of **evidence**.
- You can usually trust a *thus* or *therefore* will point to the actual conclusion.
- Usually there's only one speaker in the prompt, although about a third of the time there's still a "those who say" that the speaker opposes.

Stem

- Look for *assumption* or an obvious stand-in like *unstated premise* paired with *required, necessary,* or *underlies.*

Answer Choices

- The answers to Assumption questions tend to bounce around from topic to topic; there's often no major theme or splits to grab onto. Prephrasing becomes key.

Assumption Questions

Mastering the **Assumption** family of **Argument-Based** questions begins with the "pure" **Assumption** question, which asks you to recognize in the answer choices something that must be true if the argument in the prompt is taken to be valid.

IDENTIFYING ASSUMPTION QUESTIONS

A few examples of the way a "pure" **Assumption** question might be phrased:

- The argument depends on which of the following assumptions?
- Which of the following is an assumption made in drawing the conclusion above?
- The argument presupposes

PROCESSING THE ASSUMPTION PROMPT

Question 8 from your Diagnostic Quiz was an Assumption question, so let's practice with it. Begin by locating the conclusion. As you probably remember, in this prompt, the conclusion keyword *Thus* points the way:

> [. . .] postcolonial literature can be harmful to at least some of its readers, and thereby to society itself.

Notice the ways in which the conclusion is **qualified**. The speaker doesn't claim that postcolonial literature is *always* harmful or that it harms *every* reader, just that it *can* be harmful to *some*. When a conclusion is qualified, there's almost certainly going to be some answer choices that are wrong because they're too **extreme**, offering us information that goes further than what we'd absolutely need in order to prove the modest *some* and *can*.

Now we take stock of the argument's evidence. When you're in the hunt for an argument's assumptions, always read the evidence with the conclusion in mind. Doing so here reveals that most of the argument is just **setup** information. We're told how literature *usually* works, and that's contrasted with how postcolonial literature works. A lot of specialized humanities major jargon gets tossed around. But we're not given much evidence for the argument's conclusion.

If we remember that the conclusion was not "postcolonial literature is the worst genre of literature ever," we can breeze over the comparison in the evidence, as we don't need information about postcolonial literature's relationship to modern literature. That is pure **setup information.** We do need to know why postcolonial literature is harmful, however. So what do we learn about postcolonial literature from the evidence? First, we learn that

> it has been increasingly fashionable for postcolonial litera-
> ture to glorify these iconoclastic protagonists

and that

> postcolonial authors subtly endorse their outsider ethos

This is all well and good, but where's the harm? If the argument's conclusion is to be believed, *something* that postcolonial literature does has to harm its readers. But we're not told directly that either of these things is harmful. So does postcolonial literature do anything else?

> and may convince their readers to adopt it.

OK, postcolonial literature *may* convince people to act like protagonists from postcolonial literature. But where's the harm in that? It turns out that no harm is ever given, and thus we've found the gap between evidence and conclusion.

PREPHRASING AND PREDICTING ASSUMPTIONS

The speaker never told us *why* postcolonial literature is harmful. Thus, the speaker's assumptions must include

> ✔ At least one of the things that postcolonial literature
> does—glorifying protagonists, endorsing their "outsider
> ethos" (whatever that is), getting people to emulate
> them, etc.—can harm readers.

Otherwise, the evidence that postcolonial literature does those things would be irrelevant to the argument's conclusion.

ATTACKING THE ANSWERS

Because of our specific prediction, as we read the answers, we'd be looking for the *harm* connection that the evidence never made. If an answer choice doesn't mention *harm*, it's probably not the right answer—like Answer Choices (A), (D), and (E).

As it turns out, only Answer Choice (C) uses the word *harm* itself, but it is not the right answer. Rather, it's a clever trap meant for people reading *solely* for the word *harm*.

If we look at the rest of the answer choice, we can see that it's confusing a detail from the evidence with the conclusion. The conclusion was not that postcolonial literature is "more harmful than ever" or "more harmful than anything" or even "more harmful than other types of literature." Instead, it was the qualified "postcolonial literature *can* harm." Answer Choice (C) would only be relevant to those more extreme conclusions.

The right answer, Answer Choice (B), addresses harm in a sneaky way, the **double-negative**. Instead of saying that acting like a postcolonial protagonist is bad, the answer says that *avoiding* acting like one is *good*. Untangle the double negative knot and we end up with what we wanted.

If it's good to avoid acting like them, it's *not* good to *not* avoid acting like them—thus, it's bad to act like them, exactly what we predicted.

IDENTIFYING ASSUMPTIONS

Ironically, the main reason that finding an argument's assumptions can be difficult is that, as reasonable people, we fill in the holes in an argument that makes no sense with reasonable information. Suppose someone were to come up to you in the hall at work and tell you that

> Anna is going to be fired tomorrow because Imran saw her stealing from the supply cabinet.

Though you might not necessarily think, "Oh, this person is making an argument," they are.

Conclusion:	Anna is going to be **fired** tomorrow.
	because
Evidence:	Imran saw her **stealing** from the supply cabinet.

Seems reasonable, right? Stealing is often the sort of thing that makes a company unhappy with you, and unhappy companies tend to fire employees. But the evidence did not explicitly tell us those things—we *assumed* that they were true because if they weren't, the person coming to us in the hallway would be kind of crazy to conclude that Anna's getting fired.

Put simply, then, assumptions are everything that needs to be true so that the person making the argument isn't crazy.

Technique #4: Look for the Three Main Types of Assumptions

We can divide these "non-crazy-making-things" into three basic categories: Connecting Assumptions, Defending Assumptions, and Feasibility Assumptions. When in doubt, use these three categories as a quick checklist of items an argument needs to assume in order for it to be valid.

CONNECTING ASSUMPTIONS

If an argument is valid, the reasons given as evidence are directly relevant to the conclusion. But unless an argument is just a tautology, there will be *some* difference between what the evidence states and what the conclusion claims. For Imran and Anna:

Conclusion:	Anna is going to be **fired** tomorrow.
Evidence:	Imran saw her **stealing** from the supply cabinet.
Assumption:	Stealing results in firing. (There is a connection between **stealing** and **firing**.)

Thus, when you are analyzing an argument in an Assumption family question, look carefully at the terms used in the conclusion and those used in the evidence. If they differ (and they usually will), then the argument assumes a connection between them.

DEFENDING ASSUMPTIONS

We defined arguments originally as "a series of connected statements that demonstrate the truth of a proposition." Connecting assumptions fill in the gaps where a connection is left unstated. Conversely, defending assumptions protect the connections against possible objections or weaknesses.

For example, if it's true that Anna is going to be fired because Imran saw her stealing, it needs to be the case that not only is stealing a fire-able offense, but also that Anna is the sort of employee who can get fired. There's nothing *special* about Anna that might protect her from what is generally the case.

Assumption:	Anna isn't exempt from normal rules about firing.

The test maker will generally test these assumptions by presenting specific scenarios in which the assumption would be tested and then ruling them out.

> Anna is not the only one at the company who can make firing decisions.

> Anna is not the daughter of a boss who never fires family members.

> If this is Anna's first offense, there is no "free pass" given to first-time offenders.

Defending assumptions also cover all the things that might render a piece of evidence irrelevant to the specific case at hand. For example, even if it's true that stealing does get you fired at this company and even if it's true that Anna is fire-able, we still need to assume that

> Whoever does the firing at this company knows about what Imran saw.

If Imran never told anyone and is the only person who knows about what happened that day at the supply cabinet, then it doesn't matter whether stealing is punishable by firing.

FEASIBILITY ASSUMPTIONS

Feasibility assumptions concern unstated facts about the scenario presented that would make the argument possible. For example, if it's true that Anna is going to be fired **tomorrow**, then we must assume

> Anna is still working at the company today.

If Anna has already been fired for some other offense, then the argument that she'll be fired tomorrow is incorrect. In the same vein, we also must assume that

> Anna won't be fired tomorrow for cooking the books instead of stealing.

Remember, conclusions and arguments are not the same thing. If we found out that Anna is being fired for some reason other than what Imran saw, the argument that she'll be fired for stealing is incorrect. That argument's conclusion *is* correct, however. Anna's still getting fired. But the evidence presented in the original case does not explain why the conclusion is true anymore, so the argument based on that evidence is wrong.

Technique #5: The Denial Test

An assumption is something that MUST BE TRUE if the argument as a whole is true. Therefore, if you are uncertain about whether an answer choice contains something that MUST BE TRUE, you can ask yourself, "What if this answer choice *wasn't* true?"

Remember our argument about postcolonial protagonists?

> The most famous protagonists in literature have always been at odds with societal norms, but it has been increasingly fashionable for postcolonial literature to glorify these iconoclastic protagonists much more than any previous genre of literature has. By presenting these characters as being worthy of emulation, postcolonial authors subtly endorse their outsider ethos and may convince their readers to adopt it. Thus, postcolonial literature can be harmful to at least some of its readers, and thereby to society itself.

If we can deny the answer choice, and yet the argument can still work, that answer choice is not an assumption required for the argument. Consider tricky Answer Choice (C):

> Postcolonial protagonists who adopt an outsider ethos will harm readers more now than if they did not adopt that ethos.

What if that *wasn't* the case? Indeed, what if the *opposite* were the case? What if postcolonial protagonists who adopt an outsider ethos (whatever that is) don't harm readers *more*? What if they just harmed them *some*?

The argument's conclusion was that postcolonial literature *sometimes* harms its readers. If (C) is not true, then, the readers still get harmed *some*. The argument can survive even when the opposite of Answer Choice (C) is true, so (C) fails the test. It's not required for the argument to be true, so it's not an assumption in the argument.

III. VARIATIONS ON ASSUMPTION QUESTIONS

The other five questions in the Assumption Family still require you to understand what the argument's assumptions are, but each goes one step further than the "pure" Assumption question and asks you to do a different thing with the assumptions you've found.

Weaken questions ask you to make the argument worse, which means making an assumption on which the argument relies less likely to be true.

Strengthen questions are **Weaken**'s evil twins: find the answer choice that makes an assumption *more likely*. Note that neither requires you to absolutely prove or disprove the assumption, only to make it better or worse.

Evaluate questions are a little bit Weaken and a little bit Strengthen. The correct answer frames a question that, if it came out one way, would make an assumption more likely but, if it came out another, would make the assumption less likely. Still, these are Assumption Family questions because the only questions relevant to evaluating an argument are those questions that address the argument's assumptions. On the same note, **Flaw** questions ask you to find a problem in the argument's reasoning, but the only problems with reasoning found on the GMAT are problems with an argument's unstated assumptions—something was assumed that shouldn't have been.

And, finally, **Complete (Evidence)** questions ask you to fill in the blank with the answer choice that most logically completes the argument. On the GMAT, arguments are made more complete by providing additional evidence that *confirms* an unstated assumption.

Identifying the Question Type

It is important that you be able to distinguish these questions from one another, as the right answer to a **Weaken** question will be the wrong answer to a **Strengthen**, and so forth.

WEAKEN QUESTIONS

There are only a few ways to phrase a **Weaken** question stem, and almost all of them use that very word, *weaken*. Very rarely, the test maker will substitute *casts serious doubt* or *calls into question*.

Thus, you'll see stems like:

- Which of the following, if true, would most weaken the conclusion drawn above?
- Which of the following, if true about home heating costs, casts the most serious doubt on the conclusion drawn above?

STRENGTHEN QUESTIONS

A few examples of **Strengthen** stems:

- Which of the following, if true, most helps to justify Senior Calzoncillos's position?

- Which of the following, if true, would provide the most support for the prediction that bond prices will fall?
- Which of the following, if true, provides the strongest grounds for the doctors' conclusion?

EVALUATE QUESTIONS

Evaluate questions ask you what would be *most useful* to *determine*, *assess*, and *evaluate* arguments. Look for stems like these:

- Which of the following would be most important to know in determining whether Councilman Jamm's plan, if implemented, is likely to achieve its goal?
- In assessing the likelihood of the prediction given above, it would be most useful to know which of the following?
- In evaluating the argument, it would be most useful to compare . . .

COMPLETE (EVIDENCE) QUESTIONS

The stems for these questions are always found above the prompt and will look something like these:

- Which of the following most logically completes the passage?
- Which of the following most logically completes the argument?
- Which of the following best completes the passage below?

The trick with these is making sure not to mistake them for **Complete (Conclusion)** questions. Look for the **evidence keyword** in front of the blank (or nearby).

FLAW QUESTIONS

You'll never see *if true* in a **Flaw** question stem because the flaw is present in the text **as written**. No additional information is needed to indicate that the argument is flawed. Contrast this with the **Weaken** question, which always includes *if true*, as the argument is not necessarily bad as written.

Common **Flaw** stems include:

- The argument is flawed primarily because the author . . .
- The argument is most vulnerable to which of the following criticisms?

Occasionally, the stem will contain an indication of what the flaw actually is.

- The cheerleader's argument is flawed because it fails to consider the possibility that . . .
- The argument above is vulnerable to the criticism that the rule provided . . .

Technique #6: Use the Common Argument Patterns for Assumption Questions

Content is never king on the GMAT. The structure and function of the pieces of information are far more important to finding the right answer than the content itself. Consider these two arguments:

The city council of Bellville has enacted a new ordinance allowing police officers to issue a ticket for loitering to anyone lingering longer than five minutes outside a storefront. We can expect a general decrease in crime to follow, as vagrants will now have less opportunity to commit street crimes such as mugging or vandalism.

When salmon migrate from ocean to fresh water, they make a transition between environments few other aquatic species can manage. Significant energy resources are invested swimming upstream, and the salmon that mate after migration ultimately die. Yet the practice is to the species' advantage overall, as it allows the salmon to lay their eggs in streams unmolested by predators that threaten them in the ocean.

But for the content, they are essentially the same argument, a **net benefit** calculation: on balance, doing a thing would offer more good than harm (or harm than good). Consequently, you'll see big improvements in your GMAT Verbal subscore if you can learn to see the basic structures of arguments and the patterns that recur across many different types of questions.

Obviously, since they ask you *directly* about an argument's structure, this skill is most vital in tackling Structure family questions, but the Assumption family draws heavily on it as well. If you recognize a common pattern to the evidence and conclusion, it is often a shortcut to the argument's assumptions.

PATTERN #1: THE APPLIED RULE

Evidence:	A general rule.	All men are mortal.
	A specific case.	Socrates is a man.
Conclusion:	The rule applied to the case.	Socrates is mortal.

In these arguments, the evidence will do two things: (1) present a **general rule** and (2) establish that there is a **specific case** to which the rule is said to apply—not necessarily in that order.

Granted, the test maker can sneak a rule into the evidence in a lot of ways so that it might not always feel "rule-like" on first reading. But the pattern is possible any time an argument presents evidence establishing either (1) a **guarantee** that something will happen (or is true) if that thing means one criterion or (2) a **requirement** that something is needed for something else to happen (or to be true). For example:

> Works of art that are designed to appeal to the senses
> cannot be made with an eye toward the utility of the
> work. There is no work of art that has more visual impact
> than the ceiling of the Sistine Chapel. [. . .]

According to the **general rule** stated in the first sentence, if I show you something that we can agree is *a work of art designed to the appeal to the senses*, then we will also have to agree that that work couldn't have been *made with an eye toward utility*. (In other words, if you set out to make some pretty art, you can't also set out to make something useful.)

The second sentence presents a **specific case**: the Sistine Chapel. If we can agree that the Sistine Chapel fits the criteria of the rule, that it is *a work of art designed to appeal to the senses*, then clearly the rule's **application** must apply, and we could safely conclude that *the Sistine Chapel was not made with an eye toward its utility*. The conclusion that would be attached to our example evidence above would likely read:

> Therefore, no matter what the current use to which
> Michelangelo's masterpiece is put in the Apostolic Palace,
> that use was not part of his original artistic conception.

If this argument had appeared in a **Structure** family question like the **Method of Argument** question, we might expect the right answer to be something like

> It proceeds from a general principle to make a claim
> about what is necessarily true in a particular instance to
> which that principle applies.

If you recognized this pattern in an **Assumption** family question, you would instantly know at least one of the argument's assumptions. If the argument above were true, we would need to assume that

> ✔ having lots of "visual impact" is the same as being "designed to appeal to the senses," and

> ✔ an "original artistic conception" is the same as the "design" of a work of art.

And thus, the right answer to an Assumption question about what the argument depends upon might be

> If a goal is not one that an artist originally intended an artwork to meet, that goal cannot be said to be part of the artist's conception of the work.

Departing from the specifics of the argument above, we could say that the main assumption that all arguments that follow the **applied rule** pattern will assume is

> ✔ There is nothing **special about the case** that would keep the rule from applying or

> ✔ The rule applies to this case.

Thus, in **Weaken, Strengthen,** and **Evaluate** questions, correct answers would provide new information that addresses the link between case and rule, making it weaker, stronger, or just pointing out that it's an open question, respectively.

Flaw questions featuring invalid versions of this pattern usually involve someone mistaking a **guarantee** for a **requirement**.

> If all men are mortal, and my dog is not a man, he must not be mortal.

In other words, just because all men are mortal, it doesn't mean that men are the only things that are mortal. A possible correct phrasing for an answer choice pointing this out:

> (A) the argument treats a condition found among all members of a group as though it were exclusive to that group

You might also see a speaker sneakily swapping words as the argument moves from evidence to conclusion in a **Flaw** question, in essence assuming because a word sounds like another word or because two groups tend to be associated with each other that rules that apply to the first apply to the second:

> Car owners must register their cars with the city before they are allowed to park in this lot. Since many of the cars here clearly have expired registration stickers, their drivers should be ticketed.

In this case, the right answer could be that the argument is flawed because it

> (A) fails to establish that something true of one group is necessarily true of another.

The people who drove those cars are not necessarily the same people as the cars' owners.

PATTERN #2: CAUSE AND EFFECT

Evidence:	**correlation**:	1. X happened/is true	Fan sales rise during the summer.
		2. Y happened/is true	It is hot during the summer.
Conclusion:	**causation**:	3. X caused Y	The heat causes the increased fan sales.

From our discussion above, you already know that a **Causal Connection** is a type of conclusion. When you spot an argument concluding that something *is responsible for* something else or that one thing *brought about* another, you will find that the evidence is composed of two statements establishing only that two different things happened (or are true). The two events would be said to be **correlated**—they tend to happen at the same time or in the same place.

You've probably heard the maxim "correlation does not imply causation," often accompanied by a story like this one:

> According to folklore, there once was a czar who learned that the most disease-ridden province in his empire was also the province where the most doctors lived and worked. Accordingly, he ordered all doctors throughout his empire shot on sight in order to end the threat of plague once and for all.

Flaw questions often turn on "the czar's mistake," assuming that because there were more doctors in the diseased district (doctors and disease were correlated), it was the doctors who caused the spread of disease—and not that more doctors flocked to that district because of all the sick people to treat! Thus:

Which of the following best describes the error in the czar's reasoning?

(A) The evidence used to conclude one phenomenon is the cause of another is equally consistent with its occurrence being an effect of the other.

Certainly, there are cases where a causal connection is the likeliest explanation for two things occurring together, such as

Runners often report that a feeling of euphoria follows a long run. When runners experiencing this heightened sense of well-being have submitted to blood tests, those tests have revealed an unusually high concentration of endorphins to be present. Therefore, it is reasonable to believe that some cases of such euphoria are brought on by the release of chemicals in the brain.

The difference between the flawed argument and the convincing one all comes down to a matter of assumptions. Causal arguments all assume:

✔ There is no other factor that might have been the cause.

✔ There is a plausible mechanism by which the cause could have brought about the effect.

✔ The correlation between the cause and effect is not coincidental.

If all these considerations check out, then the argument for a causal connection is strong. Thus, each of these answer choices would **Weaken** the argument:

(A) Runners typically have heightened amounts of endorphins in their blood, as these chemicals are released when muscles regenerate from any sustained exercise.

(B) Blood tests also reveal that runners who experience euphoria following a run have unusually high concentrations of certain minerals and nonchemical agents in their bloodstream.

(C) Blood tests for endorphins are highly inaccurate.

(D) Throughout the day, the body's concentration of mood-altering chemicals fluctuates wildly, particularly in runners.

And this one would **Strengthen** it:

> (E) Runners who report never experiencing postrun euphoria have been shown in MRI tests to lack a particular receptor in the brain that mediates the effect of endorphins.

Similarly, an **Assumption** question's correct answer often states the assumption directly:

> (A) It is unlikely that a blood test would record high concentrations of a mood-altering chemical in the blood unless the person tested had recently experienced a change in mood.

Spot a **causal connection** as an argument's conclusion and you can be certain that you know at least three of its assumptions.

PATTERN #3: REPRESENTATIVENESS

Evidence:	Something is true of one party.	Toy poodles present no threat to children.
Conclusion:	The same thing is true of another.	Dogs make safe pets if you have children.

In these arguments, the evidence establishes that there is a quality that members of one group have, like *all dogs go to heaven* or *participants in the survey were more likely to report satisfaction*. From this, the argument concludes that some other group shares this quality—usually a larger group, and often the group extends to "*everybody*" or "*people in general*." Other times, the conclusion group is a group of one, a single individual.

Any time an argument relies on an analogy between two things or the similarity between two groups, or uses as its evidence a poll, a survey, an experiment, or some other way of measuring a big effect by looking only at specific cases, the argument will contain an assumption that

> ✔ the evidence group is not different from the conclusion group in a way that would be relevant to the specific quality being discussed.

Thus, a prompt built on this pattern might look like this:

> Children who live within easy walking distance of a well-maintained public playground are much more likely to be physically fit than those who must be driven to a playground further from their homes, according to a new study of children's fitness nationwide. Thus, in order to combat obesity in the very young, more playgrounds ought to be built.

Were the question attached to this prompt an **Assumption** question, this would be a credited response:

> (A) There are no other significant demographic differences between the two groups of children that would account for their differing levels of fitness.

We might **Strengthen** it by eliminating a possible difference, like

> (B) Neighborhoods with public playgrounds do not typically have more recreational sports leagues for children than those without.

And to **Weaken** it, we could point out a difference, such as

> (C) Most often, it is only young parents vigorous enough to engage with their children in physical activities that walk their children to public playgrounds.

If asked to identify the **Flaw**, we might well see:

> (D) The argument relies on the overall similarity of two groups not shown to be similar in all relevant respects

Polls and surveys are, in particular, sticking points in Critical Reasoning prompts. Because we all know that polls need to be conducted in such a way that no unintended bias creeps in, we may often suspect bias where there is no evidence of it.

Whenever we employ statistical methods to draw conclusions, it is true that we must assume many things about the polls or surveys employed if we're going to believe those conclusions.

> ✔ The sample size of the poll (or survey, etc., was large enough to draw conclusions from.

> ✔ The people selected for polling were selected in a random enough fashion to avoid bias.

But we must be careful on the GMAT that we don't assume things about answer choices that they don't say. Suppose you saw an answer choice in a Flaw question that said

> (A) Because of the risk to participants' lives, only a dozen
> patients were involved in the clinical trial.

You might be tempted to choose it, as 12 doesn't sound like a very big sample size. But the keyword in each of the assumptions above is *enough*. The poll must be large *enough*, and random *enough*. You're not allowed to use outside information to make decisions in Critical Reasoning, and the answer choice doesn't explicitly tell you that 12 is not big *enough* to draw conclusions. Thus, it would NOT be the credited answer.

When the GMAT tests these two assumptions, they have to be very specific in their wording so that the *enough* is buried in there somewhere.

> (B) The incidence of the disease is one per ten thousand
> individuals, requiring at least one hundred trials to
> evaluate the vaccine's efficacy reliably.

The same goes for the original assumption, that the two groups are similar *enough with respect to the quality in question*. If you don't spot the *enough*, then just any old difference between the two groups is not sufficient to strengthen, weaken, or evaluate. In our original playground question, this would NOT be a credited answer:

> (E) Families that live near public playgrounds tend to be
> poorer, on average, than those who live farther away.

Sounds reasonable, right? But the answer choice never hints at why wealth might affect a child's physical fitness, unlike the *recreational sports league* or the *young parents* who engage in other *physical* activities with their children. Thus, there's no way for you to know what effect wealth would have on the children's levels of physical fitness.

Just think, wealthy parents might be able to afford better coaches for their kids, but they also might tend to keep their children quiet by feeding them lots of expensive sweets and plying them with video games and other sedentary activities.

Finally, there's one special flavor of the **representativeness** pattern that often slips under the test taker's radar: **predictions**. Whenever you make a claim about what will happen in the future based on evidence about what has happened in the past, you are making a kind of **representativeness assumption**, namely, that

> ✔ things that are true of the past can be taken as representative of things that will be true of the future.

Or put another way, you assume

> ✔ nothing on which the prediction is based will change materially in the future.

or

> ✔ the future will resemble the past in all relevant ways.

Thus, credited answer choices for questions involving a prediction often introduce information that indicates that the future will or won't resemble the past in some important way.

And don't forget, **plans** and **proposals** are often themselves claims about what *will* work or what *should* be done in the future—they're predictions, too! Thus, these arguments likewise assume that the conditions that the plan or proposal was built to address won't change in some material way in the future.

PATTERN #4: NET BENEFIT/NET HARM

Evidence:	Some **advantages** and **disadvantages**, **harms** and **benefits**, **costs** and **savings**, etc.	This brand of tuna is much cheaper than the one we currently eat.
Conclusion:	Something, on balance, is **good** or **bad**.	We will save money if we switch to it.

This is in all likelihood the most common argument pattern on the test. Remember the example we began with?

> The city council of Bellville has enacted a new ordinance allowing police officers to issue a ticket for loitering to anyone lingering longer than five minutes outside a storefront. We can expect a general decrease in crime to follow, as vagrants will now have less opportunity to commit street crimes such as mugging or vandalism.

The evidence in this argument is that **one factor** that contributes to crime **has been reduced** by the plan; therefore, the plan will bring about an **overall reduction**. But what about all the other factors that might increase or decrease crime? Will they remain the same? We must assume they will. Indeed, all arguments that fit this pattern must assume

> ✔ the thing said to be beneficial or harmful will not **indirectly** cause a harm or benefit that **outweighs** its stated effect.

Consider this the old law of unintended consequences. What if we found out, for instance,

> (A) Vagrants who usually spend their time loitering will, when unable to do so, often engage in criminal activity.

Exactly. The argument would be **Weakened**. On the other hand, we can **Strengthen** such an argument by eliminating a possible side effect that would **change the balance** between the plan's advantages and any possible disadvantages.

> (B) Reducing the number of people on the street outside a business will not make that business more likely to be the target of an armed robbery.

What does *armed robbery* have to do with anything? It's a crime that might have increased due to one of the effects of the new loitering law. Since the stated prediction was that crime would go down, any crime is within the argument's **scope**.

The pattern of a **net benefit** or a **net harm** can be found attached to virtually any type of conclusion, so in most arguments, we should be on the lookout for indirect effects that are clearly relevant to the goals stated by the speaker or the benefit said to accrue from a plan.

Patterns of Flawed Reasoning

Valid arguments are not the only commonly repeated patterns. We often see the same *invalid* argument patterns again and again as well. Part of the challenge of **Flaw** questions is lining up the way the answer choice describes a flaw with the way you typically phrase it when you spot it. As you work practice questions, take note of the different ways each flaw is phrased from question to question.

CONFUSING CORRELATION AND CAUSATION

(See Causal Arguments on page 269.)

As we've discussed, just because two things *happen around the same time, tend to be true of the same group*, or are otherwise *correlated* does not mean that one thing is responsible for the other. It could be coincidence, or it could be some other factor.

CONFUSING NECESSITY AND SUFFICIENCY

Necessity and **sufficiency** describe the two ways that a pair of things or ideas can be linked conditionally. Some examples of statements expressing **necessity** would include: ·

> The car needs gas to run.
> (Gas is **necessary** for the car to run.)
>
> Without a credit score of 700, you will not be approved.
> (The credit score is **necessary** for approval.)
>
> You cannot be a man unless you are mortal.
> (Mortality is a **necessary** quality of men.)

And some sufficient statements:

> If you goof off, you won't improve.
> (Goofing off is **sufficient** to ensure no improvement.)
>
> Every good boy does fine.
> (Being a good boy is **sufficient** to know that someone is a good boy.)
>
> When you buy S-Mart, you know you're buying quality.
> (Knowing something came from S-Mart is **sufficient** to know it is of high quality.)

All sufficient statements can be rewritten as necessary statements, and vice versa.

> If your car has no gas, it definitely won't run.
> (A lack of gas is **sufficient** to keep a car from running.)
>
> You cannot be a good boy unless you do fine.
> (Doing fine is **necessary** in order to be a good boy.)

You have to be careful when changing a sufficient statement into a necessary one. The two ways a flawed argument could mess this up:

1. Assuming that because something is a requirement for an event, once the requirement is met, the event has to happen.

> You cannot vote until you turn 18. But not every 18 year old
> can vote.
> (Some aren't registered; being 18 is not the only requirement,
> nor is it a guarantee you can vote.)

2. Assuming that because one way of doing something definitely brings about a result, it's the only thing that can bring that result about.

> Everybody who entered the race got a tee shirt. Paul has a
> tee shirt, but that doesn't mean he entered the race.
> (Maybe some shirts are sold to nonracers; entering the
> race wasn't required for the tee shirt.)

CONFUSING PERCENTS AND TOTAL NUMBERS

Math, on the Verbal? Yes indeed. In **Flaw** questions, most often a rise or fall in the percentage of something (or the probability or risk) is taken as evidence that the overall amount of something rose or fell.

For example, you pour 8 ounces of coffee into a mug and add 2 tablespoons of cream, then later add another tablespoon of cream and another 10 ounces of coffee to the same mug. The amount of cream has increased, but the percentage of cream has decreased.

CONFUSING ONE THING FOR ANOTHER (AKA THE SCOPE SHIFT)

(See Representativeness on page 271.)

Whenever the evidence asserts a fact about one sort of thing, but the conclusion is drawn about some other related thing, it's possible that the two things aren't, in fact, similar at all, or at least not similar in the way that the argument's conclusion claims. You often see this problem crop up when a representativeness assumption is present, but that's not the only way it might arise.

For example: *Gold is a good investment because gold has never been worth zero.* This argument takes "never being worth zero" as essentially the same thing as "being a good investment." But—regardless of what infomercials on cable news might tell you—there's a world of difference between the two. If gold used to be worth $1,000 an ounce and has lost a couple of cents of value every decade or so, it's still true that it's never been worth zero, but such depreciation isn't the sign of a good investment.

CONFUSING THE POSSIBLE WITH THE INEVITABLE

An argument's evidence establishes reasonably that something *can* happen, but the conclusion is that it will *definitely* happen. For example, just because the lottery ticket ensures you have a chance of winning, that doesn't mean you're definitely going to win. Just because rain might break the drought, that doesn't mean that when it rains your water woes are over.

You could consider this flaw a subset of the previous two, as it is one way you could confuse necessity and sufficiency (i.e., something being possible is necessary for it to happen, but not sufficient to know it will happen), and it is also a way you could confuse one thing (possibility) with another (inevitability).

CONFUSING A BAD ARGUMENT WITH A FALSE CONCLUSION

As you no doubt remember, there is a difference between an argument for something being true and whether it is actually true or not.

For example, you might see that your friend's car is in the driveway and take that as evidence that your friend didn't go to work. If you later discover that your friend never drives to work, your argument for his being at home was a bad argument, but he might still have been at home that day. Maybe he was sick.

To borrow an old saying, *The absence of evidence is not evidence of absence.* Just because we have no reason to believe that Santa Claus is real doesn't mean he's definitely imaginary. He might exist, even if no one has ever seen him.

IV. FACT-BASED QUESTIONS

Anatomy of a Fact-Based Question

Prompt

Ironically, George Lucas's reputation as an artist has been hindered by the very technology that makes his films so dazzling. Many of the theaters that play his films lack top-of-the-line projection machinery. Such machinery is absolutely vital to the full display of Lucas's artistic skill.

Stem

Which one of the following can be properly inferred from the statements above?

Answer Choices

(A) Some theaters that play Lucas's films provide support for Lucas's reputation as an artist.

(B) All theaters that play Lucas's films and that possess top-of-the-line projection machinery display Lucas's artistic skill fully.

(C) All of the showings of Lucas's films that do not display his full artistic skill lack top-of-the-line projection machinery.

(D) If a theater possesses top-of-the-line projection facilities, it will provide a full display of an artist's skill.

(E) At least some of the theaters that play Lucas's films fail to display fully Lucas's skills as an artist.

Prompt
- There is more variation in Fact-Based prompts than Argument-Based prompts.
- Some are as short as a line and a half; others are quite long.

Stem
- Instead of using the word argument, stems often describe the prompt as "the passage" or "the statements."
- **Explain** and **Inference** questions work in opposite directions. Explain adds to the prompt; Inference deduces from it.

Answer Choices
- Pay attention to words that indicate that facts are qualified or extreme.
- Double-check the language of the answer choice to make sure you aren't glossing over a small detail.

Identifying Fact-Based Questions

Inference questions account for all but a tiny slice of the remaining Critical Reasoning questions, and they also show up among the Reading Comprehension questions.

Remember the test maker's definition of inference, which is something that **MUST BE TRUE** on the basis of some specific, definite piece of information. *Might be true, could be true,* and *really, really, really likely to be true* don't make the inference cut.

Complete (Conclusion) questions are just another form of **Inference**, as the only conclusion you are allowed to complete an argument with is one that is inferable (that MUST BE TRUE) from the facts presented.

For both, when you read the prompt, you are searching for the most definite, specific information present. Inferences come out of such information.

Explain questions rely on the same sorts of prompts—facts rather than arguments—but the task is different from that in **Inference** questions. Instead of adding the information in the prompt together to say what must be true, these questions ask you to add a piece of information *to* the prompt so that what seems like it can't possibly be true will be revealed to be sensible and sound.

As always, the stem will guide you. Possible stems for each follow.

INFERENCE QUESTIONS

- Which of the following conclusions can most properly be drawn from the information on the previous page?
- If the facts stated in the passage above are true, which of the following must be true on the basis of them?
- The claims above, if true, most strongly support which of the following conclusions?

COMPLETE (CONCLUSION) QUESTIONS

- The stems for these questions are always found above the prompt.
- Which of the following most logically completes the passage?
- Which of the following most logically completes the argument?
- Which of the following best completes the passage below?

Be sure not to mistake them for **Complete (Evidence)** questions. Look for the **conclusion keyword** in front of the blank (or nearby).

EXPLAIN QUESTIONS

- Which of the following, if true, most helps to explain the surprising finding?
- Which of the following, if true, does most to explain the phenomenon previously described?
- Which of the following, if true, best accounts for the race's anomalous results?

Processing the Prompts of Fact-Based Questions

In Argument-Based questions, your first step to untangling the prompt is to hunt for the conclusion. With Fact-Based questions, you're also on a hunt, just for different things.

INFERENCE PROMPTS

We begin with **Inference** questions, which require you to find the "most inference-y part" of the prompt—the definite rule, the principle, the thing that is *always true*, etc. The more you practice with Official Guide or GMATPrep questions, the more you will come to appreciate the way that the test maker sets up an inference question.

Technique #7: Recognize the Common Inference Keys

The content of an Inference prompt may vary, but there are certain things you learn to recognize as the test maker's way of saying "Hey, look here, we're going to build an Inference on this!"

INFERENCE PATTERN #1: UNTANGLE THE DOUBLE NEGATIVES

The test maker loves hiding information under tortuously constructed double negatives. Or perhaps we should say instead, the test maker doesn't not love hiding it there.

Thus, you might see something like this in an Inference prompt:

No one is incapable of everything.

What can you infer from that? Well, if *no one* is *incapable of everything*, then everyone (the opposite of no one) must be capable (i.e., not *incapable*) of something. Notice that negatives can be found both in little words like *no*, *not*, *nor*, and *none*, but also *inside* words through prefixes like *in-*, *un-*, and *im-*.

Combine the two, and you end up with all kinds of places in which to hide inferences.

> If everything that is not material is imperfect, then it's also true that everything that is immaterial is not perfect, and also that nothing that is not material lacks perfection.

INFERENCE PATTERN #2: KEEP TRACK OF "SO AND SO" AND "SUCH AND SUCH"

Another way to hide an inference is to separate two facts about the same thing in different parts of the prompt. The prompt starts out by talking about one thing:

> The detention of hostile combatants without specific charge has become commonplace during the modern struggle against fanaticism [. . .]

Then it switches gears to something else.

> [. . .] Throughout the era following the first two World Wars, nations generally fought other nations, rather than disparate loosely affiliated groups united only by ideology. [. . .]

Then sneakily switch back to the first topic.

> [. . .] These new methods, their proponents contend, are justified by the same principles that allow for nations to combat each other.

Take piece A and piece C, put them together, and you have the credited answer to an Inference question.

> (A) Established principles allow for some to defend the practice of detention even when that detention is not accompanied by a formal charge.

Kind of silly, right? Just remember that the right answer to an Inference question must be 100 percent justified, not merely likely or sensible. The test maker's hands are bound by this limitation, so he or she has to resort to some pretty silly tactics to cloud your ability to see the credited answer.

Thus, look for demonstrative pronouns like *this, that,* and *these,* along with place holder words like *such, one, it, there,* or the *latter* and the *former.* Trace the pronoun back to its referent and you'll often have your Inference.

INFERENCE PATTERN #3: GROUP INFORMATION BY CATEGORY

Names are important. Sometimes, you're given two names for the same concept. Other times, you're told that two concepts can both be described by a single named. Either way, keeping track of what details are said to be true of which concepts is often the key to another sort of Inference. For example:

> Disruptive thinking challenges the status quo by
> advocating for change; some disruptive thinkers work
> within existing institutions, others from without.
> Regardless, in their efforts to bring about a new social
> consciousness, those intellectual elites who would break
> with the establishment are aided by the public's growing
> consensus that institutions no longer work as they should.

Keep track of which group is which. Here, we have one group, *disruptive thinkers*, who can also be called *intellectual elites* and *people who break with establishment*. That group is further subdivided into two groups, those who work *within* institutions, and those who work *outside* them. Nothing is told to us about the individual halves; rather, another two facts are added to the original group: they *try to bring about a new social consciousness* and when they do, they're *aided by the public's consensus that institutions are broken*.

The difference between a correct inference

> (A) The success of disruptive thinkers outside an institution
>   can be influenced by attitudes toward that institution.

and an incorrect one

> (B) The public's distrust of institutions allows disruptive
>   thinkers to form a consensus for social change.

is just lining up the details with the right party.

INFERENCE PATTERN #4: BUT THAT'S TOO OBVIOUS!

Take a look back at Answer Choice (A) above and notice how modest the claim contained in it is. Success *can* be influenced—not *will*, not *is always*, not *is never*, merely *can*. Sometimes Inference prompts contain little to no definite information, no rules, no conditional statements, nothing that will allow an impressive inference to be drawn.

In those cases—when the Inference prompt lacks concrete, definite information—the correct answer is most often phrased very weakly.

(A) The atmosphere plays **some role** in the transmission of radio waves.
(B) The success of a venture is determined, **in part**, by factors beyond a capitalist's control.
(C) The ultimate temperature reached by a chemical reaction **is influenced by** the permeability of the outer valence.
(D) Cholesterol **plays a part** in blood pressure assessment.
(E) **At least one** of the factors that **contribute** to a gene's expression occurs after the organism has developed.

INFERENCE PATTERN #5: INFERRING THE CONTRAPOSITIVE (FORMAL LOGIC PART 1)

We've told you throughout this chapter that you are not required to understand the complicated or arcane rules that logicians and philosophy professors concern themselves with, and we stand by that. The most complicated logical principle you're ever asked to handle on the GMAT is the sort of thing that's covered during the first week of a Symbolic Logic or Formal Logic class.

There is one problem, though: humans are not, as a species, particularly good at Formal Logic. Psychologists even have a little experiment they've run that shows just how poorly we do with it. It's called the "Wason Selection Task." Suppose, just for the sake of this example, that you have a deck of cards. On one side of each card, there's a letter of the English alphabet printed. On the other side of each card, there's a single digit number from 0 to 9.

Now, suppose that someone told you, "All the cards that have a vowel (A, E, I, O, or U) on one side have an even number (0, 2, 4, 6, or 8) on the opposite side." Then this person proceeded to deal out four cards in front of you, like so:

Which of the four cards would you need to flip over in order to determine whether the deck follows this supposed rule?

Only about 10% of those tested correctly identify the cards that need to be flipped.

- ✔ **The "A" card**—definitely needs to be flipped. If there's a 3 on the other side of that card, the deck isn't following the rule that "all cards with a vowel have an even number on the opposite side."
- ✗ **The "K" card**—definitely does NOT need to be flipped. The rule doesn't say anything about consonants. They can have even or odd numbers on the other side.
- ✗ **The "2" card**—also does NOT need to be flipped. The rule doesn't say that even numbers are ONLY found with vowels, just that vowels always have even numbers on the other side.
- ✔ **The "7" card**—This DOES need to be flipped. If we flip the card over and find an A or an E, that means that some vowels don't have even numbers on the other side—a violation of our rule!

To beat the test at its own game, we must learn how to work with **conditional statements,** which is to say, how to think in terms of what logicians would call **sufficiency** and **necessity**.

Sufficiency and necessity describe conditional relationships two things (or concepts) can have to each other.

sufficiency—X is sufficient for Y if the presence of X is a guarantee of Y occurring or being true, with no additional requirements.

necessity—X is necessary for Y if the presence of X is required for Y to occur, but does not on its own guarantee that Y will occur.

Examples of sufficient conditions in your everyday life:

A grade of B is sufficient to pass a logic course.
Throwing a vase off the Empire State Building is sufficient to break the vase.

Examples of necessary conditions, on the other hand:

Having a lottery ticket is necessary for winning the lottery.
Air is necessary for humans to continue living.
Being four feet tall is necessary for riding this roller coaster.

· In our card example, knowing that a card has a vowel on one side is **sufficient** to know that there is an even number on the other. Likewise, having an even number on the number-side is **necessary** for there to be a vowel on the letter-side.

Shorthand for Formal Logic

If we wanted to express the sufficient/necessary relationship in a formal sort of shorthand, we would place the sufficient condition on the left side of an arrow and the necessary condition on the right side.

Sufficient	$\rightarrow$	**Necessary**
Vowel	$\rightarrow$	**Even**

The reason we use such shorthand is to make it easy to see the **_logical implications_** of conditional statements. The main implication that we're interested in is what logicians call the **contrapositive**.

Consider the conditional statement "your car needs fuel in order to run." If we believe this, we must also agree with the statement "if your car has no fuel, then it will not run." The second statement is the **contrapositive** of the first

	Sufficient	$\rightarrow$	**Necessary**
Original	running	$\rightarrow$	fuel
Contrapositive	no fuel	$\rightarrow$	not running

If the positive is true, the contrapositive must also be true. Or, to put a finer point on it, they're the same statement just expressed two different but equally correct ways.

Transforming a simple conditional statement from its original version into the contrapositive (and back again), is a two-step process: (1) reverse the order the elements are written in, and (2) negate the elements. Thus:

	Sufficient		**Necessary**
Original:	If your car is running,		then it must have fuel.
	Run	$\rightarrow$	fuel
Step 1: Reverse	fuel	$\rightarrow$	running
Step 2: Negate	no fuel	$\rightarrow$	not running
Contrapositive:	If your car has no fuel,		then it must not be running.

Going back to our original example, if "Only cards with vowels on one side have even numbers on the other," then it is also true that "All cards that have an odd number on one side have consonants on the other."

	Sufficient	→	**Necessary**
Original	Vowel	→	Even
Contrapositive	Odd	→	Consonant
	(not Even	→	not Vowel)

This is why we had to flip over both the card with the vowel on it (the A card), and the card with the odd number (the 7 card), and why it didn't matter what was on the other side of the B or the 2.

Now, if the conditional statement is complicated—that is, if it includes more than two connected ideas—then a third step is added: (3) any "ands" become "ors" and any "ors" become "ands."

Here's a complicated formal logic statement:

Sufficient		**Necessary**
If you are not wearing shoes **or** not wearing a shirt,		then you will not be given service.
no shirt or no shoes	→	no service

To transform this complicated statement into its contrapositive, just follow the 3-step process:

Sufficient			**Necessary**
Positive:	If you are not wearing shoes **or** not wearing a shirt,		then you will not be given service.
	no shirt or no shoes	—	no service
Step 1: Reverse	*no Service*	→	*no shirt or no shoes*
Step 2: Negate	*service*	—	*shirt or shoes*
	(no no service)		*(no no shirt)* *(no no shoes)*
Step 3: Or/And	*service*	—	*shirt and shoes*
Contrapositive:	If you are getting service,		then you must be wearing a shirt AND shoes.

DRILL—FORMING CONTRAPOSITIVES

For each of the statements below, write the original and contrapositive in shorthand:

1. If there is an earthquake, then the Sears Tower will fall down.

2. If the glove fits, then we must acquit.

3. If you do not take the GMAT, then you will not get an MBA and you won't get this promotion.

DRILL REVIEW

1. earthquake → ST falls
   ST no fall → no earthquake

2. fits → acquit
   no acquit → no fit

3. no GMAT → no MBA AND no promotion
   MBA OR promotion → GMAT

Distinguishing Sufficient and Necessary Conditions

If you're given a conditional statement on the test, it's imperative that you be able to distinguish an expression of sufficiency from one of necessity.

If the test maker would always use the *if . . . then . . .* construction, then recognizing conditionals would be a lot easier. Alas, there are many ways to invoke a conditional relationship. Here are the most common:

If X, then Y.	$X \rightarrow Y$	If you call me, then I'll be there. If I didn't come, then you didn't call me.
When X, Y	$X \rightarrow Y$	When you call me, I'll be there. When I'm not there, you didn't call me.
Whenever X, Y	$X \rightarrow Y$	Whenever you call me, I'll be there. Whenever I'm not there, you didn't call me.

Every X is Y.	X → Y	Every owl is able to fly. Every flightless thing (e.g., my desk) is not an owl.
All Xs are Ys	X → Y	All owls are birds. All nonbirds (mammals, for example) are not owls.
People who X, Y	X → Y	People who like birds like cool things. People who don't like cool things don't like birds.
Only Xs are Ys	Y → X	Only people who are cool like birds. Only people who don't like birds aren't cool.
X, only if Y	X → Y	You are cool only if you like birds.
X must Y	X → Y	Legal drivers must have a current license. Drivers who don't have licenses must not be legal.
X is required for Y	Y → X	Being 18 is required for voting.
X, unless Y	X → no Y	I will go to the store, unless it rains.
Can't be X unless Y	X → Y	You can't be a legal driver unless you have a license.
X, except Y	X → no Y	People are terrible, except for children.
X until Y	Y → no X	You can talk until the bell rings.
No X without Y	X → Y	You can't do well without studying. You can't (always) avoid studying without (later) failing.

INFERENCE PATTERN #6: FORMAL LOGIC PART 2—CONNECTING CONDITIONALS

When two or more conditional statements appear in an Inference prompt, that's usually a clue that you should try to combine the two. For example:

> If it rains tomorrow, then the fair will be canceled. But since it's August, days when it doesn't rain are invariably so hot that cotton candy melts.

In shorthand, the statements and their contrapositives would look like this:

Rain → no Fair   no Rain → no Cotton Candy

Fair → no Rain   Cotton Candy → Rain

The necessary condition for one set becomes the sufficient condition for the other, and vice versa. Thus:

Fair → no Rain → no Cotton Candy

Cotton Candy → Rain → no Fair

What can we infer from these two linked conditionals? If the fair is open, then no one will be able to eat any cotton candy. Also, if people are able to eat cotton candy, they won't be eating it at the fair because the fair will be closed. Each way of phrasing this relationship between the fair and cotton candy is 100 percent true if the original two conditionals are true, the very definition of an Inference.

EXPLAIN PROMPTS

Even though Inference prompts and Explain prompts both contain information you are asked to treat as true at face value, what you do with that information differs greatly between the two. Remember, Explain questions ask you to *resolve* or *explain* an apparent dilemma. Your job when attacking these prompts will be to find the two "horns" of the dilemma. Called the "horns" from the idea that a bull has two horns, and the choice between being gored by one is no better than being gored by the other. After all, if you don't know what the two things that need to be brought together are, how are you ever going to find the answer that brings them together?

Technique #8: Finding the "Horns" of the Dilemma

Explain questions present you with all kinds of weird situations. The most common are:

THE RULE VIOLATION—The prompt presents two things: (1) a **general rule** and (2) a case that seems like the rule should be applied to it, but in which **the rule *seems* to be violated**. The correct answer will usually either show that the rule **doesn't actually apply** or that the violation is itself just **further demonstration** of the rule applying.

THE FLOUTED TREND—Similar to the rule violation, in these prompts (1) **a general trend** is cited but then (2) **a specific case** that seems **counter to the trend** is given. It, too, is usually solved by the introduction of information that shows that the trend **isn't relevant to this specific case**, or that, when another factor is considered, the specific case is just **further demonstration** of the general trend.

THE UNREALIZED EXPECTATION—These prompts present (1) an **expectation** or **prediction**, but then state that it (2) **never happened** or that the **opposite happened**. Usually, the right answer will show that the expectation was based on an **assumption that doesn't apply** in this case, sometimes by showing that there was an extra **unconsidered factor** that explains things.

THE REJECTED ADVICE—These prompts establish that, in general, (1) using **one strategy is a good idea**, but that some group or actor that has been given the facts has (2) **chosen otherwise**. These paradoxes are usually explained by answer choices that provide, again, an **unconsidered factor** that show that in *this case* the advice would be bad.

When you have identified an **Explain** question, read the prompt and then try to rephrase it into either

(1), but (2) or on the one hand X, but on the other hand Y.

Only when you hold the two "horns" of the dilemma in your hand will you be able to bridge the gap between them.

Also, keep in mind that the wrong answer choices to explain questions usually fall into two camps, things that are **irrelevant to the dilemma**—that is, things that wouldn't change things at all if you knew them—or things that actually ***worsen the dilemma***, by making the weirdness in the prompt even weirder.

CRITICAL REASONING PRACTICE QUESTIONS

Argument Structure

500- to 600-Level Argument Structure Practice

1. The global increase in standard of living is the driving force behind the increased carbon dioxide emissions of the last three decades, and it is this increase that contributes the most to global climate change. As wages rise, more of the world's population can afford luxuries that, while agreeable, require substantially more energy to maintain, which causes more carbon dioxide to be emitted. Moreover, when the standard of living declined over the last few years because of the financial crisis, carbon dioxide emissions declined in turn.

    Which of the following best describes the role played in the argument above by the statement that the global increase in standard of living is the driving force behind increased carbon dioxide emissions?

    (A) It is a phenomenon whose existence is taken as evidence for a prediction later proposed.

    (B) It is the main conclusion that the remainder of the argument provides reasons to accept.

    (C) It is a phenomenon that can only be understood if all of the facts that follow are true.

    (D) It is a premise the argument presents in order to make a recommendation for conservation.

    (E) It is used to limit the extent of possible phenomenon to which a subsequent explanation can be applied.

2. In order to reduce the number of venomous cobra snakes in Delhi, the British colonial government offered a bounty for every dead cobra. Initially, this was successful, as large numbers of snakes were killed for the reward. Eventually, however, people discovered that breeding snakes to present to the government was easier than hunting them, and the cobra population rose, rather than fell. Thus, governments should not employ market-based solutions to combat biological problems.

Which of the following best describes the method of reasoning employed in the argument above?

(A) A potential solution to a problem is proposed and then discredited with the data provided.

(B) A broad conclusion is drawn by applying a narrow principle to a specific circumstance.

(C) A specific instance of a strategy in practice is taken as sufficient evidence that it ought never be used.

(D) A principle applicable to many cases is applied to a single case to make a prediction about its future application.

(E) Two potential solutions to a problem are presented, and one is discredited by data provided.

3. Despite what they profess to believe, **atheists clearly believe in a higher power**. A prominent religious activist has posted a bounty on his website offering $10 to anyone who would sign a piece of paper that says that he owns their soul, and yet after many months, there have been no takers. Why would anyone be unwilling to part with something that they do not believe exists to begin with?

Which of the following best describes the role played in the argument by the portion in **bold**?

(A) It is a statement that the author believes is valid to hold for reasons given later.

(B) It is an observation that the author uses to support a position given later.

(C) It is a pattern of cause and effect that the author believes holds true for reasons given later.

(D) It is a conclusion that the author presents in order to discredit later.

(E) It is a relationship that the author does not believe holds true in a case described later.

600- to 700-Level Argument Structure Practice

1. Last month, The Olde Tyme Creamery introduced a new milkshake flavor, Gravely Choctastic. Within a week, its main competitor, Shakez, announced an almost identical flavor named Ghastly Chocolate. Neither company has accused the other of copying its design, but **the similarity is too close to be coincidental**. Each is equal parts fruit sorbet and Rocky Road, an unorthodox combination. Moreover, **it is absurd to think that two companies working in isolation would simultaneously launch identical products with nearly identical names**.

   In the argument above, the two statements in **bold** play which of the following roles?

   (A) The first is the argument's main conclusion; the second is a condition sufficient for that conclusion to be true.

   (B) The first is a secondary conclusion used to argue in favor of the argument's final conclusion; the second is likewise evidence for the main conclusion.

   (C) Both statements are evidence given to support the argument's main conclusion.

   (D) Both statements are an explanation that the argument concludes is more likely than one the argument opposes.

   (E) Both statements are conclusions; the first is used as evidence demonstrating the truth of the second.

2. The Maillard reaction, first described in the 19th century by a French physician, is the process by which meat turns brown and crispy when cooked. Indeed, applying heat to a food is the key technique to cooking, which means that cooking should be seen as an example of applied physics, rather than as an art. Even though qualities like tastiness of browned meat or the appropriate level of crispiness may be hard to define, this difficulty alone would not relegate cooking to the ranks of the practical arts.

    Which of the following is the main conclusion in the argument above?

    (A) The Maillard reaction is the process by which meat turns brown and crispy when cooked.
    (B) It may be hard to define some qualities that are considered relevant to cooking, like crispiness and tastiness.
    (C) Something that is a practical art can never be properly considered an example of an applied science.
    (D) Cooking is better classified as an example of applied physics than as an art.
    (E) Applying heat to a food is the key technique to cooking.

3. Though there is not yet direct archaeological evidence, it would not come as a surprise to anthropologists to learn that trade routes existed between China and the West millennia ago. Those things that contributed to making the Great Silk Road such an important route during the Middle Ages—its easily traversable mountain passes, desert oases, and level terrain—would also have made it the natural route for emigration to China from Africa and the Middle East, **emigration we know to have occurred as early as 1,000,000 B.C.E.**

    The portion in boldface plays which of the following roles in the argument's reasoning?

    (A) It is given as conclusive evidence for the argument's main conclusion.
    (B) It is an intermediate conclusion about a region made plausible by evidence regarding the region's characteristics.
    (C) It is offered as evidence in support of a conclusion that is consistent with facts given elsewhere in the argument.
    (D) It is offered as evidence against a claim that the argument's main conclusion opposes.
    (E) It is the main conclusion that the argument attempts to establish regarding the region in question.

700- to 800-Level Argument Structure Practice

1. **The dividends that shareholders were expecting MegaBiz to pay this quarter were reduced at the last minute,** a sign that many analysts claim does not bode well for MegaBiz's stock price over the short-to-medium term. This analysis is not necessarily correct, however, as **often dividends are reduced in order to conserve capital in preparation for an aggressive expansion,** something only companies otherwise equipped for long-term growth can undertake.

   In the argument above, the two **boldface** portions play which of the following roles?

   (A) The first is evidence for the argument's conclusion; the second is that conclusion.

   (B) The first is a phenomenon the argument's conclusion explains; the second is a factor contributing to the likelihood of that explanation being correct.

   (C) The first is a phenomenon the argument's conclusion addresses; the second is an alternate hypothesis the argument rejects.

   (D) The first is a fact that the argument seeks to explain; the second is an alternate explanation the argument proposes.

   (E) The first is a prediction that the argument seeks to explain; the second is the hypothesis the argument presents as the likeliest evidence for that prediction.

2. Insiders within the mayor's party have called for his immediate resignation, hoping to reduce the effect that the negative publicity of the most recent scandal will have on the political future of his deputy mayor. **A swift resignation is unlikely to help the deputy mayor, however.** If the mayor resigns, he will undoubtedly be prosecuted in civil court for his indiscretions, and the deputy mayor will be forced to testify in court. If his testimony were to indicate that he was aware of the indiscretion and did nothing, the deputy mayor's political career would be over. And if he were unaware of such gross violations, voters would rightly think twice about his fitness for future political office. This is precisely why **the mayor ought to remain in office as long as possible and allow the deputy mayor to retain plausible deniability**.

In the reasoning above, the two **boldface** portions play which of the following roles?

(A) The first assesses the goal held by certain political insiders; the second presents the goal that the reasoning concludes should be favored instead.

(B) The first assesses the goal held by certain political insiders; the second presents the strategy the reasoning concludes will be more likely to succeed.

(C) The first is the main conclusion toward which the reasoning is directed; the second presents a strategy that is counterproductive.

(D) The first is the conclusion reached about one strategy for a certain goal; the second presents the strategy that the reasoning advocates.

(E) The first is the main conclusion toward which the reasoning is directed; the second is a consideration raised in order to support that conclusion.

3. Eddie: You won't be able to understand the true themes beneath the surface of the most popular alternative music of the 1990s because you were only a child when it was released. Popular music is always aimed at people in their late teens and early twenties.

   Mark: You were not alive during the ancient Roman era, nor were any of us now living, but you trust that professor Bullfinch's interpretations of the *Aeneid* do, in fact, capture that work's deepest meaning. Why should alternative music require what Roman poetry does not?

   Mark responds to Eddie's claim by

   (A) using an example from classical culture in order to delegitimize contemporary culture.
   (B) presenting an analogous situation that suggests Eddie relies on unsupported premises.
   (C) contradicting a key piece of evidence that Eddie's argument relies upon.
   (D) specifying a definition that Eddie's argument relies upon but leaves implicit.
   (E) questioning Eddie's own qualification to make judgments about a similar phenomenon.

Argument Assumption

500- to 600-Level Argument Assumption Practice

1. Because of a sharp increase in the number of commercial fishing vessels plying the waters off the coast of Peru in the past decade, the anchovy population there was largely depleted. If the stock of anchovies is ever to recover, the number of fishing vessels must be reduced by at least 50 percent. Since the Peruvian government has recently closed loopholes that allowed foreign fishing vessels to enter its waters without permits, it is likely that the population of anchovies will rise significantly in the coming decade.

   Which of the following would it be most useful to establish in evaluating the argument?

   (A) Whether high demand for anchovies in Peru or in foreign markets led to the overfishing
   (B) Whether the foreign fishing vessels use the same methods and equipment as Peruvian vessels
   (C) Whether the Peruvian government was influenced unduly by environmental lobbyists
   (D) Whether fishing vessels that previously entered without permits will be able to obtain them in the future
   (E) Whether other fish stocks have declined substantially in recent years

2. Some believe that there are a large number of gun-related homicides in the U.S., but they are simply misinformed, as this belief is itself based primarily upon the frequency with which gun-related homicides appear in news reports on television in the U.S. It is precisely because gun-related homicides are such a rare occurrence in the U.S. that they are so frequently the subject of television news.

The argument above is most vulnerable to the objection that

(A) it presupposes that most television news reports are about gun-related homicides.

(B) it presupposes, without warrant, that the television news reports are not biased.

(C) it presupposes the truth of the conclusion that it purports to demonstrate.

(D) it uncritically draws an inference from what is often the case to what will occur in the future.

(E) it uncritically assumes that a characteristic of one member of a group is shared by all members of that group.

3. *News of the Times*, the storied local newspaper, has announced it will cut its price by half, explaining that the unprecedented reduction will allow the paper to better compete with the substantially cheaper tabloid-style newspapers that have stolen much of its market share. The paper's editors reason that since the new price will be only two-thirds that of the least expensive tabloid, many former customers will resume purchasing the paper.

Which of the following statements, if true, provides the best evidence that the editors' reasoning is incorrect?

(A) The tabloid-style newspapers *News of the Times* competes against have kept their prices artificially low by reprinting material from the Internet.

(B) When the tabloid-style newspapers were introduced to the market, their prices were twice *News of the Times'* original price.

(C) Most of those who currently purchase the tabloid-style newspapers never regularly purchased *News of the Times*.

(D) Many of those who currently purchase *News of the Times* have said that they would rather the prices remained higher than risk lowering the paper's quality.

(E) During the average week, tabloid-style newspapers sell nearly five times as many copies per issue than *News of the Times* does.

600- to 700-Level Argument Assumption Practice

1. Experts have long been puzzled by how a craftsman of humble origins like Stradivarius could have developed a technique for making such exquisitely perfect violins, but a new hypothesis offers a different explanation. A drought during Stradivarius's lifetime affected the growth of Italian willow and maple trees, resulting in wood with superior acoustic properties, and thus the reputation of these violins owes more to the materials used than the man using them.

    Which of the following is an assumption upon which the hypothesis in the argument above relies?

    (A) No other Italian violin makers produced violins from the same materials as Stradivarius used.
    (B) No violin that is made with different materials could ever match the quality of a Stradivarius.
    (C) A violin made from the wood of trees whose growth was unaffected by drought would be less perfect than a Stradivarius.
    (D) The reputation of Stradivarius violins rests mostly on the name alone and not the qualities of the violin itself.
    (E) The violins made by Stradivarius were not made entirely of wood harvested before he was born.

2. There can be no doubt that Earth is currently experiencing a loss of species diversity. Though it is true that extinction is a natural process and that the rate at which species are going extinct has remained the same since the middle of the last century, it is also true that the rate at which new species emerge to replace those lost cannot be accelerated.

    Which of the following, if true, most strengthens the conclusion that Earth is experiencing a loss of species diversity?

    (A) The media that reports upon the loss of species diversity is not unduly biased in favor of environmentalists.
    (B) The climates and habitats most prone to species loss are also those most conducive to species emergence.
    (C) As no species can survive indefinitely, all species will eventually go extinct.
    (D) By the middle of the last century, fewer species were emerging than were being lost to extinction.
    (E) Scientists have made great advancements in technologies that allow species loss to be recorded.

3. Genetically modified (GMO) crops can be designed so that they are resistant to the effects of a particular herbicide. Consequently, that herbicide can be used to kill harmful weeds without fear of damaging the crop. This advantage comes with too great a price for farmers, however, as the biotech companies that create these crops also render them sterile, requiring seeds for each year's planting to be purchased where before farmers could grow their own seed.

Each of the following, if true, would weaken the conclusion above EXCEPT:

(A) The herbicides used to kill the weeds that threaten genetically modified crops require substantially fewer man-hours to apply than standard alternatives.

(B) When a company is allowed to control the dissemination of its products, it need not increase their price.

(C) The yield realized by farmers growing genetically modified crops is much larger than that of previous nonmodified crops.

(D) The herbicides designed to work with genetically modified crops are sold only by the biotech companies that produce the seeds for those crops.

(E) Crops grown for seed often require a significant investment of time and resources to harvest.

700- to 800-Level Argument Assumption Practice

1. In a typical circus troupe, acrobats perform for one-fifth of the show's duration, are involved in one-fourth of all performance-related accidents, and account for one-third of the cost of insurance premiums paid by the show. In order to remain in business, a circus cannot afford to spend more than one-fourth of its budget on any one type of performer.

   Each of the following, if true, would provide support for a ringleader's decision to reduce the performance time of a troupe's acrobats EXCEPT:

   (A) The longer a performer performs, the more likely a costly accident will occur.
   (B) Insurance premiums for circuses are primarily paid to insure its performers against accidents.
   (C) The single biggest cost a circus pays is the cost of insuring its performers against accidents.
   (D) Ticket sales for a circus's performances would not decline if acrobats performed less.
   (E) The accidents that an acrobat is likely to suffer do not occur primarily at the beginning of a performance.

2. Many businesses hire consultants to formulate plans to manage impending growth, and businesses that hire consultants do subsequently perform better than those that do not. Yet many consultants acknowledge that the advice offered by consultants is not insightful and that in many cases their advice is actually ignored. It is clear then that whatever the reason for these businesses' increased performance, it is not the advice given by the consultants hired.

   Which of the following, if true, would weaken the argument above?

   (A) A consultant can be trusted when he or she provides information about the value of his or her own advice.
   (B) When preparing for the future, the quality of potential strategies considered is less important than the quantity.
   (C) The core leadership at a business should be expected to know more about the businesses' needs than an outsider.
   (D) Businesses that are unable to afford the expense of hiring consultants are unlikely to successfully manage impending growth.
   (E) While no single consultant will be an expert on all types of businesses, consulting firms employ many consultants with different skills.

3. In the famous 1971 Stanford prison experiment, participants were sent to a derelict prison where they were randomly assigned roles as either jailor or prisoner. After a week, the experiment was ended, as in that time those acting as jailors had become so cruel to their "charges" that it was deemed unethical to risk continuing any longer.

    Which of the following is an assumption underlying the decision to end the experiment?

    (A) Whenever people are given unequal amounts of power, those with more power will abuse it.
    (B) Practical considerations are not the only grounds by which to evaluate an experiment.
    (C) If an experiment is damaging to its participants, it must be ended immediately.
    (D) Experimental methods that damage the participants of an experiment unequally are unethical.
    (E) It is possible to determine whether an experiment's results will be unethical after only a week.

Fact-Based Questions

500- to 600-Level Fact-Based Question Practice

1. Cement is composed primarily of two ingredients, calcium and silicon, mixed with small amounts of aluminum and iron. Sources of these ingredients are common—shale, limestone, basalt, and even industrial slag may be used—are not expensive, and can easily be substituted with other sources. The price of cement is, however, tightly connected to the price of oil, at least in the modern era, because the process of combining these ingredients into cement requires large amounts of energy.

    If the statements above are true, which of the following is most likely to also be true?

    (A) Oil should be considered one of cement's basic ingredients.
    (B) Oil is the primary source of the energy used in combining ingredients into cement.
    (C) If the price of shale were to increase, the price of cement would rise.
    (D) When the price of oil rises, cement manufacturers lower their overall costs by using cheaper substitutes as ingredients.
    (E) The cement necessary to build a parking garage costs more than the total cost of its basic ingredients.

2. Retail stores often use pleasant scents in order to entice customers to enter the store, a successful technique that usually results in greater sales, though the scent used by a given store need not be the same as that used by another. Indeed, bakeries that use fans to circulate the scent of baking bread to customers see similar increases in sales as clothing retailers that place potpourri strategically through their aisles. However, when a store is the only one in a mall that uses this strategy to increase sales, it generally experiences the opposite.

Which of the following, if true, most helps to resolve the apparent discrepancy described above?

(A) If only one store in a mall has a distinguishable scent, customers intuitively suspect the store of manipulation and avoid it.

(B) When several enticing smells are present in a mall, customers who fail to be enticed by one smell may find another to their liking.

(C) The presence of an enticing smell emanating from one business can sometimes increase the sales of nearby businesses.

(D) When there is only one store in a mall that uses a marketing strategy, if it is successful, others will often follow suit.

(E) If a bakery using this strategy were adjacent to a clothing store also using it, the clash of smells would not be enticing to customers of either.

3. Without the presence of Jupiter in our solar system, Earth would likely not be inhabited. Planets in solar systems with sizeable asteroid belts are subject periodically to meteor strikes that eradicate the biological precursors required for life to develop. The gravitational pull of a large gas giant such as Jupiter protects the other planets in its system from meteor strikes by attracting asteroid debris.

If the statements above are true, which of the following must also be true?

(A) If a solar system does not have a large gas giant such as Jupiter, no planet in it will be inhabited.

(B) If Jupiter were somehow destroyed by meteor strikes, life on Earth would cease to be.

(C) If Jupiter were somehow destroyed by meteor strikes, life would be less likely to develop on currently uninhabited planets in our solar system.

(D) Any planet that is found in a system with an asteroid belt cannot support life unless it is near to a gas giant such as Jupiter.

(E) No planet that is found in a system with more than one asteroid belt can support life.

600- to 700-Level Fact-Based Question Practice

1. The years between 1880 and 1905 saw a boom in timber production in Mississippi, which, by 1905, produced as much as one billion board feet of timber per year. Compare that to the rather more meager 300,000 board feet of timber produced annually in 1880. Yet in that same period, the labor force employed by timber mills in Mississippi actually shrank by about 10 percent.

   Which of the following, if true, most helps to explain the apparent discrepancy in the timber industry in Mississippi during the period indicated?

   (A) The timber industry in Mississippi has never been so productive as it was during the three decades following 1880.

   (B) Between 1880 and 1905, the total number of acres of virgin timberland in Mississippi fell substantially.

   (C) Since 1905, the majority of lumber produced in Mississippi has relied upon young second-growth timber.

   (D) Between 1880 and 1905, timber was such a large part of Mississippi's economy that many new labor saving technologies were implemented by the industry.

   (E) Between 1850 and 1950, Mississippi's economy transitioned from primarily agrarian to primarily industrial, due in part to the timber industry's success.

2. Which of the following best completes the argument below?

Moral philosophers contend that it is important for public officials to avoid even the appearance of wrong-doing. However, actions that appear wrong are not always wrong. The main reason that these philosophers give for their contention is that public officials will be unable to maintain public trust if they appear to be doing things that are considered wrong by the general public. Yet no one should be obligated to conform to the moral standards of the general public; therefore, _____.

(A) no public official should be obligated to avoid the appearance of wrong-doing

(B) all public officials have, to a degree, an interest in maintaining the public's trust

(C) public officials who have scrupulously avoided even the appearance of wrong-doing will be trusted by the general public

(D) moral philosophers will never accept that the public might trust a public official who presents the appearance of wrong-doing

(E) public officials who abuse their power without the public's knowledge are morally wrong for hiding their wrong-doing

3. Babies who are born deaf and who are raised by deaf parents who communicate with them through sign language begin to "babble" at the same age as those babies born able to hear and who are raised by parents who also can hear and who communicate with them verbally. Only in this first group of babies the babbling takes the form of repetitive hand gestures, while in the second group the babbling manifests as repetitive vocalizations. Scientists believe that these hand gestures are analogous to the vocalizations and that both represent evidence that babbling babies first babble in preparation for subsequent communication with their parents.

The information above provides the most support for scientists to also conclude that

(A) the simplest words in a language are those babies are able to understand early in their development.

(B) if babies are raised by parents who do not communicate with them in any way, they will not babble.

(C) when they first babble, babies are not aware that the sounds or gestures they make could allow them to communicate.

(D) hand gestures made by babies who are able to hear should also be interpreted as precursors to communication.

(E) when their parents are not present, babies who babble with vocalizations will continue to vocalize.

700- to 800-Level Fact-Based Question Practice

1. We intuitively know that all acts that are morally wrong should not be done because our intuition senses that these acts violate our basic autonomy as rational human beings. Any violation of our basic autonomy as rational beings ought to be avoided to the same degree as any other violation and punished accordingly. Murder is certainly wrong, whether it be the murder of one elderly criminal or a bus full of innocent children.

   Which of the following judgments follows from the principles stated above?

   (A) If it is noble to risk one's life saving the lives of others, then it is no nobler to risk one's life saving many lives than to risk it saving one life.

   (B) If stealing is morally wrong and adultery is morally wrong, then lying about one's adultery ought to be twice as intuitively obvious as merely lying.

   (C) If murdering is morally wrong, then accidentally causing a person's death is as much a violation of our basic autonomy as murdering that person.

   (D) If lying is morally wrong, then falsely claiming to have murdered someone ought to be punished to the same degree as if the liar had actually committed the murder.

   (E) If asked to choose between killing someone or letting that person kill someone else, there is no choice that is morally correct.

2. The first fishes were jawless, until 400 million years ago when one species developed jaws and branched away from its ancestors. These jawed fishes evolved into two distinct lines, those that retained the cartilage-based skeletal structure of their evolutionary ancestors, and those that replaced most of its cartilage with bone. From this latter group, nearly every land-based warm-blooded species evolved, species as different as the field mouse and the elephant.

If all of the statements in the passage above are true, which of the following must also be true?

(A) The skeletons of land-based mammals are never composed of cartilage.

(B) Fish species without jaws became extinct at least 400 million years ago.

(C) Fish species without jaws did not have skeletons that contained bone 400 million years ago.

(D) All warm-blooded, land-based species have skeletons composed primarily of bone.

(E) Field mice and elephants evolved from different species of fish, both of which had jaws.

3. The North Island trade federation is composed of three fully autonomous states: Llassu, Tragda, and Baflazam. Under their trade agreement, each of the members receives a share of the federation's total trade revenues proportional to the state's population as a percentage of the total population of the three states. Though originally Tragda received the greatest share, followed by Baflazam and then Llassu, after the most recent population survey, the federation adjusted the share of trade revenues received by Tragda downward, even though its population grew more than did Llassu's.

If the adjustment to trade revenues that followed the population survey was made in accordance with the trade federation's agreement, which of the following must be true of the three countries in the year surveyed?

(A) The three countries, if arranged from greatest population to least, would be listed Baflazam, Llassu, Tragda.

(B) The three countries, if arranged from greatest population change to least, would be listed Tragda, Baflazam, Llassu.

(C) The three countries, if arranged from greatest population growth to least, would be listed Baflazam, Tragda, Llassu.

(D) The three countries, if arranged from greatest population growth to least, would be listed Tragda, Llassu, Baflazam.

(E) The three countries, if arranged from least population growth to most, would be listed Baflazam, Tragda, Llassu.

Answer Key

500- to 600-Level Argument Structure Practice

1. **(B)**   2. **(C)**   3. **(A)**

600- to 700-Level Argument Structure Practice

1. **(D)**   2. **(D)**   3. **(C)**

700- to 800-Level Argument Structure Practice

1. **(D)**   2. **(D)**   3. **(B)**

500- to 600-Level Argument Assumption Practice

1. **(D)**   2. **(C)**   3. **(C)**

600- to 700-Level Argument Assumption Practice

1. **(E)**   2. **(D)**   3. **(D)**

700- to 800-Level Argument Assumption Practice

1. **(C)**   2. **(B)**   3. **(B)**

500- to 600-Level Fact-Based Question Practice

1. **(E)**   2. **(A)**   3. **(C)**

600- to 700-Level Fact-Based Question Practice

1. **(D)**   2. **(A)**   3. **(B)**

700- to 800-Level Fact-Based Question Practice

1. **(D)**   2. **(C)**   3. **(C)**

Explanations

500- to 600-Level Argument Structure Practice

1. **Argument:** The first sentence contains the conclusion (also the statement we are asked to find the role of), *increased standards of living contribute the most to global warming by increasing carbon dioxide*, **a causal connection**, supported by the evidence that luxuries require energy, and energy requires carbon dioxide and the evidence that when standards of living fell, the amount of carbon dioxide in the atmosphere fell. The correct role for the statement is thus described by Answer Choice (B).

   (B) The answers split 2/2/1 in the beginning: Answer Choices (A) and (C) label the statement a *phenomenon*, but the phenomenon being explained is global climate change, not the increase in standard of living itself. Answer Choices (D) and (E) label the statement as a sort of evidence, which is likewise incorrect.

2. **Argument:** The argument begins by describing a government plan, its method (paying a snake bounty), and its goal (reducing the number of cobras), and then continues to provide an unexpected negative consequence (snake breeding). With this test case taken to be **representative** of all government interventions, the conclusion is drawn in the last sentence: *governments should not employ market-based solutions*, which is precisely what Answer Choice (C) says.

   (C) Answer Choice (A) confuses the past with the present, as the solution isn't being presented now, it's being described; Answer Choice (B) is the **exact opposite** of the correct method, which goes from case to principle, not principle to case, and the same is true for (D); and Answer Choice (E) is clearly wrong, as there is only one solution in the argument.

3. **Argument:** This argument follows a familiar pattern, it's conclusion *some people say X and they're wrong*, with the people being *atheists* and the X that they don't believe in a higher power. The remainder of the argument is evidence for this claim. Through a bit of **double-negative** trickery, the bolded statement becomes the *and they're wrong (because **this** is right)*, which Answer Choice (A) nails.

(A) Answer Choices (D) and (E) can be eliminated because they are the **exact opposite,** claiming the author opposes the bolded position. Answer Choice (C) brings up the **irrelevant** concept of *cause and effect*, the **right answer to the wrong question**, and Answer Choice (B) gets the explanation backwards; the argument explains the bolded statement.

600- to 700-Level Argument Structure Practice

1. **Argument:** The argument as presented is partially flawed, as the two bolded statements are just restatements of the same conclusion, that the two companies' certainly influenced each other somehow, as Answer Choice (D) correctly points out.

   (D) The answers split 2/3 over whether the two statements play different roles. Answer Choices (A) and (B) say they are different, and can thus be eliminated. Answer Choice (C) calls the statements evidence, rather than conclusion, and Answer Choice (E) misses that the two are not *different* conclusions; the second one is just a restatement.

2. **Argument:** Rare **Role of a Statement** questions name the role and ask for the part that plays it. Here, the main conclusion is wanted, and that conclusion is *cooking should be seen as an example of applied physics, rather than as an art.* "Should" is always a good sign of a conclusion, as "should" needs support, and conclusions are supported by evidence.

   (D) The correct answer is just a slightly reworded version of the conclusion. Answer Choices (A) and (E) are evidence, and Answer Choices (B) and (C) are **misused details**, things the argument never actually said—so there's no way they could be the argument's conclusion!

3. **Argument:** This argument's conclusion is the thing that a certain yet unproven hypothesis wouldn't be surprising to archaeologists, since it fits with evidence they already have. The bolded statement is one of those pieces of evidence, thus Answer Choice (C) is the correct answer.

   (C) The 3/2 evidence/conclusion split allows Answer Choices (B) and (E) to be eliminated immediately. All that's left is to choose the proper description of the evidence. Answer Choice (A) fails because of the word *conclusive*; this evidence is only *consistent* with the hypothesis. And Answer Choice (D) is out because the speaker never *opposes* any arguments.

700- to 800-Level Argument Structure Practice

1. **Argument:** The argument begins with a phenomenon (the first bolded statement); dividends were reduced at the last minute by MegaBiz. This is followed by an explanation attributed to "analysts" who think it's bad news. The author concludes otherwise, or at least points out another explanation is possible, which is the second bolded statement. Answer Choice (D) nails this relationship of *phenomenon and new interpretation/ explanation.*

   (D) Answer Choice (A) is the only answer choice that doesn't get that the first statement is the thing being explained. Of the rest, they split over whether the second is a conclusion/alternate explanation or evidence for that explanation. Answer Choices (B) and (E) wrongly treat the second statement as evidence. Answer Choice (C) can be eliminated because it claims the speaker rejects the conclusion actually supported by the argument.

2. **Argument:** This argument begins with the recommendation of "insiders," immediately rejected by the speaker in the first bolded statement. After providing evidence that explains why the insiders are wrong, the speaker provides an explanation of a better strategy (the opposite of the one the insiders supported), as Answer Choice (D) describes.

   (D) The most fruitful split is found in the answers' description of the second statement. The goal of the strategy is *reducing the negative effect on the deputy mayor's political future,* but Answer Choice (A) confuses that with a bolded statement. Answer Choices (B) and (D) correctly describe the second statement, whereas Answer Choice (C) gets it backward, and Answer Choice (E) gets the relationship between the statements wrong (the second is counter to the first). Answer Choice (B) is wrong in a subtle way. The first bolded statement doesn't *assess the goal* but rather the *strategy* to bring the goal about.

3. **Argument:** In this two-party prompt, Eddie claims that Mark won't be able to understand alternative music because he wasn't born when it was made; Mark counters by using the example of something neither of them were alive to see, but which Eddie thinks he can understand (or that he can understand through the professor's interpretations, at least). Answer Choice (B) calls the example an *analogous situation* (which it is)

and describes the way it's used (to weaken Eddie's assumptions, just like a good GMAT test taker would).

(B) Answer Choice (A) **misuses details** from the counterexample, in a way that might be tempting to those who didn't have time to read the original (as this is an argument we hear in the **real world** all the time). Answer Choice (C) is out because Mark doesn't contradict evidence; he merely introduces additional evidence. Answer Choice (D) would be fine if it didn't say *definition*, as Mark's evidence doesn't take the form of a definition, and Answer Choice (E) is another **real-world** trap, since Mark doesn't make personal attacks (even though in this situation a person might be expected to).

500- to 600-Level Argument Assumption Practice

1. **Argument:** The argument's conclusion comes at the end of the prompt, though there is an **intermediate conclusion** in the middle, the **bare assertion** of a **requirement** for something to come about: If the anchovy population (specifically, the population off the cost of Peru) is ever to recover (and the speaker is not saying its recovery is definite or even possible), then it must be that the number of fishing vessels is reduced by 50 percent (the requirement). This intermediate conclusion is supported by a single piece of evidence, the **explanation** of the current reduction (a **causal connection**): a sharp increase in the *number* of fishing vessels. In a sense, the initial evidence is a miniargument for a **net calculation**: more vessels = more anchovy deaths. The speaker adds another piece of evidence (that recently loopholes allowed foreign fishing vessels to ply Peruvian waters). The speaker's final conclusion is found at the end, a **prediction**: the population of anchovies is going to rebound, thanks to this loophole change.

(D) Clearly, then, the speaker assumes that all the factors that went into the net calculation before, whatever they were, will continue, whereas no other factors that could change the calculation will emerge. The speaker also must assume that the **plan** will not meet with any hurdles. Answer Choice (D) would be relevant to that assumption, as it raises a possible problem with the plan. If the formerly unlicensed ships could re-enter with fresh licenses, the plan would not block the old factors that caused the decrease in anchovies from reoccurring.

Answer Choices (A), (B), and (C) are meant to mislead by bringing up things that are often relevant to fishing in the **real world**, but that doesn't matter in this specific case. Answer Choice (B) is **one step removed** from being relevant, as we don't know what would matter about the specific methods used. Answer Choice (E) is likewise **one step removed**, suggesting an **irrelevant comparison** to other fish species—whatever's happening with them, we don't know that similar things are in play with anchovies.

2. **Argument:** It might have been hard for you to find the conclusion because the speaker essentially says it twice, phrasing it differently each time. Why are people wrong to say that there are lots of gun-related homicides? Because gun-related homicides are a rare occurrence. When an argument's conclusion is the same as its evidence, the argument is said to be **circular**, and Answer Choice (C) is just one way the test maker might phrase that flaw—though it should be noted that most often circular arguments appear as distracting wrong answers on the GMAT.

   (C) Answer Choice (A) is **too extreme** to describe this argument, which merely states that there are *a lot* of TV reports on guns, not that *most* TV reports are on guns. The issue of bias, raised in Answer Choice (B) is a **real-world** distraction, the sort of accusation often thrown around when gun control comes up. There's no prediction about the future, so (D) doesn't apply, nor is there a conclusion made about a group, so Answer Choice (E) is irrelevant as well.

3. **Argument:** This question might be easily mistaken for a **Flaw** question, but notice that the stem adds the qualification *if true*, meaning that the speaker's argument isn't definitely wrong, but that it relies on an assumption that *could* be attacked and thereby the argument **Weakened**. The conclusion of the editors' argument is the **stated effect** (former customers of the paper will return to purchasing it) that a **plan** (reducing the paper's price by half) is predicted to have. As evidence, the editors point to two facts: (1) the current price of the paper is higher than tabloid prices, and (2) tabloids have been selling well. As a **prediction** the argument assumes that nothing relevant to the prediction will change (which doesn't factor into the answer of this question), and as a **plan** it assumes that there is nothing that can block the plan from having its stated effect. Answer Choice (C) points to a potential problem with assuming the latter: if the tabloids didn't steal away customers from the paper in the first place (they somehow got

non-paper readers to become tabloid readers), then the plan to steal them back probably won't work.

(C) Answer Choices (A) and (D) are **real-world** facts brought up as distractions. Answer Choices (B) and (E) are **specific numbers**, things we should know to suspect in the fuzzy-math world of the Verbal. Since we don't know if the tabloids' prices before were lower or higher than the paper's prices before or after the plan, Answer Choice (B) is **one step removed** from the argument here. Answer Choice (E) ends up just being more specific **evidence for the evidence** we already know—the argument tells us that tabloids are popular, so finding out they're five times as popular doesn't really change anything.

600- to 700-Level Argument Assumption Practice

1. **Argument:** The argument's conclusion is that *the reputation of Stradivarius violins is **more** due to the materials they're built from than the person who built them.* In support, the speaker offers evidence about how awesome the materials are and a **hypothesis** about what makes them so. There are two major assumptions here, first that such special wood requires no special artistry to work with, and second, brought out in Answer Choice (E), that *Stradivarius violins are actually made out of this special wood.* (Note that the evidence only says that this wood was *available* in Stradivarius's lifetime, not that he used it.)

   (E) Answer Choice (A) lies somewhere between the two assumptions, but it doesn't quite nail either, as the Denial test would reveal. (Even if other violin makers used the same materials as Stradivarius, it wouldn't mean that Stradivarius used the special wood or that Stradivarius's techniques were *more important* than the materials.) Since the argument is limited only to explaining why Stradivarius violins are impressive, other violins aren't relevant, so Answer Choices (B) and (C) aren't required assumptions. Answer Choice (D) contradicts the conclusion, so couldn't possibly be an assumption in the argument.

2. **Argument:** The conclusion to this argument might have been hard to spot at first, but phrasing the argument's pieces in terms of *[what] because [why]* would help. [The Earth is losing species diversity] because [The extinction rate has been the same for at least 50 years and the rate that species rise to replace can't be sped up] is essentially a **net calculation**: more species are lost than gained; thus, overall species

loss is happening. The part left out of this evidence is the *more*—the evidence only establishes that the rates have remained the same, not that one outpaces the other. Thus, Answer Choice (D) strengthens the argument by supporting the assumption that *the rate of loss is greater than the rate of gain*.

(D) Answer Choice (A) is irrelevant, but it is something that is often said in the **real world**. Answer Choice (B) is likely meant to distract in the same way, offering a possibly familiar but **irrelevant comparison**. Answer Choice (C) is almost certainly true, but it's also irrelevant. Answer Choice (E) might be relevant if there were any hint that the numbers were incorrect at any point or that it established a specific timeframe relevant to the argument (like, say, the last 50 years).

3. **Argument: Weaken EXCEPT** questions require arguments with *lots* of assumptions in order to support four correctly weakening answers. Here, the argument's conclusion is strong, though masked with colloquial phrasing: the use of GMO crops comes with *too great a price*, a **net benefit calculation** based on evidence that (as per usual) only addresses *some* of the factors that go into the calculation and assumes there are no others. Answer Choices (A), (C), and (E) provide possible advantages to GMO crops that aren't addressed in the evidence. Answer Choice (B), on the other hand, eliminates certainty about a possible disadvantage (higher price).

    (D) Answer Choice (D) is a bit of **real-world** distraction that is **one step removed** from the argument given in the prompt. There's not necessarily any disadvantage to the biotech companies selling the seeds. If there were only a small number of these companies, then maybe a monopoly would form—but that maybe and possibly isn't something we know for sure in *this* situation.

700- to 800-Level Argument Assumption Practice

1. **Argument:** This argument presents a **plan** (sneakily presented in the stem, rather than the prompt), reducing the *performance time* of acrobats in a circus, with the **stated goal** of reducing the portion of the circus's *total budget* that is given over to *insurance premiums for the acrobats*. Thus, the argument has two major assumptions: (1) *performance time is in some way related to insurance premium costs* and (2) *insurance premiums are a big part of the budget overall*. Answer Choices (A) and (B)

directly support the first assumption. Answer Choice (E) also supports the first, though a bit more obliquely. If accidents to acrobats tended to happen at the beginning of their performance, cutting time from the end wouldn't necessarily reduce the number of accidents. Answer Choice (D) is instead the confirmation of a **defending assumption**, protecting against the **unintended harm** that the budget might suffer from reducing the amount of time that acrobats perform (driving away its paying customers).

(C) The evidence says only that a single cost cannot rise above one-fourth of the budget. Answer Choice (C) doesn't strengthen the argument because insurance could still be smaller than one-fourth if it was the largest line item in the budget.

2. **Argument:** This argument is the opposite of a **causal connection**: it asserts that the advice given by consultants is *not* the cause of these businesses' increased performance. This conclusion is supported by the evidence that, even though businesses that hire consultants do better, a good bit of advice consultants give is not insightful and is ignored any way. Thus, the argument assumes that there's no way other than *being followed directly* that a consultant's advice might benefit a company. Answer Choice (B) presents this **alternative explanation** of how a consultant's uninsightful and unfollowed advice might be of benefit, by providing a greater *number* of strategies to choose between.

    (B) Answer Choice (A) is the **opposite** of what we want, as it **strengthens** the assumption that the consultants are correct when they say that they are not very helpful. Answer Choice (C) also **strengthens** the argument by making it more likely that something other than the consultants (the business's core leadership) is responsible for the increased performance. Answer Choice (D) is close, but note that it does not attribute the business's success to the consultant's *advice*, rather their *expensiveness* (so ultimately, it, too, **strengthens** the claim that it's not their advice). Answer Choice (E) addresses a **closed issue**, as the evidence already asserts that these consultants are not insightful.

3. **Argument:** The stem of this question warns us to be very careful. The conclusion we're interested in is the *decision to end the experiment*, which we're told was based on the idea that it would be *unethical to risk continuing any longer*. Thus, the argument assumes that an experiment's being *unethical* is a good reason to end it. Answer Choice (B) says this,

though in a roundabout way, substituting *nonpractical considerations* for *ethical considerations*.

(B) Answer Choice (A) is wrong because it doesn't affect the decision to end the experiment but is instead something we'd likely conclude from the behavior of the participants. Answer Choice (C) is **too extreme** for this situation, since the experiment wasn't ended *immediately* as soon as someone was damaged, only when the jailers had become "so cruel" that it was unethical. Answer Choice (D) might seem tempting, but nowhere does the argument state that the participants were damaged unequally—it merely mentions one sort of damage; there could have been other, equal damages elsewhere. And Answer Choice (E) confuses the experiment's *results* with *conducting* or *continuing* the experiment.

500- to 600-Level Fact-Based Question Practice

1. **Facts:** With **Inference** questions, always seek the most definite information in the prompt. Here, there's only one, found in the final sentence: *cement requires large amounts of energy to make.* The correct inference will need to involve this fact.

   (E) Careful with the answer choices. Only Answer Choice (B) directly mentions energy, but it is **too extreme** a claim to infer from what we have. Sentence three tells us that oil is *connected* to the energy requirement, but not that it is the main source of that energy. Answer Choice (A) is **reasonable but unsupported**, since we don't really know what the definition of an ingredient ought or ought not to include. Answer Choice (C) is **directly contradicted** by information about cheap replacements in sentence two. Answer Choice (D) is consistent with the same information about replacements, but we're never given any information about the business practices of cement makers. This leaves only Answer Choice (E), which indirectly connects to the one fact we know. Energy costs are required parts of making cement, so the cost of cement isn't entirely found in the cost of its basic ingredients.

2. **Dilemma: On the one hand**, *the pleasant smell strategy increases sales in general*, **but on the other hand** *the same strategy **reduces sales** if only one store does it.* Answer Choice (A) accounts for the apparent **unrealized expectation** that occurs in this one specific case by providing a reason for the change in outcomes for single stores: they drive away potential customers.

(A) Remember that the single smelly store doesn't just experience flat sales; its sales actually fall. Answer Choice (B) wouldn't explain the falling sales, only flat sales. Answer Choice (C) might explain why businesses around the smelly store do better, but it does not explain why the store itself does worse. Answer Choice (D) is likewise **irrelevant to the dilemma**, since in our dilemma the strategy isn't working. The same is true for Answer Choice (E), where two stores are using the strategy, but our dilemma only involves a single store.

3. **Facts:** We know from sentence one that *Without Jupiter, the chances of life developing on Earth would have been less.* The second sentence explains why in general this would be true: *something that hurts the chances of life developing (the meteor strikes) happens when there are asteroid belts.* And the third sentence ties this explanation to Jupiter: *without something like Jupiter, there'd be nothing stopping the meteor strikes.* By connecting these facts, we can infer Answer Choice (C): Without Jupiter, the chances of life developing in our solar system would be lowered. Don't be frightened by the absurd situation given in Answer Choice (C). It doesn't matter *why* or *how* Jupiter gets destroyed.

   (C) Answer Choices (A) and (D) are both **too extreme**, as our information only says the chances of developing life are *lowered* without a gas giant, not lowered to zero. Answer Choice (B) is **one step removed** from the information we have, since we don't know what causes life to continue, only what affects its chances of starting. Answer Choice (E) is both **too extreme** and a case of **mixed details** because the prompt never gives information about multiple asteroid belts.

600- to 700-Level Fact-Based Question Practice

1. **Dilemma:** The dilemma here is that two things we might assume are connected seem to be unconnected: (1) timber production went up during the period but (2) labor employed by timber mills went down. Answer Choice (D) presents the **unconsidered factor** that reconciles the two trends: labor-saving technologies were introduced during the period in question.

   (D) Answer Choices (A) and (C) are both **irrelevant to the dilemma** because they concern different time periods than the one we're interested in. Answer Choices (B) and (E) give us extra facts about the time period, but neither would account directly for a difference between production and labor.

2. **Facts:** The *therefore* in front of the blank flags this question as close cousin to the **Inference** question, since the only thing we are allowed to put in that blank is something inferable from the definite information in the prompt. Here, the correct answer, (A), is inferable by applying the definite piece of formal logic rule right before the semicolon (*no one should be obligated to conform to the moral standards of the public*) to the specific case of *public officials*. As part of "anyone," public officials, too, should not be obligated.

    (A) Answer Choice (B) could be inferred if only we knew that the moral philosophers are definitely right (and the speaker doesn't seem to think they are, anyway). Answer Choice (C) confuses **necessity and sufficiency**. Answer Choice (D) seems reasonable (if you agree with the speaker), but it is unsupported here, as we know only what moral philosophers have said before, not what they will always and forever say. And Answer Choice (E), while a laudable sentiment in the real world, is not specifically addressed here.

3. **Facts:** If we agree with the scientists' final conclusion that *babies first babble in preparation for communication with their parents*, then babies who aren't preparing for communication won't start babbling. Thus, Answer Choice (B) must be true.

    (B) Answer Choice (A) is **one step removed** from our information, which doesn't allow us to say anything for certain about *simple words*. Answer Choice (C) is explicitly **contradicted** by the scientists' conclusion. Answer Choices (D) and (E) might seem reasonable, but the scientists' evidence never provides any information about children who don't fit into the two groups in the prompt or about what happens with babies when no one's around.

700- to 800-Level Fact-Based Question Practice

1. **Facts:** The first two sentences of this prompt consist of two Formal Logic statements that can be connected: morally wrong → violates autonomy → should be avoided and punished the same. The prompt also tells us that murder is morally wrong. Each of the answer choices provide an if, but the only if that will "trigger" the chain of logic will be

"If <something> is morally wrong." Answer Choice (D) begins just this way and correctly concludes that if lying and murder are both morally wrong, then they should be punished equally.

(D) Answer Choice (A) is out because the prompt provides no rules to judge whether something is *noble* or not, and the same is true for Answer Choice (E) because there are no rules about what is morally *correct*. Answer Choice (B) concludes that something is *twice as obvious*, but all the information in the prompt is about things being *equally wrong*. Answer Choice (C) would be right if we knew that accidentally causing a person's death were morally wrong, but neither the answer nor the prompt contain this information.

2. **Facts:** This **Inference** question follows the pattern of **so and so** and **such and such**—lots of placeholder words are used to add information about groups previously mentioned. Answer Choice (C) is correctly inferable because the jawed fish split into two groups: the first group *retains* the cartilage-based skeletons of their ancestors, their ancestors being all fish that lived before Jaws.

(C) Answer Choice (A) is wrong because the only thing we know about land-based mammals is that most of them evolved from the bone-having fish. It's possible they lost their bone-skeletons after they diverged from the fish. Answer Choice (B) brings up *extinction*, a totally new concept we know nothing about. Answer Choice (D) is just (A) rephrased. And Answer Choice (E) is a **misused detail**, combining the last sentence with earlier pieces of information that we have no way to know with certainty can be combined.

3. **Facts:** Beneath this question lies one of the GMAT's favorite facts, the difference between **percentages and numbers**. According to the prompt, the trade federation's members split revenues proportional to the size of their populations. Originally, the sizes were Tragda > Baflazam > Llassu. After the census, Tragda lost revenue, which means that, as a percentage, its population was no longer as large as it had been. We're also told that Llassu's population grew *less* than Tragda's, meaning that the reason for Tragda's decrease can't be Llassu's population increase. Therefore, it must be Baflazam's increase that reduced Tragda's share. And if Baflazam grew more than Tragda, it must also have grown more than Llassu. Thus, Answer Choice (C) is inferable, the order of

population *growth* (not absolute population number) must be Baflazam, Tragda, Llassu.

(C) Answer Choice (A) concerns total population, not rate of population growth. Answer Choices (B) and (D) get the nations out of order, and Answer Choice (E) pulls a **but for one word** trick by changing the list to *least to most* instead of *most to least*.

Sentence Correction | 15

GMAT GRAMMAR 101

This chapter will go more smoothly if we take a few pages first to refresh your memory of the most basic grammatical terms. We promise that no unnecessarily complicated jargon lies ahead, only the bare bones necessary for us all to be on the same page as you learn the best ways to dominate GMAT Sentence Correction questions.

The Parts of Speech

Words can be classified many different ways; when you classify a word according to its **function** in communication, you assign it to one of the categories together called the **parts of speech**. For the GMAT, it is necessary to be able to recognize only a few: **nouns**, **verbs**, **pronouns**, **prepositions**, **adjectives**, **adverbs**, and **conjunctions**.

NOUNS

As you probably heard back in first grade, a noun is "the name of a person, place, or thing." *Dog, cat, mom, Albuquerque, sandwich, kettle, CD, elevator, Abraham Lincoln*—all are nouns.

So, too, ideas such as *love, marriage, correctness, number, sluggishness, justice,* and *symmetry.*

VERBS

Verbs are a bit trickier than nouns. We usually define them as either "an action" or "a state of being." Actions include *walk, run, sing, sit, bark,* and *love.* States of being are instead things like *is, was, will, does, shall, could, might.*

The reason we say verbs are trickier than nouns is that they can appear in a variety of different forms depending on what sort of action they're describing. The noun *dog* appears in sentences as just that: *dog* (with the occasional *s* tacked on to make it plural or apostrophe *s* to make it possessive). But *bark* appears in all kinds of different forms: *to bark, barks, barking, is barking, barked, has barked, will have been barking, were to have been barking.* The most common way a verb changes is in relation to what is called its **tense**, forms that allow us to keep track of the different times an action occurs.

The simple tenses include **present**, **past**, **and future**: *I walk today, I walked yesterday, I will walk tomorrow,* and so on. But tenses can get complicated quickly. Special ones exist for actions that are ongoing (the continuous: *I am walking now*), that occurred in the past but continue into the present (the present perfect: *I have walked for some time*), that occurred frequently in the past (the past habitual: *I used to walk*), and even that occurred in the past but that we worry might be doubted (the emphatic: *I did walk*).

PRONOUNS

While not as complicated as verbs, nouns do have one special added consideration: **pronouns**. A pronoun is a word that is allowed to "stand in for" or "replace" another noun. The noun that's being swapped for the pronoun also has a special name that we should add to our vocabulary for convenience's sake. We call these referenced nouns the **antecedents** of the pronoun.

Notice that pronouns change their form depending on the sort of noun they're replacing: people get pronouns like *he* and *us,* objects use *it* and *its;* singular nouns get *his* and *it,* plural *their* and *those,* and so on. That's because in order to be clear about a pronoun's antecedent we give the pronoun characteristics to match it.

Take comfort in knowing that on the GMAT pronouns are directly tested in just two ways: (1) whether a pronoun agrees with its antecedent and (2) whether its antecedent is clear enough or left ambiguous.

PREPOSITIONS

Prepositions come in many different varieties, depending on the way that they describe the noun or verb they've been attached to:

Time and duration: *at, on, in, during, until, after*

Movement: *to, toward, through, across, over, into, onto, after*

Agency: *by, with*

Manner or instrument: *with, by*

Location: *above, below, in*

ADJECTIVES

Some words can describe another word directly, without needing a word like a preposition to help them. These **modifiers** come in two different varieties, classified by the things that they are able to modify. The easiest and most limited of the two are called **adjectives**, words that can directly describe nouns. In the sample sentence, *noisy* was an adjective. *Small, weird, tight, gigantic, outstanding*, and *squeaky* are all adjectives.

ADVERBS

Adverbs are much more flexible than adjectives. While adjectives can only be used to describe nouns and pronouns, adverbs can be used to modify verbs, adjectives, and even other adverbs. For example:

The dogs bark **loudly**.
(*loudly* describes the verb *bark*)

The dogs have a **very** loud bark.
(*very* describes the adjective *loud*)

The dogs bark **very** loudly.
(*very* describes the adverb *loudly*)

CONJUNCTIONS

Conjunctions are the grammatical "glue" that allows us to move beyond words to the larger combinations called **phrases**, **clauses**, and **sentences**. Depending on the types of words being connected and on the type of connection made, we can further classify them.

Cats **and** dogs hate baths.
(*And* coordinates the two subjects in the sentence.)

Both cats **and** dogs make good pets.
(*Both . . . and* are used to correlate cats and dogs.)

Although dogs hate baths, they are easier to bathe than cats.
(*Although* subordinates the first clause to the second.)

SUBJECTS AND PREDICATES

As it turns out, you can't just use any old noun or verb you'd like when making a sentence. *Dogs to bark* is nonsense because *to bark*, the infinitive form of the verb, can't anchor a sentence. The noun also has to be of the type that can describe an action doer when linked to an action-describing verb. Grammarians helpfully gave these "sentence type of nouns" and "verb type of nouns" names: **subject** and **predicate**. We'll borrow them for our GMAT Grammar vocabulary list.

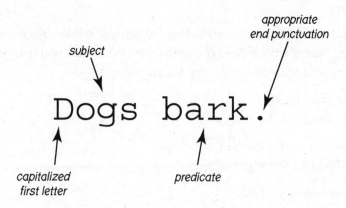

PHRASES

A **sentence** is a special type of arrangement of nouns and verbs, one we often say "expresses a complete thought." A **phrase** is just an arrangement of words that makes sense; completeness is optional. In addition to all the sentences we've used thus far, all these count as **phrases**, too:

> the noisy dogs
> a faintly speckled toad
> the long and winding road
> eating all the porridge before it got cold

NOUN AND VERB PHRASES

The most important thing about phrases is that any part of a sentence that can be occupied by a word can be occupied instead by a multiword phrase with that word as its head.

So far, we only know two parts of a sentence, **subject** and **predicate**. Swap out our single words for phrases and you can build a more respectable looking sentence like *The noisy dogs are always barking*. Subjects can thus be nouns *or* noun phrases; predicates can be verbs *or* verb phrases.

Phrases are the secret to how the test maker can build a question around the simple concept while pretending that something more complicated is happening. All the GMAT has to do is pile a cartload of complicated phrases on top of *dogs bark* and sit back confident that you'll not notice when they tried to slip *dogs barks* past you instead. Like so:

1. The violent, noisome, obnoxious dogs that typically accompany the hunter in the woods after the fox barks constantly until their prey, desperate with fear, has been run to exhaustion, much more efficiently concluding the hunt than did previous even more brutal methods.

   (A) barks constantly until their prey, desperate with fear, has been run to exhaustion
   (B) are barking constantly until to exhaustion their prey desperate and fearing is run
   (C) bark constantly until their prey is desperately with fear run to exhaustion
   Etc.

The test maker expands *dogs*, the subject, into the longer **noun phrase** *the violent, noisome, obnoxious dogs*. The verb is similarly expanded from *barks* to *barks constantly*. Yet no matter how much is piled onto the dogs or their barking, the core of the sentence remains the same: a subject and a predicate. Everything else is just some form of **modifier** or **modification**.

noun phrases

The violent, noisome, obnoxious **dogs**
previous even more brutal **methods**

verb phrases

bark constantly
has been run to exhaustion
typically **accompany** the hunter
concluding the hunt

MODIFYING PHRASES

English has many different types of modifiers, but the GMAT is most interested in testing your ability to handle modifying phrases, phrases that—like our noun and verb phrases—are built on a single head word and used in the sentence in some way to further describe or characterize the subject and predicate. We've already discussed one type of modifying phrase, the **prepositional phrase**:

prepositional phrases

> **after** the fox
> **in** the woods

Just like nouns, verbs, and prepositions, adjectives and adverbs can be used as a phrase's head word to create adjective phrases and adverb phrases.

adverb phrases

> much more **efficiently**

adjective phrases

> **desperate** with fear
> **previous** even more brutal

Such phrases can be used in a sentence any way that the head adjective or adverb could when alone.

Thus, it would be equally grammatically correct to say:

> The dogs bark until their ***desperate*** prey has been run to exhaustion ***efficiently***.

and

> The dogs bark until their prey, ***desperate with fear***, has been run to exhaustion ***much more efficiently***.

You may have noticed that in the second sentence the adjective phrase is set off from the thing it modifies by commas, whereas the adjective in the first is attached directly to and in front of the noun.

If the sentence were instead

> The dogs bark until desperate with fear their prey has been . . . .

it would be hard to tell whether the dogs are barking until ***the dogs*** are desperate with fear or whether they chase their prey until ***their prey*** is desperate with fear. In this revised sentence, ***desperate with fear*** is stranded between the dogs and their prey, rendering the thing that the modifier is meant to modify unclear.

Since "the thing the modifier is meant to modify" is a bit long, we can use that term from our discussion of prepositional phrases, **antecedent**, to indicate it.

> **Modifying Phrase.** A collection of words that jointly describe another word in a sentence.
>
> **Modifier's Antecedent.** The thing the modifier—whether adjective, adverb, or phrase—is meant to modify.
>
> **Dangling Modifiers.** Modifying phrases that don't clearly describe any one thing in a sentence.

Because English is a language that relies heavily on word order for its meaning, the general rule for modifiers is that their antecedent should be placed closest to them in the sentence.

Consider the difference between these:

> Only I love you.
> I only love you.
> I love you only.

Only is a special sort of word that is used sometimes as an **adjective** and sometimes as an **adverb**, so in the sentences above it would be allowed to modify the pronoun **I**, the verb **love** and its object, the noun **you**. Tell a person special to you "only I love you" and you're saying that people in general hate him or her; "I love only you" and there's nobody else for you. Order matters.

In fact, order matters a lot on the GMAT. Take the sentence: "Coming out of the wall, I saw termites." On the GMAT, that sentence would be considered incorrect. The initial modifying phrase *coming out of the wall* is said to have been misplaced or left "dangling" because it rightfully refers to termites, not "I."

DIRECT AND INDIRECT OBJECTS

Just as prepositions have a bit that follows them, which we say "receives" the effect the preposition provides, a sentence's predicate can have a bit that "receives" the action described by the predicate's verb. The **direct object** gets acted upon, usually in a way that completes that idea of the verb's action. Some verbs almost require objects in order to make sense. We don't often say *the dog bit* without adding what or who was bitten, or *I saw* without saying what was seen. The thing bitten or seen would be the verb's **direct object**.

Other verbs can get by perfectly well without direct objects but can take them if need be. *We danced* and *the police left* could stay as they are, or we could add that *we danced **a waltz*** and *the police left **the building***. Either works.

The **indirect objects** are rarer creatures and require that there already be a direct object in the sentence before they can appear at all. The **indirect object** is typically the recipient not of the verb but of the direct object. Usually a preposition is involved.

Take the simple sentence *Bob threw the ball*. Bob is the subject of the sentence and what the predicate says, he does. So he's the guy who throws the direct object, the ball. If we want to add an indirect object, it'll be the person who receives the ball. *Bob threw the ball to Peter*.

> **Direct Object.** The thing directly affected by the action of the sentence's predicate verb.
>
> **Indirect Object.** The thing that indirectly is affected by the action of the sentence's predicate verb; usually the recipient of the verb's action and usually connected to the verb by a preposition such as *to*.

CLAUSES

Phrases that have subjects and verbs are called **clauses**. As we already know, to be a complete sentence, a sentence must have both a **subject** and a **predicate**. Taken together, we call this **subject-predicate** pair an **independent clause**. It can "stand on its own" or "express a complete thought."

> The dog is very tall.
> They built the boat quickly.

Some clauses can't stand on their own; they aren't in and of themselves complete sentences. We call such clauses **dependent clauses**. What makes a clause dependent? Primarily, a clause is "demoted" to dependent status through the use of a **subordinating conjunction** (such as *unless, after, where, when, since, though, as,* and *if*). Thus, these clauses do not count as sentences on their own:

> before they built the boat
> because the dog is very tall
> unless you do as I say

For a dependent clause to become a sentence, it has to be attached to an independent clause with a conjunction and a comma. Without the independent clause, the dependent all by its lonesome gets labeled a **sentence fragment**.

THE FOUR-STEP METHOD FOR SENTENCE CORRECTION QUESTIONS

Let's work through a Sentence Correction question step by step:

As a vocalist and, just as importantly, as a songwriter, <u>Dolly Parton is one of the most successful cross-over artists of all time who inspired many of the singer-songwriters</u> who today routinely top the country and rock-and-roll charts simultaneously.

- (A) Dolly Parton is one of the most successful cross-over artists of all time who inspired many of the singer-songwriters
- (B) Dolly Parton was one of the most successful cross-over artists of all time, inspired the singer-songwriters, many
- (C) Dolly Parton is one of the most successful cross-over artists of all time, inspiring many of the singer-songwriters
- (D) Dolly Parton was one of the most successful cross-over artists of all time who inspired many of the singer-songwriters
- (E) and as one of the most successful cross-over artists of all time, Dolly Parton, routinely inspired many of the singer-songwriters

Step 1: Read the Original Sentence

The task is the same in every Sentence Correction question. Eliminate answer choices that contain obvious grammatical errors until you are left with one. Start by reading the sentence looking for an error. There's usually more than one error in a question, so if you spot multiple errors, just focus on the one that you know the most about. That's the error you're going to carry forward into the next step.

If nothing sticks out, that's fine, too. Answer Choice (A) is there for cases when the sentence is fine as originally written. But at this point, you shouldn't just select (A) and move to the next question. There are undoubtedly some errors that don't seem obviously wrong on the first pass. In order to make sure there aren't any lurking in this potentially correct question, you'll still want to eliminate down to (A).

Step 2: Scan the Answers

In Sentence Correction questions, the most important information to process is found in those **Decision Points**, the places where the answer choices clump together in groups of two and three that all share the same feature. These are the possible errors we must vet in order to find the credited answer choice. So Step 2 of the Sentence Correction method is to pick one **Decision Point** and compare your options. One possible decision point you might have noticed was the presence or absence of the word *who* in the answer choices. Two of the answers stick *who* between *inspired* and the rest of the sentence.

(A) Dolly Parton [. . .] **who inspired** many of [. . .]
(B) Dolly Parton [. . .], **inspired** the singer-songwriters [. . .]
(C) Dolly Parton [. . .], **inspiring** many of the [. . .]
(D) Dolly Parton [. . .] **who inspired** many [. . .]
(E) [. . .] Dolly Parton, **routinely inspired** many [. . .]

Step 3: Eliminate

Does the *who* matter? Absolutely. One of the most frequently tested errors in the Sentence Correction section concerns **phrases and clauses** and how they are **connected**.

In Answer Choices (A) and (D), the *who* does not have a comma separating it from the words in front of it, and that creates a problem. The *inspiration* becomes a description of the group of artists Dolly Parton is one of—in effect, there's a group of artists, who inspire people, and Dolly is the most successful one of them. It makes much more sense if the inspiration is an *effect* of her success. She was so successful that she inspired others.

Step 4: Repeat

That leaves us with three answer choices, (B), (C), and (E). We need another **Decision Point**! We don't need to look far. The three answer choices that lacked the *who* have a split of their own. Answer Choices (B) and (E) use *inspired*; (C) uses *inspiring*.

(B) [. . .] of all time, **inspired** many of [. . .]

(C) [. . .] of all time, **inspiring** many of the [. . .]

(E) [. . .] of all time, **routinely inspired** many [. . .]

The answer lies again in the relationship between three big phrases in the sentence. Start with the nonunderlined section. *As a vocalist, etc.* This is an introductory descriptive phrase that describes the way in which *Dolly is successful*. Her success is further described in the second big chunk of the sentence (where we learn she was a cross-over artist). So then how do we attach the third thought (that she inspired other artists) to the first two?

Using the *comma-inspired* found in (B) and (E) would create a list of two things that are each described by the first phrase, *As a vocalist, etc.* In effect, Dolly did two things as a vocalist. She was successful as a vocalist and she inspired some singer-songwriters as a vocalist. That doesn't sound right at all. As we've already said, the inspiration seems like it ought to be an effect of her *success*, not of her simply *being a vocalist*.

Can Answer Choice (C) work? It's the only one left, so it has to. If you're nearing the minute mark on time spent on this question, then it'd be best to just pick (C) and move on. You don't have to prove that a sentence is correct. You only need to prove that the other four aren't.

But, since you might be wondering, (C) does work. Changing the verb *inspired* to its -ing form *inspiring* makes it clearly a description of the stuff immediately on the other side of the comma. So now it's Dolly's *success as a cross-over artist* that inspired today's singer-songwriters, the ones who are themselves cross-over artists who can have number one hits on two different charts at the same time.

THE BIG 6: ERRORS MOST COMMONLY TESTED

As we mentioned back in the *Verbal Introduction,* the number of errors that have shown up on the GMAT is actually quite small—approximately 30 in the many decades during which the test has included some sort of grammar question. And of those 30 or so errors, only about a dozen appear with any regularity, so that the lion's share of Sentence Correction questions involve one or more of a group of just six errors. Ninety-five percent involve one of the six; about 60 percent test two or more. They are:

SUBJECT/PREDICATE AGREEMENT—The subject of the sentence (a noun) must match the predicate (the verb); singular subjects get singular predicates, and plural subjects get plural predicates.

PRONOUN REFERENCE—Pronouns must refer unambiguously to a single noun, and they must also match the noun they replace in number, gender, and case.

PARALLELISM—Parts of a sentence that play the same role must be put into matching forms. This includes words in lists, in comparisons, and in other multipart constructions.

CLAUSES AND CONNECTORS—Clauses can be either independent or dependent. Linking them incorrectly can result in a run-on sentence or a sentence fragment.

MODIFICATION—Modifying elements, such as adjectives, adverbs, and prepositional phrases, must be placed so that it's clear what they're supposed to modify and so that the modification makes logical sense.

IDIOMATIC CONSTRUCTION—Certain words are paired with other words in English not because of any logical rule, but because that's just the way they're expected to be. Usually, this involves preposition choice (i.e., you sleep *in* a bed, not *at* a bed).

In this book, we are going to call these most-frequently appearing errors "The Big 6."

The bulk of your study time should be devoted to mastering The Big 6. They will pay off more often than any other type of error, and even when other errors form the basis of a question, The Big 6 will still eliminate a couple of answer choices.

If you hit a question and have no idea where to start, always fall back on The Big 6. Use these errors as a quick-and-dirty checklist to help you find your first **decision point**.

For an even quicker quick-and-dirty checklist of The Big 6, think verbs, pronouns, modifiers, parallelism, clauses, idioms—in that order.

Any time you find yourself going back and forth on what seems like an obscure grammar point (is it "throw the ball to him" or "throw him the ball"?). Odds are, either (1) you don't know the obscure rule, or (2) there isn't actually a rule (and you're trying to create one). Either way, stop grasping at straws. Start grasping The Big 6.

Agreement Errors

The first three of The Big 6 errors—verbs, pronouns, and parallelism—all involve selecting the right *form* for a word so that it matches up with some other word.

BIG ERROR #1: SUBJECT/PREDICATE AGREEMENT

The **subject** of the sentence (a noun) must **match** its **predicate** (the verb); singular subjects get singular predicates, and plural subjects get plural predicates.

> Teacher: Would you kindly give me a sentence starting with the word "I"?
>
> Student: I is . . .
>
> Teacher: No, no! Always say, "I am."
>
> Student: All right . . . I am the ninth letter of the alphabet.

As we all know, Dogs *bark*, but a dog *barks*. Bees *fly*, but a bee *flies*. Yes, we *have* no bananas; we don't *has* no bananas. Making verbs agree with their subjects is rarely a challenge for a fluent speaker of English.

The verbs featured in GMAT Sentence Correction questions aren't difficult to conjugate, usually following the standard pattern (*I walk, you walk, he/she/ it walks, we walk, you (plural) walk, they walk).*

Never will you be asked to determine whether the verb goes *fling, flang, flung,* or *fling, flung, flung,* or *fling, flung, flinged*. (Instead, verbs follow the standard *walk, walked, has/have/had walked.*)

Moreover, questions like whether you use *fly out* or *flew out* for a baseball player and a fly ball aren't part of the GMAT's arsenal of trickery.

So how can they test subject-verb agreement in so many different Sentence Correction questions? They hide the subject or the verb—or both.

Subject-Predicate Variation #1: The Separated Subject-Predicate Pair

It is easy to disguise the subject of the sentence by either burying it under modifiers or separating it from its predicate with the same. For instance, on your Diagnostic Quiz:

       distractor   **subject**   distractor   **predicate**
The oldest fossil **organisms** presently known **has been dated** [. . .]

            subject   distractor
[. . .] **incumbent politicians,** including such once popular politicians as Charlie Crist, Florida's two-term governor, **has elected** [. . .]
                                    predicate

In the first sentence, the plural *organisms* requires the plural form *have been dated*, but if you mistook the first distractor, *fossil*, for the subject, you would have gone with the singular *has been dated*.

In the second sentence, the subject *incumbent politicians*, again plural, is separated from its predicate by 12 words and two lines! Notice how the nouns closest to the predicate—*Charlie Crist, Florida, governor*—are all singular? The predicate *has elected* agrees with these singular distractors; *have elected* agrees with the plural *incumbent politicians*.

No matter what the test makers try to put between them, do not be fooled. In English, however far apart they may be, the subject and predicate must agree.

Subject-Predicate Variation #2: The "Placeholder" or "Dummy" Subject

The phrases *there are, there is,* and *it is* can be used to delay the subject in a sentence. Even though the word *there* or *it* starts the sentence, the sentence's real subject follows the predicate verb. Suppose the test maker hit you with

> There are, without a doubt, a wealth of good reasons to invest early in one's own retirement.

you'd look after the verb (and after another distractor) to find the real subject of the sentence, the singular *a wealth*—and not the plural *reasons*. *Are* must change to *is*.

> There is, without a doubt, a wealth of good reasons to invest

In a sense, *there* and *it* are just "dummy" subjects that are holding the spot for the subject of the sentence that will be introduced later.

A related sort of place-holding occurs with words like *everybody, each, anybody, someone, no one,* and *nobody*. They're called **indefinite pronouns**, and most indefinite pronouns are treated as **singular**. Earlier, you saw

> Each of the 16 recent cases in which excessive force complaints were lodged against police officers was reviewed [. . .]

Look past the **distractors** to see the subject of the sentence is the indefinite pronoun *each*, which is here correctly paired with the singular verb *was reviewed*. *Were reviewed* would be incorrect, though it might "feel right" considering three plural nouns come between the singular subject and predicate: *complaints, cases,* and *officers*.

There are three big exceptions to the indefinite pronoun rule that we mention here for completeness's sake, not because they're tested very frequently on the GMAT.

Exception 1: A small number of indefinite pronouns are singular or plural depending on whether the noun they're replacing is countable or not. These include *all* and *some*. (More on this under *Error #6: Idioms*.)

> **Some** of the hovercrafts **are** full of eels. (You can count hovercrafts, so they are plural.)
>
> **All** of the milk **was drunk** yesterday. (You can't count milk, so it is singular.)

Exception 2: A small number of indefinite pronouns are always plural. They're easy to remember, since they all clearly describe multiple things: *both, few, others,* and *several*.

Exception 3: The word *none* switches between singular and plural depending on whether the *none* is being used by the writer to mean *not any* or *not one*. Since you can't read the test maker's mind, it doesn't really matter which one you use; either is correct. Hooray!

> She looked in the cupboard for lights, but there **were none**. (How many lights? *Not any*.)
>
> He looked in the cupboard for a flashlight, but there **was none**. (How many flashlights? *Not one*.)

Subject-Predicate Variation #3: Compound Subjects

The word *and* has a special quirk in English. When you link two subject nouns with the word *and*, you create what is known as a "compound subject," and

compound subjects are always treated as plural, no matter whether the individual items linked by the *and* are plural or singular.

Question 9 on your Diagnostic Quiz had an answer choice that ended

few landmarks and little available water exists

Subject-predicate pairs that appear in dependent clauses must agree, just as the pairs that appear in independent clauses, so here the *and* in this dependent clause means that the plural verb *exist* is needed instead of the singular *exists*—even though the singular word *water* is closer to the verb.

You can also expect the compound subject rule to be tested in the negative, too. That is, only the word *and* can create a compound subject. The word *or* does not. When *or* is used to link two subjects, the predicate agrees with whichever subject is **closest**, so it is usually the second item in an *either . . . or* or *neither . . . nor* list. This issue was also tested in Question 9, where Answer Choice (D) read

little available water or landmarks exists

Since the *plural* landmarks is closest to the verb *exists*, the plural *exist* is needed instead, because *or* does not create a compound subject. But had the answer choice instead read

little landmarks or available water exist

it would **still** be wrong because now the closest word to *exist* is the singular *water*, demanding the singular *exists*.

BIG ERROR #2: PRONOUN REFERENCE

Teacher: Beavis, name two pronouns!
Beavis: Uh . . . who, me?

> Pronouns must (1) refer unambiguously to a single noun, and they must also (2) **match the noun they replace** (or refer to) in number, person, gender, and case.

Pronouns are words that stand in for nouns. We call the word that the pronoun stands in for its **antecedent**. Pronouns must agree with their antecedents, just as subjects must agree with predicates.

As far as agreement is concerned, subjects and predicates get off easy. They merely have to agree in number (singular versus plural), but there is a whole host of ways that pronouns and antecedents must agree.

Pronoun Variation #1: Basic Pronoun Agreement

Agreement by Number

Simply put, singular pronouns must replace singular nouns, plural pronouns plural nouns, regardless of what type of pronoun is involved.

> Anyone who uses this miter saw must put it back where
> they got it from.

Anyone is singular, but *they* is plural. Thus, the credited answer to the question above might be:

> (B) All who use this miter saw must put it back where
> they got it from.

Notice that in the sentence above the verb had to change (*uses* versus *use*) to accommodate the new plural pronoun. Verb and pronoun errors are often tested in the same question on the test, so if you decide a pronoun must be changed from plural to singular, be sure that all the verbs in the sentence still match—particularly, any verbs hiding in the nonunderlined part of the sentence.

It's also important to note that on the GMAT, number agreement is really the bread and butter agreement error. Scour questions for stray *its* and *theys*. Their appearance almost always means a pronoun error is going to be among the errors tested.

Because they involve such distinctive little words, pronoun agreement by number errors makes for great **decision points**.

Agreement by Person and Gender

In grammar, "person" refers to the relationship between a subject and its verb. First-person (*I, me, we*) is used for those talking or speaking about themselves; second, for direct address (*you*); third, for speaking about an absent party (*him, her, he, they, it*).

Agreement by person is rare but does occasionally get tested, usually as a misplaced *you*. If we found both gender and person in a question, it might look like this:

INCORRECT
2nd person **you**

As Dorothy Parker observed, if a woman wants to succeed in this world, you have to play the game better than a man.

CORRECT
3rd person feminine **she**

she has to play the game better than a man

Agreement by Case

Of all the pronoun agreement error flavors, agreement by case is the one most likely to worry test takers, even though it appears much less frequently than agreement by number—probably because nobody quite remembers what "case" means anymore. Let us curse you with this rare knowledge:

Nouns in English look the same in most cases.

If *Rusty* is the subject of the sentence, you use the **subjective case** *Rusty*.

> *Rusty* is the subject of this sentence.

If *the flag* is the object of a sentence's predicate verb, you use the **objective case** *the flag*.

> We raised *the flag* to half-mast.

Only in the **plural** and the **possessive** do we change the form of a noun, and most of the time all we do then is add an *-s*, an *-es*, or a *-'s* (*apostrophe + s*).

> The *record player's* needle is broken, and who stocks *needles* for *record players* anymore?

Pronouns retain a few more case distinctions. **She** *went to the store*, but *Yoshiko went with* **her**.

The GMAT expects you to be familiar with these distinctions, but only passingly so:

If the subject of the sentence is replaced by a pronoun, you use the *subjective case*.

> *Rusty* is the subject of this sentence, and what the predicate says *he* does.

If the object of the sentence is replaced by a pronoun, you use the *objective case*.

> Throw the ball to *Regina*? Of course I'm going to throw it to *her*!

If a noun that's possessive is replaced by a pronoun, you use the *possessive case*.

> Which of the record players is *Xian's*? That one over there is *her* record player.

If both the owner and the owned noun are replaced by a pronoun, you use the *absolute possessive case.*

> Which of these is *Xian's record player*? That one over there is *hers.*

Pronoun Variation #2: Lots and Lots of Pronouns

This variation is less a grammar rule and more a matter of bookkeeping. The GMAT often gives test takers a question with a long underlined section that contains multiple pronouns, several of which agree correctly, save one that the test makers hope is overlooked.

If a GMAT question contained this sentence:

> Every **one** of the great chef's recipes were catalogued and filed according to **their** country of origin, **its** required ingredients, and **their** reception by the critics.

the correct and credited answer would be

> Every **one** of the great chef's recipes was catalogued and filed according to **its** country of origin, **its** required ingredients, and **its** reception by the critics.

because the antecedent *one* is singular, demanding a possessive singular *its* for each of the three items in the list that follows.

The more places to hide a pronoun, the more vigilant we must be.

Pronoun Variation #3: Ambiguous Pronoun Reference

Just as the test makers like to quiz you on pronoun agreement, they also like to give you sentences in which there are too many possible antecedents for the pronoun. In these cases, the trick is to replace the pronoun with a more specific word or phrase.

Faced with

> The government launched an attack on the rogue nation after **it** violated UN airspace.

we would select

> after **that nation** violated UN airspace.

You'll even see the ambiguous pronoun slipped into a single answer choice in a question that doesn't otherwise concern pronouns, most often when the answer choices are long and involve a lot of reorganizing of clauses and phrases. If you're having trouble finding a grammatical reason to choose between two answer choices, do a quick scan for a stray *they* or *it*.

BIG ERROR #3: PARALLELISM

There are two main relationships that elements in a sentence may have to each other. Take our simple sentence we used back in "GMAT Grammar 101" again: *Dogs bark.*

Suppose we wanted to add a second barker to the sentence, to have two subjects but only one predicate. Easy: *Dogs* **and** *seals bark.*

When two elements both play the same role in a sentence, we say that they are **coordinated**. Any part of a sentence can be expanded by coordinating two words or phrases.

Coordinated Subjects

> **The dogs and the three seals** barked at the waves.

Coordinated Predicates

> The dogs **barked and growled** at the mailman.

Coordinated Objects

> The dogs barked **at the mailman and his partner**.

> The dogs bit the **one mailman but not the other one**.

Parallelism Variation #1: Basic Lists and Other Compound Sentence Parts

Parallelism is most easily demonstrated with a simple sentence that would never appear on the GMAT:

> I like to hop, skip, and jump.

Here we have a simple list of things that *I like to (do)*. Each of the elements— in this case, the actions *hop*, *skip*, and *jump*—is a verb in the **infinitive** form, and they all share the same relationship to that little accompanying word *to*.

When a sentence is properly parallel, you could separate it into multiple sentences with the same form that all make sense:

> I like to hop, skip, and jump → I like to hop. I like to skip. I like to jump.

We're not allowed to mix and match our parts of speech in a coordinated list. So this sentence isn't parallel:

I like to hop, skipping, and to jump.

Infinitive, noun, infinitive isn't allowed.

We are, however, allowed to change the part of speech of members of a list, so long as we change each element. So it would still be correct for a sentence to say

I like hopping, skipping, and jumping.

Now the list is composed of three different nouns that *I like*: (1) *hopping*, (2) *skipping*, and (3) *jumping*.

And even if we were to return to our infinitive verb list, we could still change the list a different way and be in the clear—the *to* can be attached to each infinitive if we so desire. Thus:

I like to hop, to skip, and to jump.

Parallelism Variation #2: Multipart Constructions

All of the coordinating conjunctions require parallelism between the things they coordinate:

Apples *and* **peaches** will sell well.
[noun] *and* [noun]

The treasure was hidden **under Henderson's mattress** *or* **beneath the big X.**
[prepositional phrase] *or* [prepositional phrase]

What he promised *and* **what he delivered** were markedly different.
[dependent clause] *and* [dependent clause]

Tomas ate all the Ramen, *so* **Harry kicked him out of the apartment.**
[independent clause], *so* [independent clause]

Parallelism Variation #3: Comparisons

Comparisons are a special type of multipart construction that requires parallelism on two different levels. The first level you're already familiar with: compared items must be expressed as the same part of speech. Thus, regardless of what you may have heard elsewhere, it's perfectly acceptable (on the GMAT and in real life) to compare apples and oranges. Just make sure that you phrase both parts of the comparison as the same part of speech.

> Apples are denser than oranges and are more fun to throw.
>
> Oranges grow better in the winter than apples do.
>
> I like oranges just as much as apples.

But on top of being grammatically parallel, items in comparisons must also be **logically parallel**.

Because apples and oranges are both fruits, they pass the logical parallelism requirement easily. Trouble arises when you do something like this, instead:

> I like **apples** more than I like **the taste of oranges**.
>
> **Apples' skin** is thinner than **an orange**.
>
> The farmer grew more apples than in the nearby farmer's fields.

In the first sentence, a kind of fruit (apples) is compared with a particular quality (taste) that another fruit has. In the second, part of a fruit (the skin of an apple) is compared with the whole of different fruit. In the last sentence, many things might be the subject of the comparison, it's so completely muddled.

Parallelism Variation #4: I'm Sorry, You're Not on the List

Sometimes, the test maker will try to trip you up by putting something in a parallel list that actually doesn't make sense there:

> In order to improve his golf game, Mr. Morton <u>began a regimen of stretching exercises, added weight training to his daily workout, and seeing a consequent substantial</u> change within weeks.

There are three actions in this sentence, which might suggest that you need to create a parallel three-item list:

X	began a regimen [. . .]	→	began a regimen [. . .]
Y	added weight training [. . .]	→	added weight training [. . .]
Z	**seeing** a substantial change	→	**saw** a substantial change.

Now look back at that modifying phrase in the first nonunderlined section, *in order to improve his golf game*. Would it make sense to say "In order to improve his golf game, Mr. Morton saw a substantial change within weeks?" Of course not. The change Mr. Morton saw is not part of the plan to improve but rather the improvement that followed the plan. Instead, the credited answer contains a two-item list and makes it clear that the last part of the sentence is a separate thought.

> began a regimen of stretching exercises and added weight training to his daily workout, and consequently he saw a

SENTENCE ORGANIZATION ERRORS

While *agreement errors* involved the forms of individual **words**, *sentence organization* errors are built on **phrases** and **clauses**.

The larger the portion of the sentence that's underlined, the more likely it is that large chunks of the sentence (its phrases and clauses) will get moved around and reorganized in the answer choices. If the entire sentence is underlined, it's pretty much a foregone conclusion: at least one of the next two of our Big 6 will be the key to the credited answer.

BIG ERROR #4: MODIFICATION

Everything that isn't the subject or predicate of a sentence is, in some way, a **modifier**: it adds descriptive information to either the subject or the predicate (or to some *other* modifier). Consider the corrected version of the sentence from the first question on your Diagnostic Quiz:

> The oldest fossil organisms presently known have been dated at 3.4 billion years old and thus are taken as evidence that life evolved soon after a planetary bombardment 3.8 billion years ago that would have sterilized Earth of any incipient life.

When you **drilled down** to the core of the sentence, you realized that it had a simple subject (*organisms*) and a compound predicate (*have been dated* and *are taken*):

> The oldest fossil **organisms** presently known **have been dated** at 3.4 billion years old **and** thus **are taken** as evidence that life evolved soon after a planetary bombardment 3.8 billion years ago that would have sterilized Earth of any incipient life.

Organisms have been dated and are taken. The remaining 34 words all provide some sort of description of what kind of *organisms* we are talking about (the subject):

> **The oldest fossil** organisms
> organisms **presently known**

or of how they *have been dated* and what they *have been taken* to be (the compound predicate):

> have been dated **at 3.4 billion years old**
> are taken **as evidence**

or of one of the previous modifiers:

> evidence **that life evolved**
> evolved **soon after a planetary bombardment**
> evolved **3.8 billion years ago**
> bombardment **that would have sterilized Earth**
> sterilized **of any incipient life**

There are so many modifiers! And so many varieties! Adjectives, adverbs, participial phrases, verbal adjuncts, direct objects, etc.

However many modifiers appear in a GMAT sentence and whatever kind of modifier you're dealing with, the key is to make sure that the modifying element clearly and unambiguously modifies only one possible thing in the sentence and to make sure that the modifying element modifies in a logical way.

In other words, when organizing the sentence, make sure that the modifiers all make sense in their new contexts.

> Incorrect: Dangled over the precipice, the climber's
>   hands nearly slipped.
>
>   *It's **not clear** who's dangling over the precipice
>   and **illogical** to think it's the climber's hands.*
>
> Correct: While the climber dangled over the precipice,
>   his hands nearly slipped.
>
>   *Ah, it was clearly the climber dangling and not
>   his hands.*

BIG ERROR #5: CLAUSES AND CONNECTORS

> Q: What does a grammar teacher call Santa's helpers?
> A: Subordinate Clauses.

> Sentences must contain one **independent clause**; they can contain any number of **dependent clauses** (also known as **subordinate clauses**) as long as the proper connecting words are used to join them to the rest of the sentence.

Errors of parallelism crop up whenever two parts of a sentence are **coordinated**, that is, whenever two parts of a sentence play the same role. **Clause and connector** errors, instead involve cases where one part of the sentence is attached to or made dependent on another—not coordinated, but **subordinated**.

There are three levels of organization within a sentence:

Sentences are made of clauses. Clauses are made of phrases. And phrases are made of words.

Think of these levels as a hierarchy. Subordinate one word to another word and you get a phrase. In "GMAT Grammar 101," we called the main word in a phrase its "head word." Phrases can be "stacked" so that one phrase is itself subordinate to another head word.

head word + other words = phrase

Ex: *the + Secretary*   *of + the Interior*

noun phrase   **prepositional phrase**

phrase + phrase = bigger phrase

Ex: *the Secretary of the Interior*

noun phrase

BIG ERROR #6: IDIOMS

> The bit about applying the glaze to the shapely jug—
> that's where I tend to stumble.
>
> In English, it's easy enough—"I put this on that"—but
> in French, such things have a way of [coming back to
> bite you]. I might have to say, "Do you like the glaze
> the shapely jug accepted from me?" or "Do you like the
> shapely jug in the glaze of which I earlier applied?"
>
> —David Sedaris, *When You Are Engulfed in Flames*

> **id·i·om** ('i-dē-əm) n. 1. An ordering of words that relies on custom rather than grammar or logic for its meaning and correctness.
> 2. A colloquial expression in a language that cannot be understood from the individual meanings of its elements, as in *keep tabs on* or *raining cats and dogs.*

The final member of The Big 6 is in a class all by itself: errors of **idiomatic construction**.

As anyone trying to learn a new language for the first time quickly discovers, languages are *weird*. English is no exception.

You sleep *in* a bed, not *at* a bed, but why exactly is that? Things happen *at* a party, not *in* a party, but why is it that you're *in* the Army, not *at* the Army? You *get up* from your bed in the morning, but you don't *get down* when you fall asleep. We call these and other expected word combinations **idiomatic constructions** or simply **idioms**.

Logic goes out the window with idioms. There's no reason for most other than "because that's how we say it." This can be particularly galling for GMAT test takers whose first language is something other than English. But even for those who've spoken English all their lives, it can seem like there's always going to be one more idiom you've never heard of in the next Sentence Correction question that pops up on the CAT screen.

Some students react to this worry by trying to cram as many idioms into their brains as possible, which does sometimes work, but is also a lot of effort for very little reward. You've probably seen lists of 100, 200, even 1000 "Essential" GMAT Idioms floating around on the Internet. If you haven't, don't bother tracking them down, and if you have, know that there are many better ways to spend your Sentence Correction prep time.

The most important thing about idioms is that the test maker rarely makes a question whose credited answer turns *solely* on a correct idiom. Most often, incorrect idioms appear in answer choices that are wrong for some other reason, too.

Think of idioms as shortcuts. Don't make your first cut on an idiomatic issue, but when you spot something you think doesn't work idiomatically, use that feeling as a cue to look for an error elsewhere in the sentence.

MATTERS OF STYLE

There's one last area of English that the GMAT tests in Sentence Correction questions . . . sort of. The GMAT *Official Guides* often lump a lot of miscellaneous issues together under what they call "effective expression."

We've said already that you should be careful in selecting or rejecting Sentence Correction answer choices because they "feel" or "sound" wrong. While it's true that many wrong answers are clunky, repetitive, and just plain bad, there are many credited answers that feel just as weird or strange. Indeed, the correct answer is rarely the way that a normal native English speaker would phrase the sentence. An answer is correct because it avoids the sorts of errors we've already discussed, not because it "sounds good."

When you're reading explanations to GMAT questions elsewhere—on GMATClub's forums, in other test prep books, even in the *Official Guides*—you'll often see answer choices described as "clunky," "awkward," "inelegant," or "ineffective." Be careful! Much of the time, these words are just synonyms for "beats me, it just seems wrong," cases where the person explaining the question doesn't actually know the grammatical rule being tested. They're going with their gut, not their grammar.

When style is tested on the GMAT, almost always the stylistic issue is paired with *other* errors in the same answer choice, so that you don't have to use the style of the sentence as the single determining factor that rules out an answer choice.

There are, however, a couple of stylistic points that bear mentioning. These, as rules of thumb, may help you find the correct answer choices more quickly.

Redundancy

If a sentence contains two words that mean almost exactly the same thing, the GMAT will usually delete one in the right answer choice:

> Incorrect: The *new innovations* were deemed too costly.
> Correct: The *innovations* were deemed too costly.
> (All innovations are new—that's what it means to be an innovation.)

> Incorrect: The *reason why* we must sell our stocks is *because* they are tanking.
> Correct: We must sell our stocks *because* they are tanking.
> (Use "the reason" or "because," not both.)

Vagueness

If it's unclear what part of a sentence is referring to—whether that part is a pronoun, adjective, or modifying phrase—the test maker will generally rephrase the right answer to make it clear.

Incorrect: Before we left the house, we *watered,* checked to make sure the alarm was working, and set *it.*

> Correct: Before we left the house, we *watered the plants,* checked to make sure the alarm was working, and set *the thermostat.*

The GMAT doesn't consider a change from vagueness ("it") to a specific ("the thermostat") to be changing the meaning of the sentence, even if the replacement for the vague thing wasn't previously mentioned.

Wordiness

The GMAT likes to add lots of unnecessary words to wrong answer choices, so check to see if a simpler grammatically correct choice is available.

> Incorrect: Scientists have determined that eating broccoli helps *in the prevention of* anemia.
> Correct: Scientists have determined that eating broccoli helps *prevent* anemia.

> Incorrect: Alaska deposits tax proceeds into a fund *with the intention to sustain* the state's economy when oil is no longer a viable industry.
> Correct: Alaska deposits tax proceeds into a fund *intended to sustain* the state's economy when oil is no longer a viable industry.

When in doubt, shorter is better on the GMAT. That doesn't mean the answer that uses the least words is always correct, rather than when you don't have anything else to go on, go short.

SENTENCE CORRECTION PRACTICE QUESTIONS

500- to 600-Level Sentence Correction Practice

1. Tokyo, though visited by many millions of tourists each year, remains inwardly focused, largely <u>because of having</u> such strict expectations of its residents' public behavior.

   (A) because of having
   (B) because it has
   (C) because they have
   (D) on account of having ,
   (E) on account of their having

2. Although powerful enough <u>to bring down power lines, leave</u> substantial portions of the city without power, last night's thunderstorm did relatively little lasting damage.

   (A) to bring down power lines, leave
   (B) that it brought down power lines, leave
   (C) that power lines were brought down, leave
   (D) that power lines were brought down and leaves
   (E) to bring down power lines and leave

3. When attacked, slugs contract their bodies, making <u>themselves harder and more compact</u>.

   (A) themselves harder and more compact
   (B) themselves hard and the more compact
   (C) their selves harder and more compact
   (D) itself harder and more compact
   (E) it become harder and the more compact

4. Unlike the rules governing professional athletes, which require total abstention from performance enhancing substances, <u>the military actively encourages soldiers to extend</u> their capabilities artificially.

   (A) the military actively encourages soldiers to extend
   (B) with active encouragement of the military soldiers extend
   (C) the military's rules actively encourage soldiers to extend
   (D) the military does actively encourage the soldiers' extending
   (E) the military's active encouragement is for the soldiers to extend

5. <u>Without the adequate amounts of supervision, children in</u> daycare facilities can come to resemble nineteenth-century mad houses.

   (A) Without the adequate amounts of supervision, children in
   (B) Without an adequate amount of supervision, children's
   (C) If children do not get adequate amounts of supervision they need, children's
   (D) If children do not get the adequate amount of supervision, they have
   (E) If they do not have an adequate amount of supervision, children at

600- to 700-Level Sentence Correction Practice

1. On average 15 Americans die each year due to violence related to terrorism—<u>less by far than are</u> killed by falling television sets in their own homes.

   (A) terrorism—less by far than are
   (B) terrorism—fewer by far than are
   (C) terrorism, which is by far less than those
   (D) terrorism, a number lower by far than the people
   (E) terrorism, by far fewer than the ones

2. This new idea of the female's ovum as actively taking part in the acquisition of fertilizing material, rather than <u>a mere inert recipient, have emerged from the careful examination of the two *in vivo* throughout the process, including</u> immediately post coitus.

   (A) a mere inert recipient, have emerged from the careful examination of the two *in vivo* throughout the process, including
   (B) as a mere inert recipient, have emerged from extensively examining the two *in vivo*, which includes
   (C) as merely inert recipients, has emerged from extensively examining the two *in vivo* that includes
   (D) merely inertly receiving, has emerged from the extensive examination of the two *in vivo*, which includes
   (E) as merely inertly receiving, has emerged from the extensive examination of the two *in vivo*, including

3. In spite of centuries of critical inattention, Aphra Behn's long-form prose *Oroonoko* had been recently come to being regarded as an important precursor to the novel for many, a milestone of early feminist literature.

   (A) had been recently come to being regarded as an important precursor to the novel
   (B) had recently come to be regarded as an important precursor to the novel that
   (C) has recently come to be regarded as an important precursor to the novel, and
   (D) has been recently regarded as coming as an important precursor to the novel
   (E) has recently come to be regarded an important precursor to the novel, and,

4. Presently just over 7 billion, the world has a population rising at a rate of 1.1 percent with each passing year.

   (A) the world has a population rising at a rate of
   (B) world population is rising at a rate of
   (C) the world's population is rising up at the increasing rate of
   (D) the rise in the rate of the world's population is
   (E) world population has been being increased by a rate of

5. A much anticipated addition to the "extreme" candy scene is the world's largest gummy worm that is 128 times more massive than its smaller brethren, measuring 36 inches long and weighing in at approximately 3 pounds.

   (A) A much anticipated addition to the "extreme" candy scene is the world's largest gummy worm that is
   (B) As much-anticipated addition to the "extreme" candy scene, the world's largest gummy worm that is
   (C) A much-anticipated addition to the "extreme" candy scene, the world's largest gummy worm is
   (D) As much anticipated as an addition to the "extreme" candy scene, the world's largest gummy worm is
   (E) Much-anticipated as an addition to the scene of "extreme" candy, is the world's largest gummy worm

700- to 800-Level Sentence Correction Practice

1. Much of the recent musical's regard among critics <u>are due to its topical subject matter—a feature typical of musicals of the 2000s and that</u> will hinder subsequent revival.

   (A) are due to its topical subject matter—a feature typical of musicals of the 2000s and that
   (B) are due to its topical subject matter—a feature that is typical of musicals of the 2000s and they
   (C) is due to its topical subject matter—a feature typical of musicals of the 2000s, and
   (D) is due to its topical subject matter—a feature that is typical of musicals of the 2000s and that
   (E) is due to its topical subject matter—a feature typical of musicals of the 2000s and they

2. Ironically, successful candidates for a party's presidential nomination have found victory in the subsequent general election all but impossible <u>if there is an absence of support from those who directly opposed them during</u> the primary.

   (A) if there is an absence of support from those who directly opposed them during
   (B) if there is an absence of support from the direct opposition to them during
   (C) with an absence of direct support of those who were their opponents from
   (D) without the support of the direct opposition during
   (E) without the support of those who opposed them directly during

3. Although Congress's proposed ban on the use of anabolic steroids by Major League Baseball players is currently the subject of much discussion in the popular press, <u>significant revision is to be expected before it is to be passed by either chamber.</u>

    (A) significant revision is to be expected before it is to be passed by either chamber
    (B) either chamber does not expect to pass it without significantly revising it
    (C) either chamber expects significant revision to pass it
    (D) it is not expected to be passed by either chamber without it being revised significantly
    (E) it is not expected to pass in either chamber without significant revision

4. His position is rather like <u>the statement, because having a haircut reduces your total hair, and because bald people</u> have no hair, haircuts cause baldness.

    (A) the statement, because having a haircut reduces your total hair, and because bald people
    (B) the statement that having a haircut reduces your total hair, and because bald people
    (C) saying that because having a haircut reduces your total hair and because bald people
    (D) saying having a haircut reduces your hair and that because bald people
    (E) the statement that having a haircut reduces your hair because bald people

5. A majority of paleontologists contend <u>nearly all of the thousands of extinct driven species at the beginning of the Triassic were driven</u> by one single extinction event, rather than by a series of minor catastrophes.

(A) nearly all of the thousands of extinct driven species at the beginning of the Triassic were driven

(B) the thousands of species all nearly driven extinct had been so at the beginning of the Triassic

(C) at the beginning of the Triassic that thousands of species were nearly all driven so extinct and

(D) that nearly all of the thousands of species driven extinct at the beginning of the Triassic were so driven

(E) the extinction that nearly all of the thousand species at the beginning of the Triassic were driven was

ANSWER KEYS

500- to 600-Level Sentence Correction Practice

1. **(B)**   3. **(A)**   5. **(B)**
2. **(E)**   4. **(C)**

600- to 700-Level Sentence Correction Practice

1. **(B)**   3. **(C)**   5. **(C)**
2. **(E)**   4. **(B)**

700- to 800-Level Sentence Correction Practice

1. **(D)**   3. **(E)**   5. **(D)**
2. **(E)**   4. **(C)**

Explanations

500- to 600-Level Sentence Correction Practice

1. **Issues: idiomatic construction** (*because*), **pronoun choice** (*it*), **connecting clauses** (*remains inwardly focused, because it*)

   (B) Both *because of having* in Answer Choice (A) and *on account of having* in Answer Choices (D) and (E) fall short of the correct *because,* doubly required here because *because* is both the correct **idiom** and is needed as a **subordinating conjunction** to render the second half of the sentence a **dependent clause** to the **independent** *Tokyo . . . remains inwardly focused.* The only difference between Answer Choices (B) and (C) is the pronoun whose antecedent is the singular *Tokyo*; Answer Choice (B)'s *it* is singular; Answer Choice (C)'s *they* is incorrectly plural.

2. **Issues: coordination** (*powerful enough to X and Y*), **idiomatic construction** (*powerful enough + infinitive verb*)

   (E) The sentence as originally written suggests a parallel list of things the storm was: it was powerful, it left the city without power, and it didn't do much lasting damage. But since the underlined parts of the sentence do not contain the adjective phrase (*powerful enough . . .*) and the independent clause (*last night's thunderstorm did . . .*), they can't be part of such a list. The only correct option is to use **coordination** to create a compound object for the adverb phrase tacked onto the adjective *powerful*. It was powerful enough to (bring) . . . and (leave). The entire phrase is itself made **subordinate** by the word *although,* leaving a sentence with a dependent clause linked by a comma and a conjunction to an independent one. Only Answer Choice (E) lines up all those parts correctly.

3. **Issues: pronoun choice** (reflexive pronoun *themselves*), **coordination** (the comparative adjectives *harder* and *more compact*)

   (A) A compound object for the verb *making* is found in the sentence as originally written. Slugs make themselves harder and more compact. Answer Choice (B) ruins the neat **coordinated compound** with an extra *the*, as does Answer Choice (E). Answer Choices (C) and (D) introduce a pronoun error. *Themselves* already properly refers to the plural antecedent slugs, and it is in the proper case (objective) to boot. *Their selves* in Answer Choice (C) isn't a real pronoun, though it might be mistaken for one, and *itself* in Answer Choice (D) is singular. The already eliminated Answer Choice (E) also contains a singular, so it's doubly wrong.

4. **Issues: comparisons** (*Unlike the rules . . . the military's [rules]*)

(C) *Unlike* at the beginning of a sentence signals a comparison, and comparisons must be parallel. The first half of the comparison can't be changed, *the rules*, so the second half in the underlined section must also be a noun (or able to stand in for one). Comparisons must also be logically parallel, so it must be a noun of the same sort as "the rules." Answer Choices (A) and (D) compare *the military* to the rules, Answer Choices (B) and (E) compare it instead to the *military's encouragement*. Neither works, leaving only Answer Choice (C).

5. **Issues: comparisons** (*daycare facilities resemble mad houses*), **modification** (the adverb phrase *without . . . supervision* describes *facilities*), **pronoun choice** (the answers introduce ambiguous *they*)

(B) Whether the children require plural amounts or a singular amount of supervision is a distractor; both are acceptable. In fact, the question of the initial modifying phrase's antecedent doesn't work as a decision point, as we could describe both the children and the daycare as lacking enough supervision. The comparison begun at the end of the line is the key; the end of the two-part comparison (*mad houses*) is not up for grabs, so the beginning must be changed to match it. Answer Choices (A) and (E) compare the *mad houses* to *children*, Answer Choice (D) to an unspecified *they*. The choice between (B) and (C) is easy: Answer Choice (C)'s *adequate amounts of supervision they need* doesn't work as the object of the verb that precedes it, *get*. It's also redundant.

600- to 700-Level Sentence Correction Practice

1. **Issues: comparisons** (*15 Americans die due to . . . fewer than are killed by*), **modification** (the choice of a dash or comma), **quantities and counts** (*fewer/less*)

(B) The alternating *less* and *fewer* in the answer choices signals that a **quantities and counts** rule is being tested, and, as usual, tested alongside a comparison rule. Comparisons are usually easier to check than other errors and reward us with more eliminated answers. As always, items compared must be parallel: *15 die* in the unchangeable part of the sentence, so the second half of the comparison must also be a verb like *die*. Answer Choice (E) compares the noun *ones*, so it's out, and Answer Choice (D) changes the comparison to one between *number* and *people*, both nouns, but not logically parallel. Answer Choices (A) and (B) both have *are*, acceptable verbs, leaving the **quantities and counts** question as the tie-breaker. Fifteen Americans can be counted, so they must be compared with *fewer*, not *less*. (Of the other answers, only the already eliminated Answer Choice (E) gets this second issue correct.)

2. **Issues: parallelism** (*as X rather than as Y*), **subject-predicate agreement** (*this new idea . . . has emerged*), **modifiers** (*extensive/extensively*), **word-phrase-clause problems** (the choice of form for the final phrase *including immediately . . .*)

   (E) *Rather than* signals another comparison. The parts of the two part idiom as *X rather than as Y* must be parallel. The static half of the sentence establishes the first part as *actively taking part . . .* a verb phrase with lots of modifiers. Even if not so heavily modified, the second part must also be a verb (or verb phrase). Answer Choices (A), (B), and (C) all would compare nouns, *recipient* or *recipients*, and can be eliminated. Though it might not sound as graceful as we'd like, *merely inertly receiving* will still do for a verb.

   Answer Choice (D) is eliminated by both of the other issues present. The idiom must be completed with a second *as*, but Answer Choice (D) omits it [as (A) and (D) also do]. And the phrase ending in *immediately post coitus* can work as a descriptive modifying phrase with Answer Choice (E)'s *including*, but not with Answer Choice (D)'s *which* preceded by a comma. "*Comma*" *which* attaches the description that follows the *which* to whatever is on the other side of the comma, and here that would be ambiguous, with us left uncertain as to whether its antecedent is *two*, *in vivo*, or *examination*.

3. **Issues: verb tense** (had/has), **idiomatic construction** (*X is regarded as Y*), **word-phrase-clause problems** (the choice in comma placement and conjunction after *novel*)

   (C) This question contains the idiom *X is regarded as Y*, which Answer Choices (B), (C), and (D) use correctly. The verb at the beginning of the underlined section must agree with the subject. While it might not be clear what *Oroonoko* is meant to be at first, but the rest of the sentence clues us in to the fact that it's a book, and thus singular. *Has* is demanded, and *have* eliminates Answer Choices (A) and (B). The choice between Answer Choices (C) and (D) comes down to the end of the underlined section, whose form will determine whether the remainder of the sentence forms a compound object of *regarded as*, as it would in Answer Choice (D), or an **appositive phrase**, a rarer form of coordination that starts showing up on the test's more difficult questions.

Appositives link the phrases on either side of the comma, treating the comma like an equals sign, sort of. Like in comparisons, the phrases on either side of the comma need to be the same part of speech as the other and make logical sense. Logic kills Answer Choice (E). The placement of the comma would indicate that coming to be regarded by lots of people as a precursor to the novel counts as a milestone of early feminist literature. The **coordination** in Answer Choice (C) is preferable: the book has come to be regarded as two things, a feminist milestone and a precursor to the novel. The *for many* set off by commas is used here as—surprise, surprise—a distractor, meant to make it harder to see the coordination it's interrupting.

4. **Issues: modification** (the arrangement of *world, population, rising*), **idiomatic construction** (*is rising at a rate of*), **numbers and amounts** (sorting out the *rate*, *rise*, and *percentage*)

   (B) The non-underlined introductory modifying phrase modifies whatever sits on the other side of the comma. As written originally, the *world* is the thing being counted as over 7 billion. Clearly, it's the population we're counting, and Answer Choices (B), (C), and (E) do just that, while Answer Choice (D) has the *rise* as being over 7 billion. To arrive at Answer Choice (B), we can look to the number question. If the population is at 7 billion, what is rising? The percentage is rising. How is it rising? At a rate of 1.1 percent. Answer Choice (C) gets the idiom wrong, inserting an extra *up*. Answer Choice (E) changes the *at* to a *by*, which, when combined with the switch to the passive voice, would mean that the rate is the thing that's making the population number go up. The *rate* should be the amount the population is going up by, not the cause of its increase.

5. **Issues: modification** (choosing an antecedent for *A much anticipated . . .*), **connecting clauses** (**coordinating** the first two clauses)

   (C) The switch between *that is* and *is* across the end of the answer choices would be an easy decision point to start with. *That* would serve as a conjunction, making one long phrase out of the two *is* phrases, resulting in the circular statement that this giant gummy worm is the largest worm that is 128 times as big as a normal worm, or, in other words, the largest worm that is the size that it is. Out go Answer Choices (A) and (B). The remaining answer choices turn the last clause in the sentence into some sort of modifying phrase.

700- to 800-Level Sentence Correction Practice

1. **Issues: subject-predicate agreement** (*much . . . is*), **connecting clauses** (constructing a descriptive phrase after the dash)

   (D) The tricky subject *much* is singular, demanding *is*, instead of the *are* found in Answer Choices (A) and (B).

   Additionally, the tail end of the underlined section is mislinked with what follows it in all but Answer Choice (D). The correct answer coordinates two descriptions of the *feature*. It is one *that is typical . . . and that will hinder*. Answer Choice (A) drops the first *that*, and (B) turns the second into a *they*. Answer Choice (C) turns the second half of the coordinated description into a verb phrase, which doesn't match the adjective phrase *typical . . .* , and Answer Choice (E) turns the second one into an independent clause, incorrectly linked to what precedes it with an *and*, instead of the *and* and a comma that would be needed.

2. **Issues: idiomatic construction** (*X is all but impossible without Y*), **modifiers** (the migrating *direct* and *during*), **word-phrase-clause errors** (*if* versus *with* or *without*)

   (E) A slightly more obscure idiom than on easier questions, (*X is all but impossible without Y*) eliminates the *if*'s in Answer Choices (A) and (B) as well as the *with* in Answer Choice (C). The words *during* and *direct* move around a great deal from answer choice to answer choice, and the movement results in various nonsensical meanings for the incorrect choices. Answer Choice (A)'s arrangement is perfectly acceptable, but Answer Choice (B) is ambiguous (it's not clear whether the opposition happened during the primary or whether the victory is impossible during the primary). Answer Choice (C) tries to avoid the error with *from*, but the resulting phrase *were their opponents from the primary* is itself idiomatically incorrect. Answer Choice (D)'s *during* is as ambiguous as Answer Choice (B)'s. (How can the opposition support the nominee *during* the primary, the time when they are the opposition?)

3. <u>Issues</u>: **word-phrase-clause problems** (deciding what type of clauses make sense together), **idiomatic constructions** (*pass in a chamber*)

(E) Another obscure idiom appears, as they tend to do in the upper reaches of GMAT difficulty: bills *pass in Congress* (and other legislative bodies), rather than being *passed by*.

The major challenge of the sentence is organizing the subjects and predicates of the clauses so that they make sense. The bill should be the one passing or not, and the chambers aren't the ones expecting the passage.

4. <u>Issues</u>: **comparisons** (*his position is like saying*), **connecting clauses** (**coordinating** *because . . .* and *because . . .*)

(C) The choice between *the statement* and *saying* is irrelevant as far as the comparison is concerned, but the two things said in the saying/statement must still be properly coordinated in the sentence: either *that X* and *that Y* or *that X and Y* would do. Answer Choice (C)'s *saying that because X . . . and because Y* is the only good option. Answer Choice (A)'s *because . . . because* result in two dangling dependent clauses. Answer Choice (B) does the same, though with only one *because*. Answer Choice (D)'s *having* and *that because* creates a run-on instead, while Answer Choice (E)'s placement of the *because* spoils the sentence's meaning. (Bald people having no hair isn't a cause of the statement or of the reduction in hair from the haircut.)

5. <u>Issues</u>: **idiomatic construction** (two: *contend that* and *so driven by*), **modification** (placement of *so*)

(D) Two idiomatic constructions combine to form a thorny mess. The easiest idiom to track would be *contend that*. Answer Choices (A), (B), and (E) have no *that*. The organization of modifiers in Answer Choice (C), which has a *that*, suggests that the contention happened at the beginning of the Triassic, instead of the extinction.

So driven is used in the correct answer to drive the unwary away from the otherwise clearly correct Answer Choice (D), and moving the *so* around in the other answer choices only results in awkward or nonsensical phrasings. (In particular, the *so* doesn't work as an intensifier for *extinct*; nothing can be driven *so extinct*, as extinction is an all-or-nothing kind of thing.)

Reading Comprehension | 16

Reading Comprehension questions will make up about a third of the 41 Verbal questions you'll see on the day of your GMAT—about 14 in all, mixed in among the rest. Unlike Sentence Correction or Critical Reasoning questions, Reading Comprehension questions are grouped in sets of three to four that draw on the same 200- to 400-word passage.

The screen splits into two columns when Reading Comprehension questions appear, with the passage on the left and questions on the right, so it's unlikely you'll mistake them for any other type of question.

SUBJECTS COVERED

GMAT Reading Comprehension passages are drawn from three major subject areas in about equal proportions:

1. **SOCIAL SCIENCE**—History, philosophy, economics, sociology, linguistics, etc.—the "soft sciences" built on statistical analysis and studies, surveys, and other experiments involving people.
2. **PHYSICAL SCIENCE**—Biology, physics, astronomy, chemistry, etc.—the "hard sciences" where data and experiments built on physical phenomena (gravity, plate tectonics, recombinant DNA, and so on) are king.
3. **BUSINESS**—Marketing, strategic planning, sales techniques, taxation, profit margins—all the things you'd expect from a test related to the MBA.

To make the test feel more inclusive (and, for lack of a better term, "politically correct"), the test maker tends to focus on topics in the Social Science passages that relate to traditionally underrepresented minorities.

What the GMAT *Says* Reading Comprehension Tests

According to *mba.com*, Reading Comprehension questions break into three categories, "interpretive, applied, and inferential"—whatever those mean! How do you apply or infer without interpreting? Yeah, we don't know either.

On the other hand, the *Official Guide* uses a slightly different classification with twice as many categories: main idea, supporting idea(s), logical structure, inference, evaluation, application. But when you read the explanations that accompany the questions in the *Official Guide*, it's clear that the choice between "supporting ideas" and "logical structure" is almost random. (How could it be otherwise? Unless you understand the passage's logical structure, how could you understand how an idea supports the main idea?)

What's the reason for all the categories and jargon? It's all smoke and mirrors meant to disguise the very simple tasks being called for and the rigorous limitations the questions must operate under.

Truth is, the reason most people do poorly on Reading Comprehension is that they give the test maker too much credit. Test takers overthink the questions, avoiding the simpler answers because, surely, a test of comprehension requires a lot of subtle upper-level thinking. If only that were true!

What Reading Comprehension *Really* Tests . . .

The key to answering Reading Comprehension questions is understanding the limitations that the test maker operates under, the most important being that every question must be answerable on the basis of what is DIRECTLY STATED IN THE PASSAGE. No outside knowledge is allowed because the test maker doesn't want to give an advantage to test takers who happen to know about a given subject area. EVERYTHING necessary is on the screen—you just have to train yourself to find it.

In actual practice then, Reading Comprehension ought to be called Information Organization. You have 350ish words worth of information that you need to organize so that you can deal with three or four questions based on it. The 350ish words is a lot less than you usually digest in one sitting, even a 5- to 10-minute sitting (the amount of time you'll be spending on a single passage and question set).

The range of questions is limited, too, by the requirement that every correct answer be linked to something specific in those 350ish words. There really are only four basic things that the test maker can ask:

1. What was the main point the author was driving at in the 350ish words you just read?
2. What role did this small part of those 350ish words play in the overall point the author was trying to make?
3. Which of the following answer choices can be found written out somewhere in the 350ish words you just read?

4. Which of the following answer choices is directly implied (in that Critical Reasoning sense of the word) by something written explicitly in the 350ish words you just read?

Or, as you'll learn to call them soon, you can be asked to answer one of four categories of question: **Main Point, Function, Detail, and Inference.**

. . . and What It Doesn't

There are lots of things you do when you read a 350ish-word chunk of text in your day-to-day life that won't help you here.

1. **GMAT READING COMPREHENSION READING ISN'T LIKE ACADEMIC READING.** In college you no doubt learned to read with a critical eye, questioning the motives of the author, making connections to things you've read elsewhere. On the GMAT, that sort of thing will only slow you down and leave you less able to navigate the answer choices. How you feel about the text is irrelevant. Whether the text is right or wrong doesn't matter in the slightest.

2. **GMAT READING COMPREHENSION READING ISN'T LIKE PROFESSIONAL READING.** If you're out in the working world, you've probably been given assignments that involve summarizing and presenting vast quantities of written material, material you have to pore over, anticipating your boss's questions, memorizing the more salient details so you can rattle them off under pressure. Even though the GMAT will put the pressure on you, the important details will always remain on the screen for you to refer back to. Thankfully, the only questions you need to anticipate are those in that list of four from a couple of paragraphs back.

3. **GMAT READING COMPREHENSION READING ISN'T LIKE PLEASURE READING.** There is, unfortunately, a timer tick-tocking as you read on the GMAT. You'll find no leisurely beach reading here. Even more unfortunately, GMAT Reading Comprehension passages tend to be bone dry, snooze-inducing boredom bullets. Part of the challenge that's "baked into" Reading Comprehension is focusing on material that you wouldn't care to read under any other circumstance.

There are only three or four questions attached to each passage, and the test maker in no way attempts to make those four questions cover the entire passage or somehow split the content equally among them. Only a very small portion of those 350ish words will actually be relevant to the questions.

In the pages that follow, you'll learn how to identify and isolate the important bits and quickly pass over the rest.

READING THE GMAT WAY

If it always seems that the GMAT question writers have got your number or that there's always *something* you missed or that a little detail should have been paid more attention to, you're probably letting the GMAT control your attention and dictate the flow of information. You're a passive audience member and they're the master stage magician, always getting you to look somewhere else in order to hide what they're actually doing.

Think of written material on the GMAT Verbal instead as a series of puzzles that demand one of a few specific processes in order to solve. You are always *doing* something, not just reading.

You're also not skimming. You read every word. But certain words are big flashing signals that tell you "Slow down and make sure you've got this part." Others will tell you, "Nothing to see here; move along." Take this piece of a passage, for example:

> Scientists have long known that the surface of the Earth is not static, as it appears to casual observation, but rather always in motion. Even the contours of the continents change, but the rate of change is usually too slow for us to perceive. These large-scale movements of the Earth's surface layer are the chief province of the theory of plate tectonics, which asserts that the continents drift apart because of the movement of solid plates atop a hidden liquid surface.
>
> Some early models of plate tectonics treated the motion of plates as though it were similar to a flat piece of lumber riding on top of a conveyor belt, the convection cells in

Which words seem most important to you? What would you take note of?

On the GMAT, the most important words to spot have nothing to do with specifics of the content contained in the passage. The passage could be about Native American treaty negotiations during the Jackson presidency or, as here, the movement of tectonic plates—it really doesn't matter what the passage is *about*, it's what the author is *doing* that concerns us. Accordingly, to the seasoned GMAT test taker, the passage probably looks more like this:

Scientists have **long known** that the surface of the Earth **is not** static, as it appears to casual observation, **but rather** always in motion. **Even** the contours of the continents change, **but** the rate of change **is usually** too slow for us to perceive. **These** large-scale movements of the Earth's surface layer are the chief province of the theory of plate tectonics, **which asserts** that the continents drift apart **because of** the movement of solid plates atop a hidden liquid surface.

Some early models of plate tectonics treated the motion of plates **as though** it were **similar to** a flat piece of lumber riding on top of a conveyor belt, the convection cells in

Read for Structure and Function

Imagine that a power surge at the test center fried your monitor and all you could see were those words we highlighted.

long known   **is not**

        but rather   **Even**

          but   **is usually**

   These

which asserts   **because of**

  Some early   **as**

though   **similar to**

Obviously, there would be certain types of questions that you'd be unable to answer.

> According to the passage, the first theoretical model of tectonic plate movement relied on the analogy that

Notice that you would still, from just a few words, be able to tell where in the passage to start looking for the answer should the fritzed out computer monitor spontaneously start working again. It's either going to be the chunk of text following "long known" or the one after "some early."

Notice also that even without the content, you'd have a pretty good idea of how to describe the author's main point. At the least, you could eliminate some of the answer choices in a question like:

> Which of the following best describes the author's primary purpose?

Admittedly, your understanding of the passage would sound something like this:

> *Apparently, there is some phenomenon that somebody has known for a long time that can be described one way and not some other way.*
>
> *Then a bit later there's a definition of some sort of theory, probably one that describes the phenomenon they were just talking about.*
>
> *Then a little later still, there's a discussion of something else, probably a different theory, one that came before the one that was earlier described in the passage.*
>
> *This new theory or description treated the phenomenon as though it was like some other thing—and probably we'll find out later that treating it that way was wrong somehow.*

That is to say, you'd know an awful lot from only 19 of the passage excerpt's 113 words. You'd know both the **structure** of the passage and the **function** of most of the details. Many GMAT questions would be completely doable with only what we have now.

The models mentioned in the second paragraph serve primarily to

> (A) present a point of view that the author later shows to have been discredited for insufficient reasons

 (B) contrast with the author's preferred interpretation of the details of an interpretation taken as incorrect

THE KEY TO KEYWORDS

As you read any chunk of GMAT text, you should be on the alert, waiting for **keywords** that will allow you to break the information contained in the text into smaller, more useful chunks. **Keywords** come in many different flavors, each with their own use.

Timing Keys	First, second, finally, in the end, in the 1850s, later, earlier, was once
Illustrating Keys	For example, to illustrate, this can be seen in, which shows, such
Emphasis Keys	Fortunately, crucially, most important, disastrously, even goes so far as
Concluding Keys	Therefore, thus, consequently, from this we can, in conclusion
Doubt Keys	Appears, seems, was even once, some critics contend, might be taken to
Continuing Keys	Moreover, additionally, also, as well as, and, further, not only
Contrasting Keys	However, nevertheless, despite, yet, although, but, rather.
Place Holding Keys	This, that, these, those, such as, such a, the latter, the former

Be careful! It's very easy to misuse keywords. When doing pencil-and-paper practice problems, people often underline and circle these words as they read them and stop there, treating the passage like some sort of word jumble search. *Finding* the keys is only the first step to understanding the passage. It's how you *use* them that counts.

So how do we use the keywords? When you see a keyword, pause long enough to figure out what the keyword tells you about the relationship between the pieces of information that surround it in the passage. GMAT questions are, at their core, built on the relationships between details. In action, the process would go something like this:

1

2

Scientists have **long known** that the surface of the Earth is not

3 — static, as it appears to casual observation, **but rather** always in

4

motion. **Even** the contours of the continents change, **but** the rate

6

5 — of change is usually too slow for us to perceive. **These** large-scale

movements of the Earth's surface layer are the chief province of

7

the theory of plate tectonics, **which asserts** that the continents

drift apart **because of** the movement of solid plates atop a hidden

8 — liquid surface.

Some early models of plate tectonics treated the motion of plates
as though it were similar to a flat piece of lumber riding on top of a
conveyor belt, the convection cells in

1 Sets up a contrast between old and new info? No new info in this ¶.
Keep in mind for later.

2 Another contrast. What are the two parts? (1) appears static, but isn't
and (2) is in motion (though slow). What's the contrast about? Earth's
surface.

3 More info about (2) from before.

4 Contrast: actual vs. perceived. What's the contrast about? Movement
of continents.

5 Hanging contrast. No exceptions given.

6 "These" what? Connect the dots . . . this describes earlier "contours
of continents changing."

7 Definition of what? The theory of plate tectonics.

8 What causes what? Drift caused by movement of solid on liquid.

If we could get inside the head of the GMAT test taker using this approach,
we'd hear an inner monologue not too different from what we saw when we
didn't know what the content was:

> OK, so there's a phenomenon that appears one way but is
> another: the Earth's surface appears still but actually moves.
> And now more about this: blah, blah, OK I get it, it seems still
> because of how slow it is. Hmmm hmmm—wait, **these** large-
> scale movements? Which ones were those? Ah, right, the ones
> that are hard to see because they're slow. The continent ones.
> So those movements are described by a theory. And now we get
> the theory's definition. And it's about a cause. Something about
> solids and liquids—another this versus that kind of thing.

Savvy GMAT readers are always asking questions, always double checking to make sure they understand the relationship between what they've already read and what they are reading at that moment. They're looking forward to what they're going to read in the future, waiting for the second half of two-part constructions, and noticing when questions are asked but left unanswered.

These readers aren't worried that they need to know exactly how the theory of plate tectonics works, though. They're confident that should they run across the question:

> According to the passage, which of the following is a
> central claim of plate tectonics?

All they will have to do is go back to the part of the passage where they know the definition lies and reread it to make sure they can recognize the correct answer when they read the answer choices.

THE PAYOFF

As we said earlier, the authors of this book have been working one-on-one with GMAT students for a long time now. The first time we force a student to slow down and read the passage in this way, the response is, inevitably, "How am I going to have time to do all of that? I'm already going too slow."

To this, we always respond: "The reason you're going too slow now is that you skim the passage, then get to the questions and realize you don't know what's going on, so all that time spent skimming was a waste. And you read again, but still without focusing on this stuff, so you end up reading the same part over and over. Your eyes flip back to the question. You read the answers. Because you still aren't sure what the author's overall goal was, you can't recognize the answer when you see it. Then you read the answers a few more times, but slower, hoping the right thing leaps out at you."

People who move too slowly in the Verbal section are going so slowly because they spend all their time trying to rush. To quote a certain green space muppet:

> "This one [. . .] all his life has he looked away [. . .] Never his mind
> on where he was. Hmm? What he was doing. Hmph. Adventure.
> Heh. Excitement. Heh. A Jedi craves not these things."

The reason we read passages this way is because of the way that the GMAT question writers build questions.

You know that one of the things they might ask you about a chunk of text is "Do you remember what the author said about X?" If they're going to ask that question, they're not going to make it easy to find that detail. They've got to hide the right answer in some way and make wrong answers somehow seem right. From the passage we've read so far, we might see this question:

> According to the passage, the reason that the contours of
> the continents change

The correct answer would likely not be anything written within two lines of that very recognizable phrase "contours of the continents." Instead, it would be:

> (A) is the influence of the molten layer beneath the
>   Earth's solid surface

The savvier test takers already made that connection when they saw the place-holding keyword "these."

> Wait, **these** large-scale movements? Which ones were
> those? Ah, right, the continent ones. The theory says
> they're caused by this liquid stuff . . .

If the test maker wanted to make this question harder, he would go a couple of steps further in disguising that answer. In the part of the passage that we didn't excerpt above, the author introduces further ways to describe "the liquid stuff." If you're taking note of the connections between the jargon the passage is slinging around, you'd still be able to pick the right answer, even if it showed up as:

> (A) is the circulation of convection currents in the ductile
>   material below the 1300°C isotherm

Wrong answers would be phrased to attract lazier or less aware test takers.

> (B) were once the chief province of the theory of plate
>   tectonics

That answer would be great if not for the word "once." The passage does say that this movement of continents is what the theory of plate tectonics describes, but it doesn't indicate that there was a time when it was, and now it's not.

For people just reading for things that "sound right" or, worse yet, "sound like something the author talked about," this answer choice would certainly be tempting. It quotes the text of the passage almost verbatim. And there was something in the passage that was described as being one way for a while, then later another, the conveyor-belt theory from the second paragraph.

With only a vague understanding of the relationship between ideas, you might well fall for this trap answer choice.

These traps don't just appear in Reading Comprehension questions. Critical Reasoning and, yes, even Sentence Correction questions use these very same patterns to try to mislead you, and reading them in the way we've been describing in this section is, undoubtedly, the best way to avoid falling for the test maker's trickery.

Success on the GMAT isn't simply a matter of learning a collection of grammar rules or some formal logic. To succeed, you must learn how GMAT questions are designed to trap you and how to prepare yourself from the very beginning of a question to avoid those traps. Play by the GMAT's rules, know the GMAT's habits, and no score is out of your reach.

ADAPTIVE DIFFICULTY IN READING COMPREHENSION

It's not been clearly established whether the GMAT algorithm continues "adapting" during each three-to-four-question Reading Comprehension passage and question set. It's likely that the test maker has a smaller subpool of questions available for each passage, so that if you were to get the first two questions attached to a passage correct, the final question would be statistically harder than the previous two. It's also possible that the test maker assigns difficulty to the entire passage plus question set—so that missing the first two of three questions wouldn't noticeably reduce the difficulty on the third.

It's hard to tell which of these two models the test maker uses because part of what makes a question hard or easy is the passage it's attached to, and that can't change once you start a set. So, it's probably best to just not think about it. Do each question as it comes, and don't worry about whether one "feels" harder or easier.

PASSIVE VERSUS ACTIVE READING

To succeed at GMAT Reading Comprehension, you have to force yourself to read a new way, to **read actively, rather than passively**. This means that you need to read with an eye toward the specific tasks that the test maker can ask you to do.

Thus, as you read, you **interrogate the author**, taking in each piece of information one at a time. As each bit of information comes in, ask yourself, "What does this have to do with what the author already said?" and "Why is the author talking about this now?" and "Is this something new or just the continuation of a previous thought?"

Start slowly. The first sentence of a passage is not necessarily the most important. It might be a relatively meaningless bit of contextual flavor meant to throw you off the scent of the real purpose of the passage. Or it might be the author's main point, laid out as clear as day. Whichever it is, you're not going to know immediately because you have no context to put that first sentence into. The context will grow as you read each new sentence, and with that growing context, you'll be able to pick up speed.

Don't be afraid to circle back and reread a sentence or even a paragraph if something you read doesn't make sense. If you find yourself saying, "Wait, I thought this was about otters and how they clean their food, so why is the author talking about whales?" then go back and reread the otter bit. The relationship will always be spelled out somewhere.

This doesn't mean you have to understand each new bit of information completely. It's far more important to **understand the *relationship* to the author's overall point** and to the information you've already read. Your understanding of that relationship will only need to be specific enough to answer the sorts of questions that the test maker asks. (We'll discuss this more momentarily.)

Don't rush on to the next paragraph until you know what to make of the first. The second paragraph will usually go faster, and the third (if there is one) will go faster still. Build momentum by being an active reader!

When you're done reading, you won't have every answer to every possible question committed to memory or summarized in your notes, but you will know the general "shape" of the passage and the locations of the various kinds of details, and, most importantly, you will have a grasp on what the different parts of the passage contribute to the author's overall agenda.

KEYS TO READING COMPREHENSION

1. Read quickly, but don't rush.
2. Know the four basic questions and what they ask.
3. Take notes to help you answer the four basic questions.
4. Learn to predict and spot the wrong-answer traps.
5. Ignore your real-world knowledge about the passage content.

Taking Notes

Your noteboard is your best friend during Reading Comprehension passage sets, so long as you know what is helpful to write and what isn't. You don't have to summarize the passage in any detail as you read. In fact, writing out summaries of paragraphs tends to take longer than just rereading a paragraph would. Instead, let your noteboard keep track of

- the passage's basic **structure** (the role each paragraph plays, the relationship between paragraphs) and
- the author's **argument** and how it's developed (where does the author take a side, how does the author develop the argument?),

and use your notes to create

- a rough guide to help you recall where certain kinds of details are found (examples, definitions, exceptions).

Reading for Structure

Knowing the structure of a passage is much more important than knowing all the nitty-gritty details of its content. Being able to say, "in the first paragraph, the author introduced this one guy's theory, and in the second, he attacked it by giving counterexamples" will get you a lot further than trying to commit each detail of the first theory and each detail of the second to memory because **the details will stay on the screen**. If you're faced with a **Detail** question that asks

> According to the passage, the first theoretical model of
> tectonic plate movement relied on the analogy that

you can always just go back to the paragraph that talks about the first theoretical model and confirm the answer—provided your notes helped you divide up the passage into its component parts. Now, how do we find those parts?

Structural Keywords

Just as with the Critical Reasoning questions, structural keywords will help you immensely as you answer Reading Comprehension questions if you know what to do when you see them. The most important of these keywords you can think of as the "road signs" that will help you navigate the passage, telling you either "Caution: things get tricky ahead, slow down," or "Nothing to see here, move along." These are the keywords that indicate **continuation** or **contrast**.

Continuation Keywords

These words let you know that the author is continuing the same line of thought. There's no contradiction, no change in direction, no additional considerations. Some examples include:

moreover	as well as	in addition
likewise	further	by the same token
additionally	not only	along the same lines
also	thus	

However you are taking notes on the passage, continuation keywords tell you that the same note will cover what you've already read and what you're about to read. You don't need to slow down to make sure you've got a handle on a subtle distinction because *there won't be any*. Not here, at least.

Contrast Keywords

On the other hand, **contrast keywords** are signals that the author of the passage either just has or soon will make a distinction, so *slow down and be careful until you understand it*. Some examples:

however	but	except
nevertheless	rather	unless
despite	in spite of	on the other hand
yet	notwithstanding	
although	while	

Keywords and phrases aren't the only way the test maker can make a structural distinction in the passage. Some are more subtle. For example, if the author introduces something as *the usual view* or *as many believe*, that's a good sign that not too far down the screen you'll be introduced to something we might call "the unusual view" or "what a few (including the author) believe." If there's an old, established way of doing something that is specifically called something like the **original method** or **the widespread practice**, nine times out of ten you'll see a new method or a minority practice further down the screen.

To borrow a cliché, we can refer to this as "waiting for the other shoe to drop." Your upstairs neighbor takes off one shoe and drops it to the floor, so you expect to hear a second drop. The test maker tells you **some critics believe**, and you expect to be told **what others believe**. See **on the one hand**, and you expect an **on the other hand**. Indeed, any time the author starts dividing up concepts, that's a sign to slow down your reading and figure out what the division is.

Boil down the points, but don't exaggerate them for clarity. The author isn't going to say that X is the worst thing ever, just that it is really rather bad.

Using the keywords to guide us, we could see that this technical passage, for all its jargon, has a rather simple structure:

Paragraph 1

Scientists have long known that the surface of the Earth is not static, as it appears to casual observation, but rather always in motion. Even the contours of the continents change, but the rate of change is usually too slow for us to perceive.

phenomenon: crust movement

These large-scale movements of the Earth's surface layer are the chief province of the theory of plate tectonics,

theory: describes crust movement

which asserts that the continents drift apart because of the movement of solid plates atop a hidden liquid surface.

definition: explains theory

Paragraph 2

Some early models of plate tectonics treated the motion of plates as though it were similar to a flat piece of lumber riding on top of a conveyor belt, the convection cells in the molten magma gradually moving the continents apart.

older version of theory

This analogy, while intuitive, obscures more than it illuminates, for the liquid-like asthenosphere does not directly propel the solid lithosphere into motion by the force of friction.

flawed analogy (for older version)

Rather, as convection currents in the asthenosphere circulate, they pull the tectonic plates downward, causing subduction. Moreover, the weight of cold, dense plates sinking into the mantle itself drives part of their motion.

better version

Paragraph 3

But even this understanding relies upon an imperfect analogy. More recent geological research has determined that the Earth's crust is not like a brittle skin wrapped around a surging liquid mantle.

problem w/ better version

Rather, the lithosphere-asthenosphere boundary is not a physical boundary at all, but one of temperature. Below the 1300° C isotherm, material behaves in a ductile fashion; above, the material is so cool that it behaves as a rigid body would.

even better version

Essentially, the author introduces a natural phenomenon, the movement of the Earth's crust, then defines a theory that describes how it works. Then the author goes back in time to talk about an earlier version of the theory and why it was bad. A better version of the same theory is presented, but it, too, has a problem. Finally, the theory is revised one more time, and the passage is over.

Notice how little content we've included in these notes—that's because the content stays on the screen. Instead, the notes keep track of our understanding of the relationship between the pieces of information in the passage, things we can't easily spot without reading the entire passage again.

It'd be great if you actually could draw those division lines and labels right on the screen. Instead, you'll have to settle for reproducing them somehow on your noteboard. For example, you could label each paragraph or fall back on a standard outline.

Reading for Argument

When you break a passage down into its component parts, when you understand its basic structure, then the argument is easy to understand. Here, the author isn't really arguing directly with anyone. The "drama" of the passage lies in the small tweaks to the theory of plate tectonics that the author says are necessary and important. As a whole, the author seems to agree that the theory is correct, so long as the tweaks are considered.

We probably would need to add very little to our notes in order to capture this author's argument. The words "better" and "even better" already indicate where the author's sympathies lie.

Don't Look for Topic Sentences

Back in high school, you probably learned the three-part thesis statement/five-paragraph model for writing essays; consequently, you might expect that reading comprehension passages will follow something similar. Strike that thought from your mind!

The main point of a Reading Comprehension passage can be found at any point in the passage—first sentence, last sentence, thirteenth sentence, fourth-from-last-sentence, etc. There's no secret place to look, no place where the author always says, as you were once taught to do, "in this essay, I will prove that A is true, for X, Y, and Z reasons." There are, sadly, many superstitions about where to look to find the passage's topic, and if you've come across any in some other GMAT book, it's time to let it go.

In fact, the test maker **exploits** the fact that many people believe there's a "topic sentence" by often putting concise, easy-to-understand sentences that are only tangential to the main topic in those spots. The test maker is always one step ahead of the bone-headed test taker (which is why we try hard not to be one). The topic may well be expressed in the first or last sentence. It's just not always there.

THE SIX-STEP METHOD FOR TACKLING QUESTIONS

Step 1: Read and Take Notes on the Passage

What do you know? That's exactly what we've been doing these past few pages. But there's still one final thing to do before you head into the questions.

Step 2: Restate the Author's Agenda to Yourself

Most Reading Comprehension questions demand that you be able to take a step back from the passage's details and understand the author's overall agenda. So, before attempting any of the questions, take a moment and ask yourself "What was the author trying to do here?"

If you've been reading for structure and argument and taking notes accordingly, this should be a snap. First, think about the author's **overall tone**. Broadly speaking, all passages are either positive, negative, or neutral in tone.

Positive authors have something that they want to convince you of. Sometimes, there's a mysterious phenomenon that needs an explanation, and the author will present one or more explanations and then take a side, saying one is clearly the best. Other times, there's a problem, and the author likes one particular solution for it. No matter how many sides there may be, the author is on one.

Negative authors also have something they want to convince you of: that someone else is wrong about something. Again, there's a phenomenon that needs explaining, but these authors find there are problems with a presented explanation. There's a problem that *won't* be solved if one plan is used.

Neutral authors don't take sides. Sometimes they're purely descriptive: here's how something works. Other times, they present competing theories or explanations but never tell you which one is right and which one wrong.

Sometimes authors will straddle the line between these emotional charges. They're mostly negative, but at the end they cautiously present a theory they like but don't spend much time on it. Or they're neutral as they describe something, but they seem dismissive of one of the things they describe. Don't worry if you feel the author's being wishy-washy. Just make that part of your statement of the author's agenda.

In the passage we've been working with about tectonic plates, the author probably falls into the neutral to slightly positive range. Most of the passage is descriptive, but there is a growing sense as the passage goes on that there's a "best" understanding of how plate tectonics work, and a couple of not-so-good ones.

To nail our author down in a few phrases, we might put the agenda thus:

> The author describes the theory of plate tectonics and some of the earlier, less-successful versions of it, before ending by presenting the most current, best version.

Step 3: Identify the Question (Based on the Stem)

Just like Critical Reasoning questions, Reading Comprehension questions have a stem and five answer choices. You'll learn (in the coming chapter) to recognize the tell-tale words and phrases the test maker uses to delineate each.

Let's tackle the question we've been flirting with this whole chapter:

> According to the passage, the first theoretical model of tectonic plate movement relied on the analogy that
>
> (A) the solid plates that compose the Earth's crust are similar to the contours of the continents.
> (B) the brittle skin of the crust is wrapped around a surging molten layer.
> (C) the materials that compose the crust and mantle are not physically separate.
> (D) the liquid mantle is like a conveyor carrying the solid crust by friction.
> (E) the crust is like a solid, dense plate that sinks into the liquid core beneath.

In this question, the phrase "According to the passage" followed by the word "relied" indicates that the test maker wants us to find a specific **detail** somewhere in the passage that corresponds to one of the five answer choices, a question you'll soon learn to call a **Detail** question.

Step 4: Research the Relevant Text

Never be afraid to reread the passage before looking at the answer choices. Remember, the answers are *designed* to make you uncertain about what you've read. Most of the wrong answer traps rely on your not quite remembering and jumping at an answer that seems familiar but is ultimately wrong.

Don't avoid rereading the passage; just avoid aimlessly rereading. The notes you take while reading the passage will be your guide as to where to look. Our notes tell us that there was an "earlier version" of the theory described in the first part of the second paragraph, so that is what we should reread. When we do, we'd see:

> ... Some early models of plate tectonics treated the motion of plates as though it were similar to a flat piece of lumber riding on top of a conveyor belt, the convection cells in the molten magma gradually moving the continents apart. This analogy ...

Step 5: Prephrase or Predict an Answer

The best way to avoid the various wrong answer traps that the test maker has laid is to know what you're looking for in the answer choices before you go looking. Based on what we just read, we'd say something like "the solid bits were like planks, and the liquid bit was like a conveyor belt."

Step 6: Evaluate the Answer Choices

Take the answer choices one at a time, keeping in mind that the correct answer usually doesn't use the exact same words as the passage originally did.

> (A) the solid plates that compose the Earth's crust are similar to the contours of the continents.

Answer Choice (A) might seem familiar from a misreading of the first paragraph, where the "contours of the continents" phrase appears. This doesn't match our prediction, and it's a bit of nonsense. The plates aren't *similar* to the contours of the continents. They're what causes the contours to change. We'll later learn to call this a **distortion**—when the test maker purposely garbles something from the passage but uses familiar phrasing to make it seem tempting.

> (B) the brittle skin of the crust is wrapped around a surging molten layer.

Here is something else that should be familiar: a near direct restatement of an analogy in the passage, but not one attributed to the earlier version of the theory. It's found in the third paragraph and seems to be referring to the second version of the explanation, not the first. You'll soon come to recognize this as a **wrong party** trap—a true fact, but one that belongs to someone or something the current question isn't asking you about.

> (C) the materials that compose the crust and mantle are not physically separate.

Here is yet another distortion, taking pieces from the very end of the passage and repeating them incorrectly. Since the discussion of the separation of the mantle and core on either side of the isotherm came at the very end of the passage, it might trip up those test takers who didn't bother to do a little targeted rereading of the passage before looking at the answer choices.

> (D) the liquid mantle is like a conveyor carrying the solid
>   crust by friction.

Jackpot! Even though it starts with the conveyor belt and doesn't mention the planks on the belt, this is still the analogy we predicted.

If you find an answer choice that matches your prediction so closely, you might be able to click and confirm without even reading the rest. For completion's sake, what's wrong with Answer Choice (E)?

> (E) the crust is like a solid, dense plate that sinks into the
>   liquid core beneath.

It's another **wrong party** trap, taking details from the second explanation in the passage, the one that's used to correct the original interpretation.

READING COMPREHENSION QUESTION TYPES

The nice thing about GMAT Reading Comprehension questions (and Reading Comprehension questions on any standardized test, for that matter), is the limited question selection. Even though the questions might be dressed up in distracting language, at heart they boil down to two questions: (1) **what** does the author say? and (2) **why** did the author say it? Or, to use our fancy lingo: **Recall** questions and **Global** questions. Let's handle them one at a time, starting with the trickier of the two, **Global** questions.

GLOBAL QUESTIONS

Main Point

Almost every passage you see on the GMAT will have one **Global** question in which the test maker asks about the main point of the passage as a whole. Accordingly, we'll call these **Main Point** questions.

You'll recognize them easily, because their stems will usually be phrased like this:

- The **primary purpose** of the passage is to
- Which of the following best states the **main idea** of the passage as a whole?
- The author's **overall goal** can best be described as

Note the clues: some synonym for the word **primary** and another for the word **purpose** combined with some hint that you should be thinking about the **entire passage**, not just a part.

FUNCTION QUESTIONS

Function questions ask you why the author includes a particular fact or part of the passage. Why bring up the Duchess of York there in the second paragraph? Why call the critics "small-minded nitwits"? To answer Function questions, you must understand the passage's underlying logic and how the author develops the passage's main argument.

Wrong Answers to Function Questions

Function questions share wrong answer traps with **Main Point** questions (**too extreme**, the **exact opposite**, etc.), but they also have one unique pitfall to avoid: the **what not why**.

> **what not why**—These answer choices merely restate a fact from the passage instead of explaining the fact's connection to the author's overall goal.

The test maker knows that many test takers will mistake a **Function** question for a **Recall** question, and rather than looking for the answer that explains *why* the author included a specific piece of information, they'll settle for a restatement of *what* the author said.

THE MOST COMMON GMAT RC PASSAGE TYPES

In a certain sense, GMAT Reading Comprehension passages are unique. They cover a wide range of subjects. You could find yourself tackling a passage on twentieth-century jazz piano players, followed by one on the properties of mitochondrial cell walls, wrapped up with an editorial explaining the need for leash laws. But, broadly speaking, the subject areas are drawn primarily from these areas:

Natural Sciences: math, physics, chemistry, biology, astronomy, etc.
Social Sciences: economics, political theory, sociology, anthropology, etc.
Arts & Humanities: literature, art, music, film, poetry, etc.
Business: management, profit & loss, advertising, etc.

As we've already discussed, the subject of the passages is not particularly important. Regardless of the topic, you'll generally be facing the same four types of questions.

Across the various subjects, you do tend to see several common **passage structures**, however.

The Controversy Passage

These passages present a controversy in a field of study. Two or more sides on a single issue are discussed. Often, the author takes a side on the controversy, but the author may sometimes remain neutral. Other times the author decides that neither side is correct and a third option is needed to resolve the problem fully.

When dealing with controversy passages, pay special attention to the different sides and the details attached to each. Say you had a passage about physics and the Standard Model, with one side arguing that there's no need for any physics beyond the Standard Model, and the other arguing that the Model is deficient in various ways. You can be certain that several questions will turn on lining the right detail up with the right party. Keeping a jot list of details attributed to each side could prove invaluable.

The Mysterious Phenomenon Passage

These passages present something that is up for grabs in a field of study. How did the universe start? What makes the works of a particular novelist so compelling? Why does supply sometimes move independent of demand? One or more explanations are then detailed. As with the controversy passage, the author may decide one explanation is more compelling, or dismiss them all.

When confronted with a mysterious phenomenon passage, pay special attention to the initial mystery. Why does the author think this particular thing is so hard to explain? As you read through the explanations, take note of any limitations the author attributes to each. If an explanation is dismissed, why does the author dismiss it? If an explanation is lacking, how specifically does it fail?

The Short Report

Often the shortest Reading Comprehension passages on the GMAT are barely more than a book report or history lesson on a specific small thing. It could be a single war, a new type of salamander, or a fresco that was recently found beneath a city.

With these passages, don't try to memorize the details. Notes may not be necessary, as it will be easy enough to scroll quickly through the small amount of text.

Be careful, however, not to dismiss this passage as *merely* a report. There is almost always something special about the thing being discussed, some new wrinkle that the author thinks is noteworthy. When attacking the passage, don't settle for simply identifying the subject, try to understand *why* the author believes the thing being reported on is worth talking about. Is it unique in some way? Sure, it's a salamander. Is this the smallest salamander ever? Did it challenge an old view about what salamanders eat? Does it threaten a valuable crop?

Even in a very descriptive passage, there's usually a lede, some take-home point that motivates the author to write the passage.

The Problem and Solution Passage

These passages begin with a problem and present a proposed solution (or occasionally multiple solutions). Business passages in particular seem to follow this model. As with the other passages, you'll want to keep an eye on your author's opinion of the solution: does the author think it will work, or does it get dismissed? Is it almost good enough, but lacking in some small way?

Often these passages will turn on the exact goal of the people implementing the plan and the gap between their goal and the means proposed by the plan. Don't assume you understand the goal from context. Find the specific part of the passage where the author lays it out.

Pay attention as well to any prerequisites the author places on the solution. Is there some factor that any plan with a hope of success must contain? Does the author distinguish between something that is *sufficient* to meet the goal and something *necessary* to meet it?

The "Scary" Science Passage

The makers of the GMAT know their audience. They know that the typical candidate for business school admission did not study science past the sophomore year of college and that fancy technical jargon and scientific terms (cyclical self-composing systems of ligands; photocatalytic inversion; 1-3 beta-androgenase receptors) can be off putting.

When you see a lot of jargon being thrown around, a lot of highly technical terms you've never seen before, STAY CALM. All of this is for show. Remember, the test maker doesn't require outside knowledge. If a scary term is important, it will be defined. If it's not defined, don't worry about it. It's there simply for shock value.

The same goes for lots of specific numbers in a passage. If something increased by .012% in 12 hours, then by .0358% in the next 36, then returned to a pH of 3.6, don't spend time worrying about it. General trends are important in RC, specific numbers are not. Just knowing something went up or down, that it changed a little or a lot, that's usually all that's needed to get through the questions.

RECALL QUESTIONS

The remaining two types of GMAT questions are "little picture" tasks. Instead of focusing on the author's overall point, these questions just ask about something small that the author said explicitly at some point in the passage. The trick is finding that specific point and matching it up to the corresponding answer choice.

Detail Questions

Most **Recall** questions begin with the magic phrase "According to the passage/author . . . ." You'll be able to distinguish a **Detail** question from its close cousin the **Inference** question by paying attention to the verb used in the part of the stem that comes after that "According to . . . ."

INFERENCE QUESTIONS

The second type of **Recall** question and the final GMAT Reading Comprehension question type will seem familiar if you've already read the Critical Reasoning chapter: **Inference** questions. Just like their Critical Reasoning brethren, Reading Comprehension **Inference** questions ask you to select an answer choice that is directly deducible from information given in the passage but never said explicitly.

Inference questions are thus similar to **Detail** questions in that they both require you to stick religiously to the actual text of the passage; inference just asks you to go that one extra step further, to take two facts and add them together or to turn a double negative into a positive.

Both **Inference** and **Detail** questions tend to use the phrase "According to the passage/the author"; however, rather than speaking in the *is/was/says/did* voice of **Detail** questions, **Inference** questions deal in *likelihoods* and *possibilities*, things that the *author would most likely agree with*, things that are *inferred, suggested*, or *implied*. For example:

- The passage provides support for which of the following statements?
- Which of the following can be inferred from the passage about the study participants?
- The passage implies that which of the following steps must first be taken in order to achieve Olympic-level competitiveness?

Reading Comprehension Practice

Questions 1–3 are based on the following passage.

Josephus, the first-century Romano-Jewish historian notes that when the Romans destroyed Jerusalem in 70 C.E., there were so many slaves on the market that they could not be sold, even at fire-sale
Line prices. But why not buy a slave at no cost? There was certainly no
(5) ethical compunction involved; slavery was then and would remain a long-standing and popular facet of Roman life. The law of supply and demand would suggest that even as the available stock of human chattel rose, the market would find the appropriate lower (but still positive) price point. The answer, presumably, is that potential buyers
(10) owned so many slaves already that any addition to their workforce would be so marginal as to fall short of the cost of the slave's upkeep. In other words, the variable cost of maintaining the slave would have exceeded his or her output. Josephus notes in the same chapter that nearly eleven thousand men and women died from want of food, and
(15) that even the lowest forms of wheat (barley and rye, likely) used to feed the poor and servile classes were in short supply. The true price of slave ownership had, in effect, become negative and would remain there until new fields could be cleared for tillage and mills constructed to be worked. The large, sudden influx of available workers could not
(20) be matched in the near term by the meager rate of expansion of agriculture and industry.

1. What of the following best describes the main point of the passage?

   (A) To argue against slavery, given the conditions imposed upon its victims
   (B) To examine the reason for the unusually low price at which slaves were sold
   (C) To review Josephus' analysis of the slave trade in Jerusalem in 70 C.E.
   (D) To explore the applications of economics to a common problem in ancient morality
   (E) To examine the reasons for which slaves were introduced to Jerusalem

2. According to the passage, what is a reason for the low prices at which slaves were sold?

   (A) Otherwise usual food was scarce.
   (B) Ancient Romans were averse to the idea of owning slaves.
   (C) Not even the poor and servile classes could be fed.
   (D) Jerusalem's citizens were viewed as unworthy of being sold at higher prices.
   (E) Most slaves were of a working quality insufficient to merit higher sale prices.

3. The author mentions that "there was certainly no ethical compunction involved" (lines 4–5) primarily in order to

   (A) lend a historical background to the discussion at hand.
   (B) tug at the reader's ethical heartstrings.
   (C) eliminate an alternative, reasonable explanation for a phenomenon.
   (D) criticize the Romans for the cruelty inherent to their slave trade.
   (E) introduce a claim that the second paragraph will support.

Questions 4–7 are based on the following passage.

For the past ten years, the world has been experiencing a commodity price boom. From coffee to coal and platinum to pork, the general rule has been that if you took the trouble to mine it from the ground
Line or grow it on a farm, you would likely make money selling it, with
(5) one glaring exception: lobster. In 2005, Maine lobster sold for just under six dollars a pound wholesale, yet by 2013 lobster off the boat was selling for as little as two dollars a pound, less than the price of ground chuck in the supermarket. Huge lobster harvests, believed by many to be a consequence of global climate change, have glutted the
(10) market, flooding supermarkets with so much lobster that many Maine lobstermen must wonder how they can possibly remain afloat.

Paradoxically, even as the wholesale price of lobster has collapsed, the price for lobster tails in high-end restaurants has remained stable and, in many cases, increased over the same span of time. Even the less
(15) glamorous lobster roll sold at roadside stands throughout the Northeast has resisted the downward pricing trend. While restaurateurs are generally slow to reduce prices even as the cost of ingredients falls, such a substantial and extended decline in commodity prices almost invariably results in lower priced dishes. One possible explanation is
(20) that over the past fifty years, lobster has become more a luxury good than a commodity. During previous decades in which overharvesting depleted lobster supplies, it came to be associated chiefly with the wealthy, the only ones who could continue to afford it.

Moreover, restaurants rightly worry about the message that price
(25) cuts send. Studies from as far back as the 1940s strongly suggest that people wrongly assume a correlation between a product's price and quality, particularly when they cannot objectively evaluate the product before they buy it. Since few consumers follow the commodity market closely enough to know what's been happening to the whole-
(30) sale price of lobster, cheaper lobster tails could convince customers that your lobster is inferior to that at the expensive white tablecloth establishment down the street.

4. The primary purpose of the passage is

   (A) to discuss the state of the lobster industry and the consequences for those involved.
   (B) to compare the commercial success of lobster and pork in the last decade.
   (C) to examine the consequences of the collapsing wholesale price of lobster for restaurateurs.
   (D) to argue against over-harvesting and other scarce marine life in Maine.
   (E) to argue that prices have declined not solely in Maine but throughout the Northeast.

5. The author mentions "ground chuck" primarily in order to

   (A) mention another good that has steadily been declining in price.
   (B) emphasize just how low the price of lobster is, given its value.
   (C) provide readers with another way of approximating the price of lobster.
   (D) showcase that lobster prices remain elevated in comparison to the prices of some other goods.
   (E) contrast lobster with a good whose price has steadily been climbing.

6. According to the passage, what sort of product might retain its price even when wholesale prices are declining?

   (A) Products that proceed through a middleman business (e.g., a distributor of fish who sells lobsters to restaurants)
   (B) Goods that were previously regarded as luxurious
   (C) An everyday necessity consumed by a large quantity of people (e.g., coffee)
   (D) Food crafted and sold at high-end establishments
   (E) Lobster caught and sold in small, independent markets

7. According to the passage, what can be inferred about luxury goods (line 20)?

(A) Lobster is not the only luxury good whose price may have rapidly fallen in one scenario while remaining relatively elevated in another.

(B) They include all of the previously described goods: pork, coffee, and lobster, specifically.

(C) They experience declines in price according to the regions in which they are sold.

(D) There is an inconsistent demand for them even among those who can afford them.

(E) Their prices are inflated for no foreseeable reason.

ANSWER KEYS

READING COMPREHENSION TARGETED REVIEW

1. **(B)**   3. **(C)**   5. **(B)**   7. **(A)**
2. **(A)**   4. **(A)**   6. **(D)**

READING COMPREHENSION TARGETED REVIEW

1. "The main point" signals that, not surprisingly, we are looking at a **Main Point** question. This passage proceeds by introducing a Romano-Jewish historian (Josephus) who observed that Romans were unable to sell slaves on the market for high prices. It then discusses assorted possible reasons for the extremely low prices, and culminates by hypothesizing that food was insufficient to support slaves. Cumulatively, then, the passage "examines the reason for the unusually low price at which slaves were sold"— Answer Choice (B).

(B) Answer Choice (A) is not clearly done anywhere within the passage— the other, quite contrastingly, seems to just acknowledge slavery as a normal facet of Roman life. Answer Choice (C) suggests that Josephus affected an analysis that this passage is geared at critiquing, which isn't true. The main point of the passage is to explain a specific situation, too, not to explore economics [Answer Choice (D), therefore, fails]. Answer Choice (E) is not mentioned anywhere in the passage.

2. "According to the passage" points us to a **Detail** question. Reading over the passage, it is constantly emphasized that there was a food shortage—the answer to the question of low slave selling prices "presumably, is that potential buyers [would] fall short of the slave's upkeep," and we are told right after that about the thousands of men and women of even the servile classes dying without food and of agriculture's being stagnant. All this points to the idea that a food shortage would be responsible and leaves us with Answer Choice (A).

(A) We are told that Romans did not object to owning slaves, so Answer Choice (B) is invalidated. Even though Answer Choice (C) is true, this is a Critical Reasoning-esque logic trap—to say that slaves were sold for low prices *exactly because* not even the poor and servile classes could be fed is false. Both circumstances arise from a food shortage, but one does not cause the other. Answer Choices (D) and (E) aren't ever mentioned.

3. "In order to" signals a **Function** question! Look at the placement of this line inside the passage. It occurs just after we're asked why slave selling prices were so low. As such, it's highly likely that we're trying Answer Choice (C): to eliminate an alternative, reasonable explanation (moral concerns) for a phenomenon (the inability to sell slaves).

(C) Answer Choices (B), (D), and (A) are likely, reasonable answers, but they are not in any way supported by the passage. Answer Choice (E) is not true.

4. This is another **Main Point** question. Look over all of the paragraphs to arrive at the largest sense of what we're discussing: lobster, its decline (and, in some places, continued success), and the consequences of this decline. See Answer Choice (A)!

(A) Answer Choice (B) is far too specific—although both lobster and pork are mentioned, they are never compared. Answer Choice (C) is also too specific—even though we do briefly mention that restaurateurs will suffer, this is not elaborate enough to be our main point. Answer Choices (D) and (E) are completely irrelevant.

5. Here is another "in order to," another Function question. Look, again, at the part of the passage in which you find "ground chuck" (which, by the way, is a form of beef). Just after saying how glaringly lobster prices have fallen, the author mentions that lobster can cost less than ground

chuck—there's an "even less" hanging in the air there. This allows us to infer that we would typically see lobster costing more than ground chuck, and that Answer Choice (B) is a good choice.

(B) Answer Choices (A) and (E) are not mentioned, and Answer Choice (C) is useless, given that we are told a precise amount. Answer Choice (D) is untrue, as ground chuck presumably costs less than lobster.

6. "Might" signals an **Inference** question. Search the passage for details that help you make a generalization. We're told in the passage that, sure, even though wholesale prices are dropping, the lobster being sold at high-end establishments is still comparatively expensive. There's our Answer Choice (D).

(D) Answer Choices (A), (B), (C), and (E) cannot be supported on the basis of passage assertions.

7. We're directly told that this one is an **Inference** question. Look, again, for "luxury goods" inside the passage. We're told that the paradoxical state of lobster prices might be explained by the fact that lobster is a luxury good toward the end of Paragraph Two. It's not unreasonable, therefore, to think that we know this because other "luxury goods" have experienced similar patterns in pricing. See Answer Choice (A).

(A) Answer Choices (B) and (C) are never stated; while region is mentioned in the passage, it is not used to prove what Answer Choice (D) claims. Answer Choice (E) is definitely not true, as the whole passage is dedicated to finding a reason for the changes in price.

Sample Test with Answers and Analysis

ANSWER SHEET
Sample Test

Integrated Reasoning Section

1 i. Ⓐ Ⓑ Ⓒ Ⓓ

  ii. Ⓐ Ⓑ Ⓒ Ⓓ

2

Amount Needed to Spend on New Hires	Amount Each Student Expects to Make	Amount in $
○	○	0
○	○	720
○	○	1,080
○	○	1,920
○	○	2,560
○	○	3,840

3

Would Help Explain	Would Not Help Explain
○	○
○	○
○	○

4 Ⓐ Ⓑ Ⓒ Ⓓ Ⓔ

5

True	False
○	○
○	○
○	○

6

Yes	No
○	○
○	○
○	○

7.

Would Definitely be Part of the Optimite Program	Would Definitely NOT be Part of the Optimite Program
○	○
○	○
○	○
○	○
○	○

8 Ⓐ Ⓑ Ⓒ Ⓓ Ⓔ

9 i. Ⓐ Ⓑ Ⓒ Ⓓ Ⓔ

   ii. Ⓐ Ⓑ Ⓒ Ⓓ Ⓔ

10 i. Ⓐ Ⓑ Ⓒ Ⓓ

   ii. Ⓐ Ⓑ Ⓒ Ⓓ

11

True	False
○	○
○	○
○	○

12 Ⓐ Ⓑ Ⓒ Ⓓ Ⓔ

Quantitative Section

1 Ⓐ Ⓑ Ⓒ Ⓓ Ⓔ	11 Ⓐ Ⓑ Ⓒ Ⓓ Ⓔ	21 Ⓐ Ⓑ Ⓒ Ⓓ Ⓔ	31 Ⓐ Ⓑ Ⓒ Ⓓ Ⓔ
2 Ⓐ Ⓑ Ⓒ Ⓓ Ⓔ	12 Ⓐ Ⓑ Ⓒ Ⓓ Ⓔ	22 Ⓐ Ⓑ Ⓒ Ⓓ Ⓔ	32 Ⓐ Ⓑ Ⓒ Ⓓ Ⓔ
3 Ⓐ Ⓑ Ⓒ Ⓓ Ⓔ	13 Ⓐ Ⓑ Ⓒ Ⓓ Ⓔ	23 Ⓐ Ⓑ Ⓒ Ⓓ Ⓔ	33 Ⓐ Ⓑ Ⓒ Ⓓ Ⓔ
4 Ⓐ Ⓑ Ⓒ Ⓓ Ⓔ	14 Ⓐ Ⓑ Ⓒ Ⓓ Ⓔ	24 Ⓐ Ⓑ Ⓒ Ⓓ Ⓔ	34 Ⓐ Ⓑ Ⓒ Ⓓ Ⓔ
5 Ⓐ Ⓑ Ⓒ Ⓓ Ⓔ	15 Ⓐ Ⓑ Ⓒ Ⓓ Ⓔ	25 Ⓐ Ⓑ Ⓒ Ⓓ Ⓔ	35 Ⓐ Ⓑ Ⓒ Ⓓ Ⓔ
6 Ⓐ Ⓑ Ⓒ Ⓓ Ⓔ	16 Ⓐ Ⓑ Ⓒ Ⓓ Ⓔ	26 Ⓐ Ⓑ Ⓒ Ⓓ Ⓔ	36 Ⓐ Ⓑ Ⓒ Ⓓ Ⓔ
7 Ⓐ Ⓑ Ⓒ Ⓓ Ⓔ	17 Ⓐ Ⓑ Ⓒ Ⓓ Ⓔ	27 Ⓐ Ⓑ Ⓒ Ⓓ Ⓔ	37 Ⓐ Ⓑ Ⓒ Ⓓ Ⓔ
8 Ⓐ Ⓑ Ⓒ Ⓓ Ⓔ	18 Ⓐ Ⓑ Ⓒ Ⓓ Ⓔ	28 Ⓐ Ⓑ Ⓒ Ⓓ Ⓔ	
9 Ⓐ Ⓑ Ⓒ Ⓓ Ⓔ	19 Ⓐ Ⓑ Ⓒ Ⓓ Ⓔ	29 Ⓐ Ⓑ Ⓒ Ⓓ Ⓔ	
10 Ⓐ Ⓑ Ⓒ Ⓓ Ⓔ	20 Ⓐ Ⓑ Ⓒ Ⓓ Ⓔ	30 Ⓐ Ⓑ Ⓒ Ⓓ Ⓔ	

Verbal Section

1 Ⓐ Ⓑ Ⓒ Ⓓ Ⓔ	12 Ⓐ Ⓑ Ⓒ Ⓓ Ⓔ	23 Ⓐ Ⓑ Ⓒ Ⓓ Ⓔ	34 Ⓐ Ⓑ Ⓒ Ⓓ Ⓔ
2 Ⓐ Ⓑ Ⓒ Ⓓ Ⓔ	13 Ⓐ Ⓑ Ⓒ Ⓓ Ⓔ	24 Ⓐ Ⓑ Ⓒ Ⓓ Ⓔ	35 Ⓐ Ⓑ Ⓒ Ⓓ Ⓔ
3 Ⓐ Ⓑ Ⓒ Ⓓ Ⓔ	14 Ⓐ Ⓑ Ⓒ Ⓓ Ⓔ	25 Ⓐ Ⓑ Ⓒ Ⓓ Ⓔ	36 Ⓐ Ⓑ Ⓒ Ⓓ Ⓔ
4 Ⓐ Ⓑ Ⓒ Ⓓ Ⓔ	15 Ⓐ Ⓑ Ⓒ Ⓓ Ⓔ	26 Ⓐ Ⓑ Ⓒ Ⓓ Ⓔ	37 Ⓐ Ⓑ Ⓒ Ⓓ Ⓔ
5 Ⓐ Ⓑ Ⓒ Ⓓ Ⓔ	16 Ⓐ Ⓑ Ⓒ Ⓓ Ⓔ	27 Ⓐ Ⓑ Ⓒ Ⓓ Ⓔ	38 Ⓐ Ⓑ Ⓒ Ⓓ Ⓔ
6 Ⓐ Ⓑ Ⓒ Ⓓ Ⓔ	17 Ⓐ Ⓑ Ⓒ Ⓓ Ⓔ	28 Ⓐ Ⓑ Ⓒ Ⓓ Ⓔ	39 Ⓐ Ⓑ Ⓒ Ⓓ Ⓔ
7 Ⓐ Ⓑ Ⓒ Ⓓ Ⓔ	18 Ⓐ Ⓑ Ⓒ Ⓓ Ⓔ	29 Ⓐ Ⓑ Ⓒ Ⓓ Ⓔ	40 Ⓐ Ⓑ Ⓒ Ⓓ Ⓔ
8 Ⓐ Ⓑ Ⓒ Ⓓ Ⓔ	19 Ⓐ Ⓑ Ⓒ Ⓓ Ⓔ	30 Ⓐ Ⓑ Ⓒ Ⓓ Ⓔ	41 Ⓐ Ⓑ Ⓒ Ⓓ Ⓔ
9 Ⓐ Ⓑ Ⓒ Ⓓ Ⓔ	20 Ⓐ Ⓑ Ⓒ Ⓓ Ⓔ	31 Ⓐ Ⓑ Ⓒ Ⓓ Ⓔ	
10 Ⓐ Ⓑ Ⓒ Ⓓ Ⓔ	21 Ⓐ Ⓑ Ⓒ Ⓓ Ⓔ	32 Ⓐ Ⓑ Ⓒ Ⓓ Ⓔ	
11 Ⓐ Ⓑ Ⓒ Ⓓ Ⓔ	22 Ⓐ Ⓑ Ⓒ Ⓓ Ⓔ	33 Ⓐ Ⓑ Ⓒ Ⓓ Ⓔ	

Analytical Writing Analysis

Time: 30 minutes

> **DIRECTIONS:** In this section, you will be asked to write a critique of the argument presented. You are NOT being asked to present your own views on the subject.
>
> **WRITING YOUR RESPONSE:** Take a few minutes to evaluate the argument and plan a response before you begin writing. Be sure to organize your ideas and develop them fully, but leave time to reread your response and make any revisions that you think are necessary.
>
> **EVALUATION OF YOUR RESPONSE:** College and university faculty members from various subject matter areas, including management education, will evaluate the overall quality of your thinking and writing. They will consider how well you: organize, develop, and express your ideas about the argument presented; provide relevant supporting reasons and examples; and control the elements of standard written English.

Question: The following appeared as part of the business plan of By Jove, a venture capital firm:

> "In the Cleveland Heights district, the Theatre d'Arte, Purple People Pizza, and the Extra-Select Gym have all had business increases over the past two years. By Jove should therefore invest in the Playhouse Theater, the Pizza X-'Plosion, and the Curvy Gym, three new businesses across town in the Saints Row district. As a condition, we should require them to participate in a special loyalty program: Any customer who patronizes two of the businesses will receive a substantial discount at the third. By motivating customers to patronize all three, we will thus contribute to the profitability of each and maximize our return."

Discuss how well reasoned you find this argument. In your discussion be sure to analyze the line of reasoning and the use of evidence in the argument. For example, you may need to consider what questionable assumptions underlie the thinking and what alternative explanations or counterexamples might weaken the conclusion. You can also discuss what sort of evidence would strengthen or refute the argument, what changes in the argument would make it more logically sound, and what, if anything, would help you better evaluate its conclusion.

ON THE ACTUAL GMAT,
AFTER YOU HAVE CONFIRMED YOUR ANSWER,
YOU CANNOT RETURN TO IT.

INTEGRATED REASONING SECTION

Time: 30 minutes
12 questions

This section consists of four types of questions: Graphics Interpretation, Table Analysis, Two-Part Analysis, and Multi-Source Reasoning.

> **DIRECTIONS:** The new Integrated Reasoning section consists of four question types. Some require the use of both quantitative and verbal skills. Others involve the use of graphics, tables, or text material. The questions also use various response formats.
>
> For each question, review the text, graphic, or text material provided and respond to the task that is presented. *Note: An onscreen calculator is available in this section on the actual test.*

Question 1 refers to the following information and graph.

1. The graph below charts the cumulative frequency of height (in inches) of college basketball players at USC in 2002.

    Answer each question according to the information presented in the diagram.

    i. What is the range of heights within the third quartile?

    (A) 3 inches
    (B) 4 inches
    (C) 5 inches
    (D) Cannot be determined

ii. Approximately what percentage of players is within 6 inches of the median height?

(A) 66.7%

(B) 75%

(C) 83.3%

(D) 90%

---

2. The painting company Youth Pro Painters has just hired ten students this year for the 12-week summer season. Their target is to paint 1,200 houses over the summer. On average, ten students can paint four houses in 16 hours. Each student painter makes $8 per hour and is expected to work 40 hours per week.

In the table below, identify how much money the company needs to spend on additional hires in order to meet its objective. Also identify the amount of money each student can expect to make in half the summer. Choose only one option in each column.

Amount Needed to Spend on New Hires	Amount Each Student Expects to Make	Amount in $
◯	◯	0
◯	◯	720
◯	◯	1,080
◯	◯	1,920
◯	◯	2,560
◯	◯	3,840

3. The table below shows data for the percentage of the eligible population subgroups attending school.

Country	Kindergarten	Primary School	Secondary School	Post-Secondary
Argentina	71	95	90	54
Bolivia	59	91	79	38
Chile	56	88	88	22
Colombia	62	98	95	60
Paraguay	67	86	77	45
Peru	32	81	68	19
Ecuador	45	93	65	21

For each of the following statements, select *Would Help Explain* if it would, if true, help explain some of the information in the table. Otherwise select *Would Not Help Explain*.

Would Help Explain	Would Not Help Explain	
○	○	In South America, kindergartens are not as available as are primary schools.
○	○	Peru has a larger rural and agricultural population than the other countries, and most of the farms are maintained by the families that live on them.
○	○	Parents in Argentina value education more than parents in the other South American countries shown in the chart.

Questions 4–6 refer to the following documents.

Document 1:

Curlypro, a hair product manufacturing company based in Chicago, is evaluating expansion options for its product line. The company has two plants that are currently operating at full capacity. Management has finalized its top three production plant options.

Nanning, the capital of Guangxi Province in Southern China
This 30,000-square-foot plant has the capacity to produce and deliver 1,500 crates per month. The plant manager has asked for a three-year commitment and a minimum order of 1,000 crates per month. Curlypro has some concerns about shipping costs and time, but this would be an issue only if shipping the minimum amount for all three years.

Chennai, India
This 20,000-square-foot plant features a large capacity of 2,500 crates per month. The plant manager requires a three-year commitment and a minimum order of 1,000 crates per month. Similar to the Nanning plant, this plant may have prohibitive shipping costs and timing. The primary concern is that the region's reputation for underage factory workers might instigate a consumer backlash. The plant manager assures us that they do not hire anyone under the age of 18.

Sandusky, Ohio
This 18,000-square-foot plant has a capacity of 1,200 crates per month. Both Curlypro and the Sandusky plant are eager to have American workers supply the company as this will have great marketing appeal. They can also take advantage of some government assistance that will allow the Sandusky plant to require only a one-year contract and no minimum order size.

Document 2:

Curlypro produces two main products—Curlypro shampoo and Curlypro conditioner. Sales have grown substantially in the past two years. Curlypro estimates sales for the current year will reach 400 crates per month for each product line.

The current forecast for sales in the next three years is approximately a 25% to 50% increase each year for both lines. Although all the plants have significant capacity, Curlypro management wants to make the right investment for the long term. They are leaning toward the Sandusky plant due to its flexibility and the chance to keep production within the country.

Document 3:

Market research has suggested that Curlypro should launch two new lines of hair products—a Curlypro 2-in-1 shampoo/conditioner and a Curlypro dandruff control shampoo. Management is very eager to take advantage of the current success and rising brand awareness. Forecasts for the sales of each new product line are 200 crates per month, with a growth rate of 100% in year two and 50% in year three.

4. What is the difference in three-year sales forecasts for Curlypro between the most optimistic and most pessimistic forecasts, including launching either both new product lines or neither?

   (A) 1,137.5 crates per month
   (B) 2,025 crates per month
   (C) 2,337.5 crates per month
   (D) 2,800 crates per month
   (E) 3,137.5 crates per month

5. Answer the following true or false statements.

   True False

   ○   ○   If each crate sold generates $1,000 in profit, if Curlypro decides to work with the Chinese plant, if the shipping costs increase by $100,000 total, and if Curlypro's sales equal the most pessimistic forecast, net monthly profits will be over $1 million in year 1.

   ○   ○   Curlypro would sell more units overall in the first year if it launched both new products, even with the most pessimistic forecast of its current product lines, than if it continued to produce only two products and sold them at the most optimistic forecast.

   ○   ○   If Curlypro chose the Chennai plant and the subsequent negative public perception caused the sales increase to be 25% lower than the most optimistic sales forecast, launching one new product line would not entirely offset this loss over three years.

6. For each of the following scenarios, determine if the selected plant will have enough capacity to manage the production demands of Curlypro. Select *Yes* if the plant will have sufficient capacity. Otherwise, select *No*.

Yes No

○ ○ Nanning plant, year 2: Assuming Curlypro's most pessimistic forecast and the introduction of the 2-in-1 shampoo/conditioner in the second year

○ ○ Sandusky plant, year 2: Assuming Curlypro's most optimistic forecast and no new product launches

○ ○ Chennai plant, year 1: Assuming Curlypro's most optimistic forecast and the launch of both new product lines in year 1

Questions 7 and 8 refer to the following excerpt from a fictitious education report about a fictitious new school program called Optimite.

The new Optimite program has found considerable success in eastern Europe over the past two years. Two school boards on the North Shore have now called for its experimental introduction in North Chicago. The program is complex, requiring a classroom size of 60 students in grade 11. Within an Optimite class would be three teachers working simultaneously. The Optimite objective is to have collaborative learning on site via case studies and matches, physical and mental challenges, and high-level discussions. Students are encouraged to research and discuss social, political, and economic topics and to use advanced technology tools in the classroom. Optimite also requires a diverse student body of cultural and socioeconomic backgrounds, with no majority of any distinct group. Students will be evaluated before participating and again after a two-semester trial. They will be tested on skills such as leadership, innovation, quantitative analysis, verbal reasoning, and communication.

7. Based on the description in the excerpt, which of the following activities would definitely be part of the fictitious Optimite program? Which of the following activities would definitely not be part of the program? Make only two selections, one in each column.

Would Definitely Be Part of the Optimite Program	Would Definitely Not Be Part of the Optimite Program	
○	○	Capoeira martial arts
○	○	Delivering a presentation on business ethics
○	○	A case competition
○	○	A field trip to a museum of marine biology
○	○	Moderated debate on local politics

8. Which of the following issues would not be a concern to the school board in order to launch the Optimite program?

(A) Classroom size and technology resources
(B) Transportation of students to the location
(C) Finding enough students to meet the diversity requirements
(D) Maintaining a teacher-student ratio below the state standard of 24 students per teacher
(E) Finding enough qualified instructors to teach the program

Question 9 refers to the following Venn diagram and information.

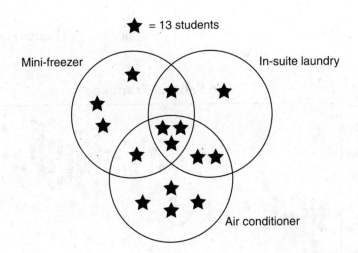

9. Refer to the Venn diagram above. Each ★ represents 13 student residents living in New College dormitories. The student dormitories have mini-freezers, in-suite laundry, air conditioners, or a combination. Complete each statement according to the information presented in the diagram.

i. If one student resident is selected at random from the New College dormitories, what is the probability that the student will have in-suite laundry?

(A) 2 out of 5
(B) 7 out of 15
(C) 3 out of 5
(D) 2 out of 3
(E) 7 out of 10

ii. If a student resident has air conditioning in the dormitory, what is the probability that the student will also have a mini-freezer?

(A) 1 out of 10
(B) 1 out of 3
(C) 3 out of 10
(D) 2 out of 5
(E) 1 out of 2

Question 10 refers to the following scatter plot and information.

The scatter plot below charts the eruptions of Old Faithful in Yellowstone National Park.

10. Complete each statement according to the information given by the graph.

i. Approximately how much time occurs between eruptions of Old Faithful?

(A) It's not possible to predict
(B) Every 55 minutes
(C) Every 80 minutes
(D) Either every 55 minutes or every 80 minutes

ii. Which of the following is closest to the length of the average duration of Old Faithful eruptions?

(A) 2 minutes
(B) 2.5 minutes
(C) 3.5 minutes
(D) 4.5 minutes

Questions 11 and 12 refer to the following table.

The table below shows data for revenues and profits of the top 13 companies globally in 2010.

Company	Revenues ($ billions)	Revenue Rank	% Change in Revenue Since 2009	Profits ($ billions)	% Change in Profits Since 2009
Wal-Mart Stores, Inc.	421.8	1	3.3	16.4	14.3
Exxon Mobil	354.7	2	24.6	30.5	58.0
Chevron	196.3	3	20.1	19.0	81.5
ConocoPhillips	185.0	4	32.6	11.4	133.8
Fannie Mae	153.8	5	429.2	−14.0	n/a*
General Electric	151.6	6	−3.3	11.6	5.6
Berkshire Hathaway	136.2	7	21.1	13.0	61.0
General Motors	135.6	8	29.6	6.2	n/a*
Bank of America Corp.	134.2	9	−10.8	−2.2	−135.7
Ford Motor	129.0	10	9.0	6.6	141.5
Hewlett-Packard	126.0	11	10.0	8.8	14.4
AT&T	124.6	12	1.3	19.9	58.5
J.P. Morgan Chase & Co.	115.5	13	−0.1	17.4	48.1

*n/a means that the actual number could not be calculated due to a negative profit change value in 2008

11. Consider each of the following statements. For each statement, indicate whether the statement is true or false based on the information provided in the table.

True False

O O The amount of revenue growth of the top five ranked companies combined is greater than that of the rest of the companies in the list.

O O The median profit amount is larger than the difference between the average of the top six profitable companies and the bottom six profitable companies.

O O If Fannie Mae's percentage change in revenue dropped by 95% in 2010 and assuming operation costs remain constant, Fannie Mae should become profitable by 2010.

12. If stock market value was based on only the average rank of three values—percentage change in revenue, total profit amount, and percentage change in profit—which company would be the best one to invest in?

(A) Wal-Mart Stores, Inc.
(B) Berkshire Hathaway
(C) Fannie Mae
(D) Exxon Mobil
(E) ConocoPhillips

STOP

ON THE ACTUAL GMAT,
AFTER YOU HAVE CONFIRMED YOUR ANSWER,
YOU CANNOT RETURN TO IT.

QUANTITATIVE SECTION

Time: 75 minutes
37 questions

This section consists of two types of questions: Problem Solving and Data Sufficiency. According to the GMAC, the directions for these question types are as follows.

Problem Solving

DIRECTIONS: Solve each of the following problems; then indicate the correct answer.

NOTE: A figure that appears with a problem is drawn as accurately as possible so as to provide information that may help in answering the question.

Numbers in this test are real numbers.

Data Sufficiency

DIRECTIONS: Each of the following problems has a question and two statements that are labeled (1) and (2). Use the data given in (1) and (2) together with other available information (such as the number of hours in a day, the definition of *clockwise*, mathematical facts, etc.) to decide whether the statements are *sufficient* to answer the question. Then fill in space

(A) If you can get the answer from **(1) ALONE** but not from (2) alone
(B) If you can get the answer from **(2) ALONE** but not from (1) alone
(C) If you can get the answer from **BOTH (1)** and **(2) TOGETHER** but not from (1) alone or (2) alone
(D) If **EITHER** statement **(1) ALONE OR** statement **(2) ALONE** suffices
(E) If you **CANNOT** get the answer from statements (1) and (2) **TOGETHER** but need even more data

All numbers used in this section are real numbers.

A figure given for a problem is intended to provide information consistent with that in the question, but not necessarily with the additional information contained in the statements.

All figures lie in the plane unless you are told otherwise.

Figures are drawn as accurately as possible; straight lines may not appear straight on the screen.

(A) If you can get the answer from **(1) ALONE** but not from (2) alone

(B) If you can get the answer from **(2) ALONE** but not from (1) alone

(C) If you can get the answer from **BOTH (1)** and **(2) TOGETHER** but not from (1) alone or (2) alone

(D) If **EITHER** statement **(1) ALONE OR** statement **(2) ALONE** suffices

(E) If you **CANNOT** get the answer from statements (1) and (2) **TOGETHER** but need even more data

1. Set T consists of 3 numbers with only one mode. Does the range equal the mode?

 (1) The largest number is twice the value of the smallest number.

 (2) The median equals the range.

2. A coin is tossed three times. What is the probability that there will be at least one head?

 (A) $\dfrac{1}{16}$

 (B) $\dfrac{3}{8}$

 (C) $\dfrac{1}{2}$

 (D) $\dfrac{5}{8}$

 (E) $\dfrac{7}{8}$

3. What is x?

 (1) $3x - 2y = 5$

 (2) $y = -\dfrac{5}{2} + \left(\dfrac{3}{2}\right)x$

4. What is the x-intercept of the equation $y = 6x^2 - 13x - 5$?

 (1) $x < 1$

 (2) $3x$ is an odd integer.

5. If $2^{x-7} \bullet 3^{2x-3} = 27^{(3x-10)/3}$, what is x?

   (A) −1
   (B) 0
   (C) 3
   (D) 7
   (E) 9

6. Is x a positive integer?

   (1) $xy = 210$
   (2) x and y are prime numbers

7. Of the 3,200 people living in town A, 25% live downtown. Of these people, 60% live in a high-rise, 40% rent, and 25% both live in a high-rise and rent. If one person is selected randomly from the 3,200 people, what is the probability that the one selected will live downtown in a high-rise but not rent?

   (A) $\dfrac{1}{10}$

   (B) $\dfrac{7}{80}$

   (C) $\dfrac{3}{20}$

   (D) $\dfrac{24}{320}$

   (E) $\dfrac{48}{320}$

8. A, B, and C are positive integers, such that A is a factor of B and B is a factor of C. Is C an even number?

   (1) AB is an even number.
   (2) B is even.

(A) If you can get the answer from **(1) ALONE** but not from (2) alone
(B) If you can get the answer from **(2) ALONE** but not from (1) alone
(C) If you can get the answer from **BOTH (1)** and **(2) TOGETHER** but not from (1) alone or (2) alone
(D) If **EITHER** statement **(1) ALONE OR** statement **(2) ALONE** suffices
(E) If you **CANNOT** get the answer from statements (1) and (2) **TOGETHER** but need even more data

9. In triangle *ABC*, what is the height from the base *AB*?

(1) The perimeter of *ABC* is 12.

(2) The triangle is isosceles with one angle measuring 60°.

10. If *r*, *s*, and *t* are integers greater than 1, what is the value of *r* + *s* + *t*?

(1) $\dfrac{100r}{st} = 70$

(2) $2rst = 462$

11. Marisa's new car gets 37 miles per gallon. She drove her new car 410 miles on a tank of gas at an average speed of 41 mph. Which of the following can be determined from the given information?

  I. Approximate capacity of the gas tank
 II. Number of days traveled
III. Cost per gallon of gas

(A) I only
(B) II only
(C) III only
(D) Both I and III
(E) None of the above

12. 1,000 tickets numbered from 1 to 1,000, inclusive, were sold in a lottery. What is the probability of selecting a ticket with a 6 as either the hundreds digit or the tens digit?

(A) $\dfrac{1}{10}$

(B) $\dfrac{12}{100}$

(C) $\dfrac{3}{20}$

(D) $\dfrac{19}{100}$

(E) $\dfrac{1}{5}$

13. Is x a prime number?
    (1) xyz has only 8 distinct factors.
    (2) xy is even when y is a prime number.

14. A set contains a parallelogram, 2 isosceles trapezoids, 3 squares, a rectangle, and 2 rhombuses that are not squares. A figure is chosen at random. What is the probability that the figure's diagonals will be of equal length?

(A) $\dfrac{3}{9}$

(B) $\dfrac{5}{9}$

(C) $\dfrac{2}{3}$

(D) $\dfrac{8}{9}$

(E) 1

15. How much older than Paul is Mary?
    (1) Peter is 10 years older than Paul.
    (2) Mary in 2 years will be twice as old as Paul.

(A) If you can get the answer from **(1) ALONE** but not from (2) alone
(B) If you can get the answer from **(2) ALONE** but not from (1) alone
(C) If you can get the answer from **BOTH (1)** and **(2) TOGETHER** but not from (1) alone or (2) alone
(D) If **EITHER** statement **(1) ALONE OR** statement **(2) ALONE** suffices
(E) If you **CANNOT** get the answer from statements (1) and (2) **TOGETHER** but need even more data

16. Nancy's family is out visiting the grandparents when Grandpa Joe decides everyone should go out for ice cream. The family takes two cars, Nancy's and Grandpa's. The ice cream shop is 10 km away, and Nancy drives at an average speed of 80 km/hr. Nancy gets pulled over for speeding, and the police officer who writes her ticket delays her by 5 minutes. Nancy and Grandpa arrive at the ice cream shop at the exact same time. What was Grandpa's average speed?

    (A) 36 km/hr
    (B) 40 km/hr
    (C) 48 km/hr
    (D) 56 km/hr
    (E) 60 km/hr

17. At a candy store, the ratio of the number of jellybeans to the number of gumdrops is 9 to 5, and the ratio of the number of chocolate bars to jellybeans is 2 to 5. If the ratio of the number of licorice sticks to the number of gumdrops is 4 to 3, what is the ratio of the number of chocolate bars to the number of licorice sticks?

    (A) 27 to 100
    (B) 27 to 75
    (C) 27 to 50
    (D) 54 to 75
    (E) 20 to 27

18. Machines X and Y, while working simultaneously at their respective constant rates, produce 1,200 widgets in Z days. While working alone at its constant rate, machine Y produces 1,200 widgets in W days. How many days does it take machine X, while working at its constant rate, to produce 1,200 widgets in terms of W and Z?

(A) $\dfrac{W}{(W + Z)}$

(B) $\dfrac{Z}{(W + Z)}$

(C) $\dfrac{WZ}{(W + Z)}$

(D) $\dfrac{WZ}{(W - Z)}$

(E) $\dfrac{WZ}{(Z - W)}$

19. For all positive integers x, y and z, $x \mu y^{z+1}$ means that y^{z+1} and y^z are divisors of x. If $162 \mu 3^{z+1}$, then what does z equal?

(A) $-3 < z < -1$
(B) $-1 < z < 4$
(C) $-2 < z < 5$
(D) $0 < z < 6$
(E) $1 < z < 4$

20. In a class graduating from medical school, the male students took an average of 9.7 years to obtain their degrees and the female students took an average of 9.0 years. What was the ratio of the number of female graduates to the number of male graduates?

(1) The average number of years for the current graduating class as a whole to graduate from medical school was 9.5 years.

(2) There were 47 female graduates.

(A) If you can get the answer from **(1) ALONE** but not from (2) alone
(B) If you can get the answer from **(2) ALONE** but not from (1) alone
(C) If you can get the answer from **BOTH (1)** and **(2) TOGETHER** but not from (1) alone or (2) alone
(D) If **EITHER** statement **(1) ALONE OR** statement **(2) ALONE** suffices
(E) If you **CANNOT** get the answer from statements (1) and (2) **TOGETHER** but need even more data

21. In city A, 72% of the employed population are blue-collar workers and the rest are white-collar workers. If 75% of the white-collar workers are male and $\frac{5}{12}$ of the blue-collar workers are female, what percent of the employed population of city A are female?

    (A) 37%
    (B) 40%
    (C) 43%
    (D) 47%
    (E) 53%

22. Is $s > -r$?

    (1) $s - 4r > 0$
    (2) $3r - s > 0$

23. At a fraternity keg party, Ogre mixes three drinks that are 3%, 8%, and 12% alcohol by volume. If x pints of 3% alcohol, y pints of 8% alcohol, and z pints of 12% alcohol mixed give $x + y + z$ pints of a 9% alcohol drink, what is x in terms of y and z?

    (A) $\dfrac{3}{(3y+z+6)}$

    (B) $\dfrac{(3z-y)}{6}$

    (C) $\dfrac{(3z+y)}{6}$

    (D) $\dfrac{(21z+17y)}{12}$

    (E) $\dfrac{3}{(3z-y)}$

24. For all positive numbers x and y, for which of the following functions is $f(x - y) = f(x) - f(y)$?

 (A) $f(t) = -2t$

 (B) $f(t) = t^2 + 1$

 (C) $f(t) = t - 1$

 (D) $f(t) = \sqrt{(t + 3)}$

 (E) $f(t) = \dfrac{3}{t}$

25. If $a^4 < b^2 < c$, which of the following statements could be true?

 I. $a > b > c$

 II. $a < b < c$

 III. $c > a > b$

 (A) I only

 (B) I and II only

 (C) I and III only

 (D) II and III only

 (E) All of the above

26. Mary needs to sort her toys. She has several identical items, including three dolls, three cars, three teddy bears, three tennis balls, and three trains. In how many ways can she arrange them?

 (A) $\dfrac{(3!)^5}{15}$

 (B) $\dfrac{15!}{(5 \cdot 3!)}$

 (C) $\dfrac{15!}{(5!3!)}$

 (D) $\dfrac{15!}{(3!)^5}$

 (E) $\dfrac{3^{15}}{15!}$

(A) If you can get the answer from **(1) ALONE** but not from (2) alone
(B) If you can get the answer from **(2) ALONE** but not from (1) alone
(C) If you can get the answer from **BOTH (1)** and **(2) TOGETHER** but not from (1) alone or (2) alone
(D) If **EITHER** statement **(1) ALONE OR** statement **(2) ALONE** suffices
(E) If you **CANNOT** get the answer from statements (1) and (2) **TOGETHER** but need even more data

27. Charles put an amount of money into each of two investments, X and Y, which pay simple annual interest. If the annual interest rate of X is 40% more than that of investment Y, what amount did Charles put into investment Y?

    (1) The amount that Charles put into investment X is three times the amount that he put into investment Y.
    (2) The interest for one year is $100 for investment X and $200 for investment Y.

28. When a bacterial culture was created, the medium consisted of 7.2×10^{20} molecules and the amount decreased every hour by a constant amount. At the end of the 7th hour, the number of molecules was $\frac{1}{8}$ less than it was at the end of the 5th hour. How many molecules did the culture medium lose each hour?

    (A) 8.8×10^{17}
    (B) 3.6×10^{18}
    (C) 9.0×10^{18}
    (D) 3.6×10^{19}
    (E) 7.2×10^{19}

29. Is $x \geq y$?

    (1) $-x \leq -y$
    (2) $x^2 - y^2 = 0$

30. What is the surface area of a cube?

    (1) The length of $\frac{1}{4}$ of the diagonal on one of the faces of the cube is $\sqrt{2}$.

    (2) The maximum distance between one vertex on the cube to another is $4\sqrt{3}$.

31. Sam plans to travel across the country by hitchhiking. He immediately gets picked up by a large transport rig that takes him k miles at an average speed of r miles per hour. He then waits 10 hours before being picked up by a van of students who are on their way to San Francisco. They agree to drive him the rest of the way. They drive at a speed of s miles per hour and finish the trip. If the total cross-country trip is D miles, how long did it take Sam to complete his trip?

    (A) $\dfrac{60k}{r} + \dfrac{(D-k)}{60s}$

    (B) $\dfrac{k}{r} + (D-k)s + 10$

    (C) $\dfrac{(k+10)}{r} + (D-k)s$

    (D) $\dfrac{k}{r} + \dfrac{(D-k)}{60s} + 60$

    (E) $\dfrac{k}{r} + \dfrac{(D-k)}{s} + 10$

(A) If you can get the answer from **(1) ALONE** but not from (2) alone
(B) If you can get the answer from **(2) ALONE** but not from (1) alone
(C) If you can get the answer from **BOTH (1)** and **(2) TOGETHER** but not from (1) alone or (2) alone
(D) If **EITHER** statement **(1) ALONE OR** statement **(2) ALONE** suffices
(E) If you **CANNOT** get the answer from statements (1) and (2) **TOGETHER** but need even more data

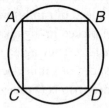

32. In the figure above, what would be the largest rectangle *ABCD* that can be inscribed in the circle?

    (1) The arc *AB* is equal to 4.
    (2) The rectangle *ABCD* is a square.

33. While in detention, Oliver is given the task of calculating the volume of 1,000 hot dogs, where each hot dog is 6 inches in length from end to end and each end of the hot dog is shaped as a half sphere with a radius r. The volume of a sphere is $V = \left(\frac{4}{3}\right)\pi r^3$.

    What is the volume of 1,000 hot dogs?

    (A) $\dfrac{(6\pi r^2 - \left(\frac{10}{3}\right)\pi r^3)}{1,000}$

    (B) $5\pi r^2 - \left(\frac{2}{3}\right)\pi r^3$

    (C) $6,000\pi r^2 + \left(\frac{4}{3}\right)\pi r^3$

    (D) $1,000(6\pi r^2 - \left(\frac{2}{3}\right)\pi r^3)$

    (E) $500(5\pi r^2 + \left(\frac{4}{3}\right)\pi r^3)$

34.   A box contains red marbles, green marbles, and yellow marbles. If a marble is randomly selected from the box, what is the probability that the marble selected will be either green or yellow?

(1) P(yellow marble) $= \dfrac{1}{3}$

(2) P(red marble) $= \dfrac{1}{4}$

35.   Each gardener employed by company ABC Estates receives the following pay: x dollars per hour for each of the first z hours in a week and $x + y$ dollars per hour for each hour over z hours per week, where $x > y$. How much less pay will an ABC Estates gardener who works $z + y$ hours earn than one who works $z + x$ hours?

(A) $x^2 - y^2$
(B) $(y - x)(x + y + z)$
(C) $yz + xz - yx$
(D) $y - x$
(E) $z(y - x)$

36.   There are at least 200 students at a cooking school studying French cuisine. The only other cuisine available for study is Indian cuisine. If 8% of the total students at this school who study Indian cuisine also study French cuisine, do more students study Indian cuisine than French cuisine?

(1)   32 students at the school study both Indian and French cuisine.
(2)   20% of the students who study French cuisine also study Indian cuisine.

37. A sequence is defined by $A_n = (A_{n-1})^2 - 2(A_{n-1})(A_{n-2}) + (A_{n-2})^2$, where $n > 2$. If $A_3 = 2$ and $A_5 = 1$, what is A_6?

(A) 1
(B) 4
(C) 6
(D) 9
(E) 25

STOP

ON THE ACTUAL GMAT,
AFTER YOU HAVE CONFIRMED YOUR ANSWER,
YOU CANNOT RETURN TO IT.

VERBAL SECTION

Time: 75 minutes
41 questions

Reading Comprehension

DIRECTIONS: This section contains three reading passages. You are to read each one carefully. When answering the questions, you *will* be allowed to refer back to the passages. The questions are based on what is *stated* or *implied* in each passage.

Critical Reasoning

DIRECTIONS: For each question in this section, choose the best answer from among the listed alternatives.

Sentence Correction

DIRECTIONS: This part of the section consists of a number of sentences, in each of which some part or the whole is underlined. Each sentence is followed by five alternative versions of the underlined portion. Select the alternative you consider both most correct and most effective according to the requirements of standard written English. Answer (A) is the same as the original version; if you think the original version is best, select answer (A).

In considering the answer choices, be attentive to matters of grammar, diction, and syntax, as well as clarity, precision, and fluency. Do not select an answer that alters the meaning of the original sentence.

Questions 1–4 are based on the following passage.

Seeking to distinguish themselves from nearby competitors, some small businesses that primarily sell their services locally—for example, nonchain restaurants, florists, and fitness studios—have begun to
Line advertise their services through "group coupons" offered at nationally
(5) known deal-of-the-day websites. Such coupons typically offer a limited number of the site's visitors (usually between 100 and 1,000) access to the business's services for a limited time (typically a month to three months) at a deep discount off the company's standard prices (sometimes reaching as much as 75 percent) if paid in advance. These
(10) group coupon arrangements have the potential to measurably increase local customers' awareness of a business's presence in the market due to the large reach of the coupon website's online presence and also due, at least in part, to the novelty currently enjoyed by these sites, many of which have been featured prominently in media outlets in the
(15) past year as the latest revolutionary trend in marketing to emerge from the much fêted realm of social media. Since customers pay before they have received the service or even spoken with the local provider, their purchases result in a large immediate influx of cash for the business.

Use of these group coupon websites is not without its risks, however,
(20) and most small businesses would do well to carefully consider their capacity for expansion and the composition of their current client base before jumping onto this "next big thing." Ironically, part of the danger of offering a group coupon through a deal-of-the-day website lies in the very thing that is most valuable about them: their reach.
(25) The number of customers who regularly check deal-of-the-day sites and who will purchase the services advertised there sight unseen is usually many times the size of a local service provider's normal client base. While a significant percentage never redeem the coupons purchased, those who do can flood the service provider with demands for service
(30) that far outstrip the business's available resources. Long-term customers may consequently feel slighted when they are unable to obtain services from these local businesses with the speed or frequency that they were once accustomed. While the business is occupied meeting the sudden demand the group coupon generated, these customers may quietly take
(35) their business elsewhere. Moreover, the new customers who discovered the business through the group coupon seldom remain loyal to the business once the discounted service has been provided, instead moving on to some other promotion advertised by the deal-of-the-day sites.

1. The primary purpose of the passage as a whole is to

   (A) account for the popularity of a practice.
   (B) explain the reasons for pursuing a strategy.
   (C) demonstrate how to institute a practice.
   (D) advocate the use of one strategy over another.
   (E) evaluate the utility of a practice.

2. Which of the following is cited in the passage as a goal of some local services providing businesses for using group coupons?

   (A) To diversify the business's normal client base
   (B) To obtain a large immediate influx of cash for the business
   (C) To differentiate the business from others offering the same services
   (D) To associate the business with the latest marketing trends
   (E) To test the business's ability to meet demands for expanded service

3. Which of the following may be inferred from the passage?

   (A) The service providers most likely to benefit by offering a group coupon are those who offer discounts lower than 75 percent off their usual prices.
   (B) The service providers least likely to benefit with a group coupon are those that operate in markets with few competitors.
   (C) If a business that offers services also sells physical goods, it will be better able to survive the loss of long-term customers caused by offering a group coupon.
   (D) If a business has excess capacity that is being underutilized, it will stand to benefit substantially from offering a group coupon.
   (E) If a business typically provides services that customers use infrequently for only a few days, it is likely to avoid the risk of offering a group coupon.

4. Which of the following hypothetical situations best exemplifies the potential problem the passage identifies for businesses offering a group coupon?

    (A) A tattoo parlor is unable to obtain permission to open a new location after their reputation spreads throughout the community.
    (B) A lawyer is forced to alter the composition of his print ads in order to avoid alienating new customers.
    (C) A business consultant's reputation for excellent service with new clients creates an expectation of continued performance she cannot satisfy long term.
    (D) A culinary school finds that its classes have declined in popularity as tastes in the community change.
    (E) A flower arranger cannot meet all the orders pending at his shop because his usual supplier cannot provide roses in sufficient quantities.

---

5. Environmentalist: Genetically engineered (GE) rice would, if introduced on a large scale, exacerbate the very problem it was designed to solve: diseases caused by malnutrition in parts of the world where rice is the primary staple crop. Use of GE rice altered so that it contains, for example, Vitamin A, further encourages a diet based on one staple food rather than the reintroduction of many vitamin-rich foods that were once cheap and available.

    The environmentalist's reasoning depends on assuming which of the following?

    (A) Whenever a genetically engineered food is introduced on a large scale, it encourages a diet that is unhealthy in at least one respect.
    (B) In areas of the world where rice is a staple crop, sufficient quantities of naturally occurring vitamin-rich foods cannot be grown without genetic modification.
    (C) The companies that typically produce genetically modified crops do so out of a desire to maximize profits.
    (D) There is no way to genetically modify grain in such a way that it will contain all of the necessary vitamins previously provided by other foods.
    (E) If the reintroduction of vitamin-rich foods is discouraged, some necessary vitamins will inevitably be absent from the diets of those vulnerable to malnutrition.

6. Karl Rove, the former senior adviser and deputy chief of staff for President George W. Bush, never graduated college. So, all other things being equal, a college degree is not required for career success.

   Which of the following would be most useful to know in evaluating the argument above?

   (A) Would Karl Rove have been named senior adviser if he had obtained a college degree?
   (B) Does a person's success in a given field relate to the jobs that person has held in that field?
   (C) Did other college dropouts find places in President Bush's administration?
   (D) Is it possible for two candidates for the same job to be equally qualified?
   (E) Would Karl Rove describe himself as successful in his chosen field?

7. Unlike previous centuries, the greatest challenges of the present era were caused by technological advancement and will likely not be solved by it.

   (A) previous centuries, the greatest challenges of the present era
   (B) previous centuries, the present era's greatest challenges
   (C) that of previous centuries, the present era's greatest challenge
   (D) those of previous centuries, the greatest challenges of the present era
   (E) the previous centuries, the greatest challenge of the present era

8. The earliest clocks relied on shadows cast by the sun, forcing primitive societies to rely on the stars alone to track the passage of time during the night, and this remained the case until at least the third century B.C.E, the earliest point when it is known that early clockmakers did perfect the water-powered escapement mechanism.

   (A) when it is known that early clockmakers did perfect
   (B) that early clockmakers are known to be perfecting
   (C) of early clockmakers who were known to perfect
   (D) at which it is known that early clockmakers had perfected
   (E) at which early clockmakers are known to have perfected

9.   Ironically, in recent years countries such as Switzerland and Denmark have been stronger advocates of the "American dream" than America, a set of ideals in which freedom includes the opportunity for success.

(A) Denmark have been stronger advocates of the "American dream" than America,

(B) Denmark have been stronger for advocating the "American dream" than has been America,

(C) Denmark have been stronger advocates than America for the "American dream,"

(D) Denmark has advocated more strongly the "American dream" than America has

(E) Denmark, stronger than America as advocates of the "American dream,"

10.   Regrettably, it has become increasingly common to find the remains of once majestic blue whales with their fatal injuries from being struck when they slept in busy shipping lanes.

(A) with their fatal injuries from being struck when they slept

(B) with fatal injuries from their sleeping and their being struck

(C) with fatal injuries from their having been struck while sleeping

(D) with fatal injuries from having been struck when they have slept

(E) with fatal injuries from having been struck as they are sleeping

11. TerraBite CFO: Recently, the popular television show *Omega Factor* ran two stories on our company that many of our staff considered unfair, one attacking the lavishness of our product launch parties, the other our generous executive bonuses. In the week since the show's airing, several of our most important sources of venture capital have all but dried up, and our available capital on hand is insufficient to meet our prior financial obligations. Obviously, the *Omega Factor*'s biased coverage is to blame for the dire fiscal straits our company now faces.

Which of the following issues would it be most important to resolve in evaluating the CFO's explanation of TerraBite's financial situation?

(A) Whether the *Omega Factor* typically runs stories that are considered biased

(B) Whether the executive bonuses paid by TerraBite are commensurate with bonuses offered by other companies

(C) Whether the venture capitalists were aware of the damaging content of the stories prior to their decision to withdraw funding

(D) What specific allegations were made in the *Omega Factor* story about TerraBite

(E) Whether the funding withdrawn by the venture capitalists would have been sufficient to meet reasonable financial obligations

Questions 12–14 are based on the following passage.

Once TED was merely a weeklong conference organized by the celebrated "information architect" Richard Saul Wurman, the letters of its name drawn from the conference's intended focus on "technology, entertainment, and design." In 2002, Wurman sold the conference to a nonprofit foundation, under whose guidance TED has grown from a disorganized brainstorming session (and vacation opportunity) for a boys club of Silicon Valley millionaires to a giant global brand.

As a nonprofit, TED is able to bring in a tremendous amount of money from members and corporate sponsorships, and, to be sure, much that is laudable is done with the infusion of resources. TED's multiple worldwide events can boast of an impressive and informative speakers list that would cost a fortune to assemble if the speakers had not agreed to donate their time for free. Much of the money brought in by these events is used to award grants to "TED-certified" lifetime achievers and up-and-coming innovators. However, to even attend a live TED conference in its present form, a donation of between $7,500 and $125,000 is required, and this in addition to a thoroughly opaque admissions process whose only stated requirement is that the applicant be "TED material." Everyone else must be content to watch the conference online.

Ironically, becoming a nonprofit has allowed what would otherwise be only a slightly interesting video podcast (the sort useful mostly as a source of factoids to wow friends at cocktail parties) to become a massive, money-soaked bacchanalia of puffed-up futurism and baseless prognostication. Today's TED is still as unclear as when Wurman first organized it, only now with its outsized delusions of grandeur masked by the thinnest veneer of public good.

12. Which of the following can be inferred from the passage?

   (A) If it were not a nonprofit, TED would be unable to afford to assemble a quality speaker's list.
   (B) If the requirements for being considered "TED material" were less obscure, more people would apply for the honor.
   (C) If the TED conference organizers did not award grants, fewer speakers would be willing to donate their time for free.
   (D) If a speaker is unwilling to donate at least $7,500, then he will not be allowed to attend a subsequent live TED conference.
   (E) If the TED conferences were still organized by Richard Wurman, they would be less successful, though just as disorganized, as they are today.

13. The author indicates that which of the following was part of the original conception of TED?

   (A) A slate of speakers whose presentations were not limited to a single topic
   (B) A requirement that all conferences concern innovation in some form
   (C) The hope that the conference would grow into something other than a Silicon Valley boys club
   (D) A thoroughly opaque admissions process without clear requirements beyond the financial
   (E) A desire to work for the public good

14. Which of the following, if true, would weaken the conclusion given in the first sentence of the third paragraph?

   (A) Much of the good that TED currently does would not be possible if the conference were still a for-profit enterprise.
   (B) Millionaires whose fortunes are built upon technology often waste their money supporting baseless ventures.
   (C) In its original form, a TED conference hosted many talks that, while disorganized, formed the basis for many successful innovations.
   (D) The standards by which an applicant is determined to be "TED material," while confusing to outsiders, are nevertheless fair.
   (E) Richard Saul Wurman made comparatively little money on the sale of the TED conference rights.

15. City Auditor: In the city of Boudreaux, municipal law demands that new adult residents moving into the city register their home and mobile telephone numbers at City Hall within two weeks of arrival. Residents moving out of the city must notify City Hall to cancel their registrations within an equivalent period of time. In the ten years since the law was put into place, registrations of new phone numbers have outpaced notifications of cancellation by at least three to one in every single year. Therefore, we can conclude with near certainty from the telephone registration data alone that the population of Boudreaux has grown substantially over the past decade.

Which one of the following, if true, most calls into question the City Auditor's claim that the population of Boudreaux has grown substantially over the past decade?

(A) In the ten years since the law was put into place, many of the people who moved out of Boudreaux later returned.

(B) Many of the people who moved into Boudreaux in the past decade did not own or have access to a telephone and were thus exempt from the requirements of the law.

(C) Many of the people who moved into Boudreaux in the past decade were young professionals who registered a work phone number in addition to their home and mobile numbers.

(D) There are stiff penalties for failing to register a number and for failing to cancel a registration, but those penalties are difficult to enforce outside the city's immediate domain.

(E) Several towns in the same county as Boudreaux with similar laws have reported their populations have increased substantially over the past decade.

16. Consultant: The goals that you have provided me are hopelessly vague. Any concrete goal a business has must either be related to the desire to maximize profits or be something the business admits is counter to its bottom line. Your business has done many things lately that are counter to your bottom line—your ill-conceived new product line and your excessive executive bonuses among them. This, therefore, is why you ought not hire any more consultants.

The consultant's reasoning is vulnerable to which of the following criticisms?

(A) It generalizes from an unrepresentative listing of the company's activities to all of its activities.

(B) It makes the unsupported claim that the company's goals are hopelessly vague.

(C) It ignores the fact that some businesses find consultants to be of great practical use.

(D) It fails to show any specific link between hiring practices and the vagueness of the company's goals.

(E) It is presented by someone who has a conflict of interests with regards to the hiring of consultants.

17. According to four out of five dentists surveyed, flossing regularly is nearly six times more likely <u>as any other method used for improving the majority of their patients' gum health.</u>

(A) as any other method used for improving the majority of their patients' gum health

(B) to improve gum health for the majority of their patients than any other method

(C) than any other method to improve gum health for the majority of their patients

(D) that the majority of their patients will improve their gum health by using any other method

(E) for the use of any other method than improving gum health for the majority of their patients

18. Crawford Long did not initially publicize his experiments with anesthesia, but when he learned, in 1849, of William T. G. Morton's public demonstration of its use in surgery, he quickly came forward.

(A) Crawford Long did not initially publicize his experiments with anesthesia, but when he learned, in 1849, of William T. G. Morton's public demonstration of its use in surgery,

(B) Crawford Long had not initially publicized his experiments with anesthesia, but when he learned of William T. G. Morton demonstrating its use in surgery publically in 1849,

(C) Crawford Long, even though he had not initially publicized his experiments with anesthesia, on learning, in 1849, that William T. G. Morton had publically demonstrated its use in surgery,

(D) Even though Crawford Long did not initially publicize his experiments with anesthesia, on learning when William T. G. Morton had a public demonstration, in 1849, of using it in surgery

(E) Crawford Long did not initially publicize his experiments with anesthesia, but on learning, in 1849, that William T. G. Morton had been demonstrating its use in surgery in public,

19. Which of the following best completes the argument given below?

A recent study has shed new light on the relationship between time spent playing violent video games and aggression in children. Aggressive behavior was noted among children who played violent games often and those who played only rarely. Differences in aggression seemed to correspond more to differences in parenting philosophy. Absent, career-focused parents with hectic schedules whose children rarely played violent games had more aggressive children than did parents with balanced schedules, even when those schedules allowed for long periods spent playing violent games. In light of this study, it is safe to conclude that

(A) even small amounts of time spent playing violent video games can be dangerous.

(B) the amount of time spent playing violent video games has no effect on the behavior of children.

(C) if career-focused parents would make time, their children would be less aggressive.

(D) prolonged sessions spent playing violent video games are dangerous only when parents are absent.

(E) time spent playing violent video games is not on its own enough to predict a child's behavior.

20. Unlike <u>the Aztec and Maya, who did not have pack animals and relied on slaves for difficult physical labor, the llama was first domesticated by the Inca</u> shortly after arriving on the South American continent.

(A) the Aztec and Maya, who did not have pack animals and relied on slaves for difficult physical labor, the llama was first domesticated by the Inca

(B) the Aztec and Maya, who relied on slaves for difficult physical labor because they did not have pack animals, the llama had been domesticated first by the Inca

(C) the Aztec and Maya, whose lack of pack animals made them rely on slaves for difficult physical labor, the Inca's first domestication of the llama

(D) not having pack animals, the Aztec and Maya relied on slaves for difficult physical labor, while the Inca first domesticated the llama

(E) the Aztec and Maya, who did not have pack animals and relied on slaves for difficult physical labor, the Incans first domesticated the llama

21. Which of the following most logically completes the argument?

Patent law exists to protect the rights of inventors to profit from their innovations, and copyright laws to protect those of artists from their art. While a chef who creates a new recipe might seem a similar case, a recipe is not a work of art, nor is it an innovation, so neither law protects the rights of a chef to profit from an original recipe. Thus, chefs' rights to profit from new recipes will never be protected by the law, since

(A) chefs lack the social capital and economic clout to convince judges to throw these laws out.

(B) there are no other laws outside the copyright and patent law systems that currently protect chefs' rights.

(C) most recipes are modifications of a previous chef's work.

(D) copyright and patent laws are considered to be so comprehensive by legislators that they will never address the gap.

(E) it is impossible to patent basic processes like mixing or baking and copyright does not protect facts.

22. The newly revised *Diagnostic and Statistical Manual of Mental Disorders* has only further complicated the controversy <u>about whether Asperger syndrome should be classified as a unique condition or if it is</u> one of the autism spectrum disorders.

(A) about whether Asperger syndrome should be classified as a unique condition or if it is

(B) about Asperger syndrome and if it should be classified as a unique condition or it is

(C) concerning whether Asperger syndrome should be classified as a unique condition or

(D) with respect to Asperger syndrome being classified as a unique condition or if it is more

(E) whether or not Asperger syndrome should be classified as a unique condition or it is

23. The recent spike in the cost of heating oil to heat homes this winter is due to a dramatic decrease in the supply of heating oil relative to demand. However, the total amount of heating oil available is greater now than it was last winter.

If the statements above are true, which of the following must also be true?

(A) The efficiency of oil-burning furnaces has not increased since the past winter.

(B) The number of homes that use oil for heating has decreased since the past winter.

(C) The demand for heating oil has increased since the past winter.

(D) The cost of transporting heating oil from refineries has increased since the past winter.

(E) The percentage of homes using oil for heating has increased since the past winter.

Questions 24–26 are based on the following passage.

In the United States, credit reports are maintained by three major credit reporting agencies: Experian, Equifax, and TransUnion. Files are only opened and information tracked once an application for some
Line form of credit has been submitted to a creditor, but as modern society
(5) inches closer to a truly cashless economy, nearly every adult has a file with at least one of the three, if not all of them.

Before consumers apply for their first credit card or make an appointment with the loan officer at their local bank, it is important that they check with each of the credit reporting agencies to make
(10) sure there is not a false credit report open in their name. More than 20,000 children and teenagers were victims of identity theft in 2008, so it is possible that someone has already used their name and stolen Social Security number to apply for credit. Moreover, all borrowers, not just first-timers, are encouraged to obtain a credit report at least
(15) once a year and to scan it for any errors or illegitimate lines of credit.

24. The author of the passage would most likely agree with which of the following statements?

(A) Cash-based societies are less prone to identity theft than cashless ones.

(B) Consumers who do not check their credit reports frequently are more likely to be poor managers of their money.

(C) It is less likely that those with a long-established credit history will have errors on their credit report.

(D) If someone has never applied for a line of credit, there would be no reason for one of the credit agencies to have a file on them.

(E) Even when a consumer has applied for a line of credit, it is possible for one of the credit agencies to fail to open a file.

25. If the information contained in the passage is accurate, which of the following groups would be most likely to not have a file at one of the three credit reporting agencies?

    (A) Consumers who have never opened a legitimate line of credit
    (B) Consumers who have not applied for a form of credit for at least seven years
    (C) Consumers who have either been victims of identity theft or who have applied for credit themselves
    (D) Consumers who have never been the victim of identity theft nor applied for a form of credit
    (E) Consumers who have avoided opening lines of credit except when such credit was necessary

26. Which of the following best describes the organization of the passage as a whole?

    (A) A financial practice is described; exceptions to the practice are presented; and recommendations to replace the practice are listed, but none are supported.
    (B) A financial practice is criticized; an explanation of the criticism is given; and the conclusion is advanced that the practice is, nevertheless, inevitable.
    (C) A financial practice is recommended; some considerations against the practice are given; and a rebuttal to those considerations is presented.
    (D) A financial practice is described; a consequence of that practice is given; and further explanation of that consequence is presented.
    (E) A financial practice is described; recommendations against that practice are given; and further details of that recommendation are provided as support.

Questions 27–30 are based on the following passage.

Civil law, as opposed to criminal law, deals with private disputes where one party accuses the other of injury—whether physical, psychological, emotional, or financial—and sues for damages.
Line However, the price of sustained legal action often exceeds several
(5) hundred thousand dollars, which prevents most investors from using a civil lawsuit to recoup damages from investment fraud. It was for this reason that lawyers and judges first developed the class action lawsuit. Such suits allow multiple parties to sue over the same legal grounds, although a single representative or lead plaintiff is the only
(10) one whose name appears on the case.

When evidence of massive accounting fraud brought down the Enron Corporation in the late 1990s, its collapse took with it nearly $65 million from the stockholders' balance sheets. In the class action suit that ultimately won damages of $8 billion for these investors, the
(15) University of California was chosen as the lead plaintiff, even though it was in many senses not representative of the other plaintiffs in the class, having lost much more than any one single investor, but far less than the investment groups that were party to the suit.

As a single entity, the university was deemed better able to
(20) coordinate the litigation, and due to the size of its losses—over $150 million lost from its pension and endowment funds—it was also seen as more likely to remain party to a suit that might stretch on for several years. Such practical considerations are not, however, counter to the justifications used by the jurists who pioneered this civil litigation
(25) device. Indeed, many initial objections to the use of the class action lawsuit were successfully answered by appeal to the principle that a system of law which could only be used by the powerful would never be used, since the powerful have and always will have other means to protect themselves from damages.

27. The passage implies which of the following things about representative plaintiffs in class action lawsuits?

    (A) It is preferable that they share at least one quality with each member of the class, though not strictly required.

    (B) It is both preferable and required that they share at least one quality with each member of the class.

    (C) If they do not share any qualities with a substantial majority of the members of the class, the suit will be unsuccessful.

    (D) Their similarity to other members of the class will have little to no effect on the ultimate success of the suit.

    (E) The likelihood that they will be eventually proved unable or unwilling to continue the suit is a factor in their selection.

28. With which of the following evaluations of the civil law system would the author most likely agree?

    (A) Although imperfect, the class action lawsuit is preferable to any other previously proposed solution to the problem of a selectively useable system of justice.

    (B) Only in those cases where a criminal judgment is impossible should a class action lawsuit be used.

    (C) Objections against a practice in civil law can sometimes be answered by appeal to concerns beyond the letter of the law.

    (D) When one party accuses the other of injury, physical and financial damages should be rewarded before psychological or emotional ones are considered.

    (E) If the financial barriers to entry in the system were relaxed, then the class action lawsuit would not be necessary.

29. According to the passage, one reason that the University of California was chosen as lead plaintiff was that

   (A) its losses from its pension fund were at least as great as those from its endowment fund.
   (B) the award for damages would have been much less than $8 billion without its participation.
   (C) the expected duration of the suit would have been unduly burdensome upon other plaintiffs.
   (D) it was more likely to see the suit through to its final conclusion than some other plaintiffs.
   (E) it was deemed to be the most similar to the largest percentage of parties to the suit.

30. The primary purpose of the passage is to

   (A) explain the factors that contribute to a plaintiff being selected to lead a class action suit.
   (B) compare strategies used in civil courts to those used in criminal courts.
   (C) illustrate the considerations involved in the development of a device used in civil courts.
   (D) describe the manner in which litigants in the Enron stock collapse were able to achieve success.
   (E) rebut the assertion that practical considerations should never be used to evaluate a legal practice.

31. Added to the tax bill that they already pay to fund their local fire departments, home owners in some cash-strapped municipalities are now being charged a hefty "accident tax."

    (A) Added to the tax bill that they already pay to fund their local fire departments, home owners in some cash-strapped municipalities are now being charged a hefty "accident tax."
    (B) Added to the property taxes that they already pay to fund their local fire departments, some cash-strapped municipalities are now charging home owners a hefty "accident tax."
    (C) Some cash-strapped municipalities are now charging home owners a hefty "accident tax" to be added to fund their local fire departments with the property taxes that they pay already.
    (D) In addition to the property taxes that they already pay to fund their local fire departments, some cash-strapped municipalities are now charging home owners a hefty "accident tax."
    (E) In addition to the property taxes they already pay to fund their local fire departments, home owners in some cash-strapped municipalities are now being charged a hefty "accident tax."

32. Fire prevention experts agree that inebriated and intoxicated people are more likely to cause fires—both accidentally and deliberately—than they are when sober. The damage done by such fires is exacerbated by the fact that the chemically impaired are also less capable at extinguishing fires they have started. Nevertheless, the damage from fires started by the sober far exceeds that done by fires started by intoxicated and inebriated people combined.

    Which of the following, if true, best explains the discrepancy above?

    (A) It can be difficult to determine who started a fire and in what condition they were in when it was started.
    (B) Naturally occurring fires or those caused by accidents do more damage than those set deliberately.
    (C) Most people who become inebriated or intoxicated do so for only a few hours each week.
    (D) Many people prone to starting fires abstain completely from alcohol or other intoxicating chemicals.
    (E) The sight of a burning fire often is sufficient to allow a person to temporarily overcome the impairment caused by intoxication.

33. The Tennessee Valley Authority brought electricity to rural Americans, <u>who had long been isolated due to its lack, and consequently no longer able to</u> operate at a complete remove from the national government.

    (A) who had long been isolated due to its lack, and consequently no longer able to
    (B) whose lack had long isolated them, due to their no longer being able to consequently
    (C) who due to its lack had long been isolated, and was consequently no longer able to
    (D) who had long been isolated due to its lack; consequently, they were no longer able to
    (E) which had long been isolated due to their lacking it; consequently, they were no longer able to

34. Because it has outgrown its current space and because that space cannot be expanded, the county animal shelter must be moved to a larger facility. Vacant buildings of sufficient size that are located near the current shelter are far more expensive than those found near the county line. Since the cost of rent is the biggest single cost associated with running the shelter, it would be cheaper to move the shelter to the county line.

    Which of the following is an assumption made by the argument above?

    (A) It is not possible to build an entirely new facility for the animal shelter.
    (B) The animals that are currently housed in the shelter will be able to be moved to a new shelter.
    (C) Volunteers who currently work at the shelter will not be dissuaded from continuing if the shelter moves.
    (D) The possible sites for the shelter near its location do not require substantially less energy to heat and cool.
    (E) City codes do not prevent the shelter from being placed in any of the buildings near its current location.

35. The biotech companies that sell genetically modified foods have always claimed that their products are no more dangerous to eat than unmodified foods. In support of this, they have widely touted the results of research published by an independent study group, the Sunbelt Foundation. But it has recently come to light that the Sunbelt Foundation's chief scientist falsified data, likely because his family was heavily invested in biotech stocks. Clearly, there is good reason to worry that these purportedly safe foods are actually harmful.

The reasoning in the argument above is suspect because

(A) the failure to prove a claim is taken as equivalent as proof that the claim has been disproven.

(B) it generalizes from a single case of wrongdoing to an insupportably broad conclusion.

(C) it fails to consider the possibility that financial interest alone is not sufficient to discredit a party.

(D) it takes the behavior of an individual as representative of a group to which the individual does not belong.

(E) it assumes without justification that independent research is sufficient to establish safety.

36. Economist #1: Rises and falls in the global economy correlate almost exactly with the amount of volatility in the currency market. Clearly, regardless of what politicians may think, the global economy's health is strictly a function of currency market volatility.

Economist #2: Absurd. Any true economist would know that in a system as complicated as the global economy, no single variable could account for its overall performance.

The second economist's rejection of the first economist's position employs which of the following argumentative strategies?

(A) Establishing by counterexample that a proposed rule is false as stated

(B) Supporting a conclusion about a specific case by appeal to a general rule

(C) Showing that an apparent correlation is actually the result of direct causation

(D) Rejecting a purely theoretical conclusion on the grounds that it has no practical value

(E) Suggesting that the argument against a conclusion is based on personal animus rather than logic

37. The tyrannical conduct of Tarquinius Superbus led to the abolition of the Roman monarchy, which ruled for nearly three centuries and had claimed to trace their royal authority to Romulus, legendary founder of Rome.

(A) which ruled for nearly three centuries and had claimed to trace their royal authority

(B) by which it was ruled for nearly three centuries and claimed to trace its royal authority

(C) ruled for nearly three centuries and which they claimed that royal authority traced

(D) which ruled for nearly three centuries and claimed to trace its royal authority

(E) who ruled for nearly three centuries and claiming to trace its royal authority

38. If asked in 1600 to predict which nation would come to dominate North America, a reasonable person likely would guess Spain, England, or France and be absolutely wrong.

   (A) guess Spain, England, or France and be
   (B) guess Spain, England, or France and it would have been
   (C) have guessed Spain, England, or France and been
   (D) have guessed that it would have been Spain, England, or France and
   (E) have guessed Spain, England, or France and would be

39. Six out of every seven long-practicing doctors agree about one thing, the *Washington Post* health editor reports: the nation's insurance system, as currently constituted, cannot long endure.

   (A) Six out of every seven long-practicing doctors agree about one thing, the *Washington Post* health editor reports
   (B) Out of every seven, six doctors of long-standing practice agree about one thing, the *Washington Post's* health reports
   (C) One thing is agreed upon by six out of every seven long-practicing doctors, the *Washington Post's* health editor reports
   (D) Six out of every seven long-practicing doctors agree upon one thing, the *Washington Post's* health editor has reported
   (E) Out of every seven doctors who have practiced for long, six agree about one thing, the *Washington Post* health editor has reported

40. The manuscript tradition of Julian of Norwich's *Revelations* is fraught <u>by ambiguity with no surviving autograph, only one of the extant manuscripts being medieval, and we do not even know if the</u> work was ever disseminated in the medieval period at all.

 (A) by ambiguity with no surviving autograph, only one of the extant manuscripts being medieval, and we do not even know if

 (B) by ambiguity: with no autograph surviving, only one of the extant manuscripts is medieval and we do not know even if

 (C) with ambiguity; no autograph survives, only one of the extant manuscripts is medieval, and we do not even know whether

 (D) with ambiguity; without an autograph that survives, only one of the extant manuscripts is medieval; and we do not even know whether

 (E) ambiguously with no autograph surviving, only one of the extant manuscripts being medieval, and us not knowing whether or not

41. Ranked first among the emotions that Aristotle thought an orator must learn to manipulate <u>are moral indignation, used both to incite citizens against injustice and for punishing those who would rise</u> above their station.

 (A) are moral indignation, used both to incite citizens against injustice and for punishing those who would rise

 (B) are moral indignation to use inciting citizens against injustice and, for punishing, those who would be raised

 (C) is moral indignation, used both to incite citizens against injustice and punish those who would rise above their station

 (D) is moral indignation for both inciting citizens against injustice and used to punish those who might rise

 (E) are moral indignation, which was used both to incite citizens against injustice and punishment of those who would have rose

ON THE ACTUAL GMAT,
AFTER YOU HAVE CONFIRMED YOUR ANSWER,
YOU CANNOT RETURN TO IT.

ANSWER KEY—SAMPLE TEST

Integrated Reasoning Section

1. i. A

ii. B

2.

Amount Needed to Spend on New Hires	Amount Each Student Expects to Make	Amount in $
●	○	0
○	○	720
○	○	1,080
○	●	1,920
○	○	2,560
○	○	3,840

3.

Would Help Explain	Would Not Help Explain
●	○
●	○
○	●

4. C

5.

True	False
○	●
●	○
●	○

6.

Yes	No
●	○
○	●
●	○

7.

Would Definitely be Part of the Optimite Program	Would Definitely NOT be Part of the Optimite Program
○	○
○	○
●	○
○	●
○	○

8. D

9. i. B
    ii. D

10. i. D
    ii. C

11.

True	False
●	○
○	●
●	○

12. D

Quantitative Section

1. B	**11.** A	**21.** A	**31.** E
2. E	**12.** D	**22.** C	**32.** A
3. E	**13.** A	**23.** B	**33.** D
4. D	**14.** C	**24.** A	**34.** B
5. D	**15.** E	**25.** E	**35.** A
6. B	**16.** C	**26.** D	**36.** B
7. B	**17.** C	**27.** E	**37.** B
8. D	**18.** D	**28.** D	
9. C	**19.** B	**29.** A	
10. B	**20.** A	**30.** D	

Verbal Section

1. E	**12.** D	**23.** C	**34.** D
2. C	**13.** A	**24.** E	**35.** A
3. E	**14.** B	**25.** D	**36.** B
4. E	**15.** D	**26.** D	**37.** D
5. E	**16.** D	**27.** E	**38.** C
6. B	**17.** B	**28.** C	**39.** A
7. D	**18.** A	**29.** D	**40.** C
8. E	**19.** E	**30.** C	**41.** C
9. C	**20.** E	**31.** E	
10. C	**21.** D	**32.** C	
11. C	**22.** C	**33.** D	

ANALYSIS

SELF-SCORING GUIDE
Analytical Writing

Evaluate your essay (or have a friend or teacher evaluate it for you) on the following basis. Read your essay completely, paying special attention to its logical organization and use of examples and facts to buttress its claims or position. Assign a holistic score between 0 and 6, using the scale below.

6 OUTSTANDING: Cogent, well-articulated analysis of the issue or critique of the argument. Develops a position with insightful reasons and persuasive examples. Well organized. Superior command of language and variety of syntax. Only minor flaws in grammar, usage, and mechanics.

5 STRONG: Well-developed analysis or critique. Develops a position with well-chosen examples or reasons. Generally well organized. Clear control of language and variety of syntax. Minor flaws in grammar, usage, and mechanics.

4 ADEQUATE: Competent analysis or critique. Develops a position with relevant reasons or examples. Adequately organized. Adequate control of language, but may lack syntactic variety. May have some flaws in grammar, usage, and mechanics.

3 LIMITED: Competent but clearly flawed analysis or critique. Vague or limited in developing a position. Poorly organized. Weak in using relevant examples or reasons. Language used imprecisely or lacking in sentence variety. Contains major errors or frequent minor errors in grammar, usage, and mechanics.

2 SERIOUSLY FLAWED: Serious weaknesses in analysis and organization. Unclear or seriously limited in presenting or developing a position. Disorganized. Few relevant examples or reasons. Frequent serious problems in language and sentence structure. Numerous errors in grammar, usage, or mechanics that interfere with meaning.

1 FUNDAMENTALLY DEFICIENT: Little evidence of ability to organize and develop a coherent response to issue or argument. Severe and persistent errors in language and sentence structure. Pervasive pattern of errors in grammar, usage, and mechanics that severely interfere with meaning.

0 UNSCORABLE: Illegible or not written on the assigned topic.

ANSWERS EXPLAINED

Integrated Reasoning Section

1. i. **(A)** The third quartile of the graph is the area between 50% and 75%. If you look at the graph, you can see where the line crosses the x-axis at 50% and at 75%. At 50%, the x-axis is at 74 inches. At 75%, the x-axis is at 77 inches. This gives you the range of heights:

$$77 - 74 = 3$$

Therefore, the answer is **A**.

ii. **(B)** From question 1, you know that the median height, or 50% of all the players, is 74 inches. Since you need to look at all players within 6 inches of that height, you should look at the graph between 68 inches and 80 inches. At 68 inches, the line is approximately halfway between 0% and 25%. At 80 inches, the line is approximately halfway between 75% and 100%. This represents about 75% of all the players. Therefore, the answer is **B**.

2. **($0, $1,920)**

(i) This is a three-tiered rate problem that tracks the number of painters, houses, and hours. Since the question asks for how many new people you need to hire, let's first calculate how many hours are required to paint 1,200 houses.

10 students paint 4 houses in 16 hours = 10 students paint 1,200 houses in 4,800 hours

From this you know that Youth Pro Painters needs 4,800 student painter hours to complete 1,200 houses. Since there are 12 weeks in the summer and 40 working hours in a week, you can calculate how many students are needed.

4,800 hours ÷ 40 hours/week ÷ 12 weeks = 10 students

The company has just enough students to paint 1,200 houses, so the total amount needed to spend on additional hires is **$0**.

(ii) To calculate the amount of money each student can make in half the summer, first calculate the amount each student will earn during the summer.

40 hr/week × 12 weeks × $8.00/hr = $3,840

To determine how much each student makes in half the summer, divide by 2. The answer is **$1,920**.

3. **(Would Help Explain, Would Help Explain, Would Not Help Explain)**

(i) This can be easily found by sorting through either the primary school column or kindergarten column. The kindergarten column ranges from 71 to 32 while the primary school column ranges from 98 to 81. This chart would help explain that kindergartens are not offered as much as are primary schools. The answer is **Would Help Explain**.

(ii) If you look at the data from the table for Peru, you can see a much lower percentage for both kindergarten and post-secondary education compared with primary and secondary. If you sort the primary and secondary school numbers, you can also see that Peru ranks among the bottom. This could suggest that farming families are keeping children away from school. Therefore, the answer is **Would Help Explain**.

(iii) You could associate the data in the chart with where education is more valued by its country's citizens. However, when you check on Argentina and how it ranks, it is the highest in the kindergarten column and is second in the other three columns. Colombia ranks first in the other three columns. Thus the table could not help you infer anything about Argentinean parents. Therefore, the answer is **Would Not Help Explain**.

4. **(C)** The best way to sort out all the information here is with a chart. In fact, if you look at the question first, you might decide to set up a chart with all the detailed information while reading the documents. Then you can reference the chart when answering the question.

	Two Current Product Lines (crates per month)		New Product Lines (crates per month)	
	Pessimistic	Optimistic	2-in-1	Dandruff
Year 0	800	800	0	0
Year 1	1,000	1,200	200	200
Year 2	1,250	1,800	400	400
Year 3	1,562.5	2,700	600	600

Most pessimistic forecast without new product launches: 1,562.5

Most optimistic forecast with new product launches: $2,700 + 1,200 = 3,900$

Find the difference: $3,900 - 1,562.5 = 2,337.5$

Therefore, the answer is **C**.

5. **(False, True, True)**

(i) Since you are looking at only year 1 and just the existing product line, you can calculate this using the information you already organized in the chart from question 5. Sales are 1,000 units × $1,000 per crate, giving you $1 million monthly. Since the shipping costs are $100,000, this brings our overall profit down to $900,000 monthly. Therefore, the answer is **false**.

(ii) Since you are looking at only year 1, you can break down this question into each scenario. Again, using a chart would help you organize the data.

Scenario 1: Pessimistic, 25% growth, 2 new product launches:

$$800 \times 1.25 + 200 + 200 = 1,400 \text{ crates}$$

Scenario 2: Optimistic, 50% growth, no new product launches:

$$800 \times 1.5 = 1,200 \text{ crates}$$

Scenario 1 does sell more units than scenario 2. Therefore, the answer is **true**.

(iii) In this case, the question is much easier if you use a chart. You also need to understand that the 25% decrease due to the negative perception affects just the sales increase, not the total sales.

	Two Current Product Lines (crates per month)		One New Product Line
	Total Optimistic Sales	With 25% Decrease	
Year 0	800	n/a	0
Year 1	1,200	1,100	200
Year 2	1,650	1,512.5*	400
Year 3	2,079.7	600	

*At this point, you may notice that the cumulative percentage increase is 37.5% per year for the current product lines. So you can easily calculate year 3.

As you can see, the total sales of the one new product line over three years are 1,200 crates. The total growth of the current lines over three years is 2,080 – 800 = 1,280. Therefore, launching one new product will not "entirely" offset the launch (even though it's pretty close). The answer is **true**.

6. **(Yes, No, Yes)**

    (i) From the chart you created for question 5, you can extract the second-year pessimistic forecast and the new product launch of just one product in one year.

    $$1,250 + 200 = 1,450$$

    Nanning's capacity is 1,500 crates per month. Therefore, the answer is **yes**.

    (ii) Similar to part (i), you can extract the second-year optimistic forecast from the chart you created for question 5, which is 1,800 crates per month. Sandusky's capacity is 1,200 crates per month. Therefore, the answer is **no**.

    (iii) Again, you can use the chart you created for question 5 to extract the optimistic forecast for year 1 and two new product launches for the first year.

    $$1,200 + 200 + 200 = 1,600$$

    Chennai's capacity is 2,500 crates per month. Therefore, the answer is **yes**.

7. **(A case competition, A field trip to a museum of marine biology)**
    This challenging question gives us a considerable amount of multilayered information. Some of it is useful, and some of it is not. You need to know the difference. The question is trying to get you to focus on the key support that is necessary to make the conclusion.

    At first glance, many of the answers seem possible, but the key here is to find what must be true based on the passage. Capoeira martial arts, delivering a presentation on business ethics, and moderated debate on local politics are all quite possible given the scope of the Optimite program. However, they are all too specific. It's equally possible that the program would have alternative physical challenges, presentations, or debates. Having a case competition, generally speaking, is the only activity that must be part of the program since the passage says "case studies and matches." Therefore, **a case competition** would definitely be part of the program.

    A field trip to a museum of marine biology would not be part of the program for two reasons. The first is that the Optimite program focuses on learning "on site." The second is that the description does not mention science. Therefore, **a field trip to a museum of marine biology** would definitely **not** be part of the program.

8. **(D)** In this question, four of the answer choices would be issues of concern to the school board.

Choice A is a concern since the program has a class size of 60 and requires advanced technology tools in the classroom.

Choice B is a concern because of the diversity of the eligible students and the preexisting concern of getting all the students to school.

Choice C is a concern because it may be difficult to find 60 diverse and talented students.

Choice E is a concern for two reasons. First, like any new program, Optimite will require teachers to learn the new curriculum. Second, the format is different than that in traditional classrooms. Optimite uses a "team" teaching structure. It's possible that some teachers may not want to get involved.

Since the Optimite program requires three teachers for 60 students, it thus has a ratio of 20 students per teacher. This is already under the standard of 24 students per teacher. The correct answer is **D**.

9. i. **(B)** This is a hard Venn diagram because it consists of three circles. The process to review and analyze the chart is the same as if it consisted of two, though. Determine the total number of residents with laundry and the total number of residents. There are 7 stars in the laundry circle and the total number of stars in the Venn diagram is 15. The probability is 7 out of 15. Therefore, the answer is **B**.

ii. **(D)** For this question, you need to consider only those residents with air conditioning. The circle for air conditioning contains 10 stars. The number of stars with air conditioning that also have mini-freezers is $3 + 1 = 4$. This gives us a probability of 4 out of 10 or 2 out of 5. Therefore, the answer is **D**.

10. i. **(D)** This is among the more tricky scatter plot distributions because it is bimodal, which means that the data suggest two distinct areas or patterns of Old Faithful's eruptions. The first significant section is on the bottom left, and the second significant section is on the top right. Since the answer choices are looking at eruption intervals, you can

approximately determine two separate ones: 55 minutes and 80 minutes. Therefore, the answer is **D**.

ii. **(C)** This question is also challenging because you need to use weighted averages to determine the duration of the average eruption. You certainly don't need to count all the plot points, but you can see that more are in the top right section than in other sections. Therefore, the average will be closer to the right side of the x-axis. If the average of the plots at the bottom left section is approximately 2 minutes and at the top right section is between 4 and 4.5 minutes, the weighted average should be more than 3 or 3.25 minutes. The only answer that fits these criteria is 3.5 minutes. Therefore, the answer is **C**.

11. **(True, False, True)**
(i) This question requires you to extrapolate new information—revenue growth. Rather than using the calculator to create an entirely new column, you should try to estimate whenever possible. If you look at the top two companies, Wal-Mart and Exxon Mobil, they have much higher revenues than the rest. In addition, Exxon Mobil's growth is substantial. In addition, Fannie Mae is in the top five. Since its revenue grew 429.2%, that would mean a revenue growth of over 80% of the total revenue, or over $120 billion. This would far outweigh the rest of the companies, two of which had negative growth. Therefore, the answer is **true**.

(ii) First, you need to sort the profit column. The median number is General Electric at $11.6 billion. Again, it is quicker to use ballpark numbers. The top half's average would be approximately $20 billion. The bottom half's average would be quite low because of the combined –$16.2 billion of Fannie Mae and Bank of America. This will bring the average profit of the bottom half to approximately $2 to $5 billion. The difference between the top half and the bottom half will be much greater than $11.6 billion. Therefore, the answer is **false**.

(iii) This question requires you extrapolate from the table. Fannie Mae's revenue change was about 430%. (Remember you don't need to use specific numbers here.) A 95% drop would give you a little over a 20% revenue increase for 2010/2011. Since Fannie Mae's profit loss was $14 billion and its operating costs are the same, you can calculate how much new revenue it will earn. Since 20% of $150 billion is $30 billion, Fannie Mae would have to earn profits. Therefore, the answer is **true**.

12. **(D)** The definition given here of a good value stock is based on only the first three columns containing numbers. So you need to sort through each column quickly and find the best company in which to invest. When you sort the column "% Change in Revenue Since 2009," you see that Fannie Mae comes out on top. However, you can eliminate it since the other two columns will decrease Fannie Mae's value significantly. Of the other four answer choices, Exxon Mobil, ConocoPhillips, and Berkshire Hathaway rank in the top five.

At this point, a quick way to solve this problem is to create a chart to track the ranks. The more complicated a question is and the more information you are dealing with, the more important it is that you add structure to the problem. Charts are a great way to do this.

Company	% Change in Revenue	Profit	% Change in Profit	Average Rank
Exxon Mobil	4	1	6	11/3
ConocoPhillips	2	8	2	12/3
Berkshire Hathaway	5	6	STOP!	

Once you get to the percent change in profit for Berkshire Hathaway, you can stop filling in the chart. This is because even if Berkshire Hathaway ranks number one in percentage change in profit (it does not), its average rank would still be greater than that of Exxon Mobil. You could have also quickly added Wal-Mart if you had thought to chart this whole question out at the beginning of this section. However, it would not have ranked high. Therefore, the answer is **D**.

Quantitative Section

1. **(B)** Let set T be $\{x, y, z\}$. If there is only one mode, then at least 2 of the 3 numbers must be the same.

Statement 1 tells us that the set looks like this: $\{x, y, 2x\}$. Since there is only one mode, $y = x$ or $y = 2x$. If we pick numbers this could be $\{2, 2, 4\}$ or $\{0, 0, 0\}$ or $\{2, 4, 4\}$. In the first 2 cases, the range, $4 - 2 = 2$ or $0 - 0 = 0$, equals the mode. However, in the 3rd case, the range does not equal the mode. *Insufficient*

Statement 2 tells us that the middle number of the set equals the range. Some of the possibilities for set T are $\{2, 2, 4\}$ or $\{0, 0, 0\}$ or $\{0, 4, 4\}$. In all three cases, the range equals the mode. Note that we cannot use the set $\{2, 4, 4\}$ because this would violate the median equaling the range.

In all cases where there is one mode in a set of 3 numbers and the median equals the range, then the range does indeed equal the mode. *Sufficient*

2. **(E)** This is a classic Mirror Rule probability problem. So we should get

$$P(\text{at least one head}) = 1 - P(\text{no heads}) = 1 - P(T, T, T)$$

$$= 1 - \frac{1}{2} \cdot \frac{1}{2} \cdot \frac{1}{2} = 1 - \frac{1}{8} = \frac{7}{8}$$

Alternatively, since there are only 3 coin tosses, you could write out all the possibilities: HHH, HHT, HTH, HTT, TTT, TTH, THT, THH.

3. **(E)** We know from the statements that to solve for x, we need 2 distinct equations and 2 unknowns. Selecting C here seems a bit too easy, so let's check and make sure that we have not missed something. If we look more closely, we see that statement 1 and statement 2 are the same equation that has just been manipulated algebraically. Thus, each statement is telling us the same thing. Since "no news is good news," the answer will be either D or E. Each statement by itself does not help us solve for x as we have 2 unknowns and only one distinct equation. Thus, even when combining the statements, no solution is possible. *Insufficient*

4. **(D)** When we factor the equation, we determine that $y = (3x + 1)(2x - 5)$, which tells us that the x-intercepts could be $-\frac{1}{3}$ and $\frac{5}{2}$.

In statement 1, if $x < 1$, then there is only one x-intercept: $-\frac{1}{3}$. *Sufficient*

Statement 2 tells us that $3x$ is an odd integer.

Again only $x = -\frac{1}{3}$ would work as the x-intercept and give us an odd integer when multiplied by 3. *Sufficient.*

5. **(D)** Since there is no multiple of 2 on the right-hand side of the equation, we can assume that the right-hand side has 2^0 (which is really just 1) in it. Thus, using the base of 2, we can calculate that $2^{x-7} = 2^0$. Therefore, $x - 7 = 0 \rightarrow x = 7$.

If you want to be sure of your answer, you can plug it into the expression with base 3, rather than calculating it all out.

$$3^{2x-3} = 3^{3(3x-10)/3} \rightarrow 2(7) - 3 = 3(7) - 10 \rightarrow 11 = 11$$

6. **(B)** Statement 1 tells us that x and y could be either both positive or both negative. *Insufficient.*

Statement 2 confirms that x is positive since prime numbers cannot be negative. *Sufficient*

7. **(B)** Since we have the percentages, we can calculate the number of people in each group. Using fractions makes the calculations much easier. There are:

$3200 \cdot \dfrac{1}{4} = 800$ people who live downtown

$800 \cdot \dfrac{3}{5} = 480$ people who live downtown in a high-rise

$800 \cdot \dfrac{2}{5} = 320$ people who rent downtown

$800 \cdot \dfrac{1}{4} = 200$ people who both live downtown in a high-rise and rent

$480 - 200 = 280$ people who live downtown in a high-rise but do not rent

Therefore, the probability of selecting someone in a high-rise and not a rental is $\dfrac{280}{3200} = \dfrac{7}{80}$.

8. **(D)** Let's first jump ahead to statement 2 because it looks easier to resolve.

In statement 2, if B is even, then C must be even because C is a multiple of B. If you are not sure of this concept, it is the same idea where 6 is a multiple of 2. Any multiple of an even number will also be even. *Sufficient*

Going back to statement 1, if AB is even, then either A or B is even, or both are even. If B is a multiple of A (because "A is a factor of B"), then B must be even, whether A is odd or even. For example, $A = 2$, $B = 6$ works because $AB = 12$, an even number. When $A = 3$ and $B = 6$, $AB = 18$, which also works. However, if $B = 9$, A cannot equal 3 because AB must be even. Since B must be even, then C must also be even. *Sufficient*

9. **(C)** We know we have triangle ABC. What we want is the height. What we need is the area and the length of the sides.

Statement 1 gives us only the perimeter. We have no idea about the lengths of any side. *Insufficient*

Statement 2 tells us we have an equilateral triangle. Because if one angle is 60° and the triangle is isosceles, then the other 2 equal angles must total 120°. Thus all the angles are 60°. However, we still don't have any values for the lengths of the sides, so we cannot calculate the area or the height. *Insufficient*

By putting the statements together, we know we have an equilateral triangle of sides 4. We can use the equilateral triangle formula $A = \dfrac{(s^2 \sqrt{3})}{4}$ to calculate the height. *Sufficient*

$$A = \frac{4^2 \sqrt{3}}{4} = 4\sqrt{3} \;\rightarrow\; A = \frac{1}{2} \cdot \text{base} \cdot \text{height}$$

$$\rightarrow\; 4\sqrt{3} = \frac{1}{2}(4)h = 2h \;\rightarrow\; h = 2\sqrt{3}$$

10. **(B)** Statement 1 gives us the equation $100r = 70st$, which reduces to $10r = 7st$. This does not give us any unique values for r, s, and t; therefore, we cannot solve for $r + s + t$. *Insufficient*

    Statement 2 gives us the equation $rst = 231$. If we break down 231 into prime factors, we get $3 \times 7 \times 11 = 231$. Since r, s, and t are integers greater than 1, they must all be prime numbers. Thus we can determine that $r + s + t = 21$. *Sufficient*

11. **(A)** Given the question, we can determine the capacity of the gas tank by dividing 410 by 37. We cannot find the cost per gallon as there is no price given for the gasoline used. Finally, we cannot determine the number of days as we do not know whether she drove continuously in one day or over two days. We also do not know if she stopped several times and drove her car over several days or even weeks. Therefore, we can determine only statement I with certainty.

12. **(D)** We need to count all the tickets with a 6 in the tens digit or the hundreds digit. Out of all the tickets sold, there are 100 tickets from 600 to 699. There are also 10 tickets each from 60 to 69, 160 to 169, all the way to 960 to 969. This occurs 10 times. The total number of tickets is now at 200. Don't forget that we need to subtract tickets that have the number $66x$ in them because we have already double counted them.

    There are 10 of them. The final total is now 190. The probability will be $\dfrac{190}{1000}$ or $\dfrac{19}{100}$.

13. **(A)** In statement 1, if xyz has only 8 distinct factors, then each of x, y, and z are prime numbers. For example $2 \cdot 3 \cdot 5 = 30$, which has 1, 2, 3, 5, 6, 10, 15, and 30 as factors. Therefore, x is a prime number. *Sufficient*

In statement 2, if xy is even and y is a prime number, then all we know about x is that it is an even number if y is odd. However, x is either odd or even when $y = 2$, the only even prime number. *Insufficient*

14. **(C)** Only an isosceles trapezoid, a square, and a rectangle will have diagonals that are equal. For example, ·

Thus, there are 6 possibilities out of 9, which simplifies to $\frac{2}{3}$.

15. **(E)** Statement 1 does not work because we have no information about Mary. *Insufficient*

Statement 2 gives us the equation

$$M + 2 = 2(P + 2) \rightarrow M = 2P + 2$$

However, when we solve this, we have 1 equation and 2 unknowns, which we cannot solve. *Insufficient*

Combining the statements gives us 2 equations and 3 unknowns, which we cannot solve. *Insufficient*

16. **(C)** We need to use $D = RT$ to solve this problem. If Nancy had driven straight to the shop, she would have taken $\frac{1}{8}$ of an hour, or 7.5 minutes. Since she was delayed by 5 minutes, then Grandpa took $5 + 7.5 = 12.5$ minutes to get there. Therefore, Grandpa drove at an average speed of $10 \text{ km}/12.5 \text{ min} \times 60 \text{ min}/1 \text{ hr} = 48 \text{ km/hr}$.

17. **(C)** The key to solving this problem is to combine the ratios by finding a common multiple. A chart is a nice way to keep track of information. Let's focus on linking the 2 gumdrop ratios first and then link that to the chocolate ratio. Let L be licorice, G be gumdrop, and C be chocolate bars.

① →	$L : G$	$G : J$	② →	$L : G : J$	$J : C$	③ →	$L : G : J : C$
	4 : 3	5 : 9		20 : 15 : 27	5 : 2		**100 : 75 : 135 : 54**
	*5	*3		*5	*27		
	20 : 15	15 : 27		100 : 75 : 135	135 : 54		

Thus, the ratio of the number of chocolate bars to the number of

licorice is $\dfrac{54}{100} = \dfrac{27}{50}$.

18. **(D)** The "job" itself is 1,200 widgets and is constant throughout the question. Therefore, we can use the standard work rate formula.

$\dfrac{1}{X} + \dfrac{1}{Y} = \dfrac{1}{Both}$ → where X, Y, and both are the time it takes machine X, machine Y, and both machines to finish a job, respectively. This gives us

$\dfrac{1}{X} + \dfrac{1}{W} = \dfrac{1}{Z}$ → We have to solve for X

$\dfrac{1}{X} = \dfrac{1}{Z} - \dfrac{1}{W}$ → $\dfrac{1}{X} = \dfrac{(W - Z)}{WZ}$

→ $X = \dfrac{WZ}{(W - Z)}$

19. **(B)** This is a symbol question that defines a unique relationship among the variables x, y, and z. Using the example given, we know that 162 is a multiple of 3. Let's break it down into prime factors first.

$$162 = 81 \bullet 2 = 9*9*2 = 3 \bullet 3 \bullet 3 \bullet 3 \bullet 2 \rightarrow$$
$$3^{z+1} \text{ and } 3^z \text{ are both divisors.}$$

To be a divisor of 162, the exponent of the base 3 can be anything from 0 to 4. Remember that $3^0 = 1$ is also a divisor! Note that the answer choices give us a range of numbers, which is a clue that z can have more than one value. The definition states that both 3^{z+1} and 3^z are divisors. If $z = 4$ then 3^z works but 3^{z+1} doesn't work. If $z = -1$, then, 3^{z+1} works but 3^z doesn't work. Therefore, z must be 0, 1, 2, or 3.

20. **(A)** This is a good example of using the jump ahead tactic, as statement 2 is less complicated. Clearly it is not sufficient to answer the problem because we have information only about the number of females and none about the number of males. *Insufficient*

Statement 1 gives us the overall average. Using a line graph, we can leverage our understanding of weighted average to determine how far away the males and females are from the overall average.

This relationship is the inverse of the overall ratio of male to female students, which means the ratio of male students to female students is 5 : 2. *Sufficient*

21. **(A)** This is a dual matrix box question because we have a group broken into two subgroups of two each with no overlap. By using the matrix box table, we get:

Employed Population of City A	Blue Collar	White Collar	Total
Males		$\frac{3}{4} \bullet 28\% = 21\%$	
Females	$\frac{5}{12} \bullet 72\% = 30\%$		x
Total	72%	28%	100%

Note that we calculated the white-collar males by taking 75% or $\frac{3}{4}$ of the total white-collar workers. Similarly, we calculated the blue-collar females by taking $\frac{5}{12}$ of 75%. Now that we have these numbers, we can easily fill in the rest of the chart. What we want, though, is x. The number of white-collar female workers is 28% – 21% = 7%. So the total percent of employed females is 30% + 7% = 37%.

22. **(C)** One of the best ways to deal with inequalities and variables in data sufficiency questions is to try picking numbers. Another strategy to keep in mind is to try to determine sufficiency by proving insufficiency. This can be done by finding two possibilities, one that gives you a yes answer and another that gives you a no answer.

Statement 1 tells us that $s > 4r$. If $s = 5$ and $r = 1$, then the expression $s > -r$ becomes $5 > -1$, which works. But if $s = -12$ and $r = -4$, then the expression $s > -r$ becomes $-12 > 4$, which does not work. *Insufficient*

Statement 2 tells us that $s < 3r$. Again we can pick numbers to try to prove insufficiency. If $s = 2$ and $r = 1$, then the expression $s > -r$ becomes $2 > -1$, which works. If $s = -5$ and $r = 4$, then the expression $s > -r$ becomes $-5 > -4$, which does not work. *Insufficient*

When we combine both statements, we know that $s < 3r$ and $s > 4r$. We could pick numbers to determine sufficiency, but let's solve instead.

Unlike most data sufficiency questions with algebraic equations, we actually have to solve the two inequalities to determine sufficiency because it's still possible to get values for r and s that are not necessarily sufficient.

$$
\begin{array}{lll}
s - 4r > 0 & \text{multiply by 3} \rightarrow & 3s - 12r > 0 \\
+\ -s + 3r > 0 & \text{multiply by 4} \rightarrow & +\ -4s + 12r > 0 \\
\hline
-r > 0 & & -s > 0 \\
\rightarrow r < 0 & & \rightarrow s < 0
\end{array}
$$

Since both r and s are negative, then any value of s would not be greater than $-r$. *Sufficient.*

23. **(B)** This is a mixture problem combined with algebra. When we express this situation algebraically, we get:

The 3 different drinks	The final mixed drink
$0.03x + 0.08y + 0.12z$	$= 0.09(x + y + z)$
	$\rightarrow$ expanding this out
	and solving for x we get

$$0.03x + 0.08y + 0.12z = 0.09x + 0.09y + 0.09z$$
$$\rightarrow 0.09x - 0.03x = 0.08y - 0.09y + 0.12z - 0.09z$$
$$0.06x = 0.03z - 0.01y \rightarrow 6x = 3z - y$$
$$\rightarrow x = \frac{(3z - y)}{6}$$

24. **(A)** There is a lot of information at play in this question. Using a chart is a great way to organize it all. First we will let $x = 1$ and $y = 2$. Then we can see what the functions in this scenario would work out to be.

Let $x = 1$ and $y = 2$ thus $x - y = -1$	$f(x) = f(1)$ What is $f(1)$?	$f(y) = f(2)$ What is $f(2)$?	$f(x) - f(y)$ What is $f(1) - f(2)$?	$f(x - y) =$ $f(1 - 2) =$ $f(-1)$ What is $f(-1)$?	Do they equal? Is $f(x - y) =$ $f(x) - f(y)$?
$f(t) = -2t$	-2	-4	2	2	YES
$f(t) = t^2 + 1$	2	5	-3	2	No
$f(t) = t - 1$	0	1	-1	-2	No
$f(t) = \sqrt{(t + 3)}$	2	$\sqrt{5}$	$2 - \sqrt{5}$	$\sqrt{2}$	No
$f(t) = \dfrac{3}{t}$	3	$\dfrac{3}{2}$	$\dfrac{3}{2}$	-3	No

25. **(E)** Let's pick numbers to determine which of the statements could be true.

I: If $a = \dfrac{3}{5}$, $b = \dfrac{1}{2}$, $c = \dfrac{1}{3}$ then $a > b > c$ AND $a^4 < b^2 < c$ could be true.

II: If $a = \dfrac{1}{3}$, $b = \dfrac{1}{2}$, $c = 1$ then $a < b < c$ AND $a^4 < b^2 < c$ could be true.

III: If $a = \dfrac{1}{3}$, $b = -\dfrac{1}{3}$, $c = 2$ then $c > a > b$ AND $a^4 < b^2 < c$ could be true.

All three statements could be true.

26. **(D)** This is a permutation problem because the order of the elements matters. This is also a special case scenario where we have repeated elements.

$$\text{Number of arrangements} = \frac{N!}{(A!B! \ldots)}$$

where N is the total number of elements at play in the questions and $A, B, \ldots$ are the number of repeated elements. In this question, $N = 15$ toys. We have 5 different elements, or toys, that repeat 3 times each. This gives us

$$\frac{N!}{A!B!C!D!E!} \rightarrow \frac{15!}{(3!3!3!3!3!)} = \frac{15!}{(3!)^5}$$

27. **(E)** All we know is that there are two investments, X and Y, and that $r_X = 1.4 r_Y$, where r_X and r_Y are the interest rates of investments X and Y, respectively.

Statement 1 tells us that $P_X = 3P_Y$, where P_X is the principal paid in investment X and P_Y is the principal paid in investment Y. However, we have no way to solve for an actual amount. *Insufficient*

Statement 2 gives us actual amounts of the interest paid on the principal. Without exact interest rates or principal amounts, though, we cannot solve. *Insufficient*

At this point we have 4 different variables at play in the question. When we combine both statements, we have $r_X = 1.4 r_Y$ and $P_X = 3P_Y$. We also have $100 = P_X \cdot r_X$ and $200 = P_Y \cdot r_Y$. We still cannot solve because the principal amounts invested could still vary in magnitude, just as interest rates could. For example, you could have $1000 invested at 10% yielding $100, or you could have $1,000,000 invested at 0.01%, yielding the same $100. *Insufficient*

28. **(D)** The key to this problem is that the decrease is constant. We can map out the timeline and let the change be y.

Hours	1	2	3	4	5	6	7
	7.2×10^{20}	y	y	y	y	y	y

The number of molecules at the 7th hour is $7.2 \times 10^{20} - 6y$.

The number of molecules at the 5th hour is $7.2 \times 10^{20} - 4y$. The 7th

hour was $\frac{1}{8}$ less than the 5th hour, so that gives us

$$7.2 \times 10^{20} - 6y = \frac{7}{8}(7.2 \times 10^{20} - 4y)$$

$$\rightarrow 8 \bullet (7.2 \times 10^{20}) - 8 \bullet 6y = 7 \bullet (7.2 \times 10^{20}) - 7 \bullet 4y$$

$$57.6 \times 10^{20} - 48y = 50.4 \times 10^{20} - 28y$$

$$\rightarrow 7.2 \times 10^{20} = 20y \rightarrow y = \frac{7.2}{20} \times 10^{20}$$

$$\frac{7.2}{20} \bullet \frac{5}{5} = \frac{36}{100}$$

$$\rightarrow y = 0.36 \times 10^{20} = 3.6 \times 10^{19}$$

29. **(A)** Statement 1 can be manipulated to give us $x \geq y$, which is exactly what we are looking for. *Sufficient.*

Statement 2 factors out to give us $(x - y)(x + y) = 0$, which means that either $x = y$ or $x = -y$. Knowing that $x = y$ answers the question, but what about $x = -y$? Well, you can just pick numbers to see.

If $x = 0$, $y = 0$. If $x = 1$, $y = -1$. However, if $x = -1$, $y = 1$, which doesn't work. *Insufficient*

30. **(D)** To find the surface area of a cube, we need to find the length of any side.

Statement 1 gives us the length of the diagonal, which is $4 \bullet \sqrt{2} = 4\sqrt{2}$. The length of a diagonal will give us the length of the side through the 45-45-90 triangle identity. The ratios of 45-45-90 triangles are $1:1:\sqrt{2}$; therefore, the triangle sides would be $4:4:4\sqrt{2}$. Thus the side of this cube would be 4.

Surface area (SA) of a cube is $6s^2$.

$$\rightarrow 6 \bullet 16 = 96 \; Sufficient$$

Statement 2 gives us the longest distance from vertex to vertex. This will also give us the length of a side through the formula for longest length in a cube, which is $\sqrt{(3s^2)}$.

$$4\sqrt{3} = \sqrt{(3s^2)} \rightarrow 48 = 3s^2 \rightarrow s^2 = \frac{48}{3} \rightarrow s^2 = 16 \rightarrow s = 4$$

$$SA = 6s^2 \rightarrow 6(16) = 96 \; Sufficient$$

31. **(E)** The best way to solve this problem is to break it down into parts.

Part 1 is the time Sam spent in the transport rig. Using $D = RT$, the total time taken is $\dfrac{k}{r}$.

The second part is the wait, which was 10 hrs.

The third part is the time spent in the van. Since the total distance is D, then the distance for the last leg was $D - k$. Therefore, the time taken was $\dfrac{(D-k)}{s}$. Therefore, the total time taken to cross the country was $\dfrac{k}{r} + \dfrac{(D-k)}{s} + 10$.

You could also have used the DiRTy chart, but you would need to account for the wait of 10 hours.

	Part 1	Part 2	Part 3	Total
D	k	0	$D - k$	D
R	r	0	s	Average rate
T	$\dfrac{k}{r}$	10	$\dfrac{(D-k)}{s}$	

Using the chart you can now sum up the total time to get the same answer as above.

32. **(A)** If we know the radius of the circle, we can find the diagonal of the rectangle, which in order to have the largest area, the rectangle must be a square.

In statement 1, the arc AB gives us the radius through the circumference formula, as we know the central angle to the arc is 90° or $\frac{1}{4}$ the total circumference of the circle. This gives us the radius through the circumference formula.

$$C = 2\pi r = 4 \bullet 4 = 16 \ \rightarrow \ r = \frac{8}{\pi} \ \rightarrow \ \text{diameter} = \frac{16}{\pi}$$

Now we can apply the 45-45-90 triangle identity to find the side of the square and then calculate its area. It's a messy calculation. The good news with data sufficiency is that you don't have to do calculations to solve; you just have to know that you can solve. *Sufficient*

The largest rectangle inscribed in a circle has to be a square, so statement 2 is redundant information. *Insufficient*

33. **(D)** Since no diagram is given, let's make sure we draw properly and understand clearly what we are calculating.

If we break this down into sections we have a half-sphere, a cylinder, and another half-sphere. The 2 half-spheres are equivalent to one full sphere, with volume $\left(\frac{4}{3}\right)\pi r^3$. The cylinder has a radius of r and a length of $6 - r - r = 6 - 2r$. This gives us

$$\text{Volume of cylinder} = \pi r^2 h = \pi r^2(6 - 2r) = 6\pi r^2 - 2\pi r^3$$

$$\text{Total volume} = V_{\text{cylinder}} + V_{\text{sphere}}$$

$$= 6\pi r^2 - 2\pi r^3 + \left(\frac{4}{3}\right)\pi r^3 = 6\pi r^2 - \left(\frac{2}{3}\right)\pi r^3$$

Since there are 1,000 hot dogs, the volume is $1{,}000\left(6\pi r^2 - \left(\frac{2}{3}\right)\pi r^3\right)$.

Alternatively, if you had to guess, imagine the entire hot dog as a cylinder. The volume would be near $6{,}000\ \pi r^2$ MINUS a spherical volume. Only D does that.

34. **(B)** Statement 1 tells us only about the yellow marbles. We don't know anything about the probability of selecting a green marble. *Insufficient*

Statement 2 tells us one thing but actually implies another. If we select one marble from the box, the probabilities are

P(red marble) + P(yellow marble) + P(green marble) = 1

The probabilities of selecting one marble must add up to 1. Since statement 2 gives the probability of selecting a red marble, then the probability of picking a green or yellow marble would be $\frac{3}{4}$. *Sufficient.*

35. **(A)** This question can get quite confusing because several numbers are at play in the question and they are all given as algebraic variables. You can either chart this out or at least sort the information in a clear way.

Pay rate for 1st z hours	Pay rate for hours > z hours
$\$x$/hr	$\$(x + y)$/hr

Gardener 1 works $z + y$ hours, so he makes $zx + y(x + y)$ dollars

Gardener 2 works $z + x$ hours, so she makes $zx + x(x + y)$ dollars

The difference in pay is

$$zx + x(x + y) - zx - y(x + y) = x^2 + xy - xy - y^2 = x^2 - y^2$$

36. **(B)** With a Venn diagram, we can compare the French cuisine students to the Indian cuisine students.

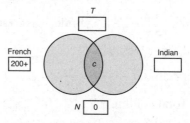

In statement 1, we have only the number for those who study both Indian and French, or the middle number. From that, we can calculate the total number of students and the approximate number of students who study Indian cuisine.

$$32 = 8\% \text{ of total or } \frac{32}{\text{total}} = \frac{8}{100}$$

Total = 400

Using the Venn formula, we get $T = A + B - c + N$

$$400 = (200+) + I - 32 + 0$$

I represents the number who study Indian cuisine and $N = 0$ because students study either French or Indian cuisine.

We cannot determine sufficiency because the number of French cuisine students is "at least" 200. If it was 200, then $I = 232$. If it was 240, then $I = 192$. Hence, the number of students studying French cuisine could be greater or less than the number of students studying Indian cuisine. *Insufficient*

In statement 2, we are told that 20% of the French cuisine students study Indian cuisine as well. This means that the 8% who study both French and Indian cuisine represent 20% of the total number who study French cuisine.

$$8\%T = 0.2F \rightarrow F = 0.4T$$

Since 40% study French cuisine, the number of students studying only Indian cuisine must be 60% and thus greater. This means that a total of $60\% + 8\% = 68\%$ of the students are studying Indian cuisine. *Sufficient*

37. **(B)** First let's make sure we understand the definition. We can actually simplify the sequence definition by factoring it out because it is one of the algebraic equation identities

$$(a - b)^2 = a^2 - 2ab + b^2$$
$$(A_{n-1})^2 - 2(A_{n-1})(A_{n-2}) + (A_{n-2})^2 = (A_{n-1} - A_{n-2})^2$$

Next, let's list the terms, leaving gaps for the ones we don't know.

$$A_3 = 2 \qquad A_4 = ? \qquad A_5 = 1 \qquad A_6 = ?$$

In order to find A_6, we first need to determine A_4. The only link we have is the sequence definition for A_5. According to the definition,

$$A_5 = (A_4 - A_3)^2 \rightarrow 1 = (A_4 - 2)^2 \rightarrow A_4 = 1 \text{ or } 3$$

Since we have two values for A_4, we have to try each value out.

If $A_4 = 1$ $A_6 = (A_5 - A_4)^2 \rightarrow (1 - 1)^2 = 0$
If $A_4 = 3$ $A_6 = (A_5 - A_4)^2 \rightarrow (1 - 3)^2 = 4$

Since there is no answer choice with 0 and there is an answer with 4, then $A_6 = 4$.

Verbal Section

The passage for questions 1–4 appears on page 430.

1. **Question:** Because it asks about the passage as a whole and inquires about the author's overall purpose, this is a Main Idea question. In this question, the short answer choices mean the correct answer will describe the author's purpose obliquely, rather than summarizing the author's central claim. Answer Choice (E) does this, as it is true that the author evaluates the utility of using group coupons (and finds the practice to be a mixed bag).

    (E) Answer Choices (A) and (B) are both **part**(s) **only** because the author is not primarily accounting for the group coupon's popularity, though reasons for its popularity and why a business might pursue the strategy are mentioned in passing. Answer Choices (C) and (D) describe things that **never happened**, as the practice is described, but never demonstrated, and there is only one strategy described (and never advocated).

2. **Question:** *Is cited* is another way of saying "is written explicitly in the text," making this a **Detail** question. The correct answer, (C), corresponds to information given in the very first line of the passage.

    (C) Answer Choice (A) is **reasonable but not said**, as this might be an expected result of the practice but is never given as a *goal* of businesses. Answer Choices (B) and (C) are **misused details**; Answer Choice (B) is mentioned, but never said to be a goal, and Answer Choice (D) is said to be trendy, but also not said to be a goal. Answer Choice (E) is very nearly the **exact opposite** of the answer: group coupons test businesses (and often find them wanting), but businesses aren't described as using group coupons as tests.

3. **Question:** *May be inferred* is the simplest way of indicating an **Inference** question is to follow. The question stem provides no guidance as to where to look for the information that will produce the inference, but it may be found via information toward the end of the second paragraph, although it's a touch tricky. It requires us to first understand that the one risk the answer choice corresponds to is the problem of a company driving away existing long-term customers and not replacing them with new ones from the group coupon pool. If the

business only needed short-term nonrepeating customers, it would not be subject to the described risk.

(E) Answer Choices (A) and (B) cannot be inferred because the author does not give us a hierarchy or a rule that any particular type of business is the most likely or least likely to do anything. Answer Choice (C) is **reasonable but unsupported**, made attractive through the red herring of "physical goods." Though the businesses in the passage are service providers, and it is their services that will be strained by the group coupons, we're never told it would be better for them if they sold physical goods, too. Answer Choice (D) is a **distorted fact**. We know that businesses should examine their capacity for expansion, but not that they should have excess, underutilized capacity, nor are we told that such a thing would equate to a substantial benefit.

4. **Question:** *Hypothetical situations* is the tipoff: since it asks us to consider something not presented in the passage, this can only be an Inference question. The information needed to evaluate these extra-passage scenarios is found throughout the passage; the correct answer, (E), is derived from information found in two places in the passage. The author mentions that (1) businesses need to carefully consider their capacity for expansion or (2) risk not being able to provide customers the service they have come to expect. This florist has overshot his capacity and thus cannot meet the demand for an arrangement that his long-term customers expect him to provide.

(E) While gaining a bad reputation is part of the risk outlined by the passage, Answer Choice (A) does not link that reputation to anything that would have come from the use of a group coupon. Alienating new customers is surely something to avoid, but this isn't the problem cited by the author, so Answer Choice (B) is **reasonable but unsupported**. The concern is alienating existing customers. The business consultant in Answer Choice (C) is surely getting in over her head because she will one day disappoint new customers, not because she will drive away existing customers. Answer Choice (E) is **reasonable but unsupported**, as changing tastes is an issue not raised by the passage at all.

5. **Argument:** The environmentalist's conclusion is a **prediction** about the **net harm** a **plan** will cause (a lot of common patterns combined), namely that the GE rice plan will *exacerbate the problem (diseases caused*

by malnutrition in places where rice is the staple crop). The evidence supporting this bold conclusion is rather meager, only that one benefit (Vitamin A) results in one harm that the plan will encourage a diet based on one staple food rather than a different option, reintroducing vitamin rich foods. Thus, the argument must assume that not doing the other option (or making it less likely) will harm people more than the benefit they'll get from the Vitamin A. Since the argument's benefit is strictly phrased in terms of missing vitamins (malnutrition), Answer Choice (E) is part of the speaker's assumption that the benefit will not be realized.

(E) Answer Choice (A) is a **closed issue** because the argument's conclusion is specifically limited to areas *where rice is the staple crop*, not *all areas*. Answer Choice (B) is the opposite of what we want, as it would **weaken** the argument's assumptions. Answer Choice (C) is reasonable but irrelevant, as *profit* is not part of this benefit/harm calculation. And Answer Choice (D) is tricky **but for one word**, though meant to appear as though it is a **defending assumption** against the possibility of an **alternate explanation**. The word that eliminates Answer Choice (D) is *grain*—if the answer said *rice,* we would have been in business.

6. **Argument:** The conclusion is the **general rule** presented at the end of the argument: *college degrees are not required for success.* It is supported by evidence of a **single case**: Karl Rove. **Representativeness** likely leapt to mind as an assumption required here, and it is, but in a slightly less direct way than usual and is better described by a **term switch**. The evidence establishes that Karl Rove had various impressive jobs, but the conclusion is that he was *successful*; thus, the argument assumes that *success* can be equated with these *impressive jobs*. **Evaluate** questions interrogate an argument's assumptions, and Answer Choice (B) pretty much does this directly.

(B) Answer Choice (A) confuses the conclusion that college degrees aren't **required** with some sort of **guarantee**. Answer Choice (C) asks for corroborating evidence, which is almost always irrelevant, **one step removed** from the argument's assumptions because it requires the additional assumption that the parties used to corroborate (other dropouts) are similar to the case (Rove) in the evidence. Answer Choice (D) is an **irrelevant comparison** (and probably also **too extreme**), as various levels of qualification are irrelevant so long as the applicant

(Rove) lacks the college degree, and Answer Choice (E) is a trap hinting at **biased evidence**, another thing the GMAT is almost never interested in.

7. **Issues: comparisons** (which must be **parallel**), **subject/predicate agreement** (with the plural *were*)

(D) This question is built on two related issues, keeping the two parties in the comparison introduced by *Unlike . . .* **parallel** both logically and grammatically. As written in Answer Choice (A), *previous centuries* are compared with the *challenges* faced by the present era, two entities that are not logically similar; either *challenges to challenges* or *centuries to the present era* (time periods) would be correct. Answer Choices (B) and (E) likewise compare centuries to challenges, though they rephrase one or the other. Answer Choices (C) and (D) correct the comparison (by using a **placeholder pronoun** to make the previous centuries a **descriptive prepositional phrase**) but introduce a new problem. The verb *were* that follows the underlined section is plural and must be linked to a plural subject. Answer Choice (C) changes the subject challenge to singular. The already eliminated Answer Choice (E) does as well, but we already have enough to know that Answer Choice (D) is the only correct option left.

8. **Issues: modification** (using the **idiomatically** and logically correct connector), **sequence of tenses** (*relied, remained, is known*)

(E) The split found at the beginning of the answer choices could eliminate only one answer, (C), as the *of* makes for modification nonsense. *When* is usually reserved for specific times on the GMAT (*when you called yesterday*), but it is probably OK here.

The verb sequence error ultimately proves deciding. Since the clockmakers' perfection/perfecting happens after the *relied* and *remained*, a tense that can occur after the past tense is required for that perfecting; Answer Choice (B) tries to avoid the error but creates nonsense with *be perfecting*; Answer Choice (D)'s *had perfected* (**past perfect***) occurs earlier in the sequence than *relied*'s **past**. [The already eliminated Answer Choice (C) does pass this requirement, however.]

Answer Choice (A)'s *did perfect* meets that requirement but is itself ruled out by a second sequence issue, the sequence between when the perfecting happened and when the knowing happened. The latter came second, so it, too, must be chronologically later than the verb for the former, and *did perfect* and *is known* are both present tense. This leaves only Answer Choice (E), that passes both sequence requirements with the sequence *are known* (**present**), *have perfected* (**present perfect**), and *relied* (**simple past**).

9. **Issues: comparisons** (logically **parallel**), **modification** (the correct object for the appositive phrase *a set of ideals . . .*), **subject/predicate agreement** (the compound *Switzerland and Denmark* is treated as plural), **sentence structure** (avoiding fragments)

   (C) This underlined section could have been tackled from either end. On the front end, a comparison error has been set up by the *stronger . . . than*. Answer Choices (A) and (C) pass this error, as **elliptical constructions** are allowed on the GMAT (the verb is left assumed, so the comparison becomes *have been stronger . . . than America [has]*). Answer Choice (B) fails (*stronger for advocating . . . than America has been*). Answer Choices (D) and (E) both *technically* pass, though the forms wouldn't be preferred by the GMAT.

   The more fruitful decision point thus becomes the modification error. In the non-underlined section of the sentence the **appositive phrase** *a set of ideals . . .* appears. Appositives must be placed next to the noun that they describe, separated only by a comma. So who or what is *a set of ideals*? Surely, *the "American dream,"* eliminating Answer Choices (A), (B), and (D) all in one fell swoop.

   That leaves only Answer Choice (E) to deal with, and it creates a fragment by deleting the verb attached to Denmark and Switzerland, creating a **sentence fragment**.

10. **Issues: modification** (which must be **idiomatically correct**), **sequence of tenses** (*has become . . . have been struck*)

    (C) The **sequence** requirement for the two events (finding the whales that were *earlier* struck) eliminates Answer Choices (D) and (E). The other answer choices avoid the error by turning the second half of the sentence into the object of the prepositional phrase with *from* as its head word, used to describe the source of the *injuries*, but in doing so other errors are introduced. Answer Choice (A)'s *when* is idiomatically incorrect, as the GMAT typically reserves *when* for specific times (*when we were at your house last Saturday*), not for general descriptions of time. Answer Choice (B) creates nonsense by using *and*, so now the whales get injuries from two different things, *sleeping* and *being struck*.

The underlined section itself is part of a modifying phrase describing *whales*, and thus must make sense logically and use idiomatically correct words to connect the description. Answer Choice (A)'s introduction of an ambiguous *there* is a pronoun error and also an illogical way to connect the description to boot!

11. **Argument:** This argument is a basic **causal connection** hidden under a few layers of distraction. The conclusion is the CFO's explanation that it was the stories that the *Omega Factor* ran that caused the company's money woes. There is precious little direct evidence given for this claim, mostly just the **setup information** that the stories were run and that the company is facing problems. To **Evaluate** an argument, the required information will help us understand an assumption the argument relies upon, and with a **causal** argument, that assumption can be stated as *there's nothing that would stop the stated cause from producing the stated effect.* Answer Choice (C) is directly relevant to that assumption, as if the venture capitalists were unaware of the story prior to pulling the funding. It would have been unlikely that the stories caused the pull, and vice versa.

(C) Answer Choices (A) and (B) rely on **real-world thinking** to distract you with some **irrelevant comparisons**, as it doesn't matter what the stories are *generally* like, only whether these two stories caused the venture capitalists to pull their money, or whether TerraBite is like *other companies*. Answer Choice (D) is more real-world thinking that would only provide **more evidence for the evidence**, which never strengthens or weakens a GMAT argument. Answer Choice (E) is the trickiest of the bunch, right **but for one word**, the word *reasonable*. It'd be reasonable to think that *reasonable* financial burdens are relevant, but we don't know if TerraBite's obligations were reasonable or not, so we don't know if this is relevant or not.

The passage for questions 12–14 appears on page 436.

12. **Question:** If you spotted the **Inference** key while reading this passage, this question would've been a snap. A definite requirement is presented at the end of the second paragraph. Between $7,500 and $125,000 is required in order to *attend* a live conference. This rule applies to everyone, including Answer Choice (D)'s *speakers*—at the conferences *subsequent* to their speaking, at least.

(D) Answer Choice (A) is a **too extreme** trap built on a potential mis-reading of another Inference key, the earlier statement that, *without the nonprofit status, the speakers list would cost a fortune*—which is not the same thing as being too expensive to put together. Maybe TED's original backers (millionaires) could have ponied up the money. Who knows? Answer Choices (B), (C), and (E) are all **reasonable but unsupported**, requiring information not present in the passage to infer.

13. **Question:** Finding the right answer to a **Detail** question is a matter of locating information through the haze of synonyms and indirect phrasing the test maker uses to disguise it. The correct detail is found near the beginning of the passage, which lists three topics originally considered acceptable for the TED conference. Thus, Answer Choice (A) is mentioned (three means not just one, right?).

    (A) Answer Choice (B) is a **misused detail**, as we know innovation is important, but not that it was considered necessary for every conference. Answer Choices (C) and (E) are both **reasonable but never said**, never the answer to a Detail question. Answer Choice (E) even throws in a bit of **heartstring-tugging** to make it extra appealing but no less wrong. Answer Choice (D) is another **misused detail**, something said in almost those exact words, but that is never linked to the conference's original conception (and seems to be a new development).

14. **Question:** Remember that sometimes the GMAT cheats a little and throws a Critical Reasoning question at you in Reading Comprehension. Treat these according to whatever strategy is appropriate in Critical Reasoning. Here, the *Weaken* requires us to find the conclusion and think about the assumptions. The correct answer attacks the assumptions. Also, remember that when a Critical Reasoning question appears in Reading Comprehension, the weakeners and strengtheners are often indistinguishable from contradictions and restatements of evidence, respectively.

    Argument: The conclusion referenced in the stem is a **causal connection**: the nonprofit status caused the conference to become something it otherwise couldn't have become, a money-fueled such-and-such. To weaken the argument, all we need to do is find an **alternate cause** that could have resulted in the stated effect. Answer Choice (B) provides this, showing us the money (that we ought to have remembered from the original description of the conference as a millionaire boys club for technology magnates).

(B) Answer Choice (A) is irrelevant to the conclusion—a bit of wishful thinking. In fact, so are Answer Choices (C) and (E)—reasonable things to believe, but not directly relevant to the stated conclusion. Answer Choice (D) is also irrelevant, a **misused detail** referencing the memorable disdain that the author had for the TED application process.

15. **Argument:** The City Auditor's conclusion is helpfully given to us in the question stem: *the population of Boudreaux has grown substantially over the past decade* and is supported by two explicit pieces of information (1) that there is a law that forces people who come to the city to register their phones and forces those who leave to cancel that registration and (2) that the number of people doing the first has gone up much faster— three times as fast—as those doing the second.

Essentially, the Auditor's conclusion is an **explanation** of the difference between those numbers: the only reasonable thing to believe is that many more people are immigrating than emigrating. The correct answer weakens the argument by suggesting an **alternate explanation**. If the law can only effectively punish you within the city, as Answer Choice (D) proposes, it is very possible that the number of people leaving the city is greater than the number of people canceling phone subscriptions.

(D) The *many*s in Answer Choices (A), (B), and (C) all render these answer choices irrelevant, as we don't know if the *many* is *many enough* to affect the calculation the Auditor is making. Answer Choice (E) is irrelevant corroboration, a form of **evidence for the evidence** that the GMAT doesn't worry much about.

16. **Argument: Flaw** questions direct our attention to an assumption and declare that assumption unwarranted. Here, the argument's conclusion (that the company shouldn't hire any more consultants) is supported by the evidence that the business does a lot of dumb things and provides vague goals to its consultants, requiring the assumption that *doing dumb things and having vague goals is a good reason not to hire any more consultants*. Answer Choice (D) calls the speaker out for never making that **linking assumption** explicit.

(D) Answer Choice (A) is a great flaw, an unwarranted **representative-ness** assumption that *this speaker* doesn't assume; Answer Choice (B) is directly contradicted by the prompt, which does offer support for the claim. Answer Choice (C) is something that the speaker ignores, surely, but it's **one step removed** from the specific case at hand, and Answer Choice (E) is the old trap of **implying bias** to the speaker. We don't attack the motives of the speaker on the GMAT, only the connections between the speaker's evidence and conclusion.

17. <u>Issues</u>: **comparisons** (which must be **idiomatically correct** and **logically parallel**), **modification**

    (B) With a sentence this messy, the best place to start is with the most obvious decision point. The first part of the underlined section splits completely on the words used to set up the comparison, an issue of the correct **idiom** to use. Answer Choice (A)'s *more likely as* doesn't work, nor does Answer Choice (E)'s *more likely for*, but Answer Choice (C)'s *more likely than* is OK, as is Answer Choice (B)'s *more likely . . . than* (the intervening words don't change the idiom). Answer Choice (D)'s *more likely that* is both wrong and nonsensical. Answer Choice (C) introduces a new **modification** error, by rearranging the words following *likely to . . .* so that the sentence seems to indicate that flossing is *to be used*, not *to improve* the health of patients.

18. <u>Issues</u>: **modification, sentence structure**

    (A) The sentence is correct as written; the various rearrangements offered in the other answers all fail in some way to make sense of the modification or of the sentence structure.

    Also, Answer Choices (D) and (C) change *did not* to *had not*, as if the **sequence of tenses** were incorrect in the original (it's not).

19. <u>Facts</u>: **Complete (Conclusion)** questions are just Inference questions with a fancy blank at the end. The correct conclusion must be *inferable* directly from the other evidence in the prompt. Here, the evidence takes the form of a study that is very **qualified**. *Some* children who were parented in one way showed less violent behavior than some other children parented in a different way. The only inference permissible in situations like this, where everything's qualified and nothing's definite will be of the **but that's too obvious!** variety, as in Answer Choice (E), which is definitely consistent with the information. On its own, time in front of the X-Station doesn't directly correlate with violent behavior, it's influenced by other factors.

(E) Answer Choice (A) is the **exact opposite** of what the evidence supports; Answer Choices (B), (C), and (D) are all **too extreme** given the qualified evidence.

20. **Issues: comparisons** (which must be **logically similar**), **modification** (placement of *first*), **sentence structure** (maintaining logical connections between ideas)

    (E) The easiest place to start when a sentence has a comparison is by checking to see that logically similar items are compared. Answer Choices (A) and (B) compare *the Aztec and Maya* (peoples) with *the llama* (an animal used by people, which is illogical and insulting to boot). Answer Choice (C) branches out and compares *the Aztec and Maya* with *domestication* (an activity), whereas Answer Choice (D) goes even further into the realm of the nonsensical by comparing the state of *not having pack animals* with *the Aztec and Maya* peoples.

21. **Argument:** In general, **Complete (Evidence)** questions can be treated just like "pure" **Assumption** questions. The best thing to add to a blank in an argument is always evidence that confirms one of the argument's unstated assumptions. Here the argument assumes that because **one way is impossible** something is guaranteed to fail, a common pattern seen in **Flaw** questions. To avoid the flaw, simply assume what really ought not be assumed, which Answer Choice (D) does. Remember, the conclusion here is that their rights will *never be protected by law*, and (D) eliminates law by eliminating those who make laws, legislators.

    (D) Answer Choice (A) simply eliminates another possibility rather than declaring that there are *no possibilities*; Answer Choice (B) is a case of **but for one word,** since the conclusion concerns the future, not just what is *currently* the case; Answer Choice (C) is **reasonable but irrelevant**, since we don't know what being a *modification* has to do with the patent process (unless we're relying on outside information, a big no-no); and Answer Choice (E) is more information **one step removed** from the argument without some **real-world thinking** covering an additional assumption.

22. **Issues: idiomatic construction** (*controversy over* as well as *whether* versus *if*), **parallelism** (demanded by whether something is X or Y)

    (C) The sentence is built upon a two-part construction that presents the classification of Asperger syndrome as a choice between two things, thus both options must be grammatically parallel. Answer Choice (C) fails to be parallel (*should be classified . . . one of*), as does Answer Choice (D) (*being classified . . . it is more*). The idiom used to create the construction is itself a fruitful decision point. The GMAT prefers *whether* for choices or options (*whether it rains or it snows*) and *if* for hypothetical situations (like *if it rains tomorrow*), eliminating Answer Choices (A), (B), and (D). Answer Choice (E) fails the idiomatic requirement on a different level, as the GMAT considers *whether or not* to be the wrong idiomatic form because *or not* is redundant.

You might have also investigated the idiom used with *controversy*. Both *controversy over* and *controversy concerning* are acceptable—if a preposition is used to connect a description to *controversy* then *over* is the one to use; otherwise, descriptions without prepositions can be correct, too. Answer Choice (D)'s *with respect* is a big red flag, not always ungrammatical, but never the sort of thing the GMAT likes to see.

23. **Facts:** This **Inference** prompt might seem more appropriate for an **Explain** question, as it appears to contain a **violated rule**. According to the law of supply and demand (one of the *very few* pieces of real-world information that you are expected to know), when supply rises, price falls as long as demand doesn't fall and when demand rises prices rise as long as supply doesn't rise. The prompt indicates that in this case, compared with last winter, this winter the overall supply of oil has risen but the price has also gone up. Thus, demand must have also gone up, as Answer Choice (C) states.

(C) Answer Choice (A) eliminates one factor that might contribute to demand falling, which isn't the same as proving that demand is up. Answer Choice (B) is feinting with a **percent versus number** flaw, but this is irrelevant here, as this is, like Answer Choice (A), just one reason demand might be down. Answer Choice (E) tries the exact same move as (B); and Answer Choice (C) brings up a sort of **irrelevant comparison**, as we can't infer any *particular* way that demand is up, only that it is up.

The passage for questions 24–26 appears on page 444.

24. **Question:** The phrase "most likely agree" indicates an **Inference** question. Unfortunately, this stem lacks any specific clue as to where the inference will be drawn from, making a firm prediction all but

impossible. A process of elimination with the answer choices will be your best strategy.

Facts: The correct answer is drawn from the last sentence of the first paragraph, which states that "nearly every adult has a file with at least one of the three [credit agencies], if not all of them." Combine this with your knowledge from earlier that files are opened once someone has applied for credit, and you can infer Answer Choice (E): sometimes one or more of the three agencies will not open a file on someone who applies for credit (though at least one almost always does).

(E) Answer Choices (A), (B), and (C) are all **irrelevant comparisons**. Answer Choice (A) is the worst of the three, as "cashless societies" never even appear in the passage. Answer Choices (B) and (C) refer to things actually mentioned by the author, but go further than the information in the passage, making stronger claims than are warranted, **reasonable but unsupported** claims. Answer Choice (D) is **explicitly contradicted** by the passage, which does give a reason a report could be opened falsely (identity theft).

25. **Question:** Parse the **double negative** trickery and you'll see this question asks for a group that could possibly end up without a credit report. The correct inference draws on the same rules as before. We know that there is only one way that a credit report is opened: when someone (and it doesn't have to be the person whose name is used) applies for credit. Thus, people who have never had any credit applied for in their name ought not have a report, as Answer Choice (D) indicates.

    (D) Answer Choice (A) forgets the identity thieves; Answer Choice (B) is something you might know from the **real world** that is not supported here; Answer Choice (C) is the **exact opposite** of the right answer, as both of these groups ought to have reports; and Answer Choice (E), like (A), forgets the identity thieves but also forgets that even necessary credit is credit.

26. **Question:** Sometimes a **Function** question is so global that it almost feels like a **Main Point** question. Rather than being asked about a specific part of the passage's function, this question asks us for the function of *all the parts* (which we would need to know if this were a **Main Point** question, regardless). Your noteboard notes probably helped you here to spot Answer Choice (D) as the correct answer. The *practice* (that begins all the answer choices) is the existence of credit

reporting agencies, the *consequence* is the need to check your credit report when you open a line of credit because of false reports, and the *further explanation* is all that business at the end explaining how identity theft works.

(D) Like a lot of **Function** questions the splits in the answer choices make for a quick process of elimination. Since credit reports are neither recommended nor criticized, only the neutral *described* will stand, eliminating Answer Choices (B) and (C) on the first past, then later Answer Choices (A) and (E), as the first also mentions a recommendation not made, the recommendation to *replace* the system and the second mentions similarly unmade *recommendations against*. The only recommendation in the passage is the recommendation that you check your credit report. (And you should, just not while taking the GMAT.)

The passage for questions 27–30 appears on page 446.

27. **Question:** Inference is by far the Reading Comprehension's favorite question type. This passage's first Inference question is built on what might seem like a throwaway detail, the explanation of why the UC system was chosen as a plaintiff. Of course, since so much of the information in this passage is **qualified** (lacking *always* and *never* rules), the correct inference, as in Answer Choice (E), is going to be of the **but that's too obvious!** variety.

    (E) The incorrect answer choices are, for the most part, **definite (but irrelevant) comparisons** that can't be supported by the **qualified** information in the passage. Answer Choice (A), on the other hand, is **reasonable but unsupported**, because since we don't know if there are any definite requirements, we also don't know that there *aren't* any, either.

28. **Question:** *Likely agreement* is just another way of asking for an Inference, and again the correct answer is a **but that's too obvious!** inference, built on the information at the end of the passage that indicates that the appeals to an extralegal principle were successful.

    (C) Answer Choice (A)'s *preferable to any other solution* is **too extreme** for our qualified and hedging author, as are Answer Choices (B)'s *only* and (E)'s *not necessary*. Answer Choice (D) is out because it creates an **irrelevant** and unsupported **comparison**.

29. **Question:** Detail questions just require us to track down information in the passage, and Answer Choice (D) can be found right there in the discussion of why the UC system was chosen, because they were more likely to stick with a long case (rephrased to more likely to stick with the case than other plaintiffs).

    (D) Answer Choice (A) is a **distortion** of a detail (no comparisons are made between the pension and the endowment, just the total from both given). Answer Choices (B) and (C) are **reasonable but never stated**, and Answer Choice (E) is another **distortion** of the discussion of why the UC system was chosen.

30. **Question:** A vertical scan of these answer choices is in order, as they all begin with verbs.

    (C) The author's overall tone was definitely neutral, more descriptive than argumentative, meaning our eyes should be drawn first to Answer Choices (A)'s *explain*, (C)'s *illustrate*, and (D)'s *describe*, as Answer Choices (B) and (E) have the **wrong tone**. Answer Choice (A) is **part but not the whole**, something mentioned but not the main point, and Answer Choice (D) is a **distortion**, as the only thing we know about the Enron case is that the UC system was picked and that they ultimately succeeded; we're never told why, in a larger sense, they won.

31. **Issues: modification** (what is being *added* or is *in addition to* what), **idiomatic construction** (the choice between *added to* versus *in addition to*), **pronoun reference**

    (E) The most obvious decision point is likely the split between Answer Choices (D) and (E)'s *in addition to* and Answer Choices (A) and (B)'s *added to*. Both are grammatically correct, but only *in addition to* is appropriate for the meaning of this sentence because the accident tax is something that the home owners are being asked to **pay** *in addition to what they have already* **paid**. Here, *added to* creates a modification error, because *added to* only works as a description of nouns and because the entire first clause acts as a modifying phrase for whatever appropriate candidate follows the comma. So, technically, the *accident tax* is being added to the *home owners* in Answer Choice (A) and the *municipalities* in Answer Choice (B). Answer Choice (C)'s *added to* might have worked, but ultimately it just makes a nonsensical construction elsewhere, *added to fund . . . with* (which has one too many prepositions to work).

492 • Pass Key to the GMAT

Of the two remaining answers, Answer Choice (D) creates a pronoun reference error by moving the *they* so that now the sentence seems to imply that it's the municipalities that are paying the taxes.

32. **Dilemma:** The discrepancy here is a sort of **net calculation** or **percent versus number** issue that seems to be out of whack. On the one hand, (1) *damage* from fires caused by the sober is greater than *damage* from fires caused by the chemically altered, yet on the other hand (2) the sober are less likely to cause fires than the chemically altered. There are two ways we might increase the damage enough to overcome this reduced likelihood: either (1) increase the number of sober people so that even though they don't, on average, commit many fires, there's enough people that the low average still results in a lot of fires, or (2) increase the *damage* from the fires that are caused by sober people, however few those fires are. Answer Choice (C) does the former, by establishing that, most of the time, people aren't drunk. Thus for most of the week, drunk people aren't drunk, they're sober, inflating the number of sober people available to start fires.

    (C) Answer Choice (A) is **reasonable but irrelevant** to our dilemma, as the comparison only concerns fires whose source can be identified; Answer Choice (B) is as well, since the dilemma doesn't concern natural versus manmade fires. If there were *enough* of these teetotalers mentioned in Answer Choice (D), it might inflate the number of the sober, as we need, but *many* on the GMAT only implies *at least one*. Answer Choice (E) doesn't affect the dilemma because the fire has already been started once the formerly intoxicated are suddenly sober.

33. **Issues: connecting clauses** (twice, between the first and second and first and third clauses), **modification** (placement of *consequently*)

    (D) As written, the sentence's *comma-and* should connect two *independent* clauses (with the *who*-clause serving dependent to the first independent clause), but the second half of the sentence lacks a noun to serve as the subject for the clause. Answer Choice (B) fixes this error, but Answer Choice (C) still suffers from it. The semicolon in Answer Choices (D) and (E) are also good solutions to how to connect the sentence's clauses up, removing the *comma-and* and making the clauses both *independent*.

    Answer Choice (E), unfortunately, breaks the relationship between the middle dependent clause and the first clause. As a rule of thumb, *comma-which* is usually part of a wrong answer on the GMAT, but the answer is usually wrong for reasons other than the use of *comma-which* itself (the old restrictive versus nonrestrictive clause issue that confuses just about everyone). The trend holds here, as *which* is the wrong connecting word to use to connect the description . . . *had long been isolated* to the *rural Americans* (as they are people, not things).

Answer Choice (B) breaks the *dependent* second clause in a different way, stranding the word *lack* so that it's no longer clear who's lacking what. Moreover, moving the *consequently* makes the sentences nonsensical.

34. **Argument:** Many difficult assumption questions ask us what a *bad* or *flawed* argument would need to assume to be correct. Here, the argument is clearly flawed. One factor that would affect the **net calculation** is mentioned (rent), but no others are mentioned. Thus, the argument assumes that there are no other factors that would affect the overall costs associated with putting the shelter close to where it is currently or out by the county line. Answer Choice (D) is a **defending assumption** that eliminates a factor that might have altered the net calculation, heating and cooling costs.

    (D) Answer Choice (A) is a **closed issue**, since the argument is only discussing which of two options is preferable, not suggesting that one option is the best of all possible options. Answer Choice (B) tugs at the heart strings but is irrelevant, **one step removed** from the evidence as we don't know if it'd be expensive to deal with these unmovable animals or not. Answer Choice (C) is also a **closed issue**, as the shelter is definitely moving, so these volunteers might be lost with either of the two proposed plans. Answer Choice (E) is tempting, but also a **closed issue**, as the argument does not need to assume that either of the two proposals is *definitely possible*, since its conclusion is limited only to a comparison of the costs of the plans if they are put into place.

35. **Argument:** Again, we see the common nestled argument structure (with a little bit of **double negative** distraction mixed in for good measure). Someone argues for something, and the speaker argues that the original conclusion is false by providing other evidence, or **somebody says X (and they're wrong)**.

    Also, always beware of prompts that invoke the issue of bias, as this is almost always a distractor on the GMAT and not a live issue. Here, the flaw is actually another familiar pattern: **disproving an argument does not disprove a conclusion**. Just because one reason to believe these foods are harmful (the evidence from the Sunbelt Foundation) has been eliminated does not mean that the conclusion of the argument (that food is safe) is itself false. Answer Choice (A) states this in an oblique but acceptable way.

(A) Answer Choice (B) springs the bias trap, but remember which conclusion we're supposed to be dealing with, the speaker's, not the Sunbelt Foundation's. Answer Choices (C) and (D) likewise hint at bias, irrelevant here because the evidence already establishes that the Sunbelt Foundation was biased. As for Answer Choice (E), it's the **right idea**, **wrong person** as the speaker *does* assume that lack of a guarantee means lack of something entirely (no proof means no truth), but Answer Choice (E) is dealing with the conclusion of those who believed the Sunbelt Foundation, not the speaker's conclusion.

36. **Argument:** The key to identifying the responder's technique is to make sure you note which parts of the original argument the responder takes issue with and which are either explicitly or implicitly accepted. Here, the second economist never mentions the argument of the first at all, instead choosing to reject the argument's conclusion with a new argument based on a rule: *nothing as complicated (as the global economy) could be accounted for by a single variable (currency market volatility)*. Answer Choice (B) states this directly.

(B) No counterexamples are present, so Answer Choice (A) is out. Answer Choice (C) is the **exact opposite** of what we want, as it describes the first economist's position, not the second one's; Answer Choice (D) is a flaw that we often see, just not in this argument; and Answer Choice (E) is, once again, the old **bias trap**, always a possibility in a two-party prompt.

37. **Issues: modification** (who ruled?), **parallelism** (of the two-part construction created by *and*), **sequence of tenses** (for the verbs *led, claimed, traced*), **pronoun reference** (who ruled or claimed what?)

(D) The first part of the underlined section splits dramatically, offering a decision point over how to connect the modifying information to the original sentence, and in a twist we might expect from a difficult sentence correction question, all of the initial words (*which, by which, ruled, which, who*) in *certain contexts* could possibly work, requiring us to lean heavily on meaning to sort out the proper grammatical relationships. So who's ruling whom and how are they ruling? The answer should be *the monarchy*, but Answer Choice (C)'s version doesn't make this clear. Answer Choice (B) introduces a new pronoun error that makes the question unanswerable, since the antecedent for *it* is unclear (what or who was ruled?)

The *and* in the underlined section sets up a two-part construction of things that describe what the monarchy did, and such constructions must be grammatically **parallel**. The already eliminated Answer Choice (C) adds an extra *they* that breaks the parallelism with *ruled*; Answer Choice (E)'s *claiming* is also wrong. All that's left to eliminate is the original Answer Choice (A), disagreeable because of *comma-which*, but unacceptable because of the stranded pronoun *their*, which has no clear antecedent.

Thus, in the end, this question breaks the *comma-which* rule of thumb in a way (which is why it's a rule of thumb and not a rule), as *comma-which* **is** part of the right answer; nevertheless, it remains the case that *comma-which* is not *itself* usually in error on the test. Remember that as questions get more difficult, the test maker will force you to "swallow a few lemons," accepting things you usually avoid.

38. **Issues: sequence of tenses** (*asked, guess,* and *be*), **pronoun reference** (*it*), **parallelism** (around . . . and . . .)

(C) The initial split between *guess* and *have guessed* is a useful decision point, but if analyzed without the content of the sentence, it would have been less than useful. (Content is increasingly important as the difficulty of questions climbs.)

Essentially, the sentence describes a sequence of events. First, the reasonable person is *asked* to make a prediction. The person then makes a guess *after* the question and *before* the person is right or wrong about the guess—and all of these things happened back around 1600, meaning *in the past.*

The **present perfect** is a flexible tense, chronologically speaking, used to describe events that started happening at some point before the present, but might continue up to it, but also might have ended before the present tense starts or before some other past event began. The correct answer, (C), relies on this flexibility to put the guessing *after* the asking. The *been* in *been wrong* is also in the present perfect, sharing the helping verb *have* with *have guessed* (an acceptable way to handle the two-part construction around *and*).

Answer Choices (A) and (B) thus fail because the guessing happens in the present tense. Answer Choice (E) adds an extra *would*, ruining the parallelism around *and*, while Answer Choice (D) ruins the parallelism a different way, by dropping the second verb entirely (*and absolutely wrong* makes no sense).

39. **Issues: modification**, **indirect and direct verbs** (*agree, reports, endure*)

(A) Another trick reserved for the more difficult Sentence Correction questions is what some grammarians call a *garden path* sentence, a sentence in which one meaning is suggested at first, but that is unsupportable the longer you walk down the sentence's "*garden path.*" At first it seems like *agree* is going to be the main verb of the sentence, but then the *Washington Post* health editor shows up to make things confusing, as the editor isn't agreeing with anything, but rather *reporting* the information in the first clause. Viewed that way, the first clause *six out of . . . etc.* works fine, even if it "sounds off."

Answer Choice (B)'s rearrangement of words creates two descriptive clauses where there was originally one, resulting in ambiguity as to what's being reported and what's out of seven (and *of long-standing practice* is itself incorrect)—a modification error. Moreover, Answer Choice (C)'s *long-practice doctors* is a bit of nonsensical modification that ruins an otherwise OK sentence.

But the much larger error present is the relationship between the agreeing by the doctors, the reporting by the *Washington Post* health editor, and the enduring that the health system won't be able to do. For verbs like *report*, which can be used to present **indirect speech**—the statement that follows the original sentence's colon—it's acceptable to use either the *present* or the *past* tenses only (a rule that has only been tested *very* rarely on the GMAT). So *has reported* in Answer Choices (D) and (E) are out, leaving us with the original sentence, as odd as it might sound.

40. **Issues: idiomatic construction** (*fraught with* and *whether* vs. *if*), **connecting clauses**, **modification**

(C) This question is built on the somewhat obscure idiom *fraught with* <noun> (usually appearing in the melodramatic phrase *fraught with danger*). The *by* in (A) and (B) is not idiomatically correct, and (E)'s switch to *fraught with no autograph* is nonsensical. Of the two remaining answers, the deciding issue is **modification**—and not, as you might have worried, the correct use of the colon vs. the semicolon (which hardly ever appears on the GMAT as the single deciding issue that makes an answer right or wrong).

In (D), the phrase *without an autograph that survives* is a dependent clause, and thus must be used as some sort of description of *only one of the manuscripts is medieval*, but there's no sensible way to manage that.

Another place to start would have been the *whether* vs. *if* choice the GMAT so loves. Remember, *whether* is for choices and options (and doesn't get an *or not*), while *if* is for hypotheticals. No hypothetical is found here, so *whether* is preferred.

41. **Issues: subject/predicate agreement, parallelism** (for the *both . . . and . . .*)

(C) The inverted sentence structure (*ranked first is moral indignation*, instead of *moral indignation is ranked first*) is used to hide a simple subject/predicate agreement error in three of the answer choices. Indignation is singular, so plural *are* in Answer Choices (A), (B), and (E) disqualifies those answers. The choice between Answer Choices (C) and (D) is made most easily by checking to see that the elements following the *both . . . and . . .* are grammatically parallel (required by all coordinating idioms). Answer Choice (D)'s *for both inciting . . . and used* is not parallel.

EVALUATING YOUR SCORE

Tabulate your score for the Quantitative and Verbal sections of the Sample Test by giving yourself one point for every correct answer, and record the results in the Self-Scoring Table below. Then find your approximate rating for each score on the Self-Scoring Scale and record it in the appropriate blank.

SELF-SCORING TABLE		
Section	**Score**	**Rating**
Quantitative		
Verbal		

SELF-SCORING SCALE—RATING				
Section	**Poor**	**Fair**	**Good**	**Excellent**
Quantitative	0–12	13–20	21–29	30–37
Verbal	0–15	15–25	26–30	31–41

Study again the Review sections covering material in the Sample Test for which you had a rating of FAIR or POOR.

*Important note: Up-to-date scoring guidelines for all sections of the GMAT can be found at *mba.com*.